Waters
Beneath My Feet

New Orleans to Nome: My 3 Year Canoe Odyssey

Jerry Pushcar

ISBN 978-0-578-41848-3

Published in Association with
10,000 Lakes Publishing

To Marilyn

Acknowledgements

This book, based upon my memoirs, has been over forty years in the making. Many people encouraged me to get it published. I tried early on to contact publishers, without much success.

Waters Beneath My Feet has finally hit the bookshelves and I would like to thank Leon Boardway for taking the time to help me whenever I asked— Often!

Barb Nickels, Thank You! For fitting this book project into your busy schedule without hesitation.

Tom Pushcar, my brother, there are not enough thank you's to go around for all your ideas, pulling slides, and communicating with Dave Setnicker in order to complete this project.

A special thanks goes to Dave Setnicker, who always felt that my story needed to be retold in book form. His printing, publishing, and marketing expertise pulled in all the pieces needed to complete the book. He, along with Barb Tucker, owner of Andrew's Cameras and cover designer, managed the project from the typewritten manuscript to the printed book.

Without these key people, Waters Beneath My Feet would still be collecting dust in my closet.

-Jerry Pushcar

Contents

9,000 miles across the North American Continent

Setting Forth

Today is January 10, 1978. I'm sitting in the corner of a ten-by-twenty-foot plywood shack in Nome, Alaska. Looking down, I can see snow-covered ground between badly worn floorboards. To my right is a roll of foil-backed insulation between me and a small fuel oil heater. A bare light bulb dangles from a rafter by a foot-long exposed cord. Another wall supports leaning sheets of plywood and sheet-rock.

Along the far wall lies my open Duluth Pack, scattered journals, and three boxes of garbage. A quart of milk, a can of root beer, and a half-pound package of bologna sit outside next to the door for refrigeration.

A honey bucket stands unused in a corner; a congratulatory letter from Vice President Walter Mondale rests on its hinged white seat and inside it is taped $210. That's all that I have. It won't go far with bread at two dollars a loaf. In the center of the room are the remnants of two foam rubber cushions butted together; over these lies a permanently smoke-impregnated sleeping bag from which I crawl each morning.

To complete the array of furnishings is a canoe paddle propped in a corner. Paddles just like that one got me where I am today—in poverty and nearly homeless. This is not the best—nor close-to the worst—place I've stayed over the last three years. Life wasn't like this three years ago. I had a good-paying job and a nice place to live; I owned a newer car and had $15,000 in the bank. At 25, what more could I want?

I wanted something that burned deep within me and could not be extinguished. Etched into my very soul was a desire—a

1

scrimshawed collage of tales about Indians, voyageurs, trappers, canoeists, homesteaders, and adventurers captured me. I made a choice. What I had then is now gone, replaced by three years of my life which I will never forget nor ever regret.

In its rough draft, the master plan was simple. It was nothing I hadn't done before, just much, much longer. Looking back, I realize that this attitude put me on a collision course with the natural order of things. It was me versus nature.

The object was to paddle a 17-foot canoe up the Mississippi River from New Orleans, cross central Canada, traverse the Richardson Mountains, then follow the Yukon River to the ocean, where a 400-mile saltwater jaunt would bring me to Nome, Alaska. Thus, would end this solitary, three-year, 9,000-mile canoe odyssey.

Months and months of planning, collecting equipment, and countless hours of introspection were over. The die had been cast. It was now only a matter of goodbyes.

I brought my first goodbye to the Smugglers Inn on the north edge of the Twin Cities. We had met there six months earlier. It was not a relaxing evening. After a dance and a few drinks, we left near midnight. In the lobby was a garden where I picked a flower and gave it to her. We drove in silence. At her apartment, she removed her coat, went straight to the bedroom, and closed the door with authority. I sat on the sofa for a few minutes, and then went in and tried to talk to her. There was no response. I kissed her on the forehead and said goodbye. At the front door, she called my name, then again. I sat beside her on the bed. She put her arms around me and cried.

At my car I noticed the yellow petal flower lying on the dashboard. Walking to her Maverick, I laid the fragile rose on the freshly fallen snow, cradled in the door handle. It was hard to leave but too late to go back.

It was 4:00 A.M. when I reached the bright red canoe and home and started packing my Cougar for the long drive to New Orleans. As I packed, I noticed something out of place. Inside the canoe was a toy truck, an apple, and a two-foot-long canoe paddle. How does a person tell his two-and-a-half-year-old nephew, who truly believes he's going to Alaska with his uncle, that he can't go? When he awoke in the morning I would be gone.

2

The backseat was stuffed, the trunk lid forced to close, the canoe paddles lashed to the carriers next to the canoe on the roof, and Blizzard curled into the black bucket seat. Blizzard was a six-week-old Samoyed, drafted to be my companion for the next three years. He didn't seem to mind yet.

It was time to leave. A goodbye call awoke my brother Tom and his wife Vickie. My sister Terry and her husband Skip were roused from a deep sleep for an embrace and a handshake. Looking in on my sleeping nephew, Scooter, one last time, I hoped he wouldn't feel too bad about being left behind. I got into my car and drove away.

My life was about to change dramatically. *For the better,* I hoped, but didn't know. *The future will be what I make of it.* I truly believed I could do this, but I coached myself anyways.

At 5:20 A.M. I stopped in Minneapolis to pick up Jim, a single, fellow Lab Tech. Having worked with me at North Star Steel for the last year, he was more than willing to take ten days of vacation to see the lights of New Orleans. There was one stipulation. Either drive my car back or sell it and send me the money. "No problem," I was informed. We were off and didn't look back. It was virtually—stop only when necessary—as we sped along the 1,200-mile road that followed the Mississippi River to my starting point. We were in New Orleans by mid-morning the next day, blurry-eyed and exhausted.

The sky was fair and the day warm, quite a contrast to the snows of Minnesota we left only yesterday. Hotel room vacancy was at a premium. So were the prices. The Super Bowl was being played here and nothing was cheap. After dropping our bags on the floor of a double room in the Holiday Inn we needed to get our bearings. That meant the famed Bourbon Street, just a few blocks away. It was early but far from inactive. After a quick beer, we had seen enough. Sleep was on both our minds.

We awoke hours later, rested, showered, and ready for Bourbon Street. It was dark and awash with people. We drifted unhindered from one establishment to the next. One bar had drag queens performing, another featured Pete Fountain. A 67-year-old Bojangles tapped his rhythm against the concrete sidewalk while money collected in a cup at his feet. Behind him, a girl swung like the bird of a cuckoo clock in and out of a doorway 15 feet above the street. People were everywhere. By midnight we had seen enough and headed for the hotel.

We awoke well before 9:00 A.M., repacked and headed for the

waterfront. The day was windy and cloudy but warm enough for tee shirts. I intended to start this voyage in the heart of downtown New Orleans, so we drove to the docks at the end of Canal Street and parked beside a massive warehouse. Standing on the dock, we saw tugs and barges everywhere in what seemed to be mass confusion. A police officer stood a short distance away, so I walked over and tried to sound frank as I said, "Where would be the best place to put a canoe into the river around here?"

"A what?" he said with disbelief.

"A canoe," I said pointing to the red craft strapped to the top of the Cougar.

"You wanna put *that*," he pointed to the canoe, "in *there*?" pointing to the river. "Hell, I can't let you put that son of a bitch in there without a permit," he informed me.

"You're telling me I have to have a permit to put a canoe in the river," I lashed back with incredulity. I couldn't believe it.

"That's right," he said. "That little building on the other side of the railroad tracks there is where you can get one." I thanked him and left. Driving past the permit station, we followed the river to the first location with river access. It was Audubon Park, a few miles from downtown.

With the canoe untied and brought to the river, Jim wandered around taking pictures while I loaded the packs, paddles, and water jugs. Two kids trying to help bring things to the canoe were a hindrance. Things were thrown in anywhere; I knew once it was just me, my things, and what I could see of the river I would need to reorganize. I had a "Charlie Rich" hat with coins tucked into the trimband and gave them each a fifty-cent piece, hoping it would impede their progress. It only made them more eager. Finally, I had to get tough. I doubled their pay and said, "Thanks for all the help, but I can handle it now," and packed according to past experience.

I was ready to leave. Blizzard acquainted himself with his new home between the first thwart and the yoke. Gathered at the top of the bank were a dozen curious spectators. Jim and I stood next to the canoe. "You sure you want to do this, Pushcar?" he questioned.

"It's a bit late to think about that now," I philosophized.

Jim seemed to be lost in thought, thinking of something to say. "You know, Pushcar, you can't do this all your life," he reasoned.

As we shook hands, I said, "I know, Jim. That's why I'm doing it now."

With the canoe launched and its bow pointed north, I was soon lost from sight. So, it began—January 10, 1975, 11:15 A.M.—A canoe, a pup, and a scrimshawed dream.

The first hour was tolerable. Then I reached the barges, three wide, 100 yards long, and fastened to shore by heavy cables. Undaunted and foolish, I pulled to their outside and faced the full might of the Mississippi's wind and current. Keeping the canoe parallel to the barges, I inched along, being overly cautious not to ram my craft's new finish against the cold rusty steel. It took 25 minutes to meet my first failure. Turning slightly outward, the current grasped the bow of the canoe and everything I had gained was lost in a matter of seconds. Gliding into the eddy below the barges, my mind had already conceived of another idea—lining. *Perhaps I can pull the canoe around the barges.*

A piece of plastic-coated clothesline was still attached to the bow's deck from when the canoe was tied to the car. To this, I affixed a towline, pushed the canoe from shore, and scrambled to the top of the first barge. It worked great as I jumped from one barge to the next, pulling the canoe, cringing each time a wake banged it up against the iron wall. I could see Blizzard eyeing me, probably pondering what he had gotten himself into. At the end of the barges, I came to a halt, dumbfounded. The front end of the lead barge sloped at a 45-degree angle and frothy water churned ominously where the current flowed beneath it. Being sucked into that cauldron would not be a good experience.

Tying the canoe in place, I walked across the front of the barges connected three-wide, assessing the situation. No way to line or paddle looked feasible. *Guess I'll portage.*

With that in mind, I bent over to untie the double half hitch. Something was wrong, the rope should have been taut but wasn't. Reeling in the slacked line produced a short piece of plastic-coated clothesline. Across the muddy water downstream I could see the canoe on its way to the Gulf. At times it would almost disappear between waves in the brown, swollen river. Occasionally a small white head would appear above the gunwale. They were moving fast.

Across the barge decks towards land I flew, hand-over-hand I went down the coarse steel cable and hit the ground running. A short sprint brought me to the dock's office. "You wouldn't happen to have a boat here, would you?" I asked an elderly man behind a desk.

After explaining the situation, he radioed one of his tugs and said, "They'll try to get it." I had to admit embarrassment as we went outside to watch. The canoe was nowhere in sight.

We waited for what seemed an eternity. My concern grew. Everything I owned was bobbing precariously in this very unforgiving situation. Finally, a twin diesel tug could be seen heading our way. Shortly a red toothpick stuck to its side was visible. It pulled near the dock and a guy threw me a rope secured to the canoe. "How much do you want for that dog?" he asked.

"He's not for sale," I said.

"Christ, he's cute. I'll give you fifty dollars more than you paid for him," he persisted.

"No, I just can't sell him," I said, ending the conversation. I thanked him for retrieving the canoe, and he waved as he resumed his business downstream.

The man who radioed the tug stood beside me. "What do I owe you for getting my canoe back?" I asked.

He put his hand on my shoulder and said, "You know, son, the best way you could pay me would be to camp here tonight. Then tomorrow take that canoe and everything in it and go back to wherever it is you came from."

"Thanks for getting it back for me. I really appreciate it," I said without acknowledging his request. He looked me in the eye for a second and then turned around and walked away. *Not a great start*, I thought, as I began the first portage.

There were many more barges to line around that first day, but I felt luck was with me each time a ribbon of water was left between land and the endless raft of barges. With much poling and pushing, I was occasionally able to squeeze through.

On one such exercise, a metal ramp blocked the otherwise clear way. I paddled under it, the bow's peak barely clearing its underside. By lying flat over the thwart in front of me, I narrowly escaped the dead end.

"What on earth are you doing?" asked a feminine voice.

What does it look like? I thought. "I'm trying to get around these barges," I replied, answering the two women standing on the ramp.

"Yes, we can see that, but where are you going?" the other lady asked.

"Alaska," I answered. I knew right then that they thought I was deranged. A sense of disbelief clouded their faces as they gave a knowing glance at each other.

"Well, good luck," one of their parting words hung emptily as I continued along the narrow channel, scraping bank and barge, headed towards Seward's Folly.

Finally, I reached the end of the barges. A quarter-mile later I could see another long string of them. *Enough for one day, I guess.* Here would be my first campsite. While the tent was pitched in a small clearing surrounded by newly planted trees, traffic flew by on a freeway just over a small grassy mound. The sun had yet to set as I rinsed the dishes from a chicken and rice dinner. Blizzard let out a howl, and I turned to see a man getting off a horse.

He introduced himself as Bill and said he hoped he wasn't interrupting. Sitting next to my small fire, we talked over a cup of tea. I had to excuse myself a few times to get the little puppy to stop barking at a big horse. Bill talked about his love of horses and things he wanted to do with his life. "I'm going to take a trip like yours someday, only on horseback," he stated, lost in dreams such as I. It appeared his life was so complex, he didn't know where to start. Wife, kids, college loans, house payments—the likelihood of his epic voyage didn't look good. With his situation unchanged and darkness near, he mounted his horse, telling me to be careful—this was "not a very safe area."

"I'll do that," I said.

Pulling the starboard rein, his horse spun around, and with a wave, he kicked his dream in the ribs and disappeared over the hill.

I did not linger in the morning. I slid my pistol back into the pack and by first light was in the canoe and making progress. Slowly, but there was at least forward motion. The barges were aligned like strings of dominos. Anchored in slackened water, a few sets allowed progress up the outside. It was still a struggle, but by traveling well ahead of the vicious fronts of each barge-column, a dash could be made from their outside to shore, avoiding those frothy cauldrons of death.

I was halfway through one of these many sorties when I sensed something amiss. It was a prelude to a storm. I had felt it many times before in the Midwest, but never like this. After a glance over my shoulder, I immediately chartered a route to safety. A wall of huge black clouds rolled up the river, pushed by a gale-force wind. Trees swayed as I rounded the barges and ruddered hard left, 150 feet from shore.

There was a moment of sprinkles, and then it poured. The canoe ran aground and Blizzard bailed out instantly. I was right behind him. The wind turned terrifying. My "Charlie Rich" hat sailed up, up and away, never to be seen again. Rain attacked like watery needles, drenching me in seconds as I threw the packs from the canoe up the increasingly muddy bank. Trying to get a tarp over them was useless. My t-shirt snapped in the wind as I called for Blizzard. Visibility was nil. It was all I could do to flip the canoe over, crawl under, and hang on. From my location I could see a white tail and two little white legs sticking out from under two packs. It was obvious about whom he was concerned.

And then in ten minutes it was over. The rain slowed to a drizzle and the wind turned to a breeze. I slid from my red cocoon to assess the damage. Everything was there, and wet, except my hat. Still, I felt fortunate. The headlines the next day read "Hurricane Touches Down in Louisiana, Killing Three." This occurred just 15 miles away.

The Mississippi River ran rampant, but the tethered barges thinned as the days drew me away from New Orleans. To lighten my spirits, some days' progress was measured in hours, not miles. Crossing the river became a regular part of the ordeal. When confronting a bit of current that couldn't be breached, there was no choice but to cross in search of lesser foes. Look both ways for barges; start straight across. Massive amounts of hard-earned ground would be lost before reaching the other side. While some days seven or eight crossings were made attempting to find an eddy on the opposite shore, other days I should have stayed where I was.

The land lay flat, broken by clumps of leafless trees. Pastures extended for miles inland. Beneath one leafless oasis, I made camp for the night. By morning, Blizzard was anxious and agitated. Whirling tight circles inside the tent, he frantically searched for a way out. Knowing danger lurked, I looked out the back screen-window, and then out the front; we were surrounded by cows.

Blizzard escaped. One quick wiggle under the nylon door, and he was off. There was a stampede as the white blur darted from cow to cow. No fear was shown as each heifer slowed down, kicked its hind legs high into the air, and then returned to full speed. The white herder was missed by inches. I shouted and shouted and shouted. There was no response until he sulked back twenty minutes later to a stern reprimand.

The next cow we encountered wasn't as fortunate. It lay bloated, floating near shore. Its only movement was at the water's whim. Flies had found a home and the stench was appalling.

Although the smell could be left behind, mental anguish lingered. The morose sight stirred something inside. It wasn't homesickness, though friends and family were 1,800 river-miles away. It was the change of lifestyles, an adjustment, and the grandeur of the endeavor. But it would fade. I had no doubts; this is what I wanted.

Miles passed without trips to town or interaction with people. I stopped in Plaquemine to obtain fresh water; carrying my five-gallon container down each long grassy bluff became a welcome respite. Struggling one afternoon brought me to the top of a hairpin turn where I spent the night, and nine hard hours the next day brought me to the outskirts of Baton Rouge, tucked inside a grove of trees, hidden from view.

Reflections after a long day on the Mississippi River.

By morning a thick wet fog hugged the ground. Only glimpses of the far shore could be seen as I left the security of the grove. It was battle with the barges all morning until I reached a high pier constructed of wooden timbers. Water surged against the battered legs of the stilted structure. A headwind didn't help. Some progress was made as I dug the paddle deep into the water, jammed it into each passing piling, and with a great shove, would surge the canoe forward a foot at a time.

Forward momentum stopped. The next piling was out of reach. Paddling in limbo, I was losing. There was but one alternative, a crossing. It was not something I wanted to do, not in this fog. The far shore appeared as a gray shadow through the haze. It looked a long way away.

As I pushed towards it, the speed of the water was amazing. It only took minutes to be swept past last night's campsite. I had to be in total concentration and full speed ahead. That helped me keep my mind off the unseen barge traffic. If there was one lurking in the fog, it could run me through and never even know it.

It took forty minutes, but I made it across. Luck was with me as the shore came into focus. Then it became clear that I was looking at another wall of steel.

Two men stood on a barge deck watching. Soon there were eight. Realigning the canoe with the river, I turned downstream. At the first opening, I ruddered hard right and slipped into calm water behind the string of barges. Even before beaching the refuge I heard, "That's a pretty dangerous river for a boat that size." I looked to the top of the barge to see two of the men that were watching moments earlier.

"Yeah," I said, "It's a little fast out there."

"Didn't think you were gonna make it for a while there. You just cost me ten bucks," the taller of the two bemoaned. *Poor you,* I thought sarcastically, and apologized for not drowning. They asked if I needed any help getting around the barges. When I declined, they asked where I was going.

"In that thing!" the shorter one exclaimed to my Alaskan reply.

"What are you making it on?" they wanted to know, "Speed, coke, heroin?"

"Just a little Seagram's seven every once in a while," I explained.

"Well good luck," they offered in sincerity. With a thanks I hoisted a pack and started another portage.

Baton Rouge was observed in passing. Once past, the river became more desolate. There were abundant trees and less habitation visible on the banks. Two days north of the city, I was trying my hardest to make headway along rectangle slabs of concrete laid in rows along the bank to prevent erosion, a steep concrete blanket, when a barge heading downstream passed within 100 yards. With a wall of water coming at me, I knew I was in trouble and had no place to go.

I abandoned ship as the wake snaked toward me, and with hands on the gunwale, feet braced on the concrete, waited for the onslaught. It arrived and I was pushed backward. The canoe rose four feet and then slammed with a sickening crunch as the initial wave receded. I tried to hold the craft in place on the concrete, gravity prevailed, and the canoe scraped the whole way to the waterline. The next wave nearly filled it. Lesser waves continued the mutilation, but with the displacement factor compromised, combined with the current, there was little to do but get the canoe away from the concrete. Carefully I entered and took a seat. With a shove of the paddle, I was away from the concrete heading backwards downstream.

Blizzard was drenched, standing in cold water up to his belly, shivering. "Don't you dare move! Not even an inch," I shouted at him while pointing my finger at him. He looked at me and whimpered, seeming to sense the urgency of the situation. We were moving farther from shore as I tried to keep the bow upstream into the current, not wanting to turn 180 degrees, which might allow more water to spill over the gunwale. Freeboard was already nil. Looking behind me caused a change of plans. I was now being swept towards a fallen tree that I had circumvented earlier.

Ever so slowly I back paddled to swing the bow downstream. A few small waves leapt the gunwale while we were broadside to the current. The fallen, floating tree was getting larger the closer we got. But with the canoe turned downstream and under minimal control, it was lucky only a few of the upper branches were scraped as we passed by them. I angled directly toward shore.

It was a very, very slow-moving balancing act. I've got to hand it to Blizzard, except for his swiveling head, he never budged. Finally, he broke ranks and leapt as the canoe bumped the concrete levee. Securing the canoe, I unloaded the water-filled packs while Blizzard shook himself dry. Narrow ledges in the concrete were the only place to set them. After bailing the canoe, I was able to roll it over to inspect the bottom. There was damage but nothing major; I was lucky. There were also losses: a new $125 tape-radio player, an unused $35 Old Town paddle, $120 worth of cassette tapes, and an untold amount of food and books.

11

Anger at the barge captain faded as I got back on the horse that had bucked me. *Comes with the territory,* I guessed. Inching the distance, I lined to the end of the levee, found a suitable campsite and started the drying-out process.

Things never fully dry in overcast skies. It took three hours the next morning before the sun burned through the overcast to reveal abundant cumulus clouds. By then I was hovering in the eddy behind a pile-dike. It was a giant wing dam installed by the Army Corps by piling rocks 100 yards into the river to focus the current in the main channel. I calculated the chances of paddling over or around this man-made obstacle. Beneath the rocks, it was calm. At the end of the wing dam, water poured unhindered, creating large whirlpools. I started toward the end, curious to see if I had what it took to get through.

The odds apparently weren't with me. I backed up slightly and accelerated full steam ahead. The bow rose as it sliced into the turbulent flow, sending me toward its apex. I knew if I could hook a rock two feet below and give a hefty push, I might make it. For an instant, my momentum and the current's equalized. Frantically I probed with the paddle for the booster rock I needed. Then it connected. With a shove, I shot forward, though imperfectly. If I had gone straight upstream things would have been copacetic. As it was, the bow turned outward, grabbed instantly by the current. I was being dragged away from shore, down-river into the main channel. The wing dam worked as its designers intended, focusing all matter towards the main channel. My curiosity had been satisfied, but I hadn't won.

I saw another whirlpool seconds before it grasped the canoe; I wasn't in the clear. The thirty-foot pool of swirling water and foam was paralyzing. If adrenaline were testosterone, I'd be set for life. There was no control. My heart raced. The canoe, and Blizzard, and our vessel were sucked into it. On the first spin, I was almost thrown backwards from the canoe. I went to my knees for a lower center of gravity and clung to the gunwales. On the second revolution, my eyes were almost level with the main surface of the river. Then as quickly as it started, it was over. After a final half-hearted spin, the canoe leveled and the whirlpool dissipated and disappeared downstream.

I was 200 yards offshore, floating sideways, and half-filled with water. With a frying pan, I bailed and then turned toward shore, feeling very fortunate. It was a lesson. Numerous as they were, pile-dikes were now overcome by dragging the canoe across their tops as close to shore as possible.

As we got further from the ocean, the river's increasing indirectness became a frustration. At times the river seemed to flow as far east, west, and south as it did north. This necessitated numerous crossings in search of an eddy. The fog was a constant factor too. So was the cold. I had packed clothing with the thought that people went south for the winter because it was warm. Yet there I was, slipping through an early morning fog with two socks on each hand and a towel wrapped around my head for warmth.

That was how I pulled into the outskirts of Natchez, Mississippi. Cold and damp, I had an overwhelming desire to eat something sweet. I passed a Coast Guard Station where bright black and red torpedo-like buoys were stacked in six-foot high rows. A man in a raincoat said hello, waving as he stepped from behind one of the piles.

As I returned the gesture, he said, "Why don't you stop in and have a cup of coffee? Bring your dog." I didn't even drink coffee but wasn't going to let that stop me.

Blizzard bound up the two flights of stairs, dashed inside, and let loose in three different places. The man introduced himself as Bill while filling two cups of coffee. After we shook hands, he got out the mop. There was a small dog in Bill's care that Blizzard assimilated with well. During our stay, they knocked over two lamps and a vase.

The heat was comforting as I sat on the couch, and Bill hopped on the pool table, legs dangling. Through a steaming cup of coffee, we discussed his tour in the Coast Guard. It seemed he would rather not be stuck here at this station. When the bottom of the cup could be seen, I felt it best to leave and asked Bill where the nearest store was. "I'll tell you what. You see that road going to the left there?" he asked while pointing out the window. "You walk along that for about ten minutes, and you'll be out of sight. It's against regulations," he said, "but I'll be along with the truck and when I slow down, you hop in and I'll get you to the store."

"I don't want to get you into any kind of trouble," I mentioned, unsure if the ruse was worth it.

"Hell," he replied, "what can they do to me? I'm the only one here."

Though no watches were synchronized, the military was right on time. An old orange pick-up, looking like no Coast Guard vessel I'd ever seen, chugged down the road and rolled to a stop. I jumped in and Bill drove the three miles to the store. "If I see you on the way back, I'll pick you up," he said as I thanked him and entered a small country grocery.

It was cluttered. A gray-haired lady stood behind a glass candy counter, greeting me as I closed the door. Strolling the two aisles, I picked up enough supplies to reach Vicksburg, 75 miles upstream. While the lady arranged the groceries in a cardboard box, I called my sister in Minnesota.

Terry was surprised and wanted to know if I had had enough of the river and was ready to come home. After a negative reply, I learned the outcome of my 1972 Cougar. It seemed Jim drove it to Florida, ran out of vacation time, and then didn't have the time to drive it back or care to sell it. So, he did the next best thing. He left it in a church parking lot and boarded a plane for Minnesota. It was subsequently stripped and what remained was towed by the city. A $125 towing fee was issued in my name. They'd have to extradite me to get that one, if they could find me first. So much for someone's word!

Terry told me to be careful, that she wished I'd just come home but knew I wouldn't, and said goodbye. Throughout the conversation I peripherally observed the unobtrusive elderly woman buffing the clean glass counter-top. It must have been real dirty for she worked on the same spot for 15 minutes, about the length of time I talked to my sister. After the call she slid the box of groceries across the gleaming counter top with a smile and wished me well.

I hadn't walked a block when a truck stopped and asked if I wanted a ride. As the windshield wipers swept from side to side, he said, "You're that guy paddling up the river, aren't you?"

"Yah," I said, "how did you know that?"

"Heard it on the radio a few days ago," he answered. I was slightly flabbergasted, thinking I was keeping a low profile.

With Blizzard and the groceries loaded into the canoe and tucked under the spray skirt, the upstream onslaught continued. The steady rain never stopped. I called it an early night and an early morning. Just before sunrise, I awoke to find Blizzard swirling around the tent, tossing something into the air. He'd catch it in his mouth, shake it, and then momentarily settle down to chew on it. I dismissed it as one of my old socks, to be dealt with an hour later.

When I woke up it became apparent that it wasn't a sock. At the foot of the sleeping bag were bits and bits of paper everywhere. Blizzard was still contentedly chewing on a small blue book, the remnants of $400 in traveler's checks. He took one look at me, dropped the mangled book, and dove for the door. I grabbed his tail just before it disappeared and pulled the squealing rebel back inside. Hoisted by the nape, feet whirling, we had quite a discussion before he continued his dash to safety.

What a wet jigsaw puzzle! It took most of an hour to get the checks back to some resemblance of their former selves. A lot of tape went a short way towards making them useful again. It took another hour of coaxing Blizzard, telling him what a great dog he was, before he was willing to board and get underway. Conferring with my nautical chart, a Shell highway map, I thought, *Vicksburg in less than a week.*

If things went as they would two days later, I wouldn't reach Vicksburg at all. The water was rising rapidly due to continuous spring rain, pushing the shoreline far beyond the dense trees abutting the bank. Progress was very, very slow. I noticed a red jerrycan wedged into the crotch of a tree as I inched along. The water was racing so fast that I headed into the trees where I literally pulled the canoe forward from tree to tree. Crosscurrents would inevitably prevent a long stint of this method as I couldn't turn in the trees. *Time to cross,* I decided four hours later.

Thirty minutes passed before it looked like I was getting anywhere. As water swirled around the canoe, I paddled hard as the distant mirage began to grow and shift. The image evolved from a combination of land, sky, and water; the phenomena created a scene where the canoe would stand still while the shoreline moved. Though I was aware it was imagined, it was still disorienting.

At the shoreline the illusion continued. I couldn't believe how fast *that* shoreline was moving. It seemed to zoom by as I dug the paddle deep. Then it became clear that this was no mere illusion. As I inched along, there would be a loud *plop* just out of sight ahead or behind me. Then *plop!* A ten-foot high section of earth fell into the river directly in front of me. Bits of earth came very close to landing in the canoe, and their wakes splashed the top of the gunwales. The brown water was decimating its banks before my eyes.

For two hours I hugged the mud bank, struggling, well-aware

of the river's tendency to undercut banks and sweep things below. I reached a niche behind a point and rested in its eddy, watching the dank water roll by. Nature put the Corps of Engineers to shame. Portaging up the near vertical bank was not an option. I pushed off the bank, hit the rushing water head on and lost. Instantly I was spun around and pointed downstream. I kept going and veered to cross.

It was a sequel to the crossing made a few hours earlier, losing ground the entire way, though upon completion the current seemed to have slackened on this side. I made headway for an hour, then faced a bout of discouragement. Wedged into the crotch of a tree, was that red jerrycan. I had been here seven hours earlier. I turned east and disappeared into the trees in search of a better way.

The canoe took a beating as the current bounced it from tree to tree. Darkness approached and I hadn't seen dry land in five hours. I kept going, hoping to find some soon. I didn't; only trees, water, and inky blackness.

I tied the stern of the canoe to a stout tree and as the rope pulled taut in the current, the canoe drifted slightly side to side in five feet of water. Lying back with the life jacket behind me, sleeping bag over me, canoe gently rocking, I tried to sleep.

It was a farce. Changing positions was near impossible and rolling over would be disastrous. I was cold and uncomfortable. Many times during the black night, the gentle rocking of the canoe was disturbed as barges plied the river, sending wakes miles through the flooded forest. In the darkness between naps, I'd probe for the gunwales and then hang on until the turbulence subsided. So it went throughout the night.

The faintest light of the morning was welcomed. I sat up groggy and stiff. The water had risen a foot overnight. After two handfuls of GORP trail mix, I set off with the intention of finding land, building a warming fire, and sleeping after a hot breakfast. This came to pass nine and a half hours later.

It took another two days before Vicksburg was reached. Before me, stood a massive concrete retaining wall. It seemed quite excessive until I reached two massive steel doors and looked up. Near the top of the wall was a vivid red line indicating the record-high water level. Beside it read 62 Feet-1926. The river now stood at 18 feet and was considered at flood stage. Walking through the massive floodgates, entering Vicksburg felt like entering the Colosseum.

Evidence of the Civil War abounded as Blizzard and I walked up and down the hilly streets. There were cannons, Confederate flags, cannonballs stacked in pyramids, and many window displays. It seemed a town proud of its past. It appeared friendly, quaint, and clean. At least, I hoped it was friendly. I was going to the bank, jigsaw in hand.

The chances were slim. A ray of hope ignited when the teller said he would have to have the traveler's checks okayed by the man seated behind him at the desk in a glass cubicle. I walked into the tiny office, handed him the checks, and pleaded my case. With upturned eyebrows, he paged through them. The checks were wrinkled, torn, taped, and still wet with dog slobber. "Exactly what happened to these?" he wanted to know. Explaining the situation the best I could, relief followed as he scrutinized them a final time and said, "Well, I guess we can go along with that." I thanked him profusely for his OK, brought them to the teller, and cashed every one of them.

Tying Blizzard to a parking meter, I walked into a sporting goods store. He was wailing before I reached the counter where a young lady asked how she could help. Through his constant barking, I produced a list from my pocket and started naming items. As she set a package of batteries on top of a growing pile, I excused myself to try and pacify Blizzard with a biscuit. "Well, why don't you just bring him in?" the young clerk suggested. I did. It was a mistake. He flew through the door, sprinting towards the shoe department at the back of the store where four older people sat. A steady stream soaked the carpet along his route. Knocking over a pile of mess kits didn't slow him.

He announced his presence by pawing and licking the gray-haired group, and then at top speed, dashed down another aisle. I caught him just as he knocked over a dozen cans of Coleman Fuel and then leashed him to a stout wooden post that supported the center of the building. Through it all, the clerk thought he was the cutest puppy she had ever seen. With "Mr. Can-Do-No-Wrong" secured, shopping resumed with relative tranquility.

"You take care of that little dog now you hear," ordered the lady as I left with a bag of warm clothes in one hand and Blizzard in the other.

"Thank you," I replied, "I will." *If she only knew*, I stewed. The next stop was the post office. Much to Blizzard's chagrin, he would be waiting at the canoe. "Do you have anything for Pushcar?" I asked the little postman behind the counter.

"Christ, have I ever," came his reply. "I don't know what the hell's in this but you're going to have to come back here and get it yourself," he grumbled. It was heavy, but I shouldered it and walked back to the canoe, anxious for any news from home.

It was a box from my sister. A letter stated that things were fine at home, and people were starting to call and ask if I was still on my quest. It also contained two pairs of clean blue jeans, four shirts, five dog treats, and all kinds of canned and dried foods. At maximum postal weight, the hoard was a very welcome sight. With provisions stowed, the quest continued.

I thought about mileage as the canoe crawled past a small town called Providence. It was February 10th—thirty days and 300 miles from New Orleans. The mileage was fictitious. It reflected no recognition for the river crossings, the lost miles, the bouncing from tree to tree, and the barges. It was just a statistic. I would be "just a statistic" too, if I didn't soon get past paddling this very fast water all day, every day.

I ferried across the river and then north, across the border into Arkansas. Artificial lines meant nothing. The water was just as fast, just as muddy, and rose just as high. Camps at night had to be made feet higher than the dusk waterline or by morning, flooding was assured. Tying the canoe to a stout tree became routine. The river was flexing its muscle.

For three days I crossed back and forth, always with a northerly intent, as the river rose. An impulsive decision was made, traveling six miles out of the way up a tributary to stop at a place called Greenville. What drew me there, I have no idea. I docked at a landing area where people watched a flock of ducks beg for bits of bread. Crossing a paved parking lot to buy a few sweets at a small shopping center, I had already seen all of Greenville that I cared for. *Why did I waste my time coming here?* I chastised myself, *now it's a six-mile paddle just to get back to the river.* A man called me as I returned across the paved lot. I walked over and said hi. He leaned against his rusted station wagon. Dirt caked its interior as tools and paper lay scattered throughout.

"Where you headed?" he asked.

"Up the river," I answered, skepticism directed at his intentions.

"I know where you're going," he stated flatly before launching into an explanation about how much boating he had done on the river. "Not in anything like that though," he said, "mine is an 18-foot aluminum with a good kicker on it." He paused mid-thought before continuing, "I'd like to help you but don't have any money to give you, why don't you take this instead? It makes a real good temporary patch," he offered me a roll of duct tape. I hated to take it, but the man seemed so sincere in wanting to help me that I couldn't refuse. "Go ahead, take it," he urged, "I can get all I want from work." His face told me it was true, so I walked back to the canoe with a huge roll worn like a bracelet.

I felt foolish standing next to the canoe, hand and roll clamped between my legs, trying to slide the thick gray bracelet back off. With an irritated red hand, I stuffed it into the side of a pack. Someone shouted from up the shore; I turned and caught, "You'd better be careful out there. There are tornado warnings!" It was one of the duck feeders; my attention turned skyward.

Half of it had turned an ominous black, and the waves had picked up enough to produce whitecaps. I made it across the lagoon then headed toward the river. It took hours, and once there, things didn't look good. The wind howled as treetops swayed to its rhythm. A large cottonmouth snake dropped from its limbed perch over the water and weaved back to safety. The nasty tailwind would have pushed me upstream but the friction between it and the rushing current created severe whitecaps, something I'd rather watch from shore. Then came the rain.

It pounded the tent well into the night. By morning, mud around the tent glistened in the sunshine. The canoe floated from its tether in the storm's aftermath. Mud oozed over the tops of my hiking boots as I carried the packs down the bank and stashed them beneath the splash cover. Kneeling on the seat and giving my heels a few claps to clean the boot's cleats, I swung the bow around and headed into the trees.

Though the sun shined for the next three days, a winter chill filled the air. The Mississippi River accepted the waters from the Arkansas River on a wide sweeping bend. It was near here that a doe crashed through the underbrush, broke through near shore, and dashed along it upstream. Seconds behind were five dogs, intent to kill. The troupe passed without acknowledging my presence just yards away. Had the pistol been more accessible, I would have tried to even the score. Blizzard attempted, as well.

It was only two hours later that I had pulled ashore, built a small fire, and was sipping a cup of tea when a commotion erupted in the woods behind me. I suspected what the barking meant and tied Blizzard up immediately. Checking the clip of the pistol, I headed for the fracas.

It exposed itself within 100 yards. The doe turned in circles defending itself as five dogs snapped at its hamstrings. Preoccupied, none noticed as I advanced to within thirty yards, braced against a tree, and shouted. For a second everything stopped. Twelve ears rose. The doe bound toward safety on one bad leg and the .22 Smith & Wesson broke the silence.

One dog went down, got up, and disappeared below the top of the grass. The rest scattered, except one. It was a Doberman Pincher with a taste for blood, apparently any blood, my blood perhaps. *Seriously?* I thought, our eyes locked together. He dashed right at me, and fast. I fired, and a slight jerk indicated a hit. Unfazed, he advanced. *No way!* Alarm bells rang in my head as his bared teeth and black collar came into sharp focus. I pulled the trigger four more times. There was one shot and three clicks. *Why had I been content loaded with only three shells!* He was but a few feet away when the bullet hit the beast. I dove behind my skinny support tree as his staggering momentum carried him past. Without hesitation, my whirling legs were beneath me, and I was headed for camp.

Christ, I have to be crazy, I reasoned, hands trembling with adrenaline as I fumbled shells into the gun. With a few deep breaths, pistol in one hand, and scavenged club in the other, I started back.

My second approach was more cautious than the first. I spotted the Doberman; he lay near our encounter, teeth sunk into the base of a scrub tree. Blood ran from his nose. A gold nameplate hung from the black collar. It was over. *Now what?* I was tempted to take the golden tag and mail it to the name and address stamped into it. Instead, I pulled the body into a small dip and covered it with leaves and pieces of wood.

I returned to camp with mixed emotions, thinking maybe the dogs were just hungry. *They weren't starving; they were pets.* I had seen it in Minnesota where dog packs killed deer just to kill. For many, it was the result of being inbred, mangy, rabid, or some combination. *They would have torn that deer apart and then moved to the next one,* I told myself. There was but one who could stop it—the owner. I left the shallow grave and despondency behind me.

The river continued its rise with no sign of cresting. The miles labored by. As I paddled the Arkansas border, skirting the tree line, a still mist enclosed the river valley. A light headwind skipped across the otherwise calm eddy I was following. Soon a heavy odor permeated the mist. It was decaying flesh. *Probably another cow or pig,* I hypothesized while paddling, scanning the murky water and tree line for its source as I went. Then I saw it at the head of a logjam, bobbing slightly in the current.

A dark brown river-victim was on its way to the ocean. Maneuvering the canoe for a closer look, I soon wished I hadn't. What I was looking at was the back of a human body burned black in the sun. A faded shirt was forced halfway over the rotting hairless head. The legs were slightly submerged and greatly bloated. The stench was overwhelming.

Pushing logs away, I was able to come broadside to the cadaver. I held my breath and gingerly slid the end of a nylon rope under its slimy leather belt. I fastened the other end to the closest tree. It was a grisly chore. After blazing a mark on a prominent tree, I started across the river, gulping the much-needed fresh air.

At the next town, Helena, Mississippi, the incident would be reported. Although one hard day's paddle should have brought me there, I made it in three. A lone man watched my approach. A biting breeze rippled the marina's quiet water as I stepped onto a snow-covered dock. "What do you want here?" the lone figure demanded. I explained the situation and was invited into a leaning, one-room dock house that seemed hardly afloat. The man who introduced himself as Porter Young brushed aside my concerned look, apparently aware that we were inside a sinking ship. He was the marina's president and owned the town newspaper. He wanted an interview and he wanted it now.

After thirty minutes he closed his notebook, asking a few more off-handed questions about what he had termed "the floater." When satisfied, he said, "You can stay here if you like. Bring all your things in out of the weather. There's a shower stall in back and a television in front, but you'll have to pay fifty cents a day for electricity." The corpse' stench still clung to my nose, its' clammy belt still touched my skin. *A shower sure sounds nice.* How could I refuse?

Porter was not finished with me as we drove to the sheriff's office and entered. "Hey, Dave, this man found a floater a few days ago, paddled a canoe all the way from New Orleans too," was my introduction to the uniformed officer.

He rattled off questions, "How far down the river is it? How long did it look like it had been in the water? Was it badly decomposed? How was it dressed? Would you be willing to ride down with us tomorrow morning and show us where it is?" and formed them into a written statement.

"Boy, that's going to be a cold ride down there tomorrow. I sure do dread it," the sheriff's deputy said with a mock shiver. His problem was solved when he learned that the floater was on the Arkansas side of the river. "Hell, no use freezing our asses off! I'll get on the phone and give them a call. Let them go get it," piped the deputy, justifying his statement.

All problems have solutions, I mused as Porter and I walked down the dock in the deepening snow. Huge flakes drifted through the air, painting everything white. Inside the tilted door of the boathouse, I removed my boots and was irresistibly drawn to an ancient overstuffed chair. Porter had started the oil stove and it created welcome problems. The heat and comforts soon took their toll, I drifted off much like the snow.

It was dark when I awoke, confused in the aftermath of sleep. This was quickly washed away with a short, hot shower, my first since New Orleans over two months ago.

The tug of war between snow and rain lasted three days before the coming season overtook the fading one. Between surges in the storm, I would walk the muddy, snow-covered ruts to the seawall and eat at Pat's restaurant. The usual fare amounted to two BLT's, a salad, a bowl of chili, two glasses of milk, and two pieces of cherry pie a la mode. I was building reserves for hard times.

The storm broke on a Friday morning. There was one chore left to do. I had left the canoe tied to the dock and did not find it floating there when I returned. Apparently, it had a hole in the hull, as only its two tips peered above the murky water. Pulled from the water, it was rolled, righted, and repacked. With a last warming blast from the oil stove, I set ten dollars on the table and left Helena.

The river continued to rise as I witnessed scenes from past floods grander than mine. One tall tree cradled a huge uprooted tree in its upper branches. Another housed a 55-gallon drum wedged thirty feet above its roots. To think of that much water and how much damage it could create was humbling.

Thirty feet of floodwater can be very intimidating.

Though the days were long, hard, and tiring, sixteen hours on the paddle were common. The scenery changed little as leafless, skeletal trees fringed the brown water.

I had finally forgiven Blizzard for the traveler's check incident and decided to again allow him to sleep inside the tent. It didn't take. Throughout the night he would continually crawl in and out. At last, he broke the zipper and I barricaded the nylon entry with a heavy pack. By morning the tent had been leveled three times. Blizzard would learn to sleep outside, leashed to the canoe.

Memphis was near, and thus were the barges. I passed one after another, making excellent time until I realized it was just too easy. Navigating a narrow space between the lines of iron, I reached shore and was surprised to see a yellow truck flying towards me then come to a dust-raising halt nearby. "What the hell do you think this is? Get that Goddamn-thing out of here!" the driver screamed while flailing his arms overhead. I managed to ask him if this was the main river and in his unrefined way, he kindly explained that it wasn't. Apparently, they were getting ready to move the string of barges when I came along. *All he had to do was ask,* I thought as I again squeezed between barges and headed for the river.

The easy paddling soon ended. A stiff headwind had developed, churning the Mississippi. I gave it a try and quickly realized it wasn't worth the effort. Gliding into an eddy behind a logjam, I weaved through ten feet of submerged standing trees to obtain shore. It was still early in the afternoon, so I tied Blizzard to a stump, took the pistol, and went for a walk. It wasn't long before a rabbit broke from cover. A shrill whistle stopped him in his tracks, and he was in the sights. He simultaneously jumped with the crack of the gun and then lay still, the .22 hollow-point hitting home.

With the rabbit roasting on a wooden spit, I turned my attention to finding leaks in the canoe. Four trees that formed a rectangle were found. Two ropes were tied between the parallel short ends, and the canoe was set upright in this cradle. With a foot of water inside, I lay underneath, felt pen in hand, waiting for seepage.

"Are you alright?" came a voice from the river. I looked over to see a man sitting in a jon boat and told him I was fine. "What are you doing here?" he demanded. I explained that I had been blown off the river and was trying to find a few small holes in the canoe while I waited. "Do you know you're trespassing?" he wanted to know.

It was hard to deny since there was a No Trespassing sign nailed to the tree directly behind me. He couldn't get ashore as his boat wouldn't fit between the trees, but when he inquired of my journey, he said I could stay as long as I wanted with one stipulation. I couldn't hunt. I assured him I wouldn't, decidedly didn't invite him for supper, and waved as he motored on down the river.

Within a day I reached another long, high, concrete levee. Memphis rose behind it. A steady headwind persisted making headway very, very slow. Reaching a bridge that spanned the Mississippi, I was aghast at the force of the water hitting its piers below. The canoe was nearly stagnant despite my best efforts. Taking a cigarette break, a man sat on an oil drum watching me with a half-smile and a shake of the head, questioning my sanity. Knowing I'd have to wait until the wind died, I stopped on the ten-foot-wide stretch of rock and broken glass at the foot of the levee. As uncomfortable as it looked, it could very well have to be home for the night.

Needing to check my surroundings, I followed a steep, worn path beneath a burned bridge and up a rugged hill. Crossing a large churchyard led to a small park high above the river. A piece of modern art glistened in the sun. It was steel and consisted of men standing on top of one another; it was dedicated to the people who died here during a cholera epidemic in the past. A small white meditation temple stood nearby. Beyond rose a Holiday Inn. There was a grand view of the river with my canoe far below. When the sights had been taken in, I started back, letting Blizzard off his leash. He never looked back as he sprinted down a ridge, over the top of another, and disappeared. I gave chase.

Then, like Captain Benteen at the Battle of Little Bighorn, from a small rise I gazed at the battle below. A girl and boy chased Blizzard. Two baseball gloves lay on the ground and a white rubber ball was locked between Blizzard's jaws. Blizzard would circle then stop near the tormented, laying on his chest, rump up, and chew on the ball. His playful mood wasn't being appreciated. Wanting nothing to do with me, he needed to be bribed with a biscuit. Sniffing the bait, he dropped the ball and was snared in the trap. After apologizing, I returned the now-cratered ball and set off for the canoe.

With Blizzard at the canoe, I again climbed to the park overlooking the river, hoping the wind would settle enough to cross the river and find a more remote place to camp. It didn't. Looking down at the canoe, it was obvious how the bottom of the levee had become covered in glass. It was thrown from right where I stood. I didn't need to be awoken by glass mortar rounds coming into camp; there seemed to be but one alternative, the churchyard. If a person wasn't safe there, where could he be?

I waited until dark. With flashlight, pistol, and sleeping bag, I climbed the steep hill. Blizzard's barking from shore was a faint solo in the background as I scanned the yard. It was lit by streetlights. On the perimeter were pine trees casting dark shadows. Here I would unroll my bedding.

Sleep came sparingly in my untrusted surroundings; my suspicions right that I wouldn't go undisturbed. Four people came running down the sloping churchyard. Now I was wide awake, edging back into the shadows. Beneath my pillow, I felt the cold security of a firearm.

As two boys and two girls came down the path leading to the burned bridge, they passed within ten feet of me, returning within minutes. I lay in the shadows unnoticed and watched as they retreated to the churchyard, confident now in my hidden position.

The four high schoolers stayed in the churchyard for well over an hour, passing joints among themselves. Soon giggling and laughter started. Then they began to play chase. Barely getting any sleep because their adolescent behavior, I was getting frustrated.

Footsteps wound to-and-fro while they chased; they became increasingly closer until something hit me in the side, just below the ribs. There was a thud as a body hit the dirt. I sat up and was knocked sideways, hit again. There was another thud. I got to my knees as one each of the guys and girls picked themselves off the ground. "SSSSorry! I, I, I didn't see you there!" he stammered, clearly surprised and frightened. All four were off on a run and disappeared, ending their game of tag.

Only a modest wind blew the next day as I lined the canoe along the base of the levee. It was a welcome alternative to paddling, but soon obstacles necessitated the use of my paddle. I was in full view of Memphis and watched as the early morning rush hour streamed past on the freeway. A siren sounded somewhere, followed by another. I had no envy.

It didn't take long for whitecaps to appear, though I had just made it into the calm waters of the Memphis Marina. Passing long rows of silent boats, I slid into the brush and trees fifty yards past the boat on the end. Here in privacy, it was time for a change. Off came the dirty clothes and on went the clean ones. That's how I entered the boathouse.

I crossed the spacious front room to address a tall sleek gentleman in white sneakers, white pants, white shirt, and a captain's hat. "Could I keep my boat here for a few hours?" I asked.

"How long is it?" he wanted to know. When I told him it was 17 feet he said, "Funny, I didn't even hear you come in."

"Well," I said, "canoes are pretty quiet." After inquiring where I was coming from and where I was going, he asked, "What are you navigating by?" I pulled the dog-eared and tattered Shell roadmap from my shirt pocket and handed it to him. The ex-barge pilot looked at it and roared with laughter. Before leaving, he offered a berth to keep the canoe and a three-inch thick book of navigational maps detailing the entire Mississippi River.

With the map book stowed and having eaten my fill at a greasy place on Second Street, Blizzard and I strolled down Third Street looking for a grocery store. It became a trial as Blizzard had obtained a huge femur bone from the waitress who thought he was "beautiful." Our stoppage was constant as Blizzard would drop his prize, panic, and refuse to go on without it. Finally, I tired of the delays and kept pressure on the leash. He sat down with total resistance trying to prevent a canine catastrophe. I gave him one more chance, and he made the most of it. So, with a foot of bone protruding from each side of his head and tail wagging, Blizzard strutted the streets of Memphis.

Blizzard was already asleep when I left the Memphis Marina, one paw holding his bone close. The current was relentless, but seeing how there was no place to stop, I fought it until dark. The shores were totally industrialized. In the fading light, I noticed two picnic tables with water covering their benches. Dry land beckoned 200 feet beyond them.

A barge had passed minutes before I had reached the picnic tables, and the wake began to home in on the canoe. I expected it would have little effect in two feet of water but couldn't have been more mistaken. The canoe rose, dropped, went crunch, and swamped in one smooth motion. Drenched, I stepped over the side and held the canoe steady as the remaining waves subsided.

Walking the canoe to shore, I was unrestrained in my abuse of the English language. By the time the canoe was emptied, rolled over, and the tent set up, it was total darkness. Probing the shoreline by flashlight produced little firewood. Even a pavilion 200 yards away with a fireplace inside proved counterproductive. It was cold, but I decided to save what little wood I had for the morning.

The night was anything but restful. Cars came and went in the growing night and whenever one stopped I would cautiously peer out, pistol in hand. Apparently, this was a lover's lane of sorts. At least there was a stout cable that prevented anyone from driving past the pavilion, and anyone approaching the tent could be seen in the bright moonlight. Besides, there was Blizzard.

Hard as I resisted, eventually I drifted into a deep sleep. Suddenly I was wide awake as my hand fumbled beneath the pillow. My heart raced. "Anyone in there?" someone said for the second time. There was a long silence. "This is the Memphis Police."

I took a very deep breath of relief and said, "Just a minute, I'll be right out." I got dressed, slid the pistol into the sleeping bag, and exited. Two police officers stood in the early morning cold, their collars pulled up over their ears. One rocked from foot to foot in the universal ritual of warmth. Condensation floated skyward as one introduced himself and his partner. Blizzard ran with his usual enthusiasm, not sensing my irritation at not so much as a single warning bark. We shook hands and they inquired about my presence.

"This is the worst part of Memphis you could have picked to camp in. I wouldn't stay around long if I were you," one said.

"We don't even like coming down here," his partner added. "You're lucky you have anything left over there." We walked to the canoe where they examined the craft and its contents. "You got all that stuff, a dog, and yourself, in that little boat and paddled it up that river, God Almighty!" the one named Bob exclaimed. We walked to a high barbecue stand where I started a fire. They held their black-gloved hands over it, rubbing warmth into them.

"What kind of heater you got in there?" officer Dave asked.

"None," I said, "Just a sleeping bag."

An "I know a nut when I see one" glance was granted.

I kept my thoughts to myself as Bob stated that he, "Didn't know the Mississippi River went all the way to Alaska."

They were obviously getting cold and offered me the morning paper if I'd walk back to the police car to get it. I declined; they wished me "the best of luck," and advised me to watch where I camped in the future.

"Well, you know, I have my trusty watchdog to protect me." We laughed at my partner.

"Yeah, we noticed. We sort of sneaked right up on you, didn't we?" were Dave's final words. With a wave, they started up the hill to their warm, idling car. On their advice, I left Memphis immediately.

What Cold Is

As the sun had yet to rise the morning was cold. But without a headwind and only a moderate current, I made good time. Once past Memphis, the absence of land worried me. None was seen throughout the morning and throughout the day; by evening I was twenty miles upstream in a place called Shelby Forest. I didn't want to spend another night trying to sleep in a rocking and rolling canoe. The sky had turned overcast, and my arms told me they had had enough. Paddling from 7:00 A.M. non-stop, I also felt my stomach groaning at its neglect after a mere cookie and handful of granola 13 hours ago.

In search of high ground, I followed a flooded road running perpendicular to the river in hopes of reaching land before dark. Within 200 yards the path opened into a clearing. In the middle stood a dilapidated shack teetering on six-by-six-inch posts. I circled the shanty in the canoe, eyeing its possibilities. Before completing the evaluation, a jon boat sped down the flooded road and crossed the clearing just as I had. Two older men eyed me as we exchanged greetings. Inquiring about any nearby land, they informed me that I could either follow the flooded road inland a mile or follow the river where a high bank would be found half a mile upstream. They made their preference known, assuring me numerous times the high bank on the river was the best decision.

With that advice I went back to the river, knowing that within the hour I'd have a hot supper and a good night's sleep. The current seemed stronger as I paddled through my deep exhaustion until reaching a mileage marker. The water was only a foot deep and somehow, I knew this was the high dry bank I was assured of.

Markers are only put on prominent points and this was one. I had to be sure and traveled in vein another half hour. The only thing that grew from the depths was the darkness that began to slowly envelop me. A curse echoed across the Mississippi as I vowed never to seek counsel again.

Nonetheless, I continued to grasp at refuge as I approached a logjam. A large stubble-filled tree extended well into the river. I veered toward its bobbing crown and slowly fought against the current. I was just beyond the crux of the obstacle, planning to head into the trees for another night spent floating, when my friend the river kicked the bucket I was standing on. I was fine, and then I was, *Oh shit! I'm goin' in—.*

The bow got caught by the turbulent water around the logjam and turned abruptly inward. There was nothing I could do. The canoe struck the bobbing tree broadside with a sickening thud and rolled before I could even take a breath. It was sucked under the log with me right behind it. The force was staggering. Somehow, I grabbed the crotch of a branch at the backside of the tree trunk and the bow decking of the canoe. There I was, doing a gymnast's iron cross, one hand grasping the canoe, the other defiantly holding the bobbing log.

I was going to be a cartoon, pulled apart at the arms. The numbing floodwater's current held a constant test against my precarious strength. With great effort I pulled the peak of the overturned craft towards the log. I was draining rapidly. Luckily branches immobilized the canoe, enabling me to boost myself onto the troublesome tree and assess the situation.

What I could see in the fading light wasn't good. Most of my gear floated, hung-up in the logjam. There was no sign of Blizzard. How long I could balance on this bobbing log was questionable at best. Needing to do something, anything, I reached down, pulled the canoe as far over the log as possible, and flipped it right side up.

I heard the *slosh, slosh, slosh* of dog paws. Having left his unseen perch to get to me, Blizzard was struggling against the murky water. I cheered him on to no avail; the current was much too strong. He veered inland and managed to get his front paws on a log. After a short rest and a final effort, he got his back feet up. Shaking himself fiercely, he walked the length of the log, inspecting his predicament. I shouted at him to sit before he fell off. He gave me a quick glance, shook himself again, sat down, and started to whimper.

Blizzard was safe, the canoe was somewhat secure, and I was out of the water. The first check-boxes were marked, but I was shivering badly. One pack floated in the canoe and luckily there was a frying pan in it. I bailed and bailed and bailed. The canoe was two-thirds empty but no matter how much effort I exerted, the last third remained unchanged. Then, in the remaining light, I noticed water gurgling through in two places. It was as good as it was going to get.

Untying the spare paddle, I maneuvered the canoe off the log. With a water-infested canoe and the powerful current, it was a trick to reach Blizzard's perch. He sat patiently on the log, showing no resemblance to a prized Samoyed. When I did reach him, persuasive force was needed to get him back into the boat. It seemed Blizzard wanted nothing more to do with the art of canoeing.

As Blizzard stood shivering in six inches of water, we passed what was left of my floating equipment. I had no intention of stopping to dig it out of the logjam. There was but one thought on my mind, *find that old cabin*.

Would it even be possible? Before long, it was as black a night as I had ever witnessed. The only variation was the different shade of black representing the tree line. No moon or stars showed through the heavy overcast. Longing for a flashlight, I bailed more than paddled. Just keeping the water-filled canoe from rolling and pointed downstream was a task. Blizzard stood in the cold water, shivering, whimpering, searching for a dry place. My knees wouldn't stop shaking. I squeezed them together as hard as I could as I drifted, bailed, and paddled for what seemed hours. *Did I pass the shack in the dark?* I prayed not, for the only other alternative was Memphis, hours and hours away. *Those Memphis cops don't know what cold is,* I scowled. In my drenched clothing, I was shaking from head to foot.

I quit looking for the flooded road that led to the shack for I'd never see it in the dark. Instead, I concentrated on the tree line. Three tall pines grew in the clearing with the cabin and their tops extended well above the surrounding forest. In daylight, they were clearly visible from the river. At night, I wasn't sure. They were my only chance.

I bailed and paddled, paddled and bailed, all the while straining into and over the black tree line. Then, I saw one. Then, the other two appeared. They were just three coal-colored spikes against a background of black space. I don't know how I ever distinguished them, and I didn't care as I forced myself and the canoe through the forest, branches raking my hands and slapping my face. The canoe crashed through thick brush and in the current bounced off menacing trees until it floated unhindered in the clearing. Since the cabin was somewhere out there in the dark, I went blindly searching for it. Little as it was, I found it, looming out there in the night.

It seemed like an eternity since colliding with the log as I paddled to the stairway and gingerly stepped on the first rotted board. The next step was missing. Standing on the third step, I pulled the canoe's bow onto the first. Then, with my feet staying over on the stringers in case of a rotted step, I advanced up to the porch.

Ghostly shadows appeared as I lit a waterproof match. The sulfur fumes soon succumbed to the musty odors of damp wood and dirt. A cobweb brushed my face as I crossed the threshold into what appeared to be the kitchen. It was barren, furnished with a rusty bed frame, half a table, and an upright metal locker-cabinet. Six wooden doors leaned against a back wall. The many windows had gaping holes, limp shreds of clouded plastic clung to their frames. There was no stove here, no warmth.

Dragging the rusted six-foot cabinet to the bedroom window, I opened the tall locker door and brushed out the few bent nails that littered its floor. Reaching out the window, a piece of crumbling wood siding was pried off and then turned to kindling across my knee. Soon smoke rolled from the top of the locker and I undressed.

Water poured from my boots. Streams of it ran to the floor as I wrung my pants and shirt. After redressing, I backed to the fire and began the slow process of drying out.

The shaking and chills diminished as my clothing slowly dried. A thick cloud of smoke clung to the ceiling, some of it eventually finding its way through the glassless windows. I was a vertical rotisserie for three hours with some success, but dampness and fatigue hinted at hypothermia. I felt I could sleep for days, but things had to be done.

The air was mercilessly cold as I left the fire to retrieve the pack wedged inside the canoe. Standing on the porch, I found a horrid surprise. I looked around, staring at reality. The canoe was gone. Squinting into the black night, I could see nothing. With a deep, lonely sigh, I walked back to the fire.

I awoke curled in a ball the same as Blizzard on the dirty wood floor, shivering, hands clenched between my knees, pondering my fate. The fire had died long ago. False dawn crept through the trees and into the building. Not a noise sounded; nothing stirred. I removed my damp, jean-jacket-blanket and assembled a fire. Condensation rose to the ceiling as I rubbed my hands, arms, and legs, followed by jumping jacks in an effort to stop shivering. A small area in front of the locker eventually warmed. Sitting as close as I dared, I leaned against the wall, absorbing as much heat as possible.

The sun's rays finally poured through the kitchen window. It found the bedroom through a knothole in the wall and puddled at my feet. Rising stiffly, I thought about the specifics of my current situation. I was in a windowless room of an old house, suspended five feet above the floodwater. There was no food, no water, and no means of escape. Though not yet a floater, I was slowly becoming another victim of this mighty unforgiving river.

It wasn't hard to visualize the canoe's disappearance. The river had been rising all week. I had left the canoe unchecked on the step for three hours. While the river rose, the canoe rose, and the current did the rest. A simple rope tied to the handrail would have sufficed. It was stupid, ignorant, and highly unprofessional. It was also history.

I walked to the railing of the sunny front porch with one hope— the canoe may have gotten caught among the trees. Scanning the edge of the clearing renewed my faith, for 100 yards away were two red points piercing the muddy waterline. I was getting a second chance.

Not many options were available to retrieve it. The water was nasty for swimming and if I could help it, I had no intention of getting back in. Waiting for someone could take weeks, and starvation and exposure would set in before the river receded. There was only one choice. Primitive as it might be, a raft would do.

If the materials were available, this type of craft could be simply constructed, especially one that only had to float 100 yards. The partial table was fit only for firewood. However, the metal locker might be watertight. In addition, there were the doors.

Bringing four from the back room, I laid them on the front porch. Two began to crumble in transit. Using a piece of angle iron wrestled from the rusted bed frame and the six bent nails from the locker, I hammered until they were sandwiched together, crumbling ones in the center. Then, with a clothesline lanyard from the front porch, I carefully slid them down the steps, eased them into the water, and securely tied them to the handrail. Gingerly, I stepped on. It sank.

Without nails, the last two loose doors were laid on the floating four. They suspended my weight a foot below the surface. Though missing the bottom panel, a one-hinged door guarding a small back room was added to the pile, and the bedroom door formed the craft's deck, if it floated.

With the caution of a cat, I boarded. Though anything but stable, no water lapped at my feet. Now I needed propulsion. Once obtained, I carefully untied the lanyard and pushed off, gliding through the water in the early morning mist.

God, I hope nobody sees me, I thought as I took aim at the two red peaks. It would be hard to explain and very embarrassing, for there is little dignity in paddling a pile of doors down the Mississippi River with a piece of siding. Though the current tried to veer me sideways, I kept the course at dead reckoning, and the expedition went according to plan.

Thrilled to finally be reunited with my canoe, I bailed to the puncture holes and exchanged crafts. With a gentle shove, the raft floated toward certain destruction while I headed for the cabin. There Blizzard waited for me. After struggling to lift the pack, items were thrown to the porch one at a time. Blizzard inspected each item for its edible qualities and escaped with a package of chicken thighs.

Now the canoe had to be repaired. Getting it up the stairway of the cabin was a grand fracas. I pulled, pushed, kicked, and cursed before it was laid keel up in the kitchen. Three punctures lay along the hull. I felt fortunate not to have collided with whatever pierced it.

I silently thanked the stranger in the Greenville parking lot as the holes were carefully duct-taped with his gift. The canoe was forced down the stairs with the help of gravity, and I immediately left for the scene of the previous nights' disaster.

The bow rose high in the water with each stroke of the empty canoe. It seemed effortless compared to last night's nightmare. Before long I spied the blue pack-frame bobbing within the knotted logjam. It was surrounded by plastic bottles, oranges, apples and boxes of Jell-O. The food pack hung fast to a log, upside down. I pulled the canoe onto the largest log and got out. Using my arms to balance among the entwined mass of wood, I log-hopped, picking up what I could and throwing it into the canoe. It took some time, but when the shapeless pile between the thwarts reached its zenith, I sat in the stern, peeled an orange, and realized it had been 36 hours since I had eaten. Those soggy chicken thighs were starting to sound pretty good.

More was retrieved than I expected. I recovered an apple a half-mile downstream on my way back. At the shack, I brought things carefully up the steps. Blizzard waited patiently. After emptying the packs, draining the water, and scattering my belongings across the floor, I counted the losses. A 300 mm Konica Hexanon zoom lens, a new Puma hunting knife, my Smith & Wesson pistol, a complete book of navigational maps, two flashlights with extra batteries, a radio, the fiberglass kit, most of four weeks of groceries, diaries, and Blizzard's dog pack. When it was all totaled, the monetary depressant totaled $2,100.

After things lay in orderly rows from wall to wall in the bedroom and the porch was crowded with drying clothes swinging from a makeshift clothesline, there was nothing more I could do. Not wanting to continue without a camera made going to Memphis necessary. It was a clear day and the weather looked promising. Hopefully, it wouldn't take long and maybe by the time I returned everything would have dried, if it was all still here.

The flooded road that left the river continued past the clearing. It was a skeletal tunnel; leafless trees sprang from both sides and in blossoming would surely obscure the sky. Turkeys flew from tree to tree as I passed. The current-free paddling was a relaxing break from the constant upstream struggle. The bow skipped systematically for 45 minutes before a gravel road rose from the murky water. I got out and pulled the canoe up, turned it over and tied it to a stout branch, and with dripping camera case in hand, started to walk.

Mud *oozed* to the brim of my boots as the road led in one direction—up. Blizzard didn't seem to mind. His dashes here and there covered twice my distance. It took most of an hour before I was out of the mud and could kick the side of a closed Forest Service Permit Station to remove the oppressive mud from my boots. I could also kick myself for bringing Blizzard. It took me two hours to realize people weren't stopping for someone with a dirty, muddy dog. I made the decision to go it alone.

We walked down the highway, Blizzard prancing in noble fashion, barking at every car that passed, unaware of his fate. Soon I found a thickly wooded area well off the highway, secured Blizzard to a tree, rubbed behind his ears a few minutes, and walked away.

Finally, a car stopped to my begging thumb. Even as I slammed the door, a mournful howl could be heard in the distance.

The back wheels of the 1957 Chevy spun as we fishtailed down the dusty dirt road. The kid tried to look nonchalant as his high-school tassels danced from the rearview mirror. Unimpressed, I got out after eight silent miles, ten miles from downtown Memphis. I walked three blocks and stuck my thumb out on the fourth. It was a two-way highway and before long a police car stopped. "If you want to hitchhike around here, you get up on that sidewalk," he said. It wasn't a request.

"Nobody can see me from there," I complained.

"Well, you either get up there or in the car."

At least I had options.

For now, the first seemed the more sensible. When his taillights vanished over a hill, I broke for the curb. Within minutes a cream-colored Cadillac stopped. I opened the door and an elderly man told me to hop in. He told me his name and stated that he was a prominent businessman. Listening to my current dilemma, he then related to a short canoe trip he accomplished 35 years ago. "One of the better times in my life," he lamented.

"I'm so impressed with what you're doing young man, I'll take you anywhere you want to go." His words were quite welcome. Then, he put his hand on my shoulder, squeezed a little, slid it down to my knee, and started rubbing. "By the way," he mentioned, "I'm a little gay and if I get out of line, just let me know."

I grabbed his wrist, put it on the steering wheel and said, "I'm not, and I will." I walked into Memphis Photo while my new friend waited in his Cadillac drinking beer.

"May I help you?" a smiling salesman asked.

"These fell into the river a couple of days ago and I need to get them fixed," I said.

"My God, they're brand new!" he exclaimed while examining the camera gear. "I hope you have insurance," he said while replacing the items into the case. I didn't. He gave me the business card of a repairman on the other side of town.

I didn't like using people, but this situation was different. My chauffer tilted a can of Grain Belt as I explained the issue. "Sure, I know where the place is. I'll take you there. You do your business, and I'll give you a ride back to your canoe at Shelby Forest."

The Cadillac was parked across from the repair shop on Sumner

Avenue. "I'll be waiting in the bar there. Come on over when you're done," he announced. Nodding, I crossed the street and entered Southern Photo.

A lady in her early thirties greeted me at the small photo counter. After a brief explanation, she said her husband was in the back and to go right in. Pepper Brewer was concentrating on a small Polaroid as I passed through a swinging half-door and stood before his desk. We exchanged greetings and before long he had removed the individual photo pieces from my soaked case. Water ran onto his desk. With raised eyebrows, he gave me a sideways glance and said, "Got a while?"

It was two hours before the verdict was reached. The 35-mm wide-angle lens could be salvaged. The cameras and zoom lens were labeled as lost. Leaving the equipment, I thanked him and agreed to return in the morning for the repaired lens.

The Cadillac waited patiently across the street. Instead Pepper opened the back door for me. It led to an alley, which I followed for a block, went right for six more, and then hopped the first bus going downtown. I still didn't like using people.

I needed a new camera. I needed money. *I needed my sister.* She answered on the third ring. After a cursory account of my incident, she said she would see what she could do and call me back. It was a tall order. The banks were closed, and it was Friday. Barely ten-dollars graced my pocket.

Within 15 minutes the phone in the booth rang. I snatched it on the first ring. *What a relief!* I don't know how she did it, but $600 would be here by morning. After a promise to be a little more careful and a grateful thank you I left the phone booth in search of a hotel room that matched my wallet.

I found a sign that said, Tennessee Hotel Rooms $3.00 and Up. I entered the lobby. Old black men sat around a table playing checkers; one read a newspaper. At the desk, I asked the gray-haired clerk to explain the difference in the price of rooms and settled on the one for $6.50. It was halfway to the penthouse. "You'll have to wait for the bellhop. He'll show you where the room is," he informed me.

"That's all right. I can find it," I said, but he wouldn't relinquish the key. Pushing a button produced an old, bent man in uniform. After inquiring about my luggage—*I didn't have any*—I followed him as he shuffled into an ancient elevator. Sliding a metal gate shut, we slowly ascended to the fifth floor. There was a ding and a jerk. When he opened the gate, we entered a long, dimly lit hallway. At the end of this plaster tunnel stood a bright light announcing an emergency entrance. It smelled of musty wood. In places, loose wallpaper lay buckled on the walls.

Unlocking room number 526, he turned on the only light, opened the curtain to expose the only dirty window, and handed me the key. If I had any money, I would have tipped him. Instead, I just said thank you; after a pause, he turned and left. The view from the clouded window was one of neatly stacked red bricks. The floor was bare wood, paint was peeling off the exposed pipes, and the ceiling apparently had a habit of losing plaster—some of which dotted the green, wool bedspread. The bed and a painted chest of drawers furnished the room.

The bathroom held most of the essentials. Leaning against a rusted sink was a small shower stall. A painted ring mounted on the wall held a single towel. The door opened inward and obscured the toilet. To use it, one had to open the door, get into the shower stall, close the door, and there it appeared. If one had long legs, you would have to use it sidesaddle, for there were only inches beyond mine to the rusty sink. As far as toilet paper was concerned, it was bring-your-own. My inspection made me wonder what the three-dollar room was like.

After showering and redressing in the same clothes, I walked to a nearby theater to see what was playing. It was called *The Black Gestapo* and was rated R. The show started in twenty minutes. I paid three dollars and went inside.

Its luxury rivaled the hotel's. There was barely enough light to see the rows of seats, of which held little comfort. *And, how could you watch a movie without popcorn?* A few people were already there as I sat down and listened to the dreamy music that played before showtime. Soon the place was packed; that surprised me for such an old hard-off place. Looking around, something seemed strange. I couldn't place it. As the title screen rolled, I noticed, *I'm the only white guy here.* Every other person I saw was black.

There were no previews, no cartoons. The music stopped and the movie started. I became increasingly aware of myself. The plot involved black people who were being pushed around by the white underground. There were payoffs, rapes, protection money, and drugs. They decided to retaliate. One black man formed an army and went against the white underground, annihilating them. Every time a white person was shot or beat up, a roar filled the theater. I could slouch no further in my seat. When one white man raped a black woman, five of the black soldiers entered his house and caught him in the bathtub. Four held him down while one castrated him. It was a bloody mess. The cheers in the amphitheater were deafening. By the time the show ended, I was five blocks away and still going strong.

A block from the hotel I passed a darkened doorway. "Hey there, handsome, wanna have some fun?" came a feminine voice from the shadows.

"No, thanks," I declined and kept walking.

"You sure there, sweetie?" I heard from behind me. They had turned out of the doorway behind me and were silhouetted by the streetlight.

I took the direct route to room 526, locked the door, and went to bed. This was not the part of Memphis for a white boy from a small town in northern Minnesota to be.

After returning the hotel key the following morning, I picked up $600 at the Western Union and headed for Memphis Photo. We dickered for thirty minutes before I spent $300 on a camera body with hopes that Pepper had repaired my wide-angle lens.

When I got to Southern Photo the Cadillac was gone. Pepper was oiling the lens when I arrived and announced that it *should* work. Securing the lens in its case, I asked him what I owed for his trouble. "Nothing," he said.

"But you can't spend all that time and not get anything for it," I suggested.

He looked at me for a few seconds and said, "Okay, I'll tell you how you can repay me. Let me give you a ride back to your canoe and we'll call it square." *What could I say?*

A light rain fell as we neared Shelby Forest. Our conversation drifted from hunting and fishing to the whereabouts of the canoe. After a few wrong turns, we stopped next to the Forestry Station. I was openly mauled by Blizzard. Nothing remained of his leash, and I felt lucky to get him back. By the time Blizzard's emotions were drained, Pepper and I were layered in mud. Pepper wanted to take a few pictures of the canoe, but when informed of the three-mile walk through the mud, it dampened his ambition. Pepper gave me his business card, telling me to look him up if I ever got back to Memphis. We shook hands, I thanked him, and he waved as his truck rolled down the muddy road.

The mud seemed worse than before. As I pulled my boots from the quagmire with each step, their prints quickly filled with water. *At least it's downhill to the canoe.* Luckily, it lay exactly where I had left it. With paddle in hand, I slipped the canoe into the water where the flooded road submerged and in a steady drizzle, headed for the old shack.

My clothes and sleeping bag swung in a slight breeze as I came to the clearing and advanced to the old house. Rain rolled off the gutter-less eaves, its rhythm against the tin obliterating all other sounds. Even though I was drenched, it was good to have returned to the old place. It was almost like coming home.

It was Sunday, March 30th, a cold, gray, windy morning. The night had been long and restless, with the small fire quickly dwindling and the sleeping bag far from dry. Sitting under the empty window, I pulled my boots on. Blizzard lay nearby with half-opened eyes. A mouse dashed through the room, heading for the safety of its hole. Blizzard pounced but the rodent squeezed through with ample time. His furious barks echoed throughout the house and died across the water. I got up and jogged away the chills. Looking toward the river, the barren trees swaying in the steady mist convinced me to stay another day. After a light breakfast, I settled beside the smoky locker to pass the time reading *Proudly They Die.*

The sound of a motorboat lifted my head from my chest. The book lay where it had slid from my sleeping hand. A jon boat came through the wooded area and was crossing the clearing. There was no doubt where it was headed.

Shortly an elderly man tied his boat to the railing and came up the steps. By the artful way he climbed, it was obvious he had experience with this particular flight. Without a greeting, he gruffly asked, "Just what do you think you're doing here?" When I explained the situation, he grunted and then barged across the porch, searching every room. The fire in the locker particularly perturbed him. "Boy, you'd better watch that fire awfully carefully," he warned. He seemed mesmerized by the wall-to-wall carpeting I had laid—my food and gear. On returning to the porch, he mentioned that the owner would kick me out if he found me here. I said I'd be gone in the morning. With another caution about the fire, he pulled his Evinrude motor to life and disappeared down the flooded road.

The sun had yet to rise when I jockeyed the last pack down the remaining steps and placed it in the bow. With Blizzard boarded, I untied the canoe and was off. At the forest's edge, I couldn't help but look back at the dirty abandoned shack in the flooded clearing and wonder what would have happened if it hadn't been there.

Instead of challenging the river, I followed a road that paralleled it. Before long, it opened to a vast expanse of water. For ten hours I battled flooded cotton fields, poling in two feet of water, which without warning, would turn deep and swift while sporting treacherous crosscurrents.

By evening, high bluffs appeared on the Tennessee horizon, the only land seen all day. After two hours, I was confronted by a barbwire fence stretching for miles in each direction. Just beyond the fence was a yellow house. To my left and behind it stood a large barn. Built on a knoll, the house had, so far, escaped any water damage, but the barn seemed to hang in two feet of water. Moving to a gate provided a view down a corral, through the open barn and across endless miles of unbroken water.

The partially submerged gate groaned loudly as I undid the loop and the locking rope and prodded it open with the paddle. Closing the gate behind me, I maneuvered through the narrow cow corral, entered the barn, and started toward a square of light at the far end of the darkened interior.

Cow stalls lined the walls and even Mother Nature failed to neutralize their odor. Nearing the back door, I began to hear quiet voices. In a dark corner, two men in waders illuminated a tractor with flashlights. Hating to be impolite and intrude on their conversation, I merely said, "Good afternoon!" as I passed through. They turned and glanced at each other as I grinned at my sense of humor and their disbelief. I had vanished through the door before either could speak and was camped at the bluffs by sunset.

Before the morning sun crowned the treetops, I was well away from the bluffs. Land vanished as one flooded field after another was crossed. Only miles of small iron fenceposts gave testimony to the twisted wire boundaries lying beneath the flowing watery silt. After nine hours in the field, I reached solid ground and the riverbank at a place called Richardson's Landing, Tennessee.

A sheer rock wall rose from the river a short way upstream from a boat dock. Three people greeted me as I passed the dock. The rock wall looked severe as it watched the rapids below. Floating, froth-capped haystacks shot past the wall, only to be whirled into submission far downstream. The canoe picked up speed as I was sucked towards it. I was in its eddy, headed where I didn't want to go.

It took some hard back-paddling to get to the dock. "You're lucky you didn't try to go out there. We pull quite a few bodies from that every year," one of the men on the dock said. *Funny he didn't warn me the first time I went by.* Maybe it was their sick entertainment. "This is the worst part of the river, about 235 feet deep out there right now," the same man said.

My inquiry regarding the whereabouts of a store was answered by another of the trio as he said, "Go back about a quarter-mile, and you'll see a small creek. It'll take you right to it."

It was a creek, very narrow and very winding. After an hour of maneuvering the hairpin turns, I stopped beneath a bridge. A dozen people stood on the bridge as I climbed the bank and walked past two outdated gas pumps and entered the store. Behind the counter was Jim Ticer. He owned and operated the store, and after purchasing a few things I asked him if there was any place I could camp for a few days in hopes that the water would recede. "Just paddle past the bridge and stay wherever you want," he said. "I doubt if anyone will bother you."

I didn't have to go far to find a secluded area that suited my needs. I spent two lazy days there. During the evenings I'd walk Blizzard to the river and watch the rapids. Inevitably, I'd stop at the store and talk to Jim. One of the more interesting things he said about the rapids was that, "People come down here in the spring to watch full-grown trees hit the rapids, spin around half a dozen times in one of the whirlpools, stand straight on end, and get sucked under to pop up a half-mile downstream." He also stated, "It's a good place to avoid in a canoe." I noted his suggestion.

The river dropped two feet in two days. On the third day, a visitor arrived. It was a state game warden. He said he saw my camp from the road and stopped to investigate. I knew there was more involved than a courtesy call, for my camp couldn't be seen from the road. I had made sure of that. But, with formalities dispensed, we had a pleasant fireside chat where he left on a cheerful note. Shortly after, Blizzard and I took our walk to the landing.

The rapids looked hardly improved, but restlessness was devouring me. With plans to leave in the morning, I was walking back to camp when a car stopped next to me. A voice said, "Where are you staying?"

It caught me off-guard, and I asked, "What?" with tongue-in-cheek.

"I said, where are you staying?" he repeated. His car window was cracked open two inches and both doors were locked.

"I'm staying up the road away," I answered.

"I know damn well you're camped up the creek in the bluff, and you're on private property, of which, I share part ownership and I want you out of there immediately!" he shouted.

Glaring at the little twit hidden behind the window, I repeated some information obtained from Jim. "Well, I happen to know that an 83-year old lady owned it, and if she told me to leave, I would."

The guy's color reddened as he yelled, "You've got my mother so scared that she won't even come out of the house!" Then added, "I'm also having you arrested for killing her dog. His whole head was smashed in with a rock!"

He seemed to be spiraling. "Well, that's too bad, but I didn't have anything to do with that," I said with little sympathy.

"You sure have a pretty dog there. Yes, you do," he replied threateningly.

His threat hit a nerve; "Yah, and if anything happens to him, I'll be looking for you," I snarled.

"Just remember," he warned as he pulled away. "You're in Tipton County now."

I waved and decided to stay one more day just to see what this county had in store for me. It came to nothing. Nevertheless, I couldn't resist one more stroll down to the landing, just to fill their hearts with terror.

Not wanting to deal with the authorities once again, I packed up early the next day and stopped by the store to see Jim one last time. After a firm handshake and a thanks, I was off. At the first bend in the little creek, I looked back. Jim still stood on the bridge watching, wishing.

I held concerns about ferrying across the river below the rapids. Even after drifting downstream a half-mile before crossing, small whirlpools still swirled beneath the canoe. As I slipped into the flooded tree line on the other side, a definite tension released.

Even so, the current was strong. It swirled around trees and through tangled logjams. It leapt and dipped, changing direction defiantly. After six hours, progress was at a stalemate. I had to recross. Knowing what lay downstream, I spared no effort as I crossed.

Darkening clouds rolled over the trees as I sought their shelter well above Richardson's Landing. There was no doubt it was going to rain. Having not seen land since leaving the landing, I was relieved when I came to a rise in a flooded road. It was as wide as a single-lane dirt road and no longer; its height arched inches above the floodwater. While gathering tall yellow reeds to pad the tent floor from along the shoulder it started to rain. There were no warning sprinkles; it just poured.

The tent snapped in the pelting rain as I shook it out over the reeds. Refusing to penetrate the hard-packed gravel, staking the tent was a problem. With my ax already at the bottom of the Mississippi, the only alternative seemed to be the cast-iron frying pan. Three hits on the first peg shattered the bottom. I found that its corpse could be skipped across the water three times before sinking.

The tent lay soaked and unerect. Wading through the water, it deepened the further I got from camp. I floated the only two meager logs I could find to the bump, tied the tent's guylines to them, and secured the fly. All in all, it was a mess. Instead of the fly being taut enough to allow water drainage, it sagged, forming pools where water seeped through. I knew it would be a long night—and it was! The deadfalls rolled inward, allowing the tent to sag farther. Soon the wet nylon blanketed my sleeping bag. Many times, I ventured into the rain to pull the logs further away from the tent.

Blizzard didn't help. There was no way he could escape the bump and if he wanted to run free, it was in tight circles. Where he ran the most was in to and out of the tent. Throughout the dark night, he'd sneak in, dog-stunk wet, shake himself from head to hind, and then curl up on the driest spot he could find, the sleeping bag.

I was not in the best of moods when I threw the wet sleeping bag aside and stepped into the steady drizzle. Everything was rolled up and stuffed under a tarp. Little remained of the bump. By evening, it would be under water. Eating half of a box of granola while standing in the rain tempered my mood enough to face hour, after hour, after hour of flooded fields.

I had just passed a huge lone tree standing defiantly in an endless world of water when a motorboat approached from behind. A loud screech echoed across the water as an aluminum propeller chopped into an unseen impediment. "Hey, you, come back here!" someone shouted from the crippled craft. I kept paddling. It was hard enough struggling against the current without having to drift fifty yards back just to talk to a couple of guys.

Later, another shout came my direction. This one I decided wasn't that far off and started drifting towards two men. They clung to a branch as I maneuvered beside them. In their backwoods way, they asked what I was doing out in the middle of this field and where I thought I was going. Upon my reply, the bigger of the two declared, "Well, there's no damn way you're getting back to the river the way you're going. If you want to get back to the river you gotta go to the town over there and cross where the damn river road got washed out."

"Well, I guess I'll have to go over that way then," I complied.

He agreed and cranked his outboard and was off, shouting, "We'll meet you there for a few beers." That was my introduction to the colorful and profane Elton Jackson.

I pulled the canoe next to their jon boat where water poured across the road. They were waiting and we walked the quarter mile to a red, two-story, wooden building that was a bar. Slabs of concrete sidewalks stood on end, uprooted by the force of the floodwaters. Faded letters on a lopsided sign said Goldwater-Unincorporated.

Every bit of the town was either mud or water except a twenty-foot area in front of the building which was covered so completely with broken beer bottles that the earth was obliterated. I tied Blizzard to the canoe, and Elton, his partner, and I walked through the frail front door and crossed the room to a well-used bar. I ordered a beer and Elton ordered a half pint. "Play any pool?" he asked me while giving his partner a knowing wink.

"Sure, I'll shoot you a game?" I said gamely.

After losing four straight, he racked his cue and with a few profanities muttered, "Let's eat, asshole!!"

After dinner Elton offered me a place to stay at his place since his wife and kids were gone. I accepted his generous offer and we both headed to the boats with two pints in hand. "By the way," Elton asked, "How you gonna get that little canoe up to the road so we can pull it across?"

"I'm going to paddle it," I said.

Laughing, Elton exclaimed, "If you think *you* can paddle that wimpy craft up *that* current, then I'm gonna just stay here and watch."

I got into the canoe, aligned the bow with the water boiling through the washout, and started up. It was strenuous and damn slow, but finally, the water's grip lessened and I was in quieter waters.

"How in hell did he do that?" Elton said in disbelief, almost to himself.

"Wasn't too hard," I lied with a shrug of my shoulders. We met at the grain elevator a small way up the road where I secured my canoe with Blizzard standing guard and got into Elton's rusted 1962 Chevy.

Mud arched behind us as the engine whined to its capacity. It was a Chevy with enough power to navigate the mud. The Chevy hit bottom twice before we slid to a stop inches from what I assumed was his front porch. "I think I know how you lost your muffler," I commented.

"Yah," he said, "It'll be four damn years next month that she dropped off on me. Sit down anywhere," Elton offered as we entered the old house. Shortly he joined me on the couch, opened a pint, and spoke mostly of his family. After a dinner of fried potatoes, beans, and half-cooked pork chops, the empty plates were returned to their niches in the sink. Elton said, "Come on, I'll give you a tour of this shitty little town."

The ride out was equal to the ride in. "See that telephone pole there?" Elton said as we drove the few miles of road not under water a second time. "There was a different one there a year ago. They just got around to putting a new one in," he said.

"Why, what happened to it?" I asked.

"That's where I killed my son, sure as if I put a gun to his head and pulled the trigger, I killed him, only 14 years old too," he said. There was a long silence. "Got drunk at some party and decided to take him home, going too fast and hit that god damn pole, crushed his whole head in. Just 'cause I went out and got drunk—now he's dead. Fourteen years old and I killed him. Don't know how long I can live with that." In the darkness, I could see tears streaming down his face. I passed him the pint and he took a long drink. Silence passed.

We were back in the house before long, and he had me read a letter from his daughter. "I never went to school much, so I don't read or write too well, and my woman ain't here to read it," he explained, "but don't ever call me dumb. Nobody can call me dumb. There are many biblical quotes from this Bible right here that I can quote by heart!" he said, thumping the Holy Book on a side table. I had no intention of calling him dumb and was more than glad to read his letter.

After reading the letter, Elton got up, took his shirt off, and mumbled something about going to bed. He walked over to the chair where his pet cat, named Tom, lay asleep. Grabbing it by the tail, he took two steps to the door, opened it, and let old tom sail off into the night. The screeching warned the three-pound chihuahua named Brownie but before he could move, a big hand clasped his scruff, lifting him off the couch. Elton walked causally to the bathroom with Brownie's four legs going every which way, gave the dog a toss in, closed the door, and said good night.

Just as abruptly as bed time came, so did Elton's greeting, "Come on, get your sorry ass out of bed!" It was early, and Elton was already making breakfast. After breakfast, Elton was in a hurry to start another day, so we created another pile of dishes in the sink, climbed into the Chevy, and drove to the canoe.

"Want a ride in a canoe?" I asked Elton.

"No way in hell anyone would get me into one of those little things and go out on that devil river," he said. He was curious to see what I was carrying so I unsnapped the splash cover and showed him. "Food, clothing, and shelter all right there. Guess that makes it your home, then."

"Yah, I guess it does," I agreed.

"You know, there's no way in hell that you're going to make it to Alaska in that thing. You doing it for money or what?" he wanted to know.

"Just doing it," I responded with a shrug. I had to explain it to myself before I could explain it to anyone else. We shook hands and I thanked him for his hospitality. With Blizzard boarded I shoved off. Looking back, I saw Elton still standing there and I shouted, "See you, old timer!" He waved and that was the last I saw of Elton Jackson.

Normal pace was maintained for but a few short hours before sunset as a strong north wind persisted throughout the day. Worries of finding land ebbed as the water level dropped drastically. Then, two days of splendid weather brought me to Caruthersville, Missouri. It was late, and the stores had already closed as darkness seeped over the town. Campsites didn't exist but a ragged ledge in the heaved concrete levee formed a tolerable niche for my sleeping bag.

It wasn't as tolerable as I had expected; sleep was fitful in the cramped cubby. Then, a blinding sun convinced me it was time to face another day. Rubbing my stiffened neck, I sat up to a wind that howled overhead and stirred the river into a dastardly state.

"Morning!" someone said behind me, making me jump. Still rubbing my neck, I turned to a man patiently perched on a stool of fragmented concrete. "I'm from the Caruthersville newspaper, and I was wondering if I could do an article about you?" he asked.

I felt it a bit early to be interrogated, but said sure. It was nothing but question, after question, after question until I felt my bladder would burst. Then he needed pictures. Finally, after one last thank you, he walked back toward town and I ran for the bushes.

Given the wind situation, I knew traveling would be futile. After maneuvering camp to the local boat landing, I flipped the canoe over to dry. Sweet destiny brought me straight to the local Dairy Queen for a banana-split breakfast just a few blocks away. Work on the canoe's hull commenced after the cold morning meal.

More talk than work was accomplished as people came and went. Around noon a geologist strutted over and bestowed much advice upon me. He told me of my past mistakes, why they happened, and mistakes I'd make in the future. He even advised me on the proper paddling of a canoe after mentioning he completed two 150-mile trips last summer. I just agreed, hoping he would go away. He left within the hour, but not without leaving me twenty pounds of cotton gin pins. "They're the best tent pegs I've ever found," he gloated. They hit the same spot in the river seven out of twelve throws.

The canoe's fiberglass shell was eventually patched and sanded. Supper was at the Dairy Queen, and I left with two hot dogs for Blizzard. He caught the first one and instantly swallowed it whole. The other was sailing through the air, doomed to the same swift fate, as a boy and girl approached through the lengthening shadows. They appeared to be in high school and said they were brother and sister. For an hour they worked on me to go home with them. Bribes such as a hot bath, good food, clean sheets, and a soft bed didn't weaken my resolve to stay with the canoe and equipment. Failing, they said discouraged goodbyes and started home.

They were more persistent than I expected. It wasn't long before a yellow pickup truck stopped, and they came running toward me, reinforced with yet another sister. "We brought you a freshly baked loaf of bread. We also brought our truck, so you can pack all your equipment and come home with us," the brother said. *What could I say?*

It was 10:10 P.M. when I met Mrs. Howard Fike. After a brief conversation, she showed me to a bedroom next to the bathroom. No doubt, the shower felt great. After a good soaking, I dried my wet shirt with their hairdryer and went downstairs. Mrs. Fike had a snack and a glass of milk waiting as I entered the kitchen. After finishing the few dishes, she excused herself, saying that they arose early on their ranch. I retired soon after.

The clean-sheeted bed beckoned, but a light knock on the door halted any progress toward it. It was John, the young brother, and he was ready to talk. We sat on the bed for hours discussing the outdoor life. Things were of great interest to him on this subject and his quest for knowledge seemed unlimited. It wasn't much before daylight when the 15-year old interviewer said, "I better get to bed before my mother finds me here."

It was cruelly early when I heard Mrs. Fike's call for breakfast. Hers sounded nothing like that of Elton Jackson. I'd hardly been between those soft clean sheets an hour. It seemed like such a waste, especially with what I observed—rain pounding on the roof. Dark gray clouds lying over the fields weren't a welcome sight. Breakfast was a healthy plate of bacon, eggs, and toast, along with orange juice and milk. Following this feast, the kids were ushered to school, Mrs. Fike did housework, and I relaxed with the morning paper.

I was nearing the want ads when Mr. Howard Fike entered the house. After introductions, we spent the rest of the day touring his ranch. There were horses, cattle, cotton gins, fields, silos, endless machinery, and crop-dusters. The man had a lot but undoubtedly worked long and hard for it. The day spent with him in the seemingly endless drizzle produced two proposals—a job offer and another night at the ranch. Only one was accepted.

By morning, sun poured through the four-paned window, fresh coffee odors drifting through the house. After another well-served breakfast, everyone sat around the kitchen table. Howard produced a Bible and his eldest daughter read a short passage. Her prayer ended with, "And please let Jerry have a safe trip to Alaska." I was touched.

Everything was packed into the truck and goodbyes were being exchanged when Mrs. Fike demanded that I return the loaf of bread given to me by her children. Upon compliance, she wished me well, placed two fresh, steaming loaves in my hands, and marched back to her kitchen. The daughters went to school, Howard returned to his ranch work, and only John waved from the landing as I continued northward.

By noon, the Delta Queen passed, its churning paddlewheel pushing it toward New Orleans. After its wake had subsided, I used my hard-earned confidence to charge towards a slightly slackened spot where the river washed over a treacherous, white-bubbling wing dam. Forward progress stopped a few feet shy of calmer water. The canoe slid slowly backwards as I groped the muddy water with the paddle for a hold among the rocks. *No way,* I thought, *surely not again!*

With one quick flex by nature, the canoe turned sideways, teetered in limbo against a snag, and then presumed to bob bottom up on its way south. I clung to the gunwale as the shoreline slid by. My survivor-dog was already there, splattering the surrounding brush as he shook from head to tail. The shore was only twenty feet away, and I tried to swim the canoe to it in vain. I didn't want to let go and lose everything that remained. Suddenly the canoe changed course in a distinctly submarine direction. All I could do was hang on as divine sunlight faded from above, sucked into the murky waters of a whirlpool.

My rig and I popped up downstream, twenty seconds later. I lustily gulped reinvigorating air and tightened my grip on the gunwale. I was weakened and could only float passively. Then to my dismay, a strong eddy grasped the canoe, forcing it back upstream. Ahead lay the same swirling water. This time I prepared with three deep breaths and disappeared again.

Upon return to the atmosphere, my mind raced for a means of escape from the watery, drowning carousel. The current took me downstream, but as the eddy again started, I kicked and broke its grasp. Floating freely, I angled toward shore.

Through all of this, where was the hero dog, the one who would lunge into the water, grab his drowning master by the collar, and bring him to safety? Tail wagging, he sat on the bank in total indifference.

Breaths came in heaving bunches as I stood on the bank,

drenched, watching most of my earthly possessions bob in the circling eddy. After emptying the water-filled canoe, I laid in wait for a paddle to circle by. With a timely shove from shore, I managed to glide close enough to snatch it. So equipped, I hovered at the head of the eddy, well away from the whirlpool, retrieving gear as it circled by.

The water-filled packs had to be towed to shore as they were much too heavy to lift over the side. When the eddy was free of multicolored paraphernalia, it became clear that some had escaped, either to the bottom or in the main channel. Either way, they were lost forever. The list of losses lengthened as an ax, radio, yoke, splash cover, tent, all my spare clothes, cooler, and a month-old camera and lens were added to it. In sum they were worth well over a thousand dollars.

It took the few hours left in the day to wring, squeeze, and drain my emaciated kit. I paddled a short distance beyond the site of my wreck, and at the top of a huge hairpin turn stood New Madrid. Historically old, the town could replace little of what I had lost. I camped on the beach that fronted a park of scrap iron and broken glass. The down sleeping bag was beyond hope for at least a few days, forcing a fitful night's sleep beside an open fire.

By May 1st the river was on the rise and summer was making a feeble attempt to oust the remaining days of winter. Before me, Cairo, Illinois glittered in the afternoon sun. Five long, tent-less days had been cataloged since my near-drowning. Barge traffic here in Cairo, where the Mississippi and Ohio Rivers fused, was oppressive for miles.

As I bobbed beside the rusted steel barges, progress was fractions per stroke. I had been traveling the west side of the river and needed to cross in order to reach town. This necessitated traveling well past the confluence and crossing, hoping that the current wouldn't sweep me below the mouth of the Ohio.

It didn't. I slid in to a park, ever so carefully maneuvering between two submerged picnic tables, with the Ohio River on my right and the Mississippi River on my left. It was a milestone of sorts, as now the volume of water to oppose should reduce drastically, since I was upstream of the Ohio River's discharge. A decrepit concrete wall loomed behind a stand of trees. I cached my belongings and gave Blizzard a tour of Cairo.

We walked from store to store and soon most of my equipment was replaced. There seemed to be but one tent in town. It was the economical kind, rated for four years old and up. With the tent on top of my load and black clouds on the horizon, I decided a hotel for the evening was in order.

I found one for nine bucks, *and they allowed pets; what a bargain!* Boy, they would soon regret that. I put all the packages on the bed, locked Blizzard in the room, and went shopping for a used guitar. I still had the original, but it had not made much of a vessel. Filled a few times with Mississippi River brew was very detrimental to its construction.

I returned with an instrument and Blizzard met me with his friendly Samoyed smile. It soon vanished as he dashed beneath the bed. The room was in shambles. Every package was torn apart and scattered. Remnants of once clean sheets lay in two mushy piles indiscriminately dumped on the carpet. Wet-dog filled the room. The curtains were pulled down and annihilated. I did what I could, hoping twenty dollars left on the bureau would help. Morning's departure was very quiet and very early. Only once underway did I quit looking over my shoulder.

Old Man River, Licked

It took six hours to reach the 13-mile marker. The Mississippi River mileage markers from New Orleans to Cairo stopped at Cairo; they then started again with Cairo being mile 0. The marker topped a twenty-foot rise with a small creek dribbling in nearby. The high dry hill silhouetted by a huge leafless cottonwood was a delicacy I couldn't resist. It wasn't long before my legs hung over the bank, thumping to the hums and strums of a six-string guitar.

"Howdy," came a call from the river below.

Looking up, I nodded saying, "Where you headed?"

"Figured on going down to Louisiana," answered a toothless man in a battered 16-foot motor-less aluminum boat.

"You've got a long way to go in that boat," I said to the disheveled old-timer.

"It's the only transportation I've got, and it's better than hitchhiking," he explained. "Thought I'd go down where the climate fits my clothes a little bit better. Come on over and have some coffee and sardines a little later. I'm camping just across the little creek." he said. "It ain't much but it's all I got." I could see one small pack in the front of the boat and had every reason to believe him.

Going through my food box, I packed coffee, sugar, flour, yeast, rice, and three cans of fruit in a sack and crossed the little creek. The tent-less traveler had tipped his boat onto a forked pole and thrown a tattered sleeping bag underneath. I made myself comfortable while he dipped a pot in the river and balanced it on the fire.

As he searched a sack for coffee grounds we talked about the river, and it wasn't long before I realized he didn't know where he was. I told him in detail about the rapids at Richardson's Landing and the trees that disappear in the whirlpools. Apprehension clouded his creased face and his jaw dropped slightly as if to allow the swallowing of more oxygen. With a stick and a sand map, I tried to lessen the severity of the situation by sketching the rock wall, the turbulent channel, and the calmer water on the west side. After kindly refusing a cup of Mississippi River coffee, I recounted my two spills and the whirlpools beneath the pile dikes. I could see this information being digested in moments of silent second thoughts.

It appeared the subject needed changing as he said, "I see you're traveling with a dog. I started out with one too but had to let him loose a week ago because I didn't have enough to feed him." The guy had come from St. Louis and was hurting.

As I got up to leave, I said, "There's some food in that sack if you want it," nodding at the lumpy pouch on the ground.

"No, I got enough to get me where I wanna go," he said half-heartedly.

"Well, I've been carrying it now for months and if you don't want it, I'll just throw it in the river," I wanted him to be comfortable taking it.

Having got his attention he replied, "Well, if you're gonna toss it, maybe I can use some of it, but I ain't gonna take it if you need it." I assured him I didn't and started toward the cottonwood. "You sure you don't want a cup of fresh coffee before you go," were his last words. I waved, loaded the new guitar, and started into the current.

The forty miles to Cape Girardeau took three days. I was having second thoughts about Cairo being a milestone. The volume of water had lessened, but the river also narrowed considerably, giving just as much authority to the current.

Lining the crushed-rock beach of Cape Girardeau were a dozen people gazing skyward at a huge, multicolored arch that had spanned the river. It was a byproduct of the storm that just soaked me. The bottom of the canoe crunched as I pulled ashore to watch the spectacle. When the rainbow faded, so did the people. I followed the group into town and toured the main street that had many of the same qualities as most of the small hamlets along the river, even a theater.

On the advice of a police officer I hid my camp a mile from town and planned to head back on foot to take in a movie. A light rain fell as I draped a twenty-foot square sheet of plastic over the incompetent tent. It overhung six feet to give Blizzard a dry place to curl up while

I was gone. Feeling sorry for leaving him alone in the cold and rain, I gave him a mouthwatering bone and folded my blue foam sleeping pad beneath the overhang to cushion his wait. With a scratch behind his ear, I was off.

The movie was mediocre. I got more of a kick out of a guy I met who wanted to take me over to Illinois, so I could go to church and be saved. I didn't even know it was Sunday. But the movie was over by 10:00 P.M., and I was back at camp in the time it takes to run a mile in the rain.

"Why you goddamn ungrateful *SOB!*" I shouted, grabbing Blizzard by the nape of his neck. "Look at what the hell you did to our camp. Just look at what you did, you ungrateful bastard." I yelled as Blizzard's paws scratched for a foothold in the rain-filled air. I cast him aside and the white blur's dash ended abruptly as the taut leash spun him around.

The camp was in ruins. The plastic sheet covering the tent was shredded. The tent lay soaked in a heap with my sleeping bag inside. The foam sleeping pad that I had graciously donated lay scattered in innumerable pieces, the largest remaining piece was the size of half a traveler's check. He kept his distance while I tried to reassemble the chaos. In the dark and steady rain, I reset the tent, crawled into the wet sleeping bag and throughout the night, contended with the constant drips.

I struggled against a paddler's worst nemeses, current and headwinds, all day; it wasn't a high mileage one. The countryside had begun changing from flooded farms to high limestone cliffs as I made my way further from the Gulf. Among cliffs, I stopped for the night. I appeared to be in a park and an apparently closed one, as not a vehicle or person was in sight. *Good, the whole place is mine.*

I walked through the area and found the best campsite available. It had a flat grassy spot, and someone had left a generous stack of cut and split firewood. A rustic sign 100 feet away read Trail of Tears Park. Having read more than one book about the infamous American atrocities, I felt awed that I could be standing right where the forced march took place. I couldn't linger on the subject, though, as last night's vigilance and today's all-day effort made for a very weary evening.

"Anyone home?" someone shouted as my eyes popped open after a long night's sleep. It was a cold morning and my breath rolled to the top of the tent. Annoyed that Blizzard wasn't barking and still half in my sleeping bag, I unzipped the door and peered out. A park ranger stood at the entrance.

"Be right out," came my reply. I dressed and entered the brisk air.

"You owe me three dollars for staying here last night," he demanded.

"I what?" I said incredulously.

"You have to pay to stay here," he answered without emotion.

"You mean I'm the only one in this whole place, and you came all the way down here in the cold for three dollars?" I said.

"Yup," he persisted. I dug into my pocket and came up with the exact amount. He thanked me and handed me a receipt, a genuine artifact from the Trail of Tears Park. It was small, but enough to start the morning's fire.

Over the next few days the weather changed drastically. It was like crossing a time warp into mid-summer. Seldom did the mercury not reach ninety degrees in the blazing sun. Blizzard was sick constantly. *Must be St. Louis,* I surmised, thinking he was sick from drinking the foul river water that was just two weeks downstream from such a major city.

My body browned as I struggled past Grand Tower, Illinois, and then ducked out of a refreshing downpour near Chester, two days later. Three people sat on a crushed rock bank watching me pass. "Come on up and have a beer!" one shouted. I tied the canoe to a rock and climbed the jagged shore. The man who had called out was a Cherokee Indian and said, "Here I am a full-blood and never rode in one of those things in my life."

"We can fix that right now," I said motioning toward the canoe. He declined wholeheartedly. I finished the beer and continued.

Blizzard's condition worsened in the coming weeks. His main activity was throwing up. I started to keep him on a short leash so that he couldn't lean over the gunwale and drink the toxic flow. Ten gallons of drinking water were obtained in Crystal City. The sun was merciless on his thick arctic coat. Many days the temperature still registered 85 degrees, even an hour after sundown. Ozone warnings on the radio explained my itching, watering eyes. Although sixteen-hour days in the ninety-plus-degree heat were at times agonizing, the biting cold, windy days of not long ago remained in my memory. So, with the seasonal scale balancing, I would make the best of the warm weather.

As I camped a mile below the first bridge on the outskirts of St. Louis, nature's scorched earth policy was finally paused, white clouds rolled over the treetops. They would obscure the moon's eclipse tonight, but it was almost worth it. I had finished a 16-mile day and was confident I would be seeing the city's sights by mid-morning.

Although I left at 7:30 A.M., by 8:30 P.M., I was still two miles from the gleaming Gateway Arch. Throughout the day I had crossed the river five times and inched around hundreds of barges that lined the shore. Most flotillas were six or seven barges wide, protruding well into the river, causing frustrating barriers. By day's end, a fireless camp on the concrete levee dampened my dreams of downtown St Louis.

Put off like most dreams, if only overnight, I reached St. Louis in three hours the next day and beached at the riverfront. The day was clear, warm, and windless. Boats with bars and restaurants lined the shore. People were everywhere. Though I was headed north, I was in the Gateway to the West. A helicopter rose from a barge and gave people tours that circled the city. The Huck Finn Excursion boat passed within fifty feet, its tourists waving. Making inquiries for a safe place to store the canoe brought me to a building a short way upstream. "Bring it up and put it in there," a man said motioning to a large building. In it went and that was that.

Finding a hotel that would accept a dog was more of a problem. The first call wanted my patronage but was very leery when dogs were involved. *If they only knew mine.* The lady gave definitive terms, saying, "If it's house-broken and you can carry it, we'll allow it." It was tempting and I filed it away as a last resort. There was no problem carrying Blizzard, but the house-broken part of her contract caused some concern. I wanted to enjoy the sheets, after all, not leave through the back door an hour before sun up again.

The seventh call went to the Holiday Inn, which warily accepted poor, unwanted Blizzard with one stipulation. I would pay for any damages. Although it was risky, I paid the nightly fee of $21 and walked Blizzard to the elevator.

A tall, elderly lady backed into the corner as I escorted Blizzard through the sliding doors. Her hawked nose towered above a mink cape while a gown flowed to the floor beneath it. Green numbers lit up as the elevator started upward. Though her face angled toward them, her eyes peripherally scanned me. Only a low hum sounded.

Blizzard's tongue dangled from his panting mouth, and I tightened my grip on his leash, knowing he was primed to leap and lick. Then it happened. His timing was so unexpected that it startled me.

Blizzard farted, and it was a long, resonant affair, which was followed by an uncomfortable silence. There was a *ping* and the metal doors slid open. The socialite walked straight out, head held high, fidgeting with her furry mantle. As the doors closed behind her, I could have sworn I heard a girlish giggle.

The next morning was a busy day with a lot to accomplish. After a hearty breakfast, I left Blizzard at a veterinarian, shopped for a new camera, lunched, toured a museum, viewed the city from atop the 630-foot tall Gateway Arch, picked up Blizzard, ate supper, saw a movie called Mandingo, showered, and was in bed by midnight.

I was awakened by a scream. The cleaning lady opened the door and finally, Blizzard thought he was a guard dog. The door slammed and footfalls faded down the hall. *What a dog!*

I had seen enough of the big city life and was ready to resume. After getting the canoe and gear back to the river's edge, I went to see about the storage fees. "Nothing, just get it out of here and have a nice trip," was the simple reply.

For almost five months I had been battling this river; it was the first of June. Ten minutes from St. Louis, Blizzard threw-up in the canoe. It was a mess; bright pink and chunky, the color of the medicine from the veterinarian. I took a piece of cardboard and scooped out what I could. The smell was ripe but there was nothing to be done about it until I could land and wash it out.

It was hours later when I pulled ashore at the Chain-of-Rocks Canal. I had no idea about the procedure involved in getting through a lock and dam; this would be the first of more than twenty that I would go through. After washing out the canoe, I walked toward a small building near the lock. Everything along the canal was fenced in, but an eight-foot chain-link fence posed no obstacle. As my leg swung over the top for the descent, an amplified voice boomed through a microphone, "If you want to get through the lock bring your boat in and we'll lock you through." I felt a little foolish at not having tried the simplest option first as I climbed down and walked back to the canoe.

The lock dwarfed the 17-foot canoe as I entered the massive concrete bin. The huge gates closed behind me. At the far end floated a giant twin-diesel tug. Massive engines started somewhere and soon the water began to rise. Ten minutes later it stabilized and the gates at the opposite end opened. I started out well behind the mighty boat's wake and passed a multitude of tugs and barges awaiting passage through the lock before continuing their journey downstream.

Evening was invading the day, so I decided to camp and watch the barges as they churned through the canal. The banks consisted of large chunks of rock, but the tops were flat enough to pitch a tent. Barges from many different states passed. By dark, I had regrets. The spotlights from every curious tug were glared at the tent. Horns and engine rumbles were constant. It was not a restful night's sleep.

Blurry-eyed, I left early the next morning with waning respect for my ability to pick campsites. When I reached the end of the rock-lined canal, there were four sheriff's cars parked at the edge of the river. A helicopter flew low overhead, and Coast Guard boats drove slowly along the shoreline. Between my transistor radio and shouted conversations, it appeared they were looking for a body. Though not wanting to find another, I scanned the shoreline all the way to the next lock at Alton. I made no sighting and the lock was navigated without incident.

Due to these locks, there was a definite slacking of the current. The wind was another matter. Unharnessed, it seemed to follow the path of least resistance, straight down the river. Though it did have a cooling effect, spring fever had infected the area. Hardly a day passed when someone didn't hail me ashore to share a beer. Beaches were lined with boats and people swarmed over the sand. Blizzard's health improved dramatically since his diet had been made to exclude the Mississippi River. I passed the Illinois River, went through lock and dam number 25, ignored the small town of Hamburg, and pulled ashore below the lock and dam in Clarksville to wait out the line of boats waiting to continue their northward journey.

Securing the canoe, I climbed the high bank and was confronted by a massive picnic. I took a right turn, heading away from the gathering when someone spotted me, "You're the guy that came from New Orleans in the canoe, aren't you? I saw you coming up the river!" From there it was chicken, ham, potato salad, punch, and sweets galore. Many questions were answered and a few true tales were told. But it was short-lived, people had to return to their various jobs in the morning. The smorgasbord patrons soon dwindled, and I was alone. Barges still languished in line so my turn through the next lock would have to wait for morning. I waited until dark then spread my bed across a picnic table and struggled to sleep until dawn.

I was through the lock and dam by 8:30 A.M. The lockmaster was one of the men whom I met at the picnic, and he sent me straight through. June 10th was upon me. To the day, New Orleans lay five months behind me. In that time, according to the Coast Guard markers, some 1,200 upstream miles had been logged. These miles are calculated by following the channel, marker to marker, usually through the middle of the river. By hugging the bank, detouring flooded fields, getting into backwater sloughs, and crossing the river many, many times, my actual mileage would far exceed 1,200.

High winds forced me ashore within sight of lock and dam number 22. I was half asleep in the beached canoe, leaning back on the deck, hat over my eyes, when a boat pulled ashore. I lifted my hat and could see Missouri Water Patrol stenciled on the side of a white tri-hull.

A husky guy in a gleaming white uniform stepped onto the deck and stood there with his arms crossed. He asked numerous questions and then, "You got an ID?" I got it from my pack and handed it to him. He read it through dark sunglasses, wrote something down in a small notebook, and handed it back. I returned it to the pack as he stood there, arms crossed, legs spread wide. "Where's your license?" he demanded.

"License for what?" I responded with a growing irritation. *I just gave him my license.*

"We don't let boats run around here unlicensed; we fine them if they aren't," he said, attempting intimidation.

"This is just a canoe," I said incredulously. "Where I come from there's no such thing as a licensed canoe."

"Well, I guess I can let you go, but you better look into that when you get back to Minnesota," he warned. With mouth shut and mind open, I imagined the guy would make a good TV commercial, gut hanging over his big buckled belt, standing like some supreme being. He was eying my equipment and then, without grace, jumped from his perch onto the sandy beach.

"That's a good-looking dog you've got there—" he was cutoff, Blizzard wasting no time before his attack, "—Why you dirty *SOB!*" he shouted at Blizzard. Two long, muddy paw prints streaked down the front of his white uniform. Without another word, the harassment ended as the guy hopped into his boat and the tri-hull disappeared around the bend. Maybe he decided to call in reinforcements.

Passage through lock and dam number 22 went smoothly. By the time I reached Hannibal a strong west wind blew, and when lock number 21 was reached, the radio was forecasting tornados. A quick stop in Owing to fill the water jugs at the North Side Boat Club turned into a two-hour conversation. By the end, the wind had switched to the North and was on the rise. Whitecaps silhouetted deep black clouds moving fast above the tree line by evening. I dashed ashore, erected the tent, and dove in with minutes to spare.

It hit hard. Rain pounded the frail structure and high winds threatened to take it airborne. The tent's attempt to stand was heroic but it soon succumbed to the elements. Then, as quickly as it started, the gale stopped. There wasn't a breeze to be felt, though the rain held fast. Crawling out revealed the tarp nowhere to be seen. With my rain suit and trash bags held over the collapsed tent by rocks, I spent a long, long night listening to the steady rhythm of water torture.

The next morning was early, gray, and wet. The torture continued. Seeing as how my condition was excessively damp and near sleepless, I defied the rain and continued closing my eyes. Early that afternoon someone shouted, "Hey, you under there!" Wrestling with my coverings, I poked my head out to see a man sitting in a boat. "You want to come over for a fresh fish dinner?" he asked. I said sure, got my boots on, and crawled out. The rain had stopped and the ride to his cabin only took a few minutes.

It was perched on high stilts, the standard fashion of many cabins along the floodplain of this unpredictable river. Two simple rooms were covered with modern wall paneling and a pot of grease boiled on top of a propane stove. Drifting throughout the cabin was the smell of deep-fried fish. The man introduced himself, his wife, and their two children. The oldest was celebrating her 16th birthday.

After fresh catfish, beans, potato salad, and warm biscuits, two verses of "Happy Birthday" were followed by a huge piece of cake and three cups of coffee. During all this celebrating, the weather had cleared and I longed for the paddle. The father handed me a still-warm, tin-foiled package of fried fish and said, "I've always wanted to do something like that. I still might one of these days." His wife in the background cleared her throat unnecessarily loud, putting a definite period on the end of his sentence.

The clear skies didn't last long. Within a day, an unrelenting drizzle streamed down my face again as I clung to the next lock's ladder, trying to keep the canoe from smashing against the concrete wall. After six tough hours in the rain, I didn't appreciate hearing the lock-master say into his loudspeaker, "You'll have to wait a few minutes. There's a Cruiser coming up the river, and I want to lock you through together."

A few minutes turned into 35 and I wondered if they would have waited for me. I didn't think so, but it made economic sense. A strong southern tailwind was making some dandy waves as it collided with the current coming from the North. The canoe would rise three ladder-rungs, then drop, scraping the concrete. My coordination was challenged as I went hand-over-hand up the rungs, then hand-over-hand back down, trying to keep the canoe both upright and uncrushed.

Finally, the Cruiser arrived. It was luxurious, to say the least. The crew hurriedly tossed large pads over the side so that the snow-white finish wouldn't be scratched against the concrete. There was a time when I had felt the same protective instincts about my craft, but that concern had aged well beyond action at this point. After the Cruiser was tied off, and I dangled from a rope behind it, the gates closed and the water rose.

"How far up the river are you going?" a captain-looking man asked while looking down at me.

"Minneapolis!" I shouted back.

"So are we!" he said and disappeared. The water reached the proper level, and the Cruiser gunned its engine, leaving me rocking in its wake. I followed it out and angled toward shore.

Fair-weather weekenders seemed to have been kept away by the rain, as for ten straight hours, empty sand beaches were passed. Then, Keokuk, Iowa, was reached, with its huge power plant and lock and dam to match. Upon pulling the rope to alert the controller, a voice said, loud and clear, "It'll just be a few minutes." I looked up at the concrete wall and a sign that stated small crafts would only be locked through at the top of each hour.

A loud horn blasted right at 6:00 P.M. and the two massive gates began to separate, exposing two towering concrete walls. I loosened my grip on the ladder I was using to anchor my place and started in. Small whirlpools spun down-river as I passed the gates. The fifty-foot walls loomed above as the huge gates clanged shut behind me. The pumps started and the water slowly rose.

After twenty minutes the surging water stopped. I was now only ten feet from the top of the wall. The lockmaster stood there with a half-smile on his face, shaking his head. "I just pumped eight million gallons of water to get that little boat of yours through here," he said. "This is the biggest lock on the river." Now I understood why they only filled it at the top of the hour; the expense had to be considerable. The gates now appeared diminutive, shrunken by the rising water; they opened, and I started for the west side of the river.

There was no place to camp. A railroad followed the river and limestone bluffs towered directly behind the tracks. Guarding the rails from the river was a jagged rock levee. A few sandy niches beckoned but I had no desire to wake during the night with a freight train rolling by a few feet from my head. Falling rocks also seemed feasible, so I kept plugging along. Eventually the tracks swung away from the river, leaving a sandy beach covered with darkness. It had been a long day, and my stomach growled from 14 hours of emptiness. By flashlight, I ate, spread the tent over the sand, threw the sleeping bag on top, and slept.

Although it was early and I didn't want to get up, I was forced to by the intense heat. It was over ninety degrees and I was drenched in sweat. I groggily slipped into the river up to my waist and splashed water over my head and torso to lower my body temperature. Figuring I should finish the job as long as I was wet, I bathed with soap and shampoo. Once the cobwebs left my head, I put in six hours before breakfast, had a quick bite, and then followed the west shore until stopping near Dallas City. The day's mileage was already 25, my best yet, *a whopping two miles per hour!*

By then the temperature had reached 100 degrees and the sun's reflection off the water was killing me. Stopping next to a large boulder, I noticed there was a brass plate affixed to it. It told of Abe Lincoln standing here on this rock in 1858 and giving a speech. I jumped up and tried it out. No crowd showed up, so I hopped down and headed toward Main Street.

It was a brief tour, lasting the time it took me to eat four Hershey Bars. A call to my sister revealed an interesting development. The people from my hometown, Biwabik, Minnesota, heard about my second capsizing and started raising money to help replace my losses. *Now that changed things.* It seemed people thought that I could actually do this. I wasn't alone anymore.

Dallas City was left with replenished groceries and a new frame of mind. The distance to Burlington, Iowa, wasn't far and by my standard supper hour, I was within a mile of it, passing cottages and buildings. From a porch came the familiar, "How about stopping for a beer!"

I stopped and went into the Cascade Boat Club. I joined two elderly men at a table while Blizzard was off with a poodle. One of the men became quite fond of Blizzard. The guy increased his popularity with Blizzard by giving him one Slim Jim after another. He had poor Blizzard sitting, barking, standing, and running in circles for those tender meat sticks.

Envious and famished, I wished a few would be thrown *my* way. After two hours of socializing, daylight was getting scarce. On the way out they invited me to their Steamboat-Days chicken fry in two nights. "An awful strong north wind would have to pick up to keep me here," I resisted temptation. Thanking them for their hospitality, I headed for the first sandy beach. Burlington could wait until morning.

For no apparent reason, it took three hours to cover the mile to the town's waterfront. Penniless, I walked to the Western Union office where my sister had sent $400. The office was gone. It had moved to a cab company. At the cab company, I learned it had moved again but they didn't know where. I found the new address and had to hurry so they wouldn't move before I got there. Finally, I found where it had relocated, at a shopping mall three miles away, ending a four-hour run-around.

On the way back to the canoe, I stopped at a bar. The sun rested on the horizon. The building was old and dark. A giant of a man handed me a can of Pabst from behind the bar and asked if I would like a glass. Declining, I put a couple of quarters in the jukebox and sat back to listen. The songs lasted the length of the beer, and I got up to use the restroom. I was washing my hands when the door opened with a clatter. In came the mammoth bartender pushing a mop and pail. He pushed it to one corner, looked at me and said, "You wanna come over to my place and have a little fun? I get off at eleven." Jesus, he looked big in that little room.

"No," I said, "I've got other plans for the evening."

"Ok," was all I heard as I left the bathroom and exited the building.

Since the locks and dams seemed to have made life a little easier, the next few days went smoothly. I had passed Bald Bluff and was nearing New Boston when I spotted the glare of a wet paddle rhythmically reflecting and then disappearing from the afternoon sun. As it headed my way my first impression was that of a kayak. When we neared, I could see it was a small open canoe being propelled by a double-bladed paddle. "Where you headed?" came the universal mutual introduction. The man said he started a few miles upstream and was on a two-day trip. As it turned out, he had taught school for twenty years in a small town forty miles from where I had grown up.

Our talk drifted to Eric Sevareid, Calvin Rutstrum, and Sigurd Olsen, but most of the conversation centered around the Boundary Waters Canoe Area of Northern Minnesota, of which we were both well-acquainted. Talk wasn't the only thing drifting and I mentioned how fast the bank seemed to be slipping by in his favor. We wished each other well and went our separate ways. By evening, camp was set up near the mouth of the Iowa River.

It took less time to travel *to* the next lock and dam than the three hours it took to go *through* it. A few more miles upstream I assumed my after-lunch pose. That is, reclined on the seat, feet on the thwart, head on the stern deck, hat over my eyes, just laid out dozing. Blizzard's welcome bark rudely roused me.

A small man approached in a canoe. In the bow sat a small dog of indistinguishable ancestry. A greeting in broken English was shouted as the bow touched shore. Off scooted the small dog with Blizzard right behind. Our conversation strained as most of what he said was not understandable. What I did comprehend was that he had come from Germany six months ago, worked in Toronto as a dishwasher, and saved enough money to float down the Mississippi River. He had a squat, foam-rubber-and-aluminum, 35-pound, birch-bark-painted canoe, and it took another twenty minutes before I understood that there was a hole in it and he wanted to know if I could fix it.

We emptied it and flipped it over for a look. There were two cracks along the keel. While I applied the healing fiberglass patches, he got across that he felt he got a good deal on his canoe, only $350 plus another $150 for shipment to Minnesota. While I didn't agree, I didn't mention it. Who's to say? He was making a lot better time than

I was.

The patches dried shortly in the searing heat and he quickly repacked. He called for his first mate and the small dog bounded into the canoe with Blizzard following, the latter pinning the small mongrel to the aluminum floor. I physically had to remove Blizzard so that the German man could be on his way. Thanking me for fixing his boat, he continued on his lifetime dream.

Back in my dream, I enjoyed that making more miles with less effort continued. That's how I docked toward evening, contented with my progress, fifty yards from a group picnic. It was only a matter of seconds before a lady started her approach. "We're leaving and you're more than welcome to use our campfire if you'd like," she informed me. Accepting the invitation, I escorted her to the fire.

After 15 more introductions were made, endless questions were answered; eventually darkness drove them to the city. Beside the pre-built fire, I was gratefully laden with ten wieners and buns, four peaches, three pieces of cake, and a lot of scraps for Blizzard. My new sponsors piled into their boats saying I must stop at the newspaper office in Muscatine. It wasn't long before their cavalcade disappeared across the water.

It took three hours the next morning in an oppressive 96-degree heat to get into Muscatine. Blizzard and my water consumption was unbelievable. Walking past the newspaper office without pause, I bought another small transistor radio at a nearby shop and left. By dusk, I was through lock and dam number 16 and camped on a sandbar two miles upstream.

I didn't think the sun could get much hotter, but it did. The river also stopped cooperating. By mid-afternoon, the miles advanced could be counted on four fingers. This part of the river was well settled, and the bank was armored with huge rocks. I approached a granite retaining wall that was 15 feet high; by staying a short distance from it I could still see over the top.

There stood a canopied rest area sheltering two picnic tables and two middle-aged women. They waved; I waved. "Stop for a beer," one suggested. I didn't want to but there was no reason to be rude. So, I stopped at the first flat rock, pulled the canoe onto it, and walked around to the gazebo. The Budweiser was cold and went well with the sweltering day. Halfway through, one of the ladies said, "Isn't that your boat?"

One quick look proved this to be true. The wake from a passing craft had lifted it from the rock and set it free. *When will I learn?* "I'll be right back," I said and ran to head it off. It was moving fast, twenty feet out from shore. Removing my shoes and socks, I scampered down the rock wall and poised myself to make the rescuing leap. Hesitating only a second to lay my wallet on a rock, I dove Tarzan-like, landing flat on the water, graciously gliding to the canoe.

With powerful strokes, I made it to the rocky shore bow in hand and tied the canoe off. Slipping my shoes back on, I walked back trying to act like this was an everyday event, hoping nonchalance would hide my embarrassment. My act was fruitless as I finished half the beer to their digs and said, "I'd better be going."

"Well, I hope you make it *all* the way to Alaska," one of them said with a chuckle.

"Don't forget your wallet!" the other teased without mercy. I thanked them, found the rock on which I left my wallet, and continued close to the wall, out of sight. The rest of the day went as planned.

Just before dark, I approached a dock with what appeared to be a clubhouse behind it. A man who introducing himself as Al was standing at the end of the dock and said he had seen me earlier and wanted to talk to me about the trip I was taking. I pulled ashore and after a few minutes, he asked, "How'd you like to run over to that island across the way for a few minutes? There's a bunch of people having a party I'd like you to meet." It was nearly dark, so I agreed.

On the short ride over, Al told me how he worked for the Coast Guard and was called upon to help find the many people that drowned each year in the Mississippi. He seemed to click on his CB radio and start his truck driving jargon to try to impress me. It didn't. A half dozen boats were strung along the beach, and we pulled up next to the last one. After introducing me to a few people, Al decided to go water skiing. There was very little daylight left. When he asked if I'd like to go along, I figured aloud, "Sure, why not."

We took a boat that wasn't the one we came over on, and five of us piled in, Al clung to the towline. Al cut through the wakes of other boats as we sped downstream. It was so dark that he was barely visible. For a mile, Al soared through the darkness. Then there was a shudder and the sick sound of metal mashing metal. The bow slowly lowered, and the craft glided to a stop. Daylight returned as flames leapt from the engine. Only the boat owner's cursing sounded in the dark. He aimed a fire extinguisher at the flaming engine, and with a *whoosh*, it was quenched. The billowing smoke was soon reduced to a few drifting wisps.

The extinguisher hit the deck with excessive force as the owner sat down and watched his boat and all aboard head downstream toward the far distant spillway of a lock and dam. Al came to the rescue. His *idea* was to swim back to the island where we had started, in the dark, against the current, and return with a boat. *That's the kind of decision people make just before the Coast Guard needs to rescue them*, I thought skeptically. "Why don't you climb in and we'll drift until another boat comes by?" I volunteered.

"Nah," he bragged, "I can swim up there in no time." Then Al disappeared into the darkness.

Someone suggested paddling upstream, so I took the only paddle while two others used Al's water skis. I ventured the idea of paddling across the current and trying to get to shore instead of fighting the current. Nobody else thought this was a practical idea. Within ten minutes both water skis lay on the boat's floor. The distance to the spillway had now decreased considerably.

I really didn't want to end this trip or my life by going over the ledge in the dark. When the lock gates opened, our worries slackened as a lighted boat sped upstream toward us. Four of the crew started shouting and waving their arms. It seemed a useless gesture in the dark and I asked the boat's owner if he had a flashlight. Rummaging through two compartments, he discovered one, and once lit, immediately the rescuers came over and threw us a rope. While being towed, the spotlight soon picked up Al. Slapping his arms against the water in slow motion, he looked awfully glad to see us. "Hey, Al!" one of his rescuers shouted. "Aren't you a little tired?"

"Is a pig's ass pork?" spat a reply from the dark water through winded breaths. Nearly finished, he was grabbed and dragged over the side. With Al spread-eagle on the floor, we headed back to the island.

The party was over, and the island was deserted. I camped next to the party's still-glowing coals, the fire a blinking, red lantern light, that signaled my presence but didn't obliterate the deserted, silhouetted island. People did though, as they swarmed my two-acre retreat by early morning. Even as I packed, boats hovered, ready to pounce on my spot. As I left the island, I thought to myself, *they can have this combat camping.*

Without a breeze, perspiration flowed freely as I made my way to lock and dam number 14, and then to Princeton, Iowa. I was interrupted from my parched stupor when I heard wild yells coming from a large commercial building fronted with windows. Waving his arms, a man stood shouting, "Canoe Man! Canoe Man! Hey, Canoe Man! Come on up here!" Tying the canoe to their dock, I rushed up the steps to a deck to see what he wanted.

There was no tragedy. Hearing I was in the vicinity, he wanted me to stop by his establishment. During my two-hour visit, the barmaid was quickly made a fan, and we played Pong on an Atari for which she received much ribbing from the small crowd we had acquired. "How about another drink, Canoe Woman!"

"You finally found your match in Pong, huh, Canoe Woman!" another customer teased.

One more patron added, "You going with Canoe Man when he leaves, Canoe Woman?" The onslaught was relentless. Feeling sorry for her, I apologized for being the cause of her torment.

She said it was all in fun; as I left, I added, "See you, Canoe Woman!!"

Waving, she laughed and said, "Have a good trip!"

People were everywhere in the time after flirting with Canoe Woman and I felt lucky to find a tiny beach on the tip of a small island to camp on; after nine straight hours in 95-degree heat I was exhausted. Just a stone's throw away from camp came the blast of stereo speakers, the river rocked to Led Zeppelin. It kept me rocking from one side of the tent to the other most of the night. By morning I was groggy but had to get out of my little fabric oven. Hardly had I crawled out when a boat neared and asked if I was leaving. *Shockingly, I know,* I felt rushed to leave, as their grill was flaming and refreshments were opened before my tent was even down.

By the time I reached Clinton I fully understood the value of that small piece of real estate. There was no unclaimed beachfront for miles. People were out in droves, enticed by the clear blue skies, the hot weather, and the Fourth of July weekend. There was a spectacle as I came into town. The high bank I followed provided no possible landing site and on it stood hundreds of spectators. Just offshore, speeding boats pulled pyramids of water skiers. I had no intention of going backwards and sitting there in the current held no promise. I went straight ahead.

The water-show continued as I inched along between it and the crowd. Some waved, some stared in puzzled disbelief. I felt very self-conscious as I inched along, as if I were crashing someone's party. Finally, I reached a small marina where I was turned away. "Already full," I was informed. That left a flat, muddy spot near a boat landing to turn the canoe over and stow the gear underneath. After exploring a small carnival and a smaller display of fireworks, I tucked my coat under my head, stretched out top of the overturned canoe, and slept away what remained of the Fourth of July.

Five hours of sleep was enough, so I rolled off the canoe and planted my feet in the mud. Dark clouds had invaded the Mississippi River Valley and held it in a fine mist, nullifying any more record-setting temperatures. It took most of the day to get to and through lock number 13, all the while darkening skies warned of worsening weather. I came to a public campground with row after row of weekend Winnebago warriors. Paddling into a small slough brought me to the edge of the many trailer campers. Before me was a baseball diamond. I pitched the tent in right field.

A break in the steady drizzle brought out the opportunity to play. Only a small bunch of young kids took interest, and though they were hard-pressed to sail a ball as far as the tent, undoubtedly most took it as a prime target. Even so, I shagged just a few ground balls.

The game had to be called due to darkness. Then, their parents came to life. Until 2:00 A.M. there were party shouts and firecrackers. The weekend campers behind home plate had their Winnebagos parked wagon-circle style with a huge fire blazing in the middle. Someone had a guitar and a dozen drunken, awful voices massacred "Old Susannah," "On Top of Old Smokey," and "Old Black Joe". The lyrics were far from the ones I learned in grade school. After every song a string of firecrackers went off, sending Blizzard into an uproar of howling and barking.

By morning the horde slept. Under overcast skies, I slipped past the quiet camp and made good time to the town of Savanna. Here I purchased a T-bone steak, onions, radishes, mushrooms, asparagus, and a carton of milk. These luxuries were rewards, something to look forward to after a hard day's paddle.

Paddling without letup for twelve hours, my appetite was not going to be disappointed. Spying a sandbar with a fifty-foot gap between boats, I knew this was as good as it was going to get. Pulling in, I started a fire with the few unpicked pieces of driftwood lying at the high-water line. When the flames were reduced to hot coals, the steak was put on the grill, the onions and mushrooms fried, the asparagus boiled, and the radishes cleaned. In less than thirty minutes all was ready. By then the gap from camp to camp was down to twenty feet.

Mileage had slowed considerably due to strong headwinds and intermittent rain for four days. In heavy seas the lock at Dubuque was reached. The canoe smashed the concrete wall numerous times before passage was attained. After four hours of hard work, the next two miles were a meager yield. Here, a man and two women stood fishing on the bank. I moved out a short way into the river so that I wouldn't run into their lines. One of the women, quite top-heavy, hooked a fish and began reeling it in. Obviously, she was excited as she got the fish ashore and dangled it by the line a foot above the ground. "Look at the big fish! Look at the big fish I caught!" she yelled at me. I wondered what she'd do if she won the lottery as she jumped up and down.

"Yah, that's a nice one!" I yelled, returning her enthusiasm. I was not two canoe lengths past them when I heard a splash and a scream. Looking back, the fisherwoman was half underwater with the man straining to pull her out. In her excitement, she must have slipped and toppled in. The other woman tried to brace the man with a hand, and even together they were hard-pressed to pull the lady out. I started to pull over but before I could she got a foothold and was able to stumble out. She dripped water the whole time they retrieved their lines and walked to the car. As they walked, beside her dangled the carp, a trophy rewarding such an effort. If she were a true fisherwoman, by the time she reached home, she laid her life on the line for that great catch.

Eight hours after the splash, I was ready for an evening break when a flash caught my eye. A walleye arched over the gunwale, gracefully glided over the canoe, and unceremoniously landed on the back of Blizzard. Within seconds the sleeping Samoyed had the intruder pinned, I had to act fast to protect my supper. We dove, and it was war. The canoe rocked and thrashed but, in the end, the fish was beneath my seat.

The walleye was cooked and cold by the time a beach-walking young man and his girlfriend approached. They were fascinated by what I was doing. "I see you don't wear a watch. I bet by now you can almost tell the time just by looking at the sun," the girl remarked.

"Usually within five minutes or so," I said as I looked up toward the sun with feigned charm and deep thought. Though my face was toward the sun, my eyes drifted to my watch affixed to the thwart. "I'd say it's about twenty minutes after eight," I professed.

The kid looked at his watch and smiled, saying, "Well, you're about 35 seconds off today."

"Guess I'll have to keep practicing then!" There was truth to this soothsaying for I had developed an uncanny ability to wake in the morning from a dead sleep and guess within a minute the correct time, most of the time.

As I entered lock number ten after a five-hour stretch the following morning, it was high noon and time was the last thing on my side. The sun beat down mercilessly. The gates closed behind me. The lockmaster, leaning on the railing above stated that the temperature was 93 degrees; he also stated that Minneapolis was only 237 more miles upstream. As the gates opened, a green aluminum canoe with two occupants entered the lock as I exited. They had come from Minneapolis, and the lock-master waited patiently as we traded information on our respective upcoming stretches. From their description, I had it made; I didn't think so. Our points of view differed—theirs downstream and mine up—and I knew a couple hundred more miles wasn't nothing.

To a canoeist, barges are one of the nemeses on the Mississippi River.

The windless, sweltering, summer days continued as I forced myself not to complain, for they would soon end. River crossings were needed much less by this far up the river. On July 15th, I passed the Wisconsin River and the Prairie du Chien Bridge, and by the time I camped on the evening of the 16th, I was a half-mile below lock and dam number nine.

It was very early and already very hot when the canoe scraped the concrete wall and I grabbed a rung of the steel ladder next to the lock. The buzzer sounded loud and clear to my pull of the request-cord. A barge chugged forward miles downstream, hazy in the distance, and I felt the economics of the situation would be to put us through at the same time; I didn't relish this.

While the canoe rocked placidly, I patiently clung to the ladder. Pulled out of my daydream and looking down-river, it seemed that those big steel blocks were getting ominously close. In fact, they were only 100 yards away and closing fast. Seconds later a loud voice boomed over the barge's loudspeaker system stating, "You've got a small canoe hanging onto the ladder down there." The barge crept onward.

"YYYYou'd better get out of there!" a winded lockmaster shouted, peering over the top of the ladder shortly.

"Where would you like me to go!" I shouted back. The lockmaster was useless; I had a decision to make. The bow of the barge was just fifty feet away and had now reached the downstream start of the concrete wall on which I clung. I was hemmed in. Gargantuan dents in the mangled hull and spots where rusted steel had peeled off bore down upon me. It was either up the ladder and watch everything I own get sucked under the barge or let go and face the whirlpool of turbulence created by the barge, hoping to stay upright and unsquished. The lockmaster continued to scream over the now-reversed engines, but I was saved not by him but by the threat itself. My decision to face the turbulence and the unknown dissipated as the floating steel halted. Looking up, I saw a huge braided loop arc to the concrete wall where it enclosed a mainstay. The huge rope groaned to full tautness as I sat feet from it, studying the rust-coated welds that descended into the brown boiling water.

The sweat-soaked lockmaster now had things well in hand as he told me to just stay where I was. There was much apologizing as he said he was on the radio and didn't hear the buzzer. He'd probably be painting handrails if word of this situation got out or had gone worse. "I'll put you through as soon as the gates open!" he shouted, and I was again alone with the steel monster. Things grew quiet as the tug shut off its engines, the only sound being the churning water that boiled from under the barge.

My camera clicked as the gates started to open. Then, a shadow slowly crept into the image in my viewfinder. It seemed that since the tug's engines were off, the current from the swinging lock gates pulled the barge away from the wall. The sturdy rope that held it and had been my salvation was now a pivot point, and the source of a new entrapment. I was surrounded by tons of iron on one side and concrete on the other.

The lockmaster lost it. He kept running somewhere and reappearing, poking his panting head over the wall to validate my existence. Each confirmation sent him again off to some post. The front barge collided with the concrete wall and I felt like I was inside a church-bell, the thunder reverberating in an echo chamber. I could feel it in my feet as the blast sent an earthquake through the water and into the canoe. Small bits of concrete fell from the wall and speckled the water before sinking. An opening appeared between the barge and the wall and widened until I could see into the fully opened gates.

I was gone. The gates shut, sealing the beast behind me. I was alone in the lock, rising, like my heartrate had moments ago. Soon I could see the beast from behind the closed wall, it peering as if to monitor its prey. But its' prey was lost; the gates opened, and I escaped into the 95-degree heat.

My environment was as oppressive as it was merciless. The sun didn't tan, it burned. Skin peeled off in opaque, silky layers and sweat flowed. Blizzard spent the day panting under a makeshift veil, only lifting his head when necessary. Lansing, Iowa, was passed without stopping and camp was erected shortly thereafter.

The early evening fire had burned to coals and I lay nearby watching a wisp of a cloud float across the blue sky. Flicking a fly from his ear, Blizzard lay at my feet. The heat had sapped my strength, and my head lolled in the tranquility of tired sleep, cradled in my interlaced fingers. Three loud blasts maliciously broke my slumber and brought me to a sitting position. 100 feet away, plowing upstream and answering to no one, the beast was loose.

The Twin Cities were well within a week's travel, and I was

anxious to get there. Finally, a steady rain squelched the heat and diminished any small boater's enthusiasm—all except one, a conservation officer. His main concern, as he drifted next to me, was my possession of a life jacket. He raised an eyebrow as I pulled it from beneath Blizzard and brushed the months of accumulated dog hair from it. "Is this craft registered with the state?" he inquired, moving on from the dog's cushion.

Is this a money thing? I thought, replying with an unassuming no.

"Take care of that when you get to Minneapolis," he sternly ordered.

Of course, officer! How could he doubt I wouldn't? The benefits of bureaucracy seemed well and alive, everywhere.

Twenty miles a day posed no problem now against this mighty river. I slipped through lock number eight without incident but nearly swamped in lock number seven. I was being locked through with three small motorboats when the gates opened with me at the front. The first boat behind me shot by. The wake picked the canoe up and slammed it against the concrete wall. Water poured over the side as I fought for control. A woman in the second boat screamed as I slid through the next trough and hit the wall again. When things settled down, inquiries were made about my safety and well-being. I replied affirmatively and the two remaining boats pulled slowly past, leaving me to paddle ashore and bail out.

Traveling occupied all the daylight hours. Late one evening I closely followed the base of a fifty-foot cliff, trying to stay out of the current. A man standing on top waved and shouted, "Come on up and have a beer!" Seeing as how my day was nearly over, I moored to a low bush and hopped out. Due to the heat, my attire consisted entirely of dirty white cutoffs. I ascended old stone steps set into the steep bank. The ragged stones scraped my bare feet, but it didn't take long to reach the top. *Surprise!* I stumbled into a party, though not for me.

A stone patio fringed with green and white crepe paper housed couples dancing to a German waltz. While the ladies wore long flowing gowns, the men's tuxedo tails swung, whirling over the cobbles. Unfortunately, there I stood almost naked, in a sea of splendor. Over seven months of growth flowed down over my shoulders and onto my chest. I hardly felt the cold beer pressed into my hand or heard the gentleman introduce his interest by explaining that he traveled to New Orleans by canoe when he was a young man, my self-consciousness prevailing.

I knew I must smell, but the closest anyone came to joining our conversation was a red-faced lady, who briefly glared at my friend from his other side. Realizing he was in trouble, and since no one asked me to dance, I thanked my host and withdrew without a bow. I knew my face was still blushed as I descended the stone steps, but my shade of crimson turned deeper as I looked down and realized my zipper was wide open. At least I wore underwear! *No more parties for me!*

I went through lock number six and then stopped at Fountain City. Checking my zipper carefully, I went into a small store and spent my remaining three dollars on dog food. The river grew more scenic as I passed through locks 5A and 5B. Limestone bluffs fronted by lively green forests stretched upwards into blue skies.

Hamm's Beer country had started and my ability to endure any more remarks about their commercial with a red canoe and a grizzly bear in the bow was growing thin. Not a day passed without a reference. "Where's the bear?" or, "Do you drink Hamm's too?" signaled the Twin Cities, and the closer I got to them, the worse it became.

Strapping a teddy bear to the front seat came to mind as I bobbed behind the gates at lock number four. Rain pelted my face and a brisk wind whistled overhead. Huge waves also crossed my mind, of which Lake Pepin was quite capable of generating, and might greet me on the other side of the gates. I didn't have to think long as they slowly opened. The lock acted as a wind tunnel, channeling a tremendous wind upon me. Lake Pepin was a blanket of white and was spreading into the open lock. Carefully I inched forward in the whitecaps, fearing disaster. Every wave lifted the canoe and set it down with a splash. Rounding the end of the concrete wall, I set a course straight toward the nearest shore.

I waited there until, finally, the wind died, giving way to a rising, lustrous full moon that peered out over the shadowed limestone bluffs. The evening smelled of the day's rain and the few remaining clouds disappeared into the night. Traveling seemed slow in the darkness, progress harder to gauge. Many lighted houses were passed. Docks were barely averted in the moonlight and the reels of set-lines screamed as their invisible threads caught on the canoe's splintered wooden keel. Some lines were cut, others screamed until silent.

I passed houseboats, party boats, lovers hand-in-hand, all unnoticed. I moved in stealth. Then a cloudbank vanquished the moon. The darkness was total. Pulling the bow ashore, I assumed my break position, waited and dozed, waited and dozed. Finally, grayness cloaked the river as the horizon brightened. A light fog preceded the morning sun. When it showed over the bluffs, I found that I was on the final, 22nd mile of Lake Pepin.

The nightshift turned into the dayshift as I continued to paddle all day. I passed lock number three, the last lock I would employ, and camp was made in the dark across from Diamond Bluff, Wisconsin.

The following day was calm and sunny. After four hours I was at my cut-off point, the St. Croix River. The Twin Cities were still miles upstream, I would not paddle through them. The water of the St. Croix was unbelievably clear compared to what I had gotten used to since leaving New Orleans.

The Mississippi River was now behind me, an everlasting memory of both good and bad. It has every right to be called the Mighty Mississippi. After spending nearly eight months on—and in—it, I felt a fondness for that dirty water. Though shortly a newspaper would proclaim it a triumph, on The Mississippi, nobody wins—you just pay your dues for passage. Without a backward glance, I started up the St. Croix.

After eight months and 1,800 miles of upstream paddling,
the St. Croix River was finally reached.

Prescott, Wisconsin, was reached on the 27th of July. It was a little way up the St. Croix and my brother Tom lived a scant twenty miles from there. It had been a good day's paddle, and one worth celebrating, so after securing my gear I walked to Bud's Bar, a local establishment, and called Tom. I asked him to come down for a beer, and he was truly surprised to hear where I was. He drove right over with his wife Vicky; their shock at me making it and them seeing me remained. I'm sure my appearance contributed to their astonishment. Almost eight months of neglect left my hair totally weather-beaten—far-reaching, snarled, and bleached white. My clothes were worn originals, but to them, it didn't seem to matter.

We packed everything into their car, put the canoe on top, and proceeded to their home for a hot shower, a well-cooked supper, and a little relaxation.

During my stay, Jim Klobuchar called and asked me to come to his office for an interview. I had called him occasionally while coming up the river and he'd done a few columns, but this was the first time I would meet him. He was a staff writer for the Minneapolis Star, the biggest newspaper in the state. We talked in his cubicle for at least an hour and had a few good laughs. I didn't think much about it until I saw the paper the next morning. In big, bold, black letters across the top of the front page, margin to margin, was printed "Canoeist Licks Old Man River on Long Haul to Nome." I was impressed.

For a whole week, I indulged in the civilized world. The dramatic change in lifestyles was enjoyable, but I missed the waters beneath my feet. So, on August 3rd, Blizzard and I left Prescott to continue our voyage.

Home Country

The St. Croix River was infested with boats of every size and shape, just the same as my previous serpentine trail. Every sandbar was overrun. It was mid-afternoon when I crossed the river to take advantage of an eddy's backwash. I headed toward the bank where the entrance to some rapids loomed. I guided the canoe to the base of the boiling chute that formed the brunt of the rapids. I beached, made a short portage, and was on my way.

Ease of travel didn't improve. Soon the river fanned wide, surrounded by pine-covered bluffs. A dismal amount of water flowed through the rocky basin. Trying to create as little draft as possible, I distributed the load evenly from bow to stern, booted Blizzard out, and started pulling through the shallows. Faithful Blizzard followed behind as I jerked and pulled the canoe over the trivial amount of water.

Already a third of the way up the St. Croix I arrived in Taylors Falls, complete with its namesake and a dam. The falls were minimal, and I pulled up them, but the dam was a huge concrete affair, with steep forested bluffs towering on both sides, a Voyageur's nightmare. Its high banks rose directly from the rounded river rocks. Finding the biggest, flattest rock, I arranged my sleeping gear upon it and assumed the fetal position. Still my feet dangled over the edge. The dam could wait until morning.

The canyon was forbidding in the early morning light, glistening with wet dew. After a dry breakfast, a search for a portage was made and shortly, a muddy path found. It wound to the top, and a barking black lab dared me to approach the house that was situated at the edge of the bluff. I was obviously on private property with

79

nowhere to go when the door opened, and an elderly man appeared. My request to use his trail for a portage was met with reluctance for fear of a lawsuit. "Normally people start portaging below the falls with a truck, drive through town, and then put in above the dam," he informed me. Seeing my despair, he said, "Well, why don't you come in for coffee?" My recent haircut and shave may have helped with that invitation.

He introduced himself as Don and his wife as Edith. Edith fixed us a snack while sneaking in questions about my origins. Having heard enough, she called a newspaper friend who came over with a camera and notebook. After the reporter's curiosity was satiated, I started down the bluff with her at my heels. After a half-dozen poses, she said thanks and started back up.

"Could you take this canoe up with you?" I called after her in jest.

The half-my-size lady gave a dubious look and after I chuckled, she called back, "At my age, I don't know if I can carry *myself* up there."

Shouldering the canoe, I started up. This was the first real portage since I had started over eight months ago, and a whole new set of muscles came into play. The incline turned into a balancing act. The bow kept hitting the ground in front but if I held it up *too* high, gravity and the weight of the canoe threatened to send me into a non-stop, backward tumble to the bottom.

With much effort the top was finally reached, the black lab skirted, and the canoe set down a quarter-mile past the dam. The two trips with the packs were much easier. When finished I stopped to say goodbye to Don and Edith. It turned out that a friend of theirs had a son who wanted to meet me, so we agreed to rendezvous six miles upriver in three hours. I left, hoping the current didn't pick up too much.

Tim White stood on the bank, a beaten-down, white pickup truck was parked behind him. It was 8:00 P.M. "You must be Tim," I said as I beached. He acknowledged the fact and invited me to spend the night at his cabin. After securing my gear and Blizzard in the back of the pickup, we were off.

A long dirt road turned into two ruts that ended at a paint-peeling two-story house. A distinct odor hung in the air. We got out of the truck and were greeted with the insistent barking of twenty-some dogs. To our right was a rusted storage container piled to the ceiling with bags of dried dog food. "You must buy in bulk." I joked.

"No, that's all from a company that sponsored me in the Iditarod Race last year," he answered. "It's a thousand-mile dog sled race through Alaska, and I got twenty miles from the finish line when some drunk hit me from behind on a snowmachine at night. Killed a couple of my dogs and broke my hip. That's where my stiff leg came from." I was familiar with the race, it ended in Nome, my destination.

We went inside. Tim lit a double-mantled Coleman lantern; there was no electricity or plumbing. A pair of snowshoes that he was weaving stood to one side of the small room, and a table and floor-to-ceiling bookshelf occupied the other. Between these stood the kitchen sink filled with dishes from previous engagements. A large, overflowing garbage can contributed its own fragrance to the room. Half-tanned caribou skins on the table didn't help. We sat at the cluttered table, drank two of his three beers, and discussed the outdoors until feeding time.

Holding a dim flashlight, I followed as Tim limped from dog to dog, pouring a gooey gruel into twenty-some coffee cans. The ruckus was deafening until all were fed. As we returned to the house, gone were all my thoughts of the glorious musher sailing behind his faithful dogs across the pristine, frozen, white land. My only thought now was how to get all their gloriousness off my boots.

The light from the Coleman lantern slowly faded as Tim turned the black knob and said good night. The lamp attempted two short comebacks then hissed into darkness. I laid tossing and turning throughout the night, listening to twenty-some dogs take turns barking. Tim snored through it all.

I was glad when Tim climbed out of bed at 6:30 A.M. and put the coffee on. The torture was over, and I climbed out of my sleeping bag seconds behind him. "How'd you sleep?" Tim asked with a knowing grin.

"Great," I said sarcastically and watched as he flipped fried potatoes in a cast iron pan, breaking his last two eggs over the lot.

After breakfast, we headed for the river. "This old truck runs pretty good for driving all the way to Anchorage and back!" he boasted over its rumble. I politely agreed as I watched out the back window to see a black and brown husky running through the dust billowing from the bald tires. Well behind was a white spot in the distance. "Your dog's not too fast, huh?" he gloated as only a dog musher could.

"It's not that he's not fast," I said, "he's just smart enough to stay out of all that dust." Tim thought about that for a second and had a good chuckle.

The canoe was already in the water and ready to go when Blizzard staggered in, tongue hanging to the ground. Tim's husky was lying beside the truck, asleep. Blizzard entered the canoe without complaint. After shaking hands and thanking Tim, I pushed the bow into the current and said farewell, "Maybe I'll see you in Alaska sometime."

"Well, I hope you get there," were his parting words.

The river was fast and shallow. I walked as much as I paddled. It took three days to get to the Highway 70 Bridge near Grantsburg, Wisconsin. A sign stood next to the bridge that read, St. Croix Information; I thought I'd stop and get some.

A brown-haired girl smiled professionally as I asked for a map of the Brule River area. "I was standing on the bridge watching you. It looked like it was pretty rough going," she said as she handed me a map. "I got a newsletter about you the other day, and it seems like Nome is a long way away."

"Yah, it's a few miles to go yet," I confirmed and thanked her as I headed for the door.

"Wait!" she cried, "I'll walk you to your canoe. Uhh, I want to see your dog." We walked the path to the canoe and talked until another information seeker stopped at the center. She wanted my full name, how to spell it, and my address before she rushed off to see about her patron. I pushed off into the current. Halfway to the building she turned and waved, shouting, "Good luck to you, Jerry!" I waved back and set my mind to the task ahead. Poor Blizzard never got so much as a pet.

A few miles past the bridge Blizzard picked up a friend, a good-looking, gray and black Husky. He'd follow us along the shore for a time, then jump in and swim behind the canoe. This went on for two hours before I stopped for lunch. Before the canoe touched shore, Blizzard was out introducing himself. They got along together splendidly.

When we left, the Husky slipped back into the water and dog-paddled behind the canoe. Blizzard craned his neck over the gunwales constantly, watching his new companion. This went on for three hours before I had to put a stop to it—I didn't need another mouth to feed. A solution presented itself as we rounded a bend; there sat an Irish Setter among camping canoeists. Edging near their canoes, the Husky got the scent of the new acquaintance and was inaugurated into camp life. As for me, I headed for the other side of the river.

By August 20th I was through the seven-mile rapids and averaging five miles a day. The evenings were now cool but still pleasant, though the cold spot in the nation was Roseau, Minnesota— already thirty degrees with a heavy frost. I planned to spend the winter near there, still 700 miles away, and I knew the fierce autumn winds on 200 miles of Lake Superior's coastline would be a major obstacle.

I wasn't worried about that then, though. I was too busy watching Blizzard catch his first weasel. He had it in his mouth and threw it into the air like a dog will do with a dead mouse. The weasel landed a few feet away and disappeared in a blur. Blizzard's full-leap attack landed him right where the weasel had been moments before. Peering under his paws produced no prey. His head came up in total bewilderment. He looked around, looked back down at his empty paws, and then looked to me for an explanation. Losing his prize lit a fire under him. He was up in a bound, puppy yapping, hot on each lead, following his killer instincts.

Things weren't so humorous in the morning when I awoke to find a spider web of fishing line woven around everything in camp. After emptying a 24-ounce bottle of maple syrup, he went on an energetic tromp with my daredevil caught in his fur. When boredom set in, he found pleasure in my wine flask, annihilating the plastic top while whetting his teeth on the leather case.

Temporarily insane, the cast iron frying pan sailed Frisbee-like through the air, dislodging a rock near Blizzard. Its broken handle rolled to the base of the tree where he cowered. Blizzard spent the rest of the day well out of my reach. Toward evening he came over to apologize.

I sat leaning against a tree as he cautiously approached and licked my hand. He then curled up at my feet, giving me quick, repentant glances. "Okay," I told him, "if that's the way you feel, it's time you trained for the Grand Portage." I took his empty nylon dog-pack from the canoe and strapped it on him for the first time.

He went nuts. It was a rover rodeo as he circled one way,

stopped, then retraced his steps in a flurry. He'd lie on his back, legs pumping, growling, and snapping over his shoulders at the encumbrance. Finally, he lay on his side, tongue panting, chest heaving. An encore ensued before resuming his former position. I hadn't laughed so hard since leaving New Orleans. After a few pets, I relieved him of his cloth burden, wondering about his capability on the nine-mile portage.

Daily mileage ebbed. For every hour I could paddle, I would have to get out and walk the canoe for two. I portaged around the Gordon Dam, crossed the St. Croix Flowage, and navigated the dwindling river to an unincorporated settlement called Gordon. It provided a few groceries and a place to eat, but finding nothing else of interest, I continued and camped on Crownwell Island.

Crossing St. Croix Lake in the morning brought me to a dead end. According to the map, a narrow inlet should take me to the Brule River. Only a trickle dribbled through a corrugated culvert there, beneath a paved highway. Cars sped by as I walked the highway toward the West. At an intersection, a dog walker informed me of a Brule River bridge two miles to the Northeast. *That has to be what I'm looking for,* I determined using the fine art of deductive reasoning.

The two-mile portage took three trips, totaling a ten-mile march. It was long after dark when the last pack fell beside the canoe. The bridge glittered in the bright, rising moon while the Brule River Bridge sign bowed in a slight breeze.

Thousands of stars shone on the ceiling of my bedroom, a wide shoulder on a country road. From the sleeping bag, I could hear the trickling sound of the Brule River. It had a special meaning; it would both take me to Lake Superior and be the first time in eight months that I would be traveling downstream toward my destination.

Mosquito hordes awoke me, and a glaring sun hampered the opening of my eyes. I looked forward to some easy downstream paddling. What I got was strife!

The Brule River's headwaters are three feet wide, three inches deep, and choked with unyielding willows. Most people who canoe the Brule River launch at Stoney Bridge, not quite a mile from here. I was there in six hours and lunched beneath a sign which stated no camping was allowed at Stoney Bridge or 16 miles downstream due to its being private property. There was little chance of getting 16 miles downstream before dark but there was an even smaller chance that I would backtrack into the willows. So, downstream I went.

I made it quite a way, but not far enough. The bannock was browning over campfire coals when a girl and a guy drifted by in a canoe. Back paddling, the Amazon of a woman said, "Are you allowed to camp there?"

"I hope so," I said. "I can't make it to the campgrounds before dark."

"Well you're on private property and you can't camp there, especially with that fire," she snarled. Another canoe had caught up with them occupied by another couple. "Is there anything we can do about that?" she spat, pointing her fat Amazonian finger in my direction.

The guy in the other canoe laxly responded, "We'll tell someone at Cedar Island Estate." I was caught and could envision the Cedar Island Estate storm troopers landing in a fleet of canoes, led by the Amazon with thick fingers, to evict me. They moved on and I didn't plan to lose any sleep over it.

There was no company that night, and none needed the next morning. A heavy fog clung to the river as the first sun's rays touched the treetops. Reveling in the effortlessness of downstream travel and astounded by how fast the trees flew by, I slid through the pristine smog. Four hours of leisurely travel brought me to a cabin nestled in tall pines and fronted by an immaculately manicured lawn. Sided in slabs of cedar, it could be none other than the Cedar Island Estates, honored by Calvin Coolidge's trout fishing visit in the summer of 1928. Two canoes tied to the dock appeared to be the ones which stopped for a visit last night. I would have stopped to offer an apology for trespassing but thought better of it. I didn't need any paddle-swinging Amazon coming after me.

At Coppermine Campsite the rapids started and were continuous. My tourist tabloid offered this statement:

"The balance of the river from the Copper Range Campground to Lake Superior contains the most dangerous rapids of the entire river and only the most skillful canoeist, one who is willing to risk frequent spills and portages, should attempt this part of the river. In this stretch of 19 miles, the river drops 328 feet, 17 feet per mile."

It wasn't bad. I was forced to portage around two ledges and shoot continuous rapids. They were shallow and extremely hard on the canoe, but I reached Lake Superior the following evening.

On a sandbar at the mouth of the Brule, I flipped the canoe over and was amazed at the amount of damage. Slices through the fiberglass ran from inches to feet. Not a square inch remained unscathed. It was a far cry from New Orleans when a small scratch in the new red paint raised my ire. *How things change.* I examined where my right heel had rested all those months. The wood had disintegrated. A half-moon of light showed through the thin scuffed fiberglass. The hull needed help. Doing what I could with duct tape, I pushed off into the vast waters of Lake Superior.

Duct tape had many uses along the Brule River.
The canoe didn't weigh 73 pounds anymore!

Surging in sharp contrast to calm winds, two-foot swells slapped the steep clay banks to taint the pulsating waters a murky red color. I paddled until dark. Limited campsites necessitated nesting on a narrow ledge of sand ominously close to the water. If I could get one calm day, I'd be in Duluth on Labor Day.

It was too much to ask. By midnight the ground shook as pounding whitecaps surged and ebbed across the precarious sands. Water swirled around my ankles and wind billowed the tent as I stepped out. One scan with the flashlight convinced me to bear hug the tent and make an exit straight up the bank. With the canoe and packs out of harm's way, I gazed across the lake as a cold wind infiltrated my long johns. Red radio lights blinking from tall towers reigned over a maze of multicolored lights extending for miles. Strobe lights blinked into oblivion as descending airplanes were devoured into the cauldron. Duluth had its chilling beauty. Finding a pothole in the hillside, I lined it with the tent and tarp. Pulling the sleeping bag over me, I snuggled in, secure against the biting wind.

Blowing day and night, the wind would not let up. I perfected a flytrap in the idle hours. While reading, a fly would land on a page. With steady hands, the fly would walk around until he reached a prearranged spot, deep in the center, and *pow!* I'd snap the book shut and add another victim. Twenty-three on one page wasn't bad. *I've gotta find something to do,* I reflected

It was five days before the wind allowed me to leave the hillside. At 4:30 A.M. I followed the south shore and crept along the backside of Park Point to a small marina. Though closed for the season, the charitable owner agreed to keep the canoe, Blizzard, and gear under surveillance while I took a sixty-mile bus ride to Hibbing.

Here I visited my sister and family whose home had withstood my preparations and mess associated with planning this canoeing endeavor. After two days of reminiscing and eating, it was back on the Greyhound, heading south.

It was a two-mile walk from the bus depot to the marina. They were waiting for me; somehow, I had been set up. There was a long van, many people, and many cameras. It was the Channel 10 news crew. "If life's rewards were regulated by redundancy, I'd be rich," I muttered to myself as I answered the same questions asked so many times. They vanished as quickly as they appeared, leaving me alone with the marina owner. He would accept nothing for his generosity but a handshake. Waving and wishing me luck, he watched me start into Lake Superior.

A slight northerly breeze reached down as I oriented the canoe in the concrete canal leading from the harbor to the lake. It looked awesome, even dwarfing the locks and dams on the Mississippi River. Looking down its mile length, Lake Superior seemed to dissipate into the blue sky.

I went slowly, feeling the height of the swells, judging the danger and not knowing what waited at its end. This was the same canal the Edmund Fitzgerald used, and I didn't want to succumb to the same fate. Soon the lift bridge loomed overhead. Meeting one of those massive ore boats did cross my mind.

Beyond the bridge, many people stood on the concrete wall.

"Look this way. Look over here," someone shouted. It was the cameraman from Channel 10. People waved and took pictures as I inched along cork-like. I may have sat up a little straighter for the camera, but I wasn't going to let go of the paddle to wave.

Before I reached the end of the two concrete fingers, time seemed endless. I felt like a yo-yo and prayed that whoever held the string wouldn't let go. The monotonous rotating light surging from the lighthouse beacon seemed to synchronize with the swells as I turned the concrete corner and headed north, parallel to shore. Although it took time for things to improve, the north winds sailed above the trees, leaving a calm corridor for advancement as I neared the protection of the shore.

To traverse this portion of Lake Superior, all I needed was a week of calm weather. That seemed like asking a lot for the middle of September, but three days of it brought me to Two Harbors.

Two hours later, I was flagged down by a lady frantically waving her hands over her head. "Want a cup of coffee?" she shouted from her porch.

"Sure," I said and beached. Entering her home produced an unexpected event. Eight elderly ladies sat around the kitchen table, all talking, and all doing very well at it. After being introduced to each in turn, I was questioned without mercy. Hating to be ambidextrous—with my mouth—I was given little choice. Questions came from everywhere. Before long, cake and cookies were placed before me to be eaten when I got the chance. It was an hour before I excused myself to leave. At the door, the homeowner handed me the rest of the cake with explicit instructions to deliver it to my sweet dog, whom I knew was already sweet enough.

Two hours away from the ladies' council, I camped. It was early, but the small pine-studded island offered the isolation to which I had become accustomed. A huge supper was consumed sitting on the dark rock that disappeared into the deep, blue water and only the campfire lit the cold night. Everything beyond its sphere was black. Huddling close, I savored its warmth and light to read a book. Well into the night, chapter after chapter was read.

"Hey, is anybody home?" came a shout that startled me from a deep sleep. *Who made it out here?* I thought I was out on a rock in Lake Superior, safe from intrusion. I deduced improperly.

"Yah, I'll be out in a minute," I said. It was seven o'clock in the morning.

The sun glaring off the calm water was blinding as I crawled from the tent. Frost smothered the island with a white blanket, punctuating a darkly clad man sitting on a rock. Two cameras dangled from cords around his neck. Beside him stood Blizzard, totally content with his petting. A kayak roped to a tree floated lazily off shore. "Hi, I'm a reporter from the Two Harbors newspaper and would like to do an interview with you. I know it's a little early, but I wanted to catch you before you left. I hope you don't mind," he said. Rubbing the sleep from my eyes, I mumbled something that sounded like a grunt and took a seat.

As the kayak disappeared, I ate a hearty breakfast of oats, bacon, tea, and toast. Within an hour of the intrusion, I was on my way. It took six hours to get to the Gooseberry Falls State Park. Dark clouds were gathering. I pulled onto the pebbled beach and took a tour. Only a trickle of water plunged scores of feet over the scenic weathered rocks. After a few pictures, I returned to the canoe and a waiting Park Ranger. "I see you made it this far. I suppose you know you're in Gooseberry Falls State Park?" he said.

"Ah, yeah, it's a pretty neat place," I answered.

"I saw you on TV the other night, and it really boggles my mind when I think of what you're trying to do," he stated.

"You should try doing it and see what it does to your mind," I chided.

"It's illegal, but you can camp here tonight if you want. I don't think anyone will bother you, doing what you're doing. Besides, we don't get many celebrities here," he said.

I didn't know what his definition of celebrities was, but it wasn't me. Maybe he said celibacies, but that wasn't me either. The only category I could ascertain was my being me. What I did know was that I needed to get a few more miles behind me.

And that's all it was, just a few.

The wind started as a whisper through the trees and then escalated until golden leaves, stripped from their life support, floated pendulum-like to earth to be consumed into nature's cycle. The first lightning bolt sent me to shore as thunder reverberated across the sky. Tiny holes appeared in the water as I dashed to beat the inevitable. I lost and was pelted relentlessly before erecting the tent. By the looks of things, I could plan on staying for a while.

For five nights and four days this niche in the forest, canopied by birch trees and well away from the windblown waters, was my home base. Beach sorties combated impatience. Reading controlled restlessness. On the fifth day, the wind had blown its course, but the cold rain continued to fall vertically. There seemed a thin line between this cold rain and snow so I didn't have the option of wasting time.

Just before dawn I pushed from shore and picked up the paddle. My slicker was cumbersome but necessary. Even though the rain never varied as I approached the Palisades, it couldn't depreciate the beauty of the high, vertical cliffs disappearing into unknown depths of blue water. As the dark walls loomed overhead, an eerie feeling of reverse vertigo prevailed. They were an hour in passing, with the wind continually at the surface of my mind.

Taconite Harbor, Cross River, Temperance State Park, Tofte, and Lutsen Ski Resort all were passed in the steady rain. After 16 hours on the paddle, a Richmoor dehydrated lunch for four did little to alleviate my appetite. Cabins were abundant but the rain kept their occupants indoors. Only one lady stepped onto her overhung deck and shouted, "Say hi to my brother in Alaska." I responded positively and continued toward the town of Grand Marais.

Compensating for the discontinuance of seemingly endless rain, a slight headwind had developed. Occasional white-tipped waves rolled under the canoe as I pulled into Grand Marais. The first stop was the forestry building for a permit to travel through the Boundary Waters Canoe Area legally. I was going through with or without one but thought it best to at least stop.

I returned the application with the desired information. It was stamped, signed, and then a copy went here, one here, another there, and I got one. "A little late to be crossing 300 miles of wilderness, isn't it?" the ranger suggested. It was September 30th and I agreed, but 300 miles just didn't seem that far anymore. I returned to the canoe, set up camp, and never gave it another thought.

I was up early. While I strolled the city's main street, no lights beckoned early morning shoppers. Dawn extinguished the streetlights, but few spectators appeared. A door slammed somewhere and quickened footsteps sounded behind me. "Hey!" a stranger shouted. "Richard Humphrey wants to buy you breakfast at the cafe across the street." Knowing no one here, I was suspicious, but hungry enough to accommodate him.

Richard was pleasant, maybe ten years older than me, and

obviously ambitious. An early riser, mayor, and owner of the Lake Superior Trading Post, he seemed fascinated by canoeing. Breakfast and tea lasted the better part of two hours, which led to a tour of his Trading Post. I was then assigned a personal clerk who found everything I could possibly need for the next 300 miles. Some things I could use and some were mere conveniences, but purchases were made which I could afford. When I think back on it, I didn't really need most of the things and buying my own breakfast would have been much cheaper. Richard will do well in this world.

The weather couldn't have been better as I left Grand Marais. Blue skies and calm winds dominated the area. Many hours later, Grand Portage appeared as a square speck across a blue mirror. When I neared the stockade, some ancestral stimulant surged through me. Visions of short, barrel-chested Voyageurs plying the fur trade for thousands of miles could be conjured. They were strong men who once sang and left their namesakes behind them as they crossed a vast empty wilderness.

The visions didn't diminish as I docked next to the pickets of the old fort and crossed the courtyard. In its center was the American flag, hanging limply from a whitewashed wooden pole. I entered the main building. There was a fascinating array of exhibits depicting the height of the fur trade. Observing some rusted number 4 traps, somebody behind me said, "Are you Pushcar?"

Turning, I said, "Yes." A man stood there wanting to shake my hand.

"I wish I could do something like that. How do you manage alone? Aren't you scared?" the man asked as my hand kept going up and down. Only Nancy, the attendant, saved my arm as she said it was late and she had to close the doors to the Post.

By evening, everything I owned was gone through to lighten the load. Every pack was emptied and necessities were neatly arranged into two packs. My 300-mile dash against freeze-up would start in the morning with the nine-mile Grand Portage. With the packs situated, all I needed was a good supper and a long night's sleep. The sleep was no problem. The supper involved a two-mile walk to a newly constructed hotel.

When I crossed the lobby of the Radisson Hotel on the Grand Portage Indian Reservation, it wasn't much before dark. I was dearly craving a steak when I asked the hostess for a table for one. "Not without reservations, or you could wait until 9:30," was the disappointing answer. The place was far from crowded but with nothing to do, I moved to the bar and nursed a bottle of beer for two hours.

As the clock crept to 9:45, it was obvious I was being avoided. A suited man was counting the night's take at the cash register so I walked over and asked if I could get supper. "Kitchen closes at ten o'clock," he said looking at his watch. It appeared I was being blackballed because of my attire. But then again, I might have smelled a little smoky. Because this was the last stop for 300 miles, I used my ace in the hole.

"Jim Klobuchar told me to tell you 'Hi' when I reached Grand Portage," I ventured.

"You're not the guy paddling the canoe, are you? Well, I guess I can get you in. Just wait at the bar," came the reply. Sometimes it just helps to know the right people.

It was 10:30 when he came over and said, "Your table is ready." Hastily I walked into an empty restaurant. There wasn't even a waitress. I didn't know if I ordered from the chef or the dishwasher, but his first words were, "Sorry, kitchen closed at 10:00." All I wanted was a steak dinner, but the only thing available was a Grand Portage Salad. It appeared to be left-overs from the celebrities. The only thing "grand" about the shriveled-up thing was the bill. Pocketing any tip, I walked back to my world.

A fog hung over the old fort. The sun had yet to rise. Shouldering the 100-pound pack, I started down the old portage, tumpline straining my neck. Blizzard walked behind me encumbered with his loaded pack. The rope tied from my belt to his collar kept him on a straight and even course. Near the two-mile mark, I set the pack aside, secured Blizzard, and returned for the second load.

Footing on the dew-covered rocks was treacherous, but the day was flawless. Clear skies, cold air, and a bright sun peering over the treetops set the fall colors ablaze. Nancy was hoisting the colors to a cheerful, "Good morning!" as I passed through the yard for the second load. Placid Lake Superior was totally unmenacing in the early morning. I said my goodbyes to it while adjusting the shoulder straps of the sixty-pound pack. With rusted agility, I raised the canoe to my knees and flipped it overhead. The yoke pads landed squarely on my shoulders, and I was off across the Voyageur's trace.

Skirting the fort, I crossed the highway and was swallowed by the boundless wilderness just as the singing Frenchmen had centuries ago. No lyrics escaped my clenched teeth. Within a mile, strange twinges erupted from shoulders to toes as the load forced my nose toward the ground. Desperation clouded my eyes until they zeroed in on two narrowly-spaced pines. The bow slipped between them and wedged tightly. The stern thumped the romantic trail as I went to my knees and crawled to safety. Singing like a modern Voyageur, I dumped the pack. Nine months of sitting in a wicker seat didn't prepare me for this.

Given a chance, I could justify my wretched condition. It was the canoe. In New Orleans, it weighed a mere 73 pounds. Now it was badly waterlogged and covered with layer upon layer of fiberglass patches. Tied to the thwarts are the paddles and fishing rod with a combined estimated minimum weight of 120 pounds, easily. Add to this the sixty-pound pack and I was carrying my own weight for nine miles, plus another trip with a 100-pound pack. It was about what the ancient voyageurs carried day after day. I had a challenge ahead.

With everything united at the two-mile mark, I decided to march the lighter load the remaining seven miles to the end of the portage. Adjusting Blizzard's doggie-pack, I hoisted mine and was off. Blizzard looked pathetic, ten-pound pack skewed, head down and defeated. Fitfully looking back, he would whine at his degradation to a draft animal. He crawled along unleashed, encouraged, and prodded from behind. Over the next two hours, his condition deteriorated. We were nearing the end of the portage, and I talked to him, trying to keep his spirits up, hoping he would make it. Then, he disappeared in a sprint, oblivious of his burden.

"Come on over for coffee," the man named Doug Berg said as he petted Blizzard. With a handshake I graciously declined, wanting to end this portage before dark.

"Keep it hot," I said and returned for the canoe. Picking up the pace as the portage wound through the miles of poplar, birch, and pine, the smell of the northern woods in the fall was invigorating. I seemed to be flying without the weight of the pack. That shortly ended.

Many times, I thought about leaving the canoe and coming back for it in the morning. But persistence told me to do it and get it over with. I could smell smoke a mile from the trails end that lifted my spirits but did little to lift the oppressive weight on my shoulders. The golden forest had lost some of its luster by the time I set the canoe next to the pack. The sun had set long ago. Having just walked 27 miles and leapfrogging almost 300 pounds of gear, I felt every mile of it as I stiffly eased down and sat next to Doug.

Twelve teenagers peered through a blazing campfire. They were from the Mini-School Program at Minnetonka High School. The group was ending a 250-mile canoe trip across the Boundary Waters Canoe Area. Coffee, soup, and jokes went on for hours. After the campfire was stoked a final time until its death, bodies were sent scampering from its ring of warmth to chilled sleeping bags. Mine was truly appreciated after the long day.

I must admit there were a few aches as I opened my eyes to voices outside the tent. At 7:00 A.M. I joined the crowd around the fire. After breakfast, the whole group posed in front of their sixty-pound Kevlar canoes while I snapped a picture. The girls in front smiled widely while the boys behind held deep breaths, augmenting squared-shoulders. The final shutter's click sent them scurrying to break camp. I watched until all was ready. On command, packs were lifted and canoes were thrown on sets of young shoulders. With a wave they were heading off for civilization, I for isolation.

Blizzard takes a break on the Pigeon River after finishing the nine-mile Grand Portage.

The Pigeon River at the end of the portage was upstream, rapid-filled, and cold. Snow swirled through the darkened skies before noon. Soaked to the crotch by capillary action, I teetered on numbed feet, walking the canoe through numerous rapids. Dreaded groans were heard as entrenched rocks battered the canoe's hull. As water seeped in unchecked, drainage efforts were necessary. I wasn't saddened upon reaching the 300-rod portage to South Fowl Lake. Dry footwear was put on immediately, but shortly I curled my toes, not knowing whether to laugh or cry. Each toe throbbed like a banged funny bone. Mercifully they soon warmed to a dull tingle.

The 300-rod portage was paltry compared to yesterday's jaunt. Camp was erected on the far side of the portage. Something had to be done to the canoe. The hull was a mess. Gaping gashes peered through tendrils of shredded tape. The keel appeared as a 17-foot fuzz-stick. Again using duct tape, I covered the obvious trouble spots. Content with my work, I was startled to look up at a huge moose, inspecting my handiwork, hardly fifty-feet away. Its humped back glistened in the evening sun as he lowered his head to drink. With total arrogance, he ignored my presence, lifted his massive rack, and indifferently disappeared without a sound. I was breathing rapidly as the monstrosity vanished. Soaring adrenalin left me standing ten feet behind the canoe. After retrieving the tape that floated in South Fowl Lake, I returned to my chores.

By morning a lip of ice ringed the lake. Frost-tipped trees signaled an end to autumn's brightness. A loon seemed to mourn its passing as his lonely cry reverberated to silence. South Fowl, North Fowl, and Mountain Lakes were crossed.

On a portage from Rove Lake, I met a young man and his wife who had hiked from their cabin a few miles away. We shared lunch on a log and discussed trivial niceties. Upon their departure, I sat down and relaxed against a tree. Within minutes he was back, slipping the strap of his Nikon camera from a branch stub. "Better take my camera with me," he remarked.

"You might as well since my Konica lenses won't fit it anyway," I said jokingly. With a stern look of reprimand, he ambled down the trail to catch up with his wife.

Days started at 6:30 A.M. in the dark. Turning to thin strands of baldness, the forest lost its thickness as leaves layered the frozen earth. Only the towering pines broke the biting fall winds as I paddled and portaged through Daniels, Birch, Mayhew, Crab, Loon, and Gunflint Lakes. Few people trod the BWCA at this time of the year. The tourists had had their fun and were gone.

The Gunflint Lodge was desolate and closed for the season. I bobbed in the whitecaps, staring at it, willing it to life, looking for any movement. Shutters covered its windows like pennies over a dead man's eyes. I accepted its dimness and crossed lakes that sprang from childhood memories, the Gunflint, Saganaga, Knife and Basswood. These names brought back fond memories of elders returning with stringers laden with record-sized walleye pike, canoeing, wilderness camping, long, hard portages, men of everlasting strength.

There must have been things they forgot to tell me because here I was, unable to catch a fish. In addition, the canoe needed a shipwright, and I was cold to the bone, almost out of food. It all seemed like an illusion.

Sometimes even this wilderness area seemed like an illusion. Portages resembled well-groomed bike trails with canoe rests every quarter mile. Resting places were designated campgrounds with grills and picnic tables. It seemed man had taken some of the wild out of the wilderness in his quest to preserve it.

One thing that definitely wasn't an illusion was the rain. It had held for days as I crossed Saganaga, Seagull, Juniper, and Knife Lakes. Three men fishing on Knife Lake reported a three-day catch at zero, soothing my troubled mind regarding my ability to catch fish. Rain rolled off the side of the canoe as I peered from underneath while crossing the Basswood Falls Portage.

The yoke bit into my shoulders, but the sight of each U.S. Forestry "goal-pole" brought instant relief. These log-supported crossbars are constructed so the weary traveler may tip the bow of the canoe upward, advance two steps, set the canoe's bow on the wooden crossbar, and walk away. When rested, all that is needed is to walk under the canoe, lift, and resume the portage.

Expertly I raised the bow and advanced. It was a cruel joke. The canoe defied my will and slid smoothly under the crossbar. I reversed and reapproached but was brought to a halt with a shuttering direct hit. For my next attempt I reversed and powerlifted. With arms fully extended skyward and a slow advance while dragging the stern, the bow barely cleared the crossbar. On extended toes, a final thrust moved the bow's deck over the crossbar. Paul Bunyan must still be alive and well.

One of the many portages in the Boundary Waters Canoe Area (BWCA).

Canoes are known for their silent maneuverability. This was true as mine slid off the crossbar and silently headed for the ground. I turned just in time to witness its last gesture before coming to a final rest. A major thump was surpassed by a loud crack, as the yoke bore the total weight and shattered both inside gunwales. At the time I had no use for the Forest Service and its canoe rests, and loudly stated so.

With fishing line and whittled willow, the gunwales and yoke were lashed and secured enough to proceed. The yoke made unfamiliar sounds as the foam rubber pads settled onto my shoulders. It was springy, so springy that at full stride my head would knock against the bottom of the canoe. A stocking cap with three socks inside became mandatory on portages until other arrangements could be made.

The rain followed me as I portaged Curtain Falls, paddled Iron and Bottle Lakes, crossed Bottle Portage, and got into Lac La Croix. Then, on October 17, the rain ended. It helped my foul mood somewhat as I had just spent three and a half hours looking for Blizzard. He was dining on the remnants of a dead fish. I couldn't blame him for only a small package of rice lay in the bottom of the food box next to a twelve-inch fillet of northern pike. Finally, fishing had picked up.

The situation wasn't the best. Blizzard was upset because he wasn't fed properly. Trying to explain to him that he wasn't doing much paddling either didn't help his mood. He would just look at me and whimper. The canoe leaked badly. When the water rose above my makeshift pole floor, which was used to keep my feet dry, it was time to bail. It was an hourly chore. It was cold, and I was ready to reach the sanctuary of International Falls, fifty miles away.

At last the rice was gone and the food box was empty. The Canadian Channel, a long narrow waterway, was reached in two hours of morning darkness. As trees swayed in the early morning wind, I followed the channel to a point of land tipped with a flashing beacon. Spray flew five feet into the air over the rocky point as I climbed a small knoll to view endless rolling whitecaps. It was Rainy Lake. On the other end, miles away, was International Falls.

The wind held me huddled behind the knoll throughout the day. By evening there was hope. An hour after dark I doused the fire and entered the relatively calm Rainy Lake.

Progress per stroke decreased as Rainy Lake seeped in. Soon water lapped around my feet and it was time to bail. What little warmth was left from the campfire was soon replaced by frigidity as the night breeze crept into my bones.

Darkness seemed to intensify everything, from bailing, shivering, and the silence, to the unwelcome stupor of disorientation and numbness. Startled shore creatures bounded as I slid through the night. Some scurried while some crashed through the dark underbrush. Their fearful flights created nervousness not easily contained. It kept a person alert, on edge. I traveled all night and it seemed dawn never arrived. Only a lighter shade of darkness appeared as sleet poured from a cold, dark gray sky. It seemed a contest to see how the most water could get into the canoe. I paddled and bailed, paddled and bailed. Hours slid by. By nightfall, after a hungry 23-hour shift, I was ready to camp almost anywhere.

I awoke tired with no desire to rise. I watched as rivulets of water rolled down the tent, only to change course as a wind billowed the nylon tent. Grudgingly I crawled out, ate half a cold fish and challenged the rain and headwind until dark. I landed eight miles from International Falls. Numb, water-wrinkled hands sheathed the paddle between two packs by midday the next day.

International Falls appeared like a lighted snow globe as I squinted through the falling flakes. I couldn't feel the cold water that I heard squirt between my toes as I jumped ashore. The International Boundary Bridge stood to my right. Before me, trees planted pattern-like resembled a park. Beneath these stood ragged, statuesque Natives trying to stay out of the falling snow. I tied Blizzard to the front of the canoe as a visual deterrence and walked to the Customs Office next to the bridge.

As I wasn't leaving the United States, I probably didn't have to stop, but thought it best. I was immediately smothered with a barrage of questions. Snow piled on the windowsill in alarming amounts as the officer silently scrutinized my driver's license. After an extended triple-take, positive identification was established, and I asked where I could keep my canoe for a few days. "If you leave it there," he said, "by dark, it'll be gone. Why don't you bring it up and set it next to the building here?" Gratefully I accepted and headed for downtown.

The paved streets were terribly slick. Blizzard walked in show class form in front, behind, and both sides of me. The town was neither big nor ugly. It was small-town America bearing a reputation of record cold temperatures and a Western Union office for much-needed money. After counting out $250, the lady suggested the city pound for Blizzard. After many inquiries, one friendly local finally admitted that it was one and the same as the Sewage Plant. There was no dignity in being a dog.

After a steak dinner, I checked in at the Rex Hotel. It left nothing to the imagination with a bed, shower, sink, toilet, and towel, just the essentials. Check out was at 11:00 A.M. sharp or it would be another ten dollars. I must have used that much in hot water. The pressure was far from adequate, but what dripped out was refreshing. The shower proved to be a nightcap for the evening; the last thing I remembered was the constant *hiss* and occasional *bang* of the old iron radiator struggling to keep the antiquated Rex warm.

A rattling reveille sounded at 7:00 A.M. when the heat was turned back up, forcing hot water to circulate throughout the Rex. The bed did little toward a good night's sleep. I wandered around town until the store opened at 9:00 A.M. to shop and wash a few clothes. That left me with only eleven dollars. It was time to leave.

While packing my new possessions, there was a knock at the door. It was a lady who introduced herself as Nina Helmer from the local newspaper. Same questions—same answers. At one time during our discussion, she pointed at my diaries stating, "I'd give anything to read those." I shook my head and smiled.

I left shortly after Nina. The weather wasn't great, but better than it had been in days. Blizzard was ecstatic, prancing through six inches of snow to the canoe. He was head-up and proud. The Sewer Plant was behind him now, and he never looked back.

The portage around the Rainy River Dam wasn't bad. It followed a muddy, snow-filled, rutted road to the river's edge. Not wanting to re-soak my now-dry feet, I stopped on an island a half-mile down-river and fiberglassed the worst holes in the bottom of the canoe. After building a huge fire, I tipped the canoe on its side to allow the bottom to absorb as much heat as possible. It still took hours before the resin cured in the swirling snow.

A comfortable campsite along the Rainy River.

With a relatively dry canoe, a downstream current, and a steady headwind, twenty miles was accomplished only to sleep on top of a picnic table in a campground next to Highway 1. Across the river on the north bank sat the tiny Canadian settlement called Emo. By dark, it turned scenic as the nightlights reflected off the newly formed shore ice and Northern Lights danced above them.

In the morning light Emo was just a few buildings on the bank. It was almost November, and winter had no intention of waiting for me. Snow flurries filled the air as I shot Little Sioux Rapids and reached Baudette, Minnesota. It was near here I would have to spend the winter. I could go no farther without entering Canada. Ten months and 2,500 mostly-upstream miles had gotten me this far. Now I had all winter to reflect on those miles and ponder the next 6,500. All I needed was a place from which to do it.

Winter Doldrums

Knowing no one sometimes made things difficult. I needed a place to spend the winter. I thought about building a small log cabin in some out of the way place, so my first stop was the Forestry Station. Wrong choice! With so much bureaucratic B.S. spewed in such a short time, my head spun all the way to the land office. At the city auditor's desk, I was informed that the man I needed to talk to wouldn't be in that afternoon because he was paving his driveway. I walked the streets, thinking of my dilemma. A small building set back from the street caught my eye. Above the building swung a sign stating Realtor. He had vacation homes on Lake of the Woods, two- and three-bedroom houses, farms, cabins, and lakeshore property. I sat there shaking my head negatively. Then, "There's an old farmhouse 25 miles from here, no plumbing, no electricity, $35 a month," he said.

I had only three words to say about a dump like that: "I'll take it."

My brother Tom and his wife Vicky came to Baudette late that afternoon. After a quick lunch, we headed for my winter home.

It stood in a clearing just off the road. The glassless windows appeared as dark square pits. Many harsh winters had faded the stucco on the exterior of the two-story building. A small, weathered, red shed stood leaning nearby and a tall elbow to elbow square structure reclined at an odd angle behind that. No other buildings were in sight.

Upon crossing the threshold where a door once hung, we entered the house through a battered, screened-in porch. The door bottom scraped the floor as we entered the kitchen. A wood-burning range dominated the area. Along one wall stood the cupboards and counter, another stood empty, and along another wall, more nothing. A back door led to an attached woodshed and the well. The rest of the plumbing consisted of a sink that drained beneath the house and the small outhouse perched over a dark pit.

One huge room made up the rest of the downstairs. Except for a bed, a barrel stove, and an out-of-tune piano, it was empty. The upstairs was no better. Within the three rooms were a table, a broken, high-backed chair, and a rotting, stained mattress. Glass speckled the floors as every window opening stood vacant except for a few jagged fingers of shattered pane. If one were trusting, it appeared electricity could still be forced through the exposed frayed wires. I wasn't. Tom and Vicky agreed that with a bit of work it could be comfortable. More precisely, the phrase used was, "Quite a bit of work." The month of May seemed like a long way away.

Going back to Baudette, we put my gear inside the Mach 1 and tied the canoe on top. While Tom and Vicky drove the first load to my winter quarters, I headed for the grocery store.

The narrow aisles weren't crowded as I made my way through them. It took two hours to fill the three shopping carts, though a quarter of that time was spent talking to the butcher/manager of the store. It was time well spent, for, in exchange for a few tales, I received a cart filled with canned goods at a discount and a gunnysack loaded with dog bones.

"You're Mister Pushcar aren't you," a lady stated as I walked out of the store with a bag in each arm. I replied affirmatively, and she said, "Welcome to Minnesota." Instead of telling her that I was born, raised, and lived here for 25 years, I just said thank you.

Tom and Vicky picked me up with my winter supplies, and it was well into the afternoon before the groceries were stored in the well-scrubbed cupboards. They decided to help clean the old house and then spend the night. Many buckets of water were hoisted from the well because dirt layered everything. It was a chore, but when it was accomplished, the house was probably cleaner than any time in recent memory. As a reward, we decided to see the nightlife of the nearest town.

Williams was small, with a population of 52, only six miles away. There was a hotel, bar/liquor store, a grocery store, and a post office. The bar was crowded with red-shirted hunters in from the fields, discussing deer stories and leaving after "just one more." Most were still there when we left two hours later.

Tom and Vicky departed around noon the next day. I hated to see them go, but I had much to keep me busy. In the next few days, I built a sawbuck, sealed all the windows with plastic, struggled the heavy old Wurlitzer piano into the kitchen, and cut the downstairs room in half by nailing in a plywood wall. A heavy, solid oak chest of drawers was found in an upstairs closet. It was all I could do to maneuver it to its tipping point at the top of the steps. When the stairwell stopped shaking and the dust settled, I righted the wooden beast, sealed the door going upstairs, and shoved it into the corner.

On November 3rd, the snow and ice disappeared. The temperature soared to 71 degrees. It seemed unbelievable that a few weeks ago I was racing winter with fear of losing. This heat awoke the dormant residents. The house was overrun with flies and summertime insects. Opening both doors in hopes of thinning out the masses was ineffective. It probably let more in than out. Only the cold night air would once again settle them.

The following week, the old house was winterized as much as possible. Then, my thoughts turned to the woodpile. Four days ago, my landlord Tom stopped and said he'd send a pulp truck loaded with slab wood from a local lumberyard that I could use as firewood. My patience lasted only so long, and after a few weeks, I knew the wood stove must eat. So, I shouldered my Duluth Pack, and with saw and ax in hand, walked the quarter mile to the nearest trees.

The forest was composed of pines, scattered with poplar and white birch. Finding the driest pine, I went to work cutting the log into four-foot sections. With these strapped to the pack and hoisted onto my back, I headed home.

It looked like a pitiful amount when I dumped it in the woodshed. However, after nine trips that day, I could tell some progress was being made. For ten straight days I cut, carried, split, and stacked wood. One and one-half cords lay neatly stacked in the woodshed. On the eleventh day just after a bachelor's breakfast of six servings of oatmeal topped with chocolate chips and sugar, half a bag of cookies, and two large tumblers of Tang, I heard a commotion outside. It was a pulp truck loaded with slabs. It was a relief, as I was already weary of a winter spent delivering wood to the wood stove.

With the wood worries settled, I sat down to matters of a more relaxed importance. It amounted to a six-hour session with the guitar, four hours with John Jakes' continuing novel *The Seekers*, and a short time with a harmonica. Blizzard had never heard the tones of a mouth organ before, and after a few notes his head picked up and a long, mournful, wailing howl filled the room. It almost appeared he was singing. After a short time, I was laughing so hard I had to quit and go back to reading.

It was getting late, and I was leaning against the wall with my bare feet propped near the barrel stove. Feeling hungry, with flashlight in hand, I walked into the dark kitchen for a late-night snack and stopped cold. Rising between my toes was a warm mushy substance. If I hadn't known what it was, I would have explained the situation as not unpleasant. Not so for Blizzard! His nose was shoved into it, accompanied by a stern lecture, whereas he was escorted out of the building with the door slammed behind him.

My pace of life slowed considerably. Days slid by as I read *The Dogs of War*, *The Marathon Man*, *Jaws*, *The Night of the Long Knives*, and *The Lost Universe*. Between novels, I would write letters to companies, trying to interest a sponsor in what I was doing. Before leaving for New Orleans, I had written 120 letters asking for some sort of sponsorship. Seven replied with only one saying "maybe."

But now, how could they resist? After 2,500 upstream miles, certainly one of these sporting goods companies would be overjoyed for the advertising possibilities, and the empty upstairs rooms would be stockpiled to the ceiling with everything from Richmoor dehydrated dinners to Gerry Mountain tents.

Three letters out of thirty were returned that winter. First, "We only sponsor religious groups;" second, "We'll give you 10% off on select merchandise;" and third, "We're sorry." *Curses!*

The ground was white, and the wind howled across the farmlands as I walked the lonely highway to Williams to post the letters. Few cars passed as most people didn't venture into the storm. After mailing the thirty letters, I managed a ride home in a garbage truck, first class, front seat.

It was eleven o'clock the next morning when a light gray Volkswagen pulled into the front yard. A tall, bearded man, briefcase in hand, advanced toward the door, introducing himself as Bill, from the Baudette Gazette. For three hours we sat at the kitchen table drinking tea until the interview was terminated. Then the canoe was dragged from the dilapidated garage. We posed in the snow for a few authentic photos with Blizzard toting a doggie pack. After a quick thank you, Bill's Volkswagen chugged down the icy road.

The weather turned colder, and daylight hours shortened as the end of November neared. Snow blanketed the earth, enhancing the nightly dance of Aurora Borealis. Wind and wolf howls melded as each dusk approached. A feeling of comfort prevailed as the woodshed was piled to the top with firewood and the cupboards were full. It was like having money in the bank.

Now that I was set to spend a long, cozy winter, I turned my efforts to writing. It took a while to get started as *Helter-Skelter*, and *The Adventurers* took priority. Reading and writing held my spare time interests until midnight. Then, the toilet trained Blizzard would be let out for a few minutes, and I would end the day listening to a Chicago radio station that broadcast E.G. Marshall's *Mystery Theater*, complete with suspense-building static.

Without electricity, reflector ovens can be used for more than cooking.

For activity, Blizzard and I would walk through the woods, checking the half-dozen rabbit snares I had set. On one such trip, Blizzard found a porcupine under a log. He circled the log, using every bark in the canine language. I finished resetting a snare and literally dragged him away from his invisible adversary. Some squirmy time was spent with the pliers that afternoon.

The snow had been piling up the last few days. I was just returning from a three-hour snowshoe trek when a red Suburban pulled into the yard. It was my sister Terry, her husband Skip, and their son Scooter. After we exchanged greetings, I gave them a tour of the old place while a bottle of milk heated on the wood stove for Scooter. It seemed that their impression of my situation was not good. "You're sure you don't want to come down and stay with us for the winter?" Terry asked seriously. It was tempting, but I couldn't, not after cutting all that firewood.

They couldn't stay long because it was a three-hour drive to their home and dusk was already approaching. After final goodbyes, I unpacked boxes of clothes, meat, groceries, and sweets. I was being well taken care of.

The days leading to Christmas turned cold. Minus 35 degrees was the norm. It was enough to keep me inside stoking the barrel stove. The well and the drain for the kitchen sink froze, making it a good time to get to know the temperamental wood range in the kitchen. I never could get a well-balanced fire in it.

Splintered kindling lay on crumpled newspapers. On top of this rested larger sticks that hopefully would produce the long-lasting coals desired. Over the intricate maze, I sprinkled a small amount of the white gas that remained from a gallon can. Taking two steps back, I lit a match and threw it toward the dark, round hole in the cast iron top. Nothing happened as the match disappeared into the firebox. Repeating the sequence produced nothing. After sprinkling more white gas, the third match produced instant success. The room filled with a *vrhoooomph!* of ignition. The violent flame simultaneously slammed down the oven door, made two cast iron lids do flips, and sent two sections of stovepipe into flight. They lay rocking on the floor.

A haze filled the now silent room. Black soot and ashes gradually settled everywhere. Cautiously peering over the crater's edge, I feared another eruption. Only a small flame flickered in the firebox, taunting me. I found the problem, *aside from the white gas*, after a thorough inspection of the stove. A small lever tucked under the stovetop opened the draft to allow smoke to enter the chimney. Though it took two days to clean the kitchen, the newly cleaned stove worked adequately the rest of the winter.

The cold weather held, and it now took eleven drops of a concrete block to open the frozen well. While the icy water heated in the teapot, I sat down to construct a splash cover for the canoe. The Mississippi River owned the original, and I could see no sense in purchasing another for $400. I would make my own out of ripstop nylon for under fifty dollars and with a bit of labor.

After working on the splash cover most of Christmas Eve morning, I decided to walk to town. The six miles was covered quickly in the zero-degree weather. The first stop was the Williams Post Office. There, awaiting me were a half-dozen newspapers rolled up and taped shut. I opened one and Blizzard and I were featured on the front page. "New Orleans to Nome by Canoe—Alone" flashed the headlines. It seemed poor Blizzard was just a prop in the scheme of things. I stuck the papers into my pack and walked across the street.

The tiny bar was full. With both people and spirits. I had stopped for a Christmas drink and the first one was free. The people here seemed extra friendly and many asked about my trip. Surely the newspaper article had something to do with that. After a second beer, I shouldered my pack, went out the door, and headed home.

On Christmas Day morning, I sat at the kitchen table sewing the splash cover when there was a knock on the door. It was the landlord's son Ed inviting me to their home for Christmas dinner. I accepted, dressed warmly, and hopped on the back of his snowmachine. Dinner was already being served when we walked in the door, so we immediately sat down at a long table with seven kids and their parents. A short "grace" was said, and plates of food appeared from the kitchen. A platter of fried chicken was set in the middle of the table and was soon surrounded by plates filled with trimmings.

The few presents were opened after dinner, and I was glad when Ed asked me to go fishing. He had made an embarrassing ruckus because all he received for Christmas was a Minnesota Vikings stocking cap. When we got on the snowmachine in a light snowfall, we headed for Lake of the Woods.

His plywood icehouse was small, but everything we needed was there. After cleaning twenty-six sauger, we were back on the snowmachine before it was very dark because there was no headlight attached.

By the time we reached my front door, a storm seemed imminent. The wind had picked up, and snow swirled across the road. "Looks like you had visitors while you were gone," Ed remarked while we looked at the fresh snowmachine tracks and footprints leading to the door. After I wished Ed the best of luck, he whisked away into the developing storm. I followed the unknown boot tracks to the house.

I had left the house open, for I hadn't expected to be gone long. Nothing seemed to be amiss, but Blizzard didn't rise to greet me as usual. He lay sprawled in the corner, gazing at me, moving his tail slightly. I fried a three-pound fish and then did the dishes. Blizzard got up, walked halfway to the door, and vomited. I opened the door and he staggered out. After cleaning the mess, I called him continuously. There was no response.

The light snow had accelerated, and the wind turned the night into a squall. Donning my winter gear, I started searching the stormy night for him. Calling and whistling proved futile. The flashlight barely pierced the storm's wrath. I walked continually larger circles around the house until I found a faint trail in the deepening snow. Following this for fifty yards through knee-deep snow, I shone the flashlight under a willow bush and there lay Blizzard, breathing heavily. He wouldn't respond to my coaxing and just touching him produced a whimper. Gently picking him up, I carried him back to the house.

The strength of the storm intensified. I had to follow my trail back as the light from the window was not visible. Blizzard vomited as soon as we entered the house. I wrapped him in a quilt, and he just lay there, breathing heavily with froth forming at his mouth. I knew why he wandered into the storm. It was an ageless custom preceding death.

Struggling with the quilt, Blizzard staggered to his feet and started walking along the wall. He got stuck in the piano bench and cried mournfully. I pulled him out and he continued his walk, using the wall as a guide. He walked into the counter, the stove, then stumbled over a box before getting to the door. There he lay, sniffing the cold air coming over the threshold. Again, struggling to his feet, he stood wobbling and fell as he tried to dig under the door for more fresh air. An attempt to arise failed. It was a hard event to witness. Shining a flashlight into his eyes produced no reaction. Blizzard appeared to be blind.

He lay in front of the door, his body occasionally convulsing, his cries of agony almost human. For hours I sat by helplessly. By morning the only sounds were the cry of the wind and the heavy gasping breaths of Blizzard. Then he was gone. I sat alone in the kitchen, head down and hands between my legs, lost in sorrow, listening to the wind blow through this old house.

The sun finally rose. I wrapped Blizzard in the quilt and carried him into the field next to the house and laid him next to a pile of rocks. Though the sun shone brightly, the wind still blew bitterly. I covered Blizzard with rocks and walked away. There became an emptiness in this journey.

It was hard to believe Blizzard's death was natural. I had left him for four hours, and he was fine. Within an hour of my return, he was on the verge of death. There was nothing in the house that would have made Blizzard sick. Could it be possible that someone had stopped here and poisoned him? There are a lot of great people living in this area, and I found that hard to believe. Still, I'll never know. It was Christmas. What a present! I had to get away.

Nine long hours of hitchhiking brought me to my sister's home on Ely Lake, a few miles from my hometown of Biwabik. I don't know how, but word of Blizzard reached this part of the country before I did. My sister stated that donation cans to replace Blizzard were already in most business establishments in Biwabik. The following day, there was more than $75 raised over the price of a $350 Samoyed.

Just before New Year's, a friend and I stood in front of a fenced cage near Cook, Minnesota. Inside scampered seven small Samoyeds. It was a hard decision. Three were females so that cut my choice to four. The one that caught my eye was a frisky tyke that would chastise his siblings and take no backward steps, another formidable watchdog. Even though he was the runt of the litter, he was chosen to become Vagabond.

That same evening my friend convinced me to show what slides I had to him and two other friends. It was the least I could do. The four of us were to meet in the back room of one of the bars in Biwabik at 7:00 P.M. I arrived ten minutes early, and the only available parking was four blocks away. Something was off. I finally parked behind the building, blocking someone in. It didn't take long to discern the situation. Opening the back door, my greatest fears were realized. The back room was packed with people. Retreat was out of the question; I had been spotted. In comparison, the challenge of whirlpools and attacking dogs seemed nominal. My mind raced in terror as I was guided through the crowd to a long table. Behind it was a folding chair. In its center stood a microphone and a controller to the slide projector.

I should have been kicking and screaming as I crawled toward the door. But these were people I knew, people that were supporting me. Still, I was well out of my element and knew it. I am not a public speaker nor am I a narrator. I yearned to be by myself, gliding down a river, but here I was, facing reality.

The lights went out. Except for the hum of the slide projector, there was no sound. A picture of a Samoyed puppy appeared on the screen. *I am supposed to be speaking.* This wasn't easy for someone that thought a half-dozen words constituted a speech.

"This is Blizzard," I said with an unexplained pause, "when he was six weeks old."

"We can't hear you!" came a voice from the back of the room. Boy, it sure sounded like one of my buddies. *I'll kill him when this is over. What am I doing here?* I raised my voice enough to make it through the first slide. The litany wore on.

Drinks appeared. After two dozen slides, things were still very quiet. Momentum didn't appear to be going my way. After another dozen slides, people started asking questions. Then, the more they saw, the more questions they asked. Some even laughed at my wry humor. Halfway through, I felt I had reached some degree of competency.

When the last slide was shown, people were standing and applauding. I felt a sense of embarrassed pride. These people were really behind me and believed in what I was trying to do. I felt obligated to them. Doc Dewhurst, who cut my hair as a kid, said I shouldn't. "It may seem kind of selfish on our part, but most of us would give most anything to do what you're doing," he said. "I guess we're just living our dreams through your experiences."

My stint in town ended, and Terry and Skip gave Vagabond and me a ride home to the old farmhouse on Sunday. They couldn't stay as both had jobs to attend to Monday morning.

The mound of rocks in the empty field caught my eye as I carried Vagabond through the snow-filled porch, unlocked the door, and entered the kitchen.

The old house seemed desolate, devoid of life. Clouds of condensation left my mouth and disappeared against the paint-peeled ceiling. The minus thirty-degree temperature had completely penetrated the old building. Despite the loss of heat, one thing concerned me even more. It was $2,100 worth of camera gear I had hidden in the bottom of the wood-box. Thankfully, it was still there.

While a roaring fire in the rusted barrel stove slowly radiated warmth to all but the far corners of my winter retreat, my mind fell to securing water. A look down the culvert shaft didn't look promising. After numerous attempts at securing water access by my conventional method, the concrete block lay shattered on the ice. The situation appeared more severe than anticipated.

The desire to not melt snow for water all winter tested my ingenuity. My solution required a herculean effort that yielded slow results. With a stout, weathered timber laid across the top of the culvert, I fastened a twelve-foot rope to its center and followed my dropped hatchet into the hole, shimmying down the rough strands. Claustrophobia was imminent as my feet touched the ice. *Glad I tied knots in the rope*, I thought. There was no chimney climbing out of this one and I didn't need to be found here in the spring.

Ice chips flew as I swung the hatchet, trying to keep the hole a uniform size and big enough to insert a five-gallon bucket. I found little discomfort in the hole at thirty degrees below zero given the level of effort required, and finally, I broke through at the two-foot mark. Water gushed through and my mission was accomplished. Hand-over-hand I grasped the knotted rope until I could grab the rim of the culvert and pull myself out. At the bottom of the hole, water glistened. To avoid repeating this procedure daily I built a makeshift ladder.

Things returned to normal over the next few days, and I decided it was time for a trip into town to check the mail that had been neglected for nearly three weeks. After making a small collar and leash for Vagabond, we started the mid-morning hike. The temperature had warmed to twenty below. As we walked down Highway 2, it was very quiet. Suddenly a full-grown lab "attacked" from a trailer. Tail wagging, he advanced full bore. Vagabond gave out a mighty *yap!* then let loose a shot of digested dog food and desperately tried climbing my leg to safety.

I scooped him up as the Lab skidded in. Trembling, the wide-eyed warrior lay in my arms. The lab sniffed around, stood for a petting and then loped back home. Setting Vagabond down produced a few victory yelps. Although we continued our walk into town, canine eyes never left the trailer.

The Post Office held a surprise. Eleven letters from all over the Midwest expressed sorrow and sympathy over the loss of Blizzard. One of them read:

Dear Mr. Pushcar,

I read about your dog in the Minneapolis paper. I have a dog that looks like your dog. I don't want him though. You can have him for free if you want him. I am Jay Becker, age eleven. Good luck on your canoe trip. I will keep track of your progress if I can.

Jay Becker
Deer Creek, MN
56522

The letters weren't the only surprise that this small town held. Just a block away stood a pile of blackened ruins. It was a mass of tin, timbers, and broken glass. Still smoldering was the bar and liquor store, remnants of social gatherings in Williams.

According to reports, it was the day before New Year's that the fire started. A teenage boy was in custody for arson. He sure knew when to hit where it hurt. But people are resilient. A new bar was already erected in the nearby hotel.

By the end of my first week back home, with letters answered and chores done, I found the true depths of boredom. What else could it be called when you sit unmoving, waiting for a mouse to dash across the floor so you can throw a hatchet at it again? The mouse soon tired of the challenge, so on impulse, I dressed warmly, leashed Vagabond, and headed for Baudette 24 miles away.

It took three rides and four hours. In my youth, I could have run there in less time. So, I thanked my third ride, a reverend, and promised to attend his Sing and Praise the Lord Fellowship that evening. *White lie!* Religion was never my strong suit, not then, not now.

As I roamed the main street of Baudette, many unknown people offered condolences over the loss of Blizzard. Little Vagabond seemed to be quite a hit. Stopping to see the friendly editor of the newspaper produced different results. I was informed that many locals weren't happy about a story published in the Minneapolis paper. It stated that Blizzard was poisoned, and it made the town look bad. "Nobody around here would have done that," the editor said with a tinge of malice.

"I suppose nobody would set a torch to the only bar in Williams just before New Year's Eve either?" I retaliated in the name of justice. Ending the discussion, I added, "Were his next plans to level the grocery store and then the post office?" I didn't leave mad, just not as congenial as when I went in. It was time to head home.

A smoke-belching, vintage auto rolled to a stop twenty feet past my outstretched thumb. It was two-toned, white and rust. Holding my breath through the oil smoke, I reached the passenger's door. Opening it revealed two bearded, gruff individuals that could have just stepped off the set of *Deliverance*. Neither of them was Burt Reynolds. "Hop in!" the driver said with cheer.

"Better get in front," his partner said, "it's a little crowded back there."

The back seat was jammed with cases of beer and whiskey. One small box of groceries was crammed under the back window. As I wiggled in enough to close the door, two smells filled the interior—strong body odor and whiskey. Vagabond lay curled on my lap as the car shivered in high idle, jerked as it hit first gear, and then rolled noisily down the road.

We never went over thirty miles an hour. I never figured out if the driver wouldn't or the car couldn't. "Have a swallow," offered the voice behind the Windsor bottle. The small swallow scorching soon turned to warmth but did little to ease the apprehension as the truck kept veering toward the ditch.

The two Finnish, deer hunting, trapping, logging bachelors were friendly enough. They had just hit town for the first time in a few weeks and were blowing off a bit of steam. A person couldn't help liking the old guys with their carefree, uncomplicated lives. "We live a few miles down the road, but we'll give you a ride all the way home," the driver said as we left the main highway.

I was relieved as the sociable hermits stopped in front of the house and I got out. With a toast of their bottle, they wished me well and were again on their way, leaving me in a cloud of blue smoke.

Time traveled slowly. February 1st found Vagabond still not

housebroken, but he could sit up and scratch behind his ear without falling over. The nightly temperatures dropped to minus 39 degrees. This held for over a week, necessitating daily work on the woodpile. It also inspired me to become a pianist.

Standing alone in the kitchen, old, cold, and dusty, the piano seemed a relic of the past as I plunked one key after another. There was an instruction booklet in the piano bench. Placing it on the rack before me, I opened it to page one. Within the week, it was mastered. Then, my career was over. There was no sequel to *Teaching Little Fingers*.

After a ten-mile snowshoe trek, Vagabond takes a much-needed rest.

After that, trips to town became more frequent, and it didn't take much to convince me that one was necessary. On one of these tedious trips, I made it three miles before a car stopped. A man and his son offered me a ride, which I accepted. Endless questions concerning my trip were asked. The answers must have been right for this was followed by an invitation to coffee.

While the coffee brewed, my host shared a "fantastic video tape" called *A World Without Cancer*. It was not exactly what I needed to hear, as I had lost my sister, father, mother, grandfather, and grandmother to the disease.

Fortunately, the movie also built an appetite as coffee and a tray of pastries appeared from the kitchen. With cup in hand and hardly a doughnut gone, the doorbell rang, and four people entered the living room. My hosts seemed overjoyed. Benches at the organ and piano were immediately filled.

What followed was a conglomeration of off-key gospel composition. All six struggled in vain to blend voices and instruments. I sat patiently, toughing it out, wondering how my rendition of "Twinkle, Twinkle, Little Star" would go over on the piano. Amazingly, after it was over, they all clapped and hugged each other. Maybe I was missing something here. Anyway, I thanked my hosts for their coffee and music, and then decided to walk home. It was a day meant for walking. The temperature had soared to 55 degrees and spring filled the air. I guess it was a day to sing after all.

The 1st of March approached. The well didn't freeze, and no fire was required in the barrel stove during the day. I could feel the wanderlust in my bones. Just thinking about getting back into the canoe brought out the maps. Writing and reading were out of the question. Warm weather made it extremely difficult to stay indoors. Still, no letters had arrived offering to shower me with camping equipment. I would do with what I had.

One interesting letter did arrive though. It was from a man in Duluth starting a 1,000-mile Canoe Club. The first meeting was to be held March 8th and would feature a slide presentation of a world-record canoe trip. It was appealing. I left within the hour.

I dined at a local restaurant with my friend Rick, and it took most of our meal to convince my old friend it would be a very worldly experience for him to join me at this new 1,000-mile Canoe Club meeting.

It was held in a church, and we were late. A cold blast of air entered with us. We were puzzled. Roughly fifty people had their heads bowed and a preacher was standing at a podium blessing their souls. "I think we're in the wrong church," I whispered to Rick. Spotting a poster stating that two men had paddled 7,000 miles in one season and were having an eight o'clock slideshow, we felt it had to be the right place and slid into the last pew.

Our disappointment lasted the entire program despite feeble attempts at sound effects from nature. It was a prayer meeting in disguise. Rick's head was bowed with a sullen expression masking his red-tinted face as his eyes stared unblinkingly. His thumbs twiddled.

115

"I've at least got to introduce myself to the guy," I pleaded. We hovered in the back pew until most of the people left the church before introducing ourselves. An interesting half-hour of bush talk followed before I was invited to Lake Superior the following day. Apparently, a lead had opened in the ice, and the guy was going to paddle his canoe in circles in it. With a lame excuse, I declined having already turned enough circles in that lake.

After handshakes were finished, we climbed into Rick's Plymouth and headed downtown. His attention was already upon the long-frozen six-pack in the car. I had seen enough.

By noon the next day I again stood on Highway 53, wondering what happened to the 55-degree weather. Minutes slid into hours before a Suburban's red backup-lights twinkled through the blowing snow. I jogged toward them. Opening the door, someone said, "How you doing, Push?" It took a second to recognize the old high-school classmate whom I hadn't seen in nine years. He introduced his wife and their two children, offering me a ride to my doorstep.

"Seeing how I teach school twenty miles from Williams and go right through there, it would be no problem," he said. Boy, that was great news to hear. With many good laughs about old basketball games and classmates, we had a lot of catching up to do. Time flew and after stopping for lunch, he left me at the Williams Post Office. With a promise to keep in touch, we departed.

Nothing had changed in Williams except the ashes of the burned bar and liquor store were now a leveled gravel lot. The post office box was empty, but the new bar at the hotel was full. Sitting next to a man named Jack Lauffin, a local farmer, I listened as the bar population discussed the fate of the northern Minnesota timber wolf. As their fate oscillated, Jack challenged me to a friendly game of pool. It was an hour before we hung up the pool cues. I hardly beat him, but he opened his wallet and crammed a twenty-dollar bill into my shirt pocket. "That's for your trip," he explained. As much as I told him I didn't need it, he told me I did. The guy was twice my size so what could I do?

Before it got too late, I left and walked the six miles home in the dark. It was still cold for mid-March. I retrieved Vagabond from his stay with friends on the way. He seemed to enjoy the exercise after being at the hotel for two days.

The old house was dark and uninviting. Little scurrying noises sounded as the door creaked open. Vagabond dashed to the hunt.

The single-mantle Coleman lantern hissed to life after twenty pumps. Wood was just starting to crackle when bright lights shone through the kitchen's windows, penetrating its darkness.

Closing the door to the barrel stove, I walked into the kitchen and the lights vanished. Two car doors slammed shut. Then, there was silence. Alone in the dark kitchen, apprehension mounted. Rays of a flashlight flashed across the window. Faint voices sounded. Footfalls crossed the porch, and two loud knocks echoed through the kitchen. Opening the door, I was blinded by the beam from a flashlight. "How you doing, Push?" came a voice from the night. It was two of my friends from Biwabik who had helped set the stage for the slideshow.

I was amazed they had found me. They admitted to a few wrong turns and stated they were here and ready to spend the night, which was just fine with me. Then, after having a beer and a few laughs, they showed me the ticket. At the top read "Jerry Pushcar Benefit Dance." It was in two days and I was expected to be there. They had come to make sure.

Gary had rented the Biwabik town pavilion, got local bar owners to donate a few kegs, and Mike's rock and roll band was to provide the live music. Instructed to be there early, I was overwhelmed with nervousness.

People filtered in and soon the tables were filled. The event became standing-room-only, and small groups now loitered around the dance floor. I didn't recognize many faces. The band started promptly at eight o'clock and played for five hours before the bright lights were turned on. Through the P.A. system, Mike thanked everyone for coming. The experience was better than I had anticipated. Many new people were met, and I was reunited with people I grew up with and hadn't seen in years. After we cleaned the pavilion, Gary handed me a shoebox. It contained almost $800. Friends like that are very hard to find.

Mike and Gary gave me a ride back to Williams the next afternoon. They spent the evening, leaving the following morning with my heartfelt thanks.

April Fool's Day brought splendid warmth. It provided an opportunity to renovate the canoe. Pulling it from the dilapidated garage, I laid it keel down across two sawhorses and filled it with water from the now open well. With pen in hand, I crawled underneath. The carnage was remarkable.

Circle after circle was drawn around the dripping water before I refilled the canoe and kept circling. I was soaked, but when finished, 49 points of entry had a black halo around them. There was no sense in applying many small patches. I stripped the entire bottom of fiberglass. Although it took a week to strip, fiberglass, sand, paint, and varnish, when the gunwales and keel were reattached, it looked nearly new.

The following week I had a work offer and accepted it. I made friends with another guy on the job named Lowell. We put in some very long days packaging potatoes in 100-pound sacks and then stacking them ten bags high. It was hard work and for the entire first day it seemed as if all eyes were on me. Few make it through the first day. I wasn't one of the quitters.

Lowell and I became partners in crime. On a warm Sunday, we finished early and decided to take a ride in the country. The liquor store was closed, but Lowell had no trouble finding a cache under his friend's house.

He was in and out of the ditch twice within the hour. The third time, we had to flag down a tractor to pull us out. I offered to drive. "Next stop you can take over," Lowell slurred. I took that to mean the next time we hit the ditch. A few miles down the road smoke billowed over the treetops to our right. "Something's sure burning, looks like someone's barn!" An excited Lowell yelped.

"Look out!" I shouted at the distracted Lowell. In the nick of time he looked back to the highway, swerved out of the oncoming lane, and missed a vehicle that had slowed to look at the fire by inches. "Good thing nothing was coming," I said in a voice brimming with spite.

Already there was a fire truck, hosing the inferno to no avail. The burning garage was built from creosoted railroad ties. Five or six cords of cut and split birch firewood were stacked against the building. Everything was engulfed in flames. As he slapped his knees, Lowell howled with laughter and said, "Look at the son of a bitch burn!" Standing helplessly, the fire truck soon ran dry as flames and black smoke billowed into the clear blue sky. People ran ant-like through an adjoining pasture trying to control a growing grass fire. I grabbed two wet gunnysacks and joined in.

Two hours later I returned to the car, black with soot and sweat-soaked. Lowell leaned against the hood, sipping a beer. "About time," was his only comment. Although the garage had collapsed, flames still reached upward ten feet. People milled around watching the dying fire. "Can't do anything more around here," Lowell theorized. I agreed. This time I drove. The next day Lowell and I put in another ten-hour workday carrying 100-pound sacks of potatoes.

Mid-April was warm. We'd work all day wrestling 100-pound sacks of potatoes, eat a huge supper and then close the bar with a few games of pool and foosball. The next day we would do it all again. It almost became competitive. I carried 500 sacks into the backroom and stacked them the day the potato job ended. It was a workout.

Plans were progressing at the farmhouse. With the potato job a thing of the past, more important matters could be undertaken. I checked the mousetraps one last time and recorded the winter's catch at 36.

The kitchen cupboards were emptied. What wasn't going into the canoe was either given or thrown away. There was a pile in the kitchen and one in the bedroom, both ready to be packed. The canoe was ready as was I, anxious to feel the waters beneath my feet once again.

But, for now, I was as lost as any time since leaving New Orleans. I didn't know what to do. Everything was done except to wait. My time in Williams was drawing to a close. Blocks of ice still choked the river but when they left, so would I.

Sometime during this period of purgatory, a newsman from Warroad drove up and requested an interview. Peering past me, he scrutinized a cluttered kitchen, and then stated, "I'm an outdoors person myself. Why don't we sit outside?" I agreed as it was a fantastically clear, warm day.

I followed him across the porch and out the door as he sat in a nice pile of dead grass next to the door. *Good God,* I shivered. How could I tell him that particular parcel of grass was dead for a reason? On cold winter nights, when nature called, hiking to the outhouse was not an option. Instead, I used a mayonnaise jar. In the morning, it was dumped.

We sat there for the better part of an hour—he on the brown grass, me on the green. Whenever the breeze would abate his nose would twitch. When finished, he got up, brushed the back of his pants off, thanked me for the great interview, and drove away. Now that's a real outdoors person!

Resumption

While the sun had yet to rise, a fog lay low over the river. Last night's chilled temperature held as I positioned the three packs inside the canoe. Vagabond turned tight circles in his designated area, seeking a comfortable niche for the long journey. Ripples fanned from the canoe as I pushed into the calm bay of Rainy River. There were no farewells as each stroke raised the bow slightly, pushing me toward Canada. In a matter of hours, I passed bridge columns heavily initialed with graffiti and docked on foreign soil. Climbing a steep bank to the highway, I walked into the Customs Station at the Baudette-Rainy River International Bridge.

They were friendly but firm. "What's your name? Where are you from? What's your final destination? We'll need to see some sort of identification. Any liquor, drugs, firearms, or expensive equipment?" It was all the information needed at the border crossing. Impersonal phrases were repeated hundreds of times a day. When all was said and done, the officer handed me a sheet of paper and said, "Now if you'll sign this Temporary Admission Permit and leave $377.54 with us you can be on your way.

"Do what?" I asked incredulously.

"That's what the duty and excise taxes come to on your equipment," he said. "It should be twice that, but we're already giving you a handsome break."

The duty on the camera equipment was $301.60. The canoe was rated at $63.70 and the rifle at $12.24. "It's only a deposit and when you leave the country with everything you brought in, you'll get it back. Just don't lose that pink slip," he warned. That left slightly over $200 with which to enter the country. In a few months, I could be

121

facing vagrancy.

When the door had almost closed behind me, I heard, "Just a minute, I'm going to take a look at what you have down there." A young officer donned his blue hat and jacket, followed me along the pavement, over the guardrail, and then down the steep hill to the canoe. Between him and the canoe stood a barrier, ten feet of mud. As he peered at the canoe's contents from the edge of the goo, I could see grave indecision. I asked if he wanted me to carry him over, but he reacted to the facetious challenge by tiptoeing across with extra-long strides, arms flailing like wings in the wind. His goal was a piece of driftwood where he teetered on the sinking trivial castaway. Rapping his knuckles on the long white tube containing my 800 mm camera lens, he hit the E string beneath the nylon guitar case and then announced, "Everything looks in order, so have a pleasant trip."

Spring 1976. Packed to face customs before entering Canada.

"Thanks," I said as he crossed the barrier and started up the hill. Loading Vagabond, I sloshed through the mud and floated the canoe into another country. Looking up, I saw the officer standing on top of the hill with one-foot resting on the guardrail. His hands were a blur. It reminded me of a train station in my youth.

But no trains ran here. It was eight o'clock and the fog was melting in the morning sun. Rainy River's sluggish water slowly widened, only to be smothered on its flanks by wide, thick reed beds. Soon these reeds spread to expose clear blue white-capped water. It looked ominous both on the map and in front of me. It was Lake of the Woods. The thousands of islands on this huge body of water could be a nightmare to orient.

Defying the wind as much as possible, I set a course straight north, island hopping. Sometime during the afternoon, I passed what I hoped was Pine Island. By now my body was revolting; even potato piling didn't prepare me for this. Pounding up and down, bucking the wind and waves had taken its toll. This was the contribution of the long lazy winter. By sundown, I had had enough.

My feet dragged as I shuffled along the sand beach collecting driftwood for a fire that never passed the incendiary stage. Dumping the load of wood, I grabbed a length of salami from the food box and sat down for supper. My bed was a hollow in the sand with my sleeping bag pulled over me.

The last thing I remembered was a strong wind developing, and Vagabond curled at my feet. By morning I sat up stiffly, knowing I shouldn't have tried to get to Nome in one day. Sand sifted from the sleeping bag and only a shoelace disclosed the sandy grave entombing my pants, shirt, and shoes. Sand was in my eyes, ears, hair, and nose. It grated between my teeth and sunk to the depths of my armpits.

Only after much digging, picking, shaking, scraping, and the use of some very cold water could I function properly. *I must have slept through quite a blow*, I thought as I arranged a campfire to start the day consuming healthy portions of oatmeal, bannock, and Tang. With diminishing stiffness, I washed the few dishes, rolled the sleeping bag, and pushed the canoe into day two, doubtful of matching yesterday's 25 miles.

Most of the morning was calm until a wind arose with a small gale not far behind. I tucked behind a small nameless island for lunch. It was more of a large rock dotted with trees, but while Vagabond explored the archipelago, I gave fishing a try.

When pulling the tackle box from the pack, a piece of paper fluttered to the ground. Opening it, I found a dollar inside with the following written note:

"I don't think you know me, but I graduated from Biwabik High School in 1973. I was surprised to see your outfit here and wished I could have met you." It was signed but I couldn't quite make out the signature. The first name was Susan; the last was a blur.

Fishing proved futile and I debated challenging the five-mile stretch of open water to Bigsby Island. I pulled to the leeward side of the island. From there I could see Tomahawk Island. Its beacon light beckoned, but I was going nowhere.

West winds lessened but lingered over the next few days as I island hopped northward. Vagabond lay before me, nestled in my lifejacket. Looking down, I was amazed by his growth. Suddenly there was movement on the island that caught my eye. A black bear had just emerged from the underbrush. Rocks and fallen logs were cast aside as the bear searched for grubs.

Replacing my paddle with the camera, I shot. Its head rose instantly to the click of the camera, and his nostrils flared as he sniffed the air. It took minutes before he was satisfied with his surroundings and then started for the water's edge to drink. His muscled body rippled as he filled the viewfinder. His smell was as offensive as my mouth was dry. It was a picture of a lifetime.

Suddenly Vagabond reacted to the bear's stench. The attack sent my heart palpitating. Water sprayed everywhere. The bear was a blur of black. Vagabond's uproar reverberated across the water. I was vocally irate at his sense of duty, and he dove for cover as the bear disappeared. I couldn't punish him, as his response was only natural. Besides, someday a brown bear might wander into camp and Vagabond could just sit down and look at me. Knowing you reap what you sow, I paddled away from the picture of a lifetime.

By the next morning, rain dotted the calm waters where Voyageurs once ventured. A hurried breakfast sent me on an identical course, following a compass instead of a lop pole. For ten hours the maze continued in and out of dead-end sloughs, between islands, and around islands, only to camp on another pine-studded rock thirty miles away. Since the water was smooth and it was my kind of country, I had no complaints.

Soon rain approached in earnest, necessitating the use of the splash cover. Vagabond was confused as his world turned dark. At regular intervals, his white head poked from beneath the green nylon, swiveled left and right, and then disappeared. *At least one of us remained dry.*

Lunch sites were picked with care as dog lessons were quickly learned. Big islands meant frustrating hours of searching and screaming pleas that the voyage was ready to resume. Since small islands only took minutes to scrutinize, the mission could continue without maddening the master as nothing is more irritating than having the water calm and the dog gone.

Kenora lay on the north shore of Lake of the Woods. I knew I was close when boats zigzagged between islands, buoy markers abounded, and power poles dwarfed the tree line. Finding an island without a cabin was arduous. Anything that could support a structure was occupied, except the rock.

I found a bald hump surrounded by swamp with a power pole rising skyward from its center. Everything had to be moved to its zenith as boat wakes nearly covered the wood tick sanctuary. By morning, dozens crawled over me, searching for a place to bury their heads and start their vampire habits. I fled to the mainland.

A strong west wind swayed the treetops. House after house lined the shore, each fronted with a long board landing pier where boats floated lackadaisically, tethered by ropes. It was Sunday and I needed to replace my fishing rod that now rested on the bottom of Lake of the Woods. In the nearby town of Keewatin, only a few hours out of the way, a store was advertised as being open.

What appeared to be a public landing was soon reached, and Vagabond was tied to a low bush while the canoe was secured to a huge concrete block. *Now to find the store.*

"Can't miss it" came directions from a gas station attendant. After a half-mile uphill walk on a narrow shoulder of a highway, I finally reached a sidewalk and entered the store.

A woman named May greeted me as I entered the double doors. Somehow, I managed to choose the cart that veered sideways when pushed forward and wrangled it up and down the aisles. Only six oranges and a half pint of maple nut ice cream caught my attention.

The door to the sporting goods section had to be unlocked. Pocketing the key, May directed me to the back wall where a slim variety of fishing rods hung from wooden pegs. I needed a compact one, and May had just the answer. It was telescopic, just like the one being replaced. It had broken on the first cast. I knew it was a mistake, but I accepted it anyway, setting it on top of the ice cream carton while May operated the cash register. With change in hand, I started the descent to the canoe.

Sweltering heat melted the ice cream and it soon dripped through the paper bag, trailing puddles down the hill. Vagabond waited patiently with tail wagging. He stared at me eagerly as I ate the remaining frozen ice cream from the core of the carton. With him on cleanup, I dug my thumb into the thick orange peel savoring its released aroma.

With better things to think about than oranges, I headed east, ducked under a railroad trestle, rounding a bend to stop at a boat hoist. There appeared to be a ten-foot drop to the Winnipeg River, and I could see narrow-gauge tracks disappearing into the water that were meant to help ease the descent. Apparently, a cradle on a cart slid under a boat, and the whole contraption was winched over the tracks to the opposite side where the boat slid into the water, allowing the boater to be on his way. I read the multitude of signs: price per boat length, weight restrictions, keep off, restricted, danger, and — open May 21st. Fortunately, it was a short portage.

After a little over a day on the Winnipeg River, the small settlement of Minaki, Ontario, 25 miles north of Kenora, was reached. It was a place that seemed to offer little as I landed the canoe near the Forestry and RCMP buildings. The RCMP, or Royal Canadian Mounted Police, are Canada's federal police force, but they provide local support all over, too. Past these structures stretched a dirt road with a closed, dusty Co-op store on its far side. Threatening to open in an hour stood a Hudson's Bay Store, just a short distance away.

Across the street, a restaurant sign dangled at an odd angle. Since it seemed a good place to spend an hour, I ordered a hamburger, with no amenities. "It's already seasoned," answered my request for salt and pepper. *No wonder the masses avoid this place.* I finished the dollar-a-bite burger and left the premises. I'd rather wait outside for the store to open.

A phone booth leaned toward the street. I decided to call my brother. I dialed 0 and waited. Only a dial tone filled the earpiece. It was becoming more and more evident that this Canadian bush life was going to require some adaptation.

Leaning against a telephone pole, I watched as the crowd thickened to six. Then a Buick Riviera stopped next to the store, and a Caucasian got out, wearing dress slacks, a fine cotton shirt, white tie, and a wide leather belt that couldn't hide a protruding stomach. After he entered a back door, chains soon rattled, and the front door swung open. The crowd of older Indian ladies filed in. Their dress was ragged, with nylons bunched around their ankles and caved-in shoes. Most wore long patterned-dresses and combed their hair straight back from their brown, wrinkled faces. I waited, entering the store behind them.

Splitting the store in two was a divider. While one side

contained groceries, the other held clothes, sporting goods, and hardware. It wasn't a Walmart; it was a store of necessities. The most impressive feature was a map. Mesmerized, I stood looking for many minutes. The depiction was from the days of the Voyageurs. It portrayed their 6,000-mile trade route from Ottawa to Fort Chipewyan through a roadless wilderness.

Heading in that same direction, I was back on the Winnipeg River. Minaki was not impressive, but 15 miles downstream, the Minaki Resort was. It was situated on the right bank and was massively constructed of stone, huge logs, and cedar shakes. Even though incomplete, the building's esthetic value couldn't be denied. I stopped for a closer look, but the groundskeeper halted my advance.

Near, if not sixty, gray hair poking beneath his billed hat, he stated bluntly, "Government owns it." He also informed me that it contained a swimming pool, two restaurants, a boat landing underneath the building, a bar, a dance hall, and a huge golf course. "Yup, eight million dollars is being dumped into the place, and they can't get it right. A green roof would have looked a lot better from the air," he critiqued disapprovingly.

Neither agreeing nor arguing, I left. His departing words were a clear, stern warning. "You be real careful at Dog Rapids just a few miles downstream. Wasn't many years back a 16-foot fishing boat capsized in the rapids. We found the boat pretty quick, but it took a long, long time to find the two guys and girl."

He was right; it wasn't far downstream. The huge red letters on the white sign read Danger Fast Water. The canoe, Vagabond, and I went through a series of small whirlpools, shot a small chute over what appeared to be a string of huge boulders, sped down a stretch of fast-moving water, and then passed a similar sign pointing in the opposite direction. Such were Dog Rapids.

With the help of the current, White Dog Dam was reached in just a few hours. Well below the dam floated a log chain used to keep boats at a distance. A heavy, steel chain connected the logs as they stretched from bank to bank. The dam gates opened automatically without warning, and any boat caught close to the gushing water would be in for a rough ride.

I had a hard time crossing. Taking aim at the center of a log, I advanced. The canoe would slide onto the log but not over. Crawling over the packs, I stood on the water-soaked log. It was precarious but held my full weight. With balanced bouncing and timed tugs, the canoe inched across. Once free, I angled toward shore and docked beneath the dam.

Dust settled from a car passing the top of the dam. Following a dirt road that climbed a faraway hill, the car disappeared, leaving only a thin trail of dust. There was no portage. It was just a major inconvenience as I climbed the road bank, crossed the road, slid down a fifty-foot embankment, crossed a campground, and inched down a precarious glass-impregnated rock bank to a glass-covered beach. I never did understand the fixations that people have with glass, especially bottles. I guess they were just made to be broken.

As I traveled through light turbulence far below the dam, sunset was yet a few hours away. Drifting downstream lethargically, I enjoyed the evening with a setting sun in my eyes as the small village of White Dog came into view on the north bank. This was the first of many such villages. Boats, mostly wooden, lay docked on the muddy beach. Each weather-beaten house attached itself to the river by a narrow, hard-packed trail.

I watched as an old, bent-backed Indian lady swayed down the steep trail to the water's edge with two pails. She filled them and started back. Halfway up she stopped, set the pails down, and with wrinkled hands on old hips, straightened her old back. Her pulled back white hair contrasted with her long, black, tattered dress. Her stooped posture emphasized her fragility. She turned toward the river, saw me, and swiftly resumed her climb, seeming to fear being caught at rest. Water slopped over the pails as she disappeared into a faded, green house. Shortly she reappeared with a man and a young boy. Unmoving they watched as I passed.

Upon receiving orders and a shove, the boy ran to the house next door, then to another and another. Soon people stood in doorways, looked out of windows, and watched from the bank. None spoke, and none waved. Few visitors must have passed this way. *Those shacks must be cold in the winter,* I thought. It looked as if half the windows were broken, and the other half were boarded; it made Minaki look pretty good.

A dilapidated log cabin stood on a small hill, slightly away from the other buildings. A thin stream of white, wood smoke curled from its stone chimney while a smoldering fire in the front yard poured thick smoke through what appeared to be meat suspended from a tripod. A woodpile was stacked against the cabin and a muddy path switch-backed to the river. Apparently, an archaic Indian lived there, clinging to threads of the past. He was probably living life the best he could—the life he knew.

I spent the night with the river separating me from the village. The community slept. The next morning, only one light shone as I pushed the canoe into the river. That was from the log cabin. Sparks flew from the chimney as the early morning fire was stoked. Only a few howls from chained huskies mourned my passing.

It was Friday, May 21st, and I had soon portaged around another dam and reached Point DePois. By the following day, I stood on top of Seven Sisters Dam. It was a warm, lazy day. From this vantage point, one could see huge water-worn rocks where water once flourished. Now only small pools appeared intermittently beneath the crisscrossed power lines. Making my way off the dam, I crossed the public campgrounds and found the restroom. This was no hole-in-a-box operation. It was clean, warm, had running water, no mosquitoes, and even had toilet paper. I checked every stall but couldn't find the Winnipeg Gazette. If I wanted a paper, I'd have to stop at Lac Du Bonnie.

But first, I needed to get past this dam, and my heart wasn't in it. After a drawn-out orientation run, I shouldered the heaviest pack, picked up the guitar, and was off. The trail led to a trestle road bridge, down forty feet of very steep stairs, and then along an overflow channel for a quarter-mile.

Upon reaching the stairs I discovered a generous amount of blood. Soaked into every other step with regular intervals, it was splattered across the dam. I reasoned it must have happened minutes ago since it wasn't there on my orientation run. At the bottom of the steps was a bloody, barefooted imprint pressed into the muddy trail. It appeared to be a young, teenaged-size foot bleeding badly. The blood trail continued to the end of the portage.

It took little investigating to see what had happened. A few feet from the last bloodstain lay the bottom of a broken beer bottle, its sharp, jagged teeth protruding like punji sticks. Picking it up, I found a small pool of blood swayed inside. It was an awesome thing to step on, especially if the victim was running. With a shutter, I threw the bloody glass into the channel and returned for another load.

Although the two packs weren't bad, the canoe was awkward, especially descending the flight of stairs. If they were much steeper, they could have been called a ladder. The bow hung well below my feet in order to keep the stern from hitting the steps behind me. A very slow, well-balanced pace prevented a headlong flight. It took four hours to drag myself across the portage. It should have taken only two.

The afternoon heat was relentless as I reached Lac Du Bonnie hours later. I didn't stop as homes, docks, and motorboats slid by. Some people waved from lawn chairs, but mostly I passed unobserved. Traveling until dark compensated for time lost on the portage. Through the dimming light, a small, mounded, treeless island came into view. A rock finger rose from one end. It could have been the grave of a giant, but it was just a stone chimney, reminiscent of a dream shattered when the dam system was built, forcing the owners to flee. It appeared they took their log home with them.

In the morning light, I studied the finger of rock while eating a dry breakfast. In the back of my mind, I tucked away how it was drafted, the unique way the log wall had tied into it, the hearth, and the mantle. Mentally I reconstructed the log walls on the still-existing rock foundation, knowing that someday I could live out my days in a place like this. *Just one dream at a time,* I told myself and started towards McCarthy Dam ten miles away.

Typical of the other dams, the portage started by going up a hill, over a road, down a steep rock embankment, and through a campground that sat next to the water below the dam. The only difference was that this campground was packed. I stepped over tent guylines, skirted Winnebagos, maneuvered around people in lawn chairs, and tramped through a Boy Scout encampment. Vagabond was kept on a very short leash.

People dotted the shoreline casting every conceivable type of lure to attract a fish. Just below the dam, two Natives threw a net basket on a long rope into the water, waited a few minutes, and then pulled it out hand-over-hand. Their catch soon flopped on the ground behind them. There had to be envy from the anglers. *Native fishing rights,* I presumed.

By midday, I arrived at Great Falls Dam. The water between these dams was under so much control that it posed no problems. Getting across the log chain was no worse than the preceding ones, but the portage proved short, steep, and precarious.

It started out facing a twelve-foot wall of rock and huge pieces of concrete. There was no place to land so I tied the canoe to a rock and struggled the packs to the road. Then came the canoe. There was no room to maneuver. Balanced on a two-foot rock, I grabbed the yoke, jerked the craft to my thighs, and then onto my shoulders.

I sidled up next to the wall, carefully picking one foot-hold at a time. It was like climbing a ladder with an awkward, imbalanced 120 pounds rocking on your shoulders. Repeat twelve times. Nothing was flat, and the course veered considerably from ledge to ledge. Muscles that had previously been dormant protested. It was slow and precise. I didn't think about what would happen if I fell.

With the balancing act behind me, I departed from below the dam next to a half-sunk, rusted iron barge. Huge flat rocks made an indirect route to open water. Another day's travel in slackened currents brought me to the town of St. George.

Nothing moved at the dock. A light green Pinto and an old Chevy decorated a small graveled area. A diminutive weather-beaten shed stood to one side, its half-open door harboring a crescent moon. *Definitely a hole in a box.* I headed for downtown.

A scuffed, green and white sign announced St. George's population at 347. It was a five-minute walk to the first house and another five-minute walk to the last. Only a paint-peeled Dairy Queen showed signs of life. After a quick soda, I strolled the empty streets back to the dock and settled in for the night under a grove of budding birch trees.

From my perch on top an Arctic Cat snowmachine crate, I noticed kids heading to school at 8:30 A.M. Then, as if on cue, shades came up in the only store in town, and I followed two elderly ladies through the opened door. Minding my own business, I paid for two Cokes, two apples, and two Hostess Twinkies. With breakfast done, I wrapped four rolls of film in a Twinkie wrapper, enclosed it in a brown paper bag, and sent the package to my brother from the smallest post office I had ever seen.

Within two hours, I was at the last dam on the Winnipeg River. Concrete had been used to the maximum to change the river from what it had once been into what is now gone forever. I was glad the dams were behind me.

From here, northward, the civilization to which I was accustomed, would be sparse. Fort Alexander lay a short distance downstream. There I would fill the pantry with a month's worth of provisions, for beyond Fort Alexander lay Lake Winnipeg, a thinly populated body of water spreading over 9,396 square miles notorious for bad weather. I welcomed its challenge.

Topping the hill above the river, I viewed Fort Alexander. The village was on the other side of a cemetery of white crosses. By the number and condition of the graves, it appeared the town had been here for many years. I passed an outdoor altar littered with broken glass and desecrated with initials. Side-stepping graves I looked at some of the dates on the few granite headstones. Most graves weren't elaborate, only marked by rotting, wooden crosses.

My expectations for provisions were discouraged by the view from the highway. Walking to a small trailer court, I asked a man sitting on his steps where the store was. "No store here for a long time now. You have to go eleven miles down the road now," came the reply I did not want to hear. I wasn't going eleven miles down the road, and I wasn't paddling back to St. George. *I'll make do,* I reassured myself. The next habitation was Matheson Island, 100 miles away.

The remains of the 200-mile long Winnipeg River sluggishly fanned into Traverse Bay. Towering pines, birch, and poplar oversaw the long sand beaches strewn with decaying driftwood. Water turbidity increased as the 15-mile bay suddenly exposed the main body of water. Huge brown swells, originating miles and miles out of sight, rolled southward. I was at the mouth of Traverse Bay, an advisable place to camp and study the maps.

I hadn't been there long when a canoe landed next to mine. An older man and a boy jumped out. "Hi, I'm John and this is my 14-year-old son," the elder said. Still grasping his .30-30 Winchester, he shook hands with me.

Camped a short distance down the shore, they usually came to this spot to hunt black bear. "We see them almost every night along this stretch," he informed me. *Great,* I thought with dread as he sent his boy off to look for fresh tracks. We sat next to the fire talking over a cup of tea until his son returned with negative results, and they decided to hunt elsewhere.

I was in bed early, not overly worried about black bears. They seemed to have a natural fear of dogs that bark. If the dog won't bark, the loaded .30-06 beside me would.

Arising at 5:20 A.M., it was cold, dark, and silent. Laying a fire, I hoped my breakfast of fried potatoes, sausage, and tea would attract no unwanted visitors. A short walk afterward revealed their tracks all over the beach.

As I traveled near the eastern shoreline, a light fog was my ceiling on the calm water. Swells rippling outward from the canoe revealed large, potentially damaging rocks ominously close to the surface. Deep in a nameless bay, a loon throated an unanswered call. Its dying echo seemed a comfort.

By noon, black clouds rolled over the tops of the tall pines. Lightning cracked as I found a niche in which to camp, arranged the tarp, and secured the canoe. The storm moved across the water, directly toward me. Shortly the brown waves surged high onto the beach. The tarp snapped in the wind. Like Moses, I stood defiantly challenging the storm. Then at the first raindrop, I dove under the dancing tarp. The fire hissed in its attempt to turn back the penetrating rain. Building a quick driftwood roof over it, I opened a book and settled in until Mother Nature exhibited a little more cooperation.

The storm bled the sky for two days, producing a week of clear, nearly calm days. This allowed me to pass Observation Point, cross five miles of open water at Manigotagan Bay to Clements Point, and reach Black Island. Here pelicans abounded in a sheltered bay, feeding in the shallow waters. It was a photographer's delight, much the same as calm water was to a canoeist. After a few quick photos and a dash to reach the end of Black Island called Gray Point, daylight had faded.

Leaving Gray Point early in the morning, I weaved through five miles of small islands. The days were lengthening with daylight extending from 4:00 A.M. to 10:00 P.M. I used it to my advantage to cover a 45-mile stretch of water that passed through Loon Straits, traversed eight miles of open water to Little Bullhead Point, and finally went through a narrows to dock across from Matheson Island.

It seemed that a road ended here as five dusty trucks stood waiting in a dirt parking area. A large, overloaded, wooden boat had just left the parking area and started the one-and-a-half-mile ferry to the tiny village on the island. A beacon light pulsating yellow rays into the darkening night guided their way. I decided to wait until morning to cross and pitched the tent at the end of the parking area.

That was a mistake. An angry wind had developed overnight, blowing the length of the island. Without breakfast, I started into the crosswind. By the time this ordeal was over, I had made it to the end of the island.

It took nearly two hours of struggling into the headwind before reaching the dock in front of the small village. I found the store by following a local's finger. No sign advertised it; only a heavily-used path betrayed its existence. A broken picket fence framed the building. A white-painted, wooden door swung on rusted hinges as I entered. There was no conceivable order.

What seemed to be the hottest selling item was Shasta pop. Case upon case was stacked head-high next to the door, in the middle of the room, and against the walls. Next to these were stacked cases of canned goods. Meat and produce were nonexistent. There were few shelves and no aisles. A person just wandered through the piles.

A small room to one side held a few items of clothing and a half-dozen pairs of boots. There was no dog food so Quick Quaker Oats would be on the menu. While I shopped, a woman sat patiently behind a caged window, glancing through a newspaper. A post office sign above the cage proclaimed her position. While her husband tended to his chores, he asked if I had found everything I needed. "I could use some toilet paper and a can of Raid," I answered. Amazingly, he went into a back room and returned with both.

"Let me tell you a little story," he volunteered as he placed the items on the counter. "A couple of years ago a kid came through here and stopped for a few groceries. 1973 I believe it was. All alone he was too. Anyway, the waves got him over on Bloodvein Bay, and he lost his whole outfit. Amazing he didn't lose his life, the crazy kid. He had a canoe just like yours, same color even. Said he was going all the way to Churchill." This ended his story with a chuckle and a shake of his head. "Don't know whatever happened to him," he said as an afterthought.

"The crazy kid never made it," I said. "He got to Hudson Bay and the tide smashed his canoe at the mouth of the Nelson River. Then he walked 110 miles to the railroad and got out by train."

"You know the guy?" he asked incredulously. Redness crept into his face as I admitted to being the crazy kid. "Well, I'll be damned," he said with a laugh, "and you're still at it." By this time his wife had emerged and was listening intently.

"That's amazing," she said while looking at me if I were an apparition. I don't know what he thought of my destination, but there were no chuckles. After I paid the grocery bill, he reached behind the counter and placed two cans of pop in the grocery bag. "No doubt you'll be getting thirsty along the way," he said as he slid the bag

134

toward me. They weren't Shasta but top-shelf, genuine Coke. "Be a little more careful this time, will you," he said with a grin.

"I'll sure try," I replied and pulled the door shut behind me.

I left Matheson Island bucking the wind, covering just one mile an hour. Soon the sun's glare changed to a golden sunset. As the wind slackened, darkness replaced the fading brilliance. Mud replaced the sandy beaches. For hours I probed the darkness with the flashlight looking for a place to land. I'd paddle and probe, paddle and probe. The mud seemed infinite. Finally, the canoe came to a jarring halt as the bow sliced into it. It immediately infiltrated the tops of my boots as I stepped in past my ankles.

With rifle and flashlight in one hand and sleeping bag in the other, I sloshed toward the comfort of the tree line. Vagabond was right behind me. Not many hours were left until daylight. Soon after sunrise I stuffed the down sleeping bag into its nylon sack, trudged back through the mud, and covered the hour to the village of Jackhead.

The bow touched gravel and I quickly grabbed Vagabond as he had his eye on two kids passing on bicycles. The dirt path ascending the hill dodged rusted car bodies half-sunk into the mud, discarded stoves and refrigerators, bicycle frames, 55-gallon drums, and an assortment of trash I didn't need to identify. It appeared that if it weren't wanted, over the bank it would go.

Topping the bank, I saw a middle-aged man pushing a vintage mower over a grass-free lawn. It must have just been seeded, or there wasn't much to do here. My attention shifted from the mower to the business district. There wasn't any. The closest resemblance was a window-broken town hall and a rusted gas pump. I asked one of the Natives walking by where the store was. After a quizzical look, he pointed south saying, "Down that way." Only tall pine trees stood where his finger pointed, the store at Matheson Island lay twenty miles behind them.

I returned past these cloned government houses and weighed the odds of reaching the next area of civilization with the food I had. The odds weren't in my favor, nor was the north wind, but I was going to try. Grand Rapids was 225 miles away.

The glorious days of summer were upon me, at least for now. Late morning suns lifted cool, morning fogs. Days were long and warm. Kinwow Bay was apprehensively crossed in a choppy north wind. The options had been weighed. I could go six miles, straight across; twenty miles following the bay's shore; or sit and wait for calmness. A successful four-hour bounce across the wide-open expanse fueled me with added confidence, but I hadn't lost the realization that confidence can be a deadly cross to bear.

The coastline slid slowly by. Two miles an hour offered a view of nature that few ever see. Foxes ran the beach and unidentified birds soared the skies. Coming to McBeth Point necessitated a detour. The long pine-covered arm extended well into Lake Winnipeg. At its terminus stood a ghost town. From the rotted dock to the rustic boardwalks, nothing was more enjoyable to explore. What once had been was now nothing, reduced to rot and relics, a spot near nowhere where dreams were dreamed and lost. Only a weatherworn, crudely etched sign linked its past to the present. It read, Murdochville, pop. 9.

Vagabond went in first. I followed with the .30-06, exploring each building. While some leaned dangerously, others lay flat with their roofs on their floors. Thick sawdust still covered the floor of the huge ice-house as loosened boards dangled from a bedroom ceiling. A mouse scurried through the kitchen, avoiding blue, speckled, porcelain plates, their chipped edges ravaged by rust, to disappear beneath a large, dented coffee pot. Nothing was salvageable except a wet, musty western by Louis Lamour. Lucky, since I was expecting wind-bound days.

Vagabond was quickly nowhere to be found. I located him behind the icehouse digging in the biggest accumulation of pop cans I had ever seen. In the center was Vagabond. Cans flew in all directions as he dug for some buried treasure only a dog could covet.

His coveting came to naught and we soon rounded the end of McBeth Point. Whitewashed from the thousands of seagulls inhabiting the point were low, smooth rocks. It stank. As he stared, drooling intently at the diving birds, Vagabond was willing to camp there, but it was not an option. Instead, a rocky beach fifty-feet wide, miles away proved suitable. The beach ended at a five-foot bank topped with thick willows that shortly yielded to the pines. While the tent was set up, mosquitoes were out in masses. With Vagabond tied to the canoe, sleep came easily.

It would not last. A frightening cry broke the dark silence and my slumber. Then came a thump as Vagabond's leash pulled tight. I could hear him straining against the canoe scraping along the rocky beach behind him. My eyes shot open but were useless in the night. Choking down adrenaline dipped fear I groped frantically for the flashlight. The rifle was already across my knees and ready to go, the result of reflexes, not conscious thought. I sat motionless, listening intensely, trying to regain some composure, willing my heartbeat to slow down. Vagabond's initial excitement had abated, and all was quiet. Dry-mouthed, I unzipped the door enough to peer out.

A dark form was barely visible fifty yards down the beach. It would advance teasingly, then playfully retreat. It was a deadly game. This was repeated numerous times as Vagabond stood wagging his white tail like a surrender flag in the night. Obviously, the animal wanted Vagabond to follow it. The rouse ended as the flashlight picked up its two yellow, glowing eyes. They disappeared immediately. Shortly a chorus sounded behind the tent as six timber wolves lamented their loss of a meal. After one thunderous round into the trees from the .30-06, their haunting echoes faded across the water. Vagabond curled back into a ball of naive innocence, only raising an ear as I ejected the spent casing from the chamber. He never realized the seriousness of his situation.

Sleep came slowly and in fits as heightened instincts reacted to minute sounds amplified in my head. The last sound before sleep was a light wind through the trees. The next was water dripping on top of the sleeping bag. As the night began clear, I saw no immediate need to erect the fly over the tent. Now the sky had turned for the worse. I took my chances and lost.

At least the rain was intermittent, which allowed a pan of potatoes to be fried. Vagabond drooled as I ate; he sat with a staring, head-down, hangdog look. It was more obnoxious than pitiful, but I gave in and filled a bowl with potatoes, covered it with peach juice, then placed two peach slices on top. It vanished, and the self-pity-act soon returned.

As a drizzle-filled fog descended over the lake near dawn, I packed the wet tent, donned my rain gear, and faced it. Visibility was limited. Passing the sheer rock cliffs along Lynx Point, I consulted the map often to keep some semblance of where I was in the fog. By hugging the coast, I passed Turnagain Point and Bush Dega Point, making a bouncy three-mile crossing to Inner Sturgeon Island. A short hop to a rock called Tree Island ended the wet, uneventful day. No wolves would be serenading the pooch tonight: we were halfway across ten-mile-wide Sturgeon Bay.

Monday, June 7th was a long, eerie day. Waking well before the sun, I watched a thick band of fog move across the lake. It looked like a twenty-foot wall of thick smoke rolling toward me, soon engulfing my small island.

My next haven, Cochrane Island, lay two miles away. Visible one minute and gone the next, it sat along with Vagabond and I among a group of islands in the mouth of Sturgeon Bay. Four miles beyond was Clark's Point, my destination, totally obliterated by the undulating fog. It was bizarre, but looking straight up, I could see stars in the blue morning sky.

After a quick breakfast, I watched as the warming sun tried to dissipate the fog. A window opened. Cochrane Island was clearly visible, so I shoved off. I couldn't see anything past the island and apparently wasn't worried or thinking about it. If all went well, I'd be there in two hours, three at most.

Very quickly the swells got my attention. They'd lift the canoe high on each crest and then drop it hard into each trough. I misjudged angling over one and took in a splash of water. After 15 minutes, Cochrane Island had vanished. *Enough*, it was back to the island for me. I turned my head to find my retreat, and all I could see was fog. The window had closed.

Trying to find the small acreage of Tree Island in the fog was a fool's errand. If I missed it, there were miles and miles of open water, and the wind had surpassed a breeze. Using the compass, I tried to get a west bearing to Clark's Point. It was hopeless. The canoe agitated so much that the needle just spun. Although I thought about fastening the splash cover, that would require a break from paddling and thus a loss of control. I couldn't afford that. An hour had passed as things escalated.

Quartering into a swell, I rolled the canoe with my hips over the crest, and on the way down, jerked the life jacket from beneath Vagabond. When cresting the next one, I put it on. From each trough I couldn't see over the next crest, and it was creating much anxiety. The yet-increasing north wind made things more difficult, the rolling swells becoming whitecaps.

In a way, the wind was a gift in disguise. By keeping it to my right, I could be somewhat sure I was on a westerly course to land. That was my only salvation, for visibility was not much beyond the bow of the canoe. Forward progress, if any, was not recognizable. I truly had doubts about a future in this business.

It had been hours since I left Tree Island. More than once I didn't make the crest of the wave, and the bow would be thrown back sideways into the trough, dumping cold water into my lap. *Lord, just let me get to shore and I'll never do wrong again,* I pleaded, religion again entering my life by necessity. Totally concentrating, I explained the situation to myself. *Okay Pushcar, just take it easy and concentrate on each wave. You haven't come that close to going over, and if you take each wave, one at a time, you'll be okay. Just watch each carefully and roll over them.* Bloodvein Bay, in the year of 1973, did enter my mind.

Kneeling in the cold sloshing water to lower my center of gravity, I was totally soaked. My jaws ached from the tension. Bailing occurred when necessary. I should have hit land hours ago. I kept on, calling myself every locker room adjective there was. The one "stupid" seemed to come up more than once. Occasional shivers raced through my legs. I lost track of time with my watch stored inside the waterproof ammo box-camera case, the only place it would stay dry.

Then, I saw it. An angel flew above the fog, just twenty feet from my head. It was in the form of a pelican, and I prayed he was headed toward land.

Within ten minutes a dark towering hazy outline appeared through the fog followed by trees. Approaching shore with too much force, I jumped into waist-deep water, for if the canoe was driven into the rocky beach by one of *these* swells, major repairs would be in order. Timing the swells, I dashed up the beach and made a quick landing, dragging everything well beyond the water's reach. Finally, being able to relax, I stretched out supine on a sandy spot and said my thanks. I had been out there for over six hours.

Needing to spend some time on land, I poured water from the canoe as I tipped it on its side and built a fire to dry out. Though the fog situation seemed to be improving, canoeing was finished for this day. It was still early afternoon and for an hour I skirted the fire, turning, switching from side to side, avoiding the smoke. Unfolding the map, I concluded that the end of Clark's Point was about three miles away. A plan was formulated to explore the peninsula: to walk along one side of the point, round the tip and then return along the opposite side. With the rifle, camera, and an extra wool shirt, I started into a stiff wind.

The walking was rocky and slow, but I didn't mind. Coming to what appeared to be a clearing, I climbed the low bank and approached a grassy opening. A cabin foundation could be seen through the grass. The roof and walls lay rotting where they fell. No bottles or artifacts could be found, but many piles of mushy, reddish droppings were scattered throughout the clearing. The bears were being well fed on berries.

Finding nothing of interest, I continued toward the point. Skipping rocks into the oncoming waves resulted in failure. After covering two and a half miles, I noticed something orange washed ashore ahead of me. I didn't think much of it and continued along the edge of the surf. Small tufts of fog lingered, but for the most part, visibility was to the horizon. Waves rolled in and being on top of them was not some place I wanted to be. I was close enough to the orange object now to see that it was a coat. A few more steps and I abruptly stopped. The orange object turned out to be the inside-out lining of a coat. It was pulled over the head of a corpse with lifeless arms reaching above its head.

I stood there transfixed, almost expecting it to get up and walk. Keeping my distance, I passed it, peering. It would rise with the waves, linger a moment, then settle back among the rocks. Two waxy hands appeared above the pulled-over coat, their bones protruding profoundly. The gray shirt and blue baggy pants had long been faded. Rotted, green cut-off waders were turned down at the ankles. I sat on a nearby rock to ponder the situation.

There was little I could do. A large rock rested near the tree line. Getting it into a bear hug, I waddled across the beach and dropped it next to the body. Using a rope found while beachcombing, I knotted one end around the slippery belt. A shiver shook my shoulders as a wave forced the cadaver against my leg. After hurriedly finishing the half hitch knot, I tilted the rock up and fastened the rope's other end to it, hoping to prevent the body from washing back into Lake Winnipeg.

Searching the beach provided a 15-foot, limbless, dead tree. Finding a suitable place between two rocks, I wedged the pole in vertically and piled rocks around its base. It would be visible a long way from shore.

Peering from the back-right pocket was a wallet. Stooping down, I timidly pinched it, working it back and forth until it pulled free. I felt like a grave robber. The black slimy leather stank. Even though it could be weeks before I might see anyone, if the body did break loose, there would be some record of it. It was the least I could do to turn the wallet in at the next town.

Running the wallet through the lake did little to alleviate the smell. The first thing I saw upon opening it were gold letters ironically stating, "Good Luck Employee." In the pouch were ten faded twenty-dollar bills. There were also lottery tickets, prophylactics, credit cards, licenses, receipts, and a blurred picture of two kids. I laid the wallet open on a nearby rock, hoping it would dry by the time I passed on the way back. Picking up the rifle, I continued down the beach.

It occurred to me that I could walk away 200 dollars richer; nobody would know. It may never reach its rightful owner anyway, but that just wasn't in my upbringing. While pondering this and that, I looked up and saw three boats battling southward in the waves. I couldn't fathom anyone being out in that water.

The first boat was a large blue and white runabout. Two smaller open fiberglass crafts followed slowly behind it. I took off my wool shirt and waved it overhead. They held their course. I yelled and waved and yelled and waved to no avail. Chambering a shell, I pointed toward open water and pulled the trigger. Again, I circled the shirt overhead. The nearer of the smaller boats broke formation.

The boat bobbed 150 feet offshore, afraid to come any closer. In the craft were two men, two women, and two kids. "There's a body over there," I shouted against the roar of the water as it smashed against the rocks.

"What?" came a faint reply.

"A body, there's a body washed ashore over there," I shouted as loud as possible. One of the men was on the deck with a long aluminum pole, probing the water's depth. They were taking a beating in the swells.

Finally, one of the women understood and shouted, "We'll send help."

"Are you okay?" I could make out as one of the men shouted through cupped hands. After giving them an OK sign, I waved. They turned and joined the other two boats and soon were just specks among the swells. My voice was hoarse from shouting as I put my shirt back on, hung my camera around my neck, picked up the rifle, and again started for the end of the point.

When I reached it, to my surprise, eight men sat around a fire drinking coffee. Three aluminum boats were pulled well out of the surf. Since the lake was much too rough for their boats, they had been stranded here since early morning. "What did you shoot? We heard a shot." one questioned.

"Just a tin can," I lied. I wanted to tell them about the body, but some instinct prevented it. Besides, help was on the way.

After a cup of coffee with the stranded men, I returned along the same route and stopped fifty yards from the pole marker. Wedged between two rocks was a small blue book. I picked it up and opened it. It was empty. At one time something had been glued to the inside. On the cover in faded gold was stenciled "Royal Canadian Air Force." Sliding it into my shirt pocket, I retrieved the wet wallet and dropped it to the depths of a bread bag that was recovered along the beach. Wrapping the excess plastic around it and securing it with a string, I slid it next to the little blue book, hoping it wouldn't leak. I took one last look. Was this a warning from above? Only hours ago I was in a situation that could have held the same results. But I felt fortunate. Fate had its finger pointed elsewhere.

Smoke from the campfire rose straight into the air. Gone was the wind, and the sun wasn't far from it. The drone of a motor broke the serenity. Soon an aluminum boat edged toward shore. A wader-clad Indian jumped out and guided the boat safely onto the rocky beach. Another Indian followed with a man dressed in blue. "Hear you found a body?" the man in blue asked. I told him I did and where it was. By this time another RCMP officer was out of the boat and introduced himself as Vince. None of the four could have been over thirty, but Vince was obviously their superior. The three subordinates were left without introductions.

It caught my eye that both RCMP officers wore life jackets, while neither of the Natives did. "How old would you say it is?" Vince asked.

How the hell should I know? "Probably this spring or late last fall. His wallet's over on that rock," I said pointing with a slight sideways nod of my head. The second in command went over, released it from the plastic bag, and at arm's length, thumbed through it.

"From The Pas!" he exclaimed while handing it to Vince. Without a glance, it disappeared into his pocket.

"We'll go pick it up and come back to get a statement from you," Vince said as they boarded.

"There's a 15-foot pole sticking up as a marker," I volunteered.

"Okay," was the reply as the motor was started; they were gone.

Thirty minutes later they returned, using the same docking procedure. Wrapped in brown canvas, a bundle lay heaped on the floor of the boat. "Come over here and we'll get a statement," Vince said as he took off his gloves. I followed to a sandy area and sat down beside him. He took out a pen and patted his coat pocket. Opening his coat, he indicated an empty pocket and sheepishly asked, "Got any paper?" I got my logbook, opened it to the back, and handed it to him.

Writing in longhand he formed a statement based on my story. All questions were answered: Why are you here? Where are you going? Where did you stay last night? What pocket was the wallet in? Are you sure? What did you do after you found it? Name and address? The final statement came to a page and a half. He handed it to me and said, "Read it and if it's all correct, just sign it on the bottom." "Anything more you can think of that we'll need?" Vince asked his partner.

"Maybe we should ask if he ever saw him before?" Vince disregarded the thought and I could see why he was in command.

Halfway through reading the statement the Native in waders stood right in front of my tent urinating. I flushed with anger. Looking at Vince, he puckered one corner of his mouth and shook his head in frustration. After signing the statement, I ripped it from the journal and handed it to him. He got up, brushing sand from the seat of his pants. "Oh, yeah, I found this about fifty yards from the body," I said handing the small blue book to Vince. He looked at it, opened it, and then closed it.

Slapping it against his palm twice, he said, "This is worth more than you'll ever know." Vince thanked me for the help as they embarked, waving as they pulled away. *Now, that would not be my kind of work;* it would be a long time before their day was done.

Things went relatively well throughout the next few days. Even though usable light extended for 19 hours, travel time was short due to strong winds. Early mornings and late evenings were most productive. Food was getting low; pancakes without butter or syrup became a staple. Between gusts of wind, I hugged the shore past Carscallen Point, fished the mouth of Warpath River, and rounded Dancing Point. My nemesis switched from north to south, and shoreline mileage accelerated.

The canoe seemed to fly across the white-capped water. Tipping over was of little concern as I could spit to shore and was only in three feet of water. Six miles later, the dash was over. The canoe came off the top of a swell and shuddered hard as it beached on a shallow reef. Since the next wave didn't float it, I could not continue the ride. The next wave came in over my head. Soaked in an instant, I rolled over the port side gunwale, grabbed the bow, and beached. The floating packs were rescued, and the canoe was drained and left to dry.

Stranded again I made the standard inspection tour along the beach. Within sight of camp, I found a smooth-faced piece of concrete, mostly buried in the sand. *Now what could that be doing 100 miles from nowhere,* I asked myself. Curiosity got the better of me as I set the .30-06 aside and started scooping sand. Shortly thereafter, sweat began.

I pried, pushed, and pulled until finally, I could get my fingers underneath it. The thing was bigger and much heavier than I imagined, and I had no idea why I was doing this in the first place. With one last grunt, the slab flipped over and thudded on its back. The smooth concrete face was covered with very legible print. Only black paint inside the sunken letters showed wear.

Brushing away the sand, I read etched block lettering:

ON THIS SPOT JOHN TRUMAN
OF ST. MARTIN, MB BURNED TO DEATH
WHILE FREIGHTING FISH ON FEB. 3, 1933.
BORN JUNE 23, 1914. THIS CROSS WAS
DONATED BY FRIENDS COLLECTED BY
G. KOLOMYA

The top of the marker was rounded, exhibiting two deep holes, which could have supported a cross. None was in the vicinity. Behind the monument stood a clearing. Only a rusted stove half-buried in the tundra gave testimony to this tragedy. With lack of much debris, I speculated an overnight camp resulted in a tent fire. But then, 42 years can obliterate much.

The wind allowed only three hours of travel the following morning. An eagle soared above, my landing having frightened it from its nest. The huge, high nest was visible through the forest. It was the kind of day for taking a picture fit for a calendar. I pictured a spectacular photo, with the eagle landing in its nest, wings spread gloriously, fish in claws, coming home to feed its young.

Many days were lost as the wind raged on Lake Winnipeg.

I stood below the half-dead poplar tree with the nest at its top. Next to pieces of eagle eggshell, two rotted whitefish lay in the dead leaves. Splattering the leaves and ground were dried white droppings. The eagle continued to soar high above the treetops. Making an opening in a brush pile big enough to accommodate the tripod and myself, I donned my camouflaged hat and vest for the occasion. A log was rolled in to sit on and strategically placed branches left an opening for the 800-mm lens. Everything was in position. The camera was in line and focused, and the light meter was set. All that was needed was an eagle to land, and I'd squeeze the bulb release.

Hours passed. My neck ached from continually looking up. Two white globs arched over the side of the nest and painted a small pine tree below. More hours passed, and the daylight was fading, necessitating an adjustment of the light meter. Mosquitoes came to feast. The wet log had long ago soaked my britches. Finally, a shadow crossed the blind.

Only my eyes moved as the eagle circled the nest once, then twice. I could hear the air flowing across its wings. Then there was a flutter as the huge wings flapped and the claws touched the edge of the nest. At that instant, I squeezed the bulb, and the camera did the rest.

For seven hours I was perched on that wet log, motionless,

craning my neck, being devoured by mosquitoes, just waiting for that one opportunity. It was a lesson in patience, for when it landed, it came directly over me, allowing the best picture of an eagle's posterior you'd ever want to see. With the camera, lens, and tripod, I left the blind, wondering what month on the calendar would be honored with *that* photo. The eagle smugly circled as I left the next morning.

Within two hours a horrific wind swamped me. It was getting to be routine: swamp, dry out, walk; swamp, dry out, walk. Before the walking part of the routine, I pitched the tent with the door facing the wind. I knew it would be dry by the time I returned, blown balloon-like as it was.

I reached a small clear river that emptied into the churning brown water of Lake Winnipeg shortly into my walk. It looked like ideal fish country. Deciding to return to camp for my rod and reel, I called for Vagabond. He was chasing seagulls on the other side of the river. I don't know how he crossed, but he was sure fitful about how he would get back. Vagabond has not the personality that likes to swim, or really anything to do with water except drinking it.

"Come on! Let's go!" I shouted and walked away. He ran whimpering up and down the riverbank, afraid of being left behind and reluctant to get wet. The distance between us increased. He tested the water with one paw, slowly waded in, and then took the plunge. Emerging, he shook himself and ran happily to catch up, diverting his course twice to chase seagulls. I never saw a dog that could chase so much and catch so little.

Returning to the clear river, casting produced six nice walleyes in half an hour. Thrown on the bank behind me, my stash would be guarded by Vagabond. At the first flop, he'd spring into action, pinning them with his front paws until they ceased to struggle. Stepping back, he'd stare, pouncing again at the slightest twitch. Twice he was caught sneaking one off, only to drop it and sulk with his head and tail held low. Back at camp they were cleaned, split, roasted on a board, and divided evenly. I had four; Vagabond had two.

Throughout the night the wind slowly shifted to the west. It didn't lessen; it just shifted. This left a narrow avenue of navigable water protected by the swaying trees. Beyond this, the high-swelling waves looked ominous, white capping as far as the eye could see. Rain came shortly but on water as temperamental as Lake Winnipeg, travel had to be conducted whenever possible.

I clung to the shore for ten nonstop hours. This brought me to Wicked Point, and I was ready for a break before crossing twelve miles of open water. The wind had died but a steady drizzle still fell from the gray sky. It wasn't a pleasant place to take a break. The only land was 100 yards away through a field of mud. Taking what little food was left and with teapot in hand, I started trudging.

Just a high spot in a field of mud, a lone pine tree sprouted from its center. It may have been hit by lightning or just succumbed to the wind as ten feet up its trunk, it had toppled, leaving a crude shelter beneath its branches. By lopping branches beneath the fallen tree then throwing them on top, most of the rain was held at bay.

A small fire was soon arranged with scattered wood, and hot water was ready for tea. With cup in hand, I leaned against the broken tree trunk devouring bannock and cold-hardened fish. For what it was, it was starting to taste pretty good. With a somewhat satisfied stomach and comforted by the warmth of the small fire, I dozed.

I awoke chilled. Only an occasional hiss sounded as a raindrop slipped through the fallen pine tree in its attempt to quench the smoldering fire beneath it. Totally relaxed, I opened my eyes and gazed across the lake. Amazingly, it lay flat. Nothing would have felt better than to rekindle the fire and retain my repose against the tree. But Lake Winnipeg was calm, and I had to take advantage of it. Dousing the fire, I retraced my steps through the thick mud. The fire left a smoky halo dissipating above the lonely pine, held to earth by humidity.

Even though I felt revived, twelve miles across open water looked like a long way away. Long Point, my destination, was barely visible through the mist. As the canoe cut through the muddy water, there was much skepticism but little choice. Every so often a light breeze would arise, sending ripples scurrying across the top of the water. *God don't start blowing now,* I silently pleaded, trying to keep the wind calm for a few more hours. Digging the paddle deep, I kept the craft on a straight course. There was still apprehension as I reached the point of no return. Confidence was gained as the shore became closer and closer. Once the dormant instinctual fear had disappeared from my heart, I knew I'd make it, even if the wind picked up.

Although weariness enveloped me from paddling 15 hours on a

very substandard diet, the five-hour crossing proved to be more mentally than physically fatiguing. The wind remained calm as the sun dropped into the lake. I had plans to travel throughout the night, all the next day, and reach Grand Rapids late that evening. In anticipation, I drank two pots of tea and studied the map in the growing darkness. I determined my location along the southern shore of Long Point, a heavily wooded, 25-mile long, thick finger that protruded eastward into the lake.

With little light left, I pulled a stocking hat over my head and started out. The temperature was falling but I hoped it would stabilize shortly. The shore and trees soon combined to create a large black mass, topped with twinkling stars. No moon appeared to alleviate the eerie feeling of gliding through the night, nor from wondering what was twenty feet away. Only a silhouetted tall tree passing in front of a star testified to forward progress. A growing wind scurried through the trees, its low howl magnified by the darkness and my mind. Still, the water remained calm on the leeward side of Long Point.

There was no hurry. As the canoe mounted unseen rocks, bumps and scrapes could be felt. The howling increased as trees began to sway, but still, I was able to continue through the night, cradled in their protection. It came to an end at 3:30 in the morning.

Standing at the end of Long Point, I held onto my hat. The north wind and spray weren't merely magnified by the darkness, and neither were the whitecaps. They were the real thing. Grand Rapids by evening would have to wait.

Crawling out of the tent in the morning I could feel that I had covered 55 miles in 21 hours. The food pack was empty except for a few tea bags and two fish fillets. With no grease or butter for frying, beachcombing produced a board and a few rusted nails. These were employed in the "stake and bake" method of fish preparation. *This type of baking is a lost art,* I understood, as the fillets curled, sprung from their crucified positions, and slid down the board into the sand. Vagabond had no qualms.

It was a full day and night before the wind ceased, the rolling water pacified. Paddling around the end of Long Point, I greeted a clear, calm day. It was two weeks into June and my mind wandered aimlessly. I stroked toward Grand Rapids, fifty miles away.

It was past noon when an eagle circled low overhead, breaking my wandering concentration. To my left was a very tall pine tree. Nestled in a fork at its top was a ball of interwoven sticks. What really caught my eye was the tree next to it. It stood ten feet higher and if a person gained that vantage point, it would provide a direct view into the nest. No doubt, there would be a fuzzy, little baby bald eagle occupying it. I pulled ashore.

It looked like a long, long way up as I stood at the base of the tree, gazing toward heaven. The pine's girth dwarfed my outstretched arms as they failed to span even a third of the way around it. Ten years ago I would have scampered to its top like a squirrel, but now the ten feet of limbless bark seemed a bit more daunting. It took a few tries, but by wedging fingers and jamming toes, I was able to reach the first limb. Once I had pulled myself onto it, the belt ax and camera were secured, and I started up.

It took a contortionist to weave through the countless limbs. They snagged clothes, camera straps, bootlaces, ax handles, and hair. But persistence paid off as I neared the top. Shortly a gray, down-covered baby eagle peered over the nest, bewildered by the commotion. Beyond the nest lay miles of rolling green forest meeting a clear blue sky. Lake Winnipeg was a long, flat mirror extending north and south. I climbed higher to get above the nest. The wind that swayed the treetop so precariously at this elevation did not go unnoticed, though not one rustled pine needle hit the ground.

From where I clung, I could almost touch the top of the tree, but there was no overwhelming desire to do so as its width was already smaller than the size of my wrist. Affixing the zoom lens, I focused and shot whenever the featherless fowl would look my way. I followed him through the lens as he stood up, stuck his backside toward the side of the nest, and released a white glob that splattered the branches below. Hopping around, he would stumble, only to right himself and ruffle his scrawny wings.

There was nothing but concentration through the lens when I heard it. It wasn't the loud *crack* of catastrophic failure, but instead a spine-chilling *screech* and the *whoosh* of wings a foot from my head. Dropping the camera onto its strap, I instinctively ducked and hugged the skinny trunk. My heart raced. Mother was mad! But she wouldn't knock me from my perch.

She came out of her dive, gained altitude, circling once, descending like a Spitfire. By then I had the hatchet out, circling it over my head in a last-ditch attempt at defense. This really set the puny treetop in motion. "OK, OK!" I shouted, conceding retreat as a brown blur again disappeared over my shoulder, missing by inches. I don't know which one of us was screaming louder as she did tight circles overhead. She was lining up for another round. I hastily sought the sanctuary of the limbs below.

Questioning my sanity, I weaved down, making good time. Hanging from the bottom limb, I dropped to the ground. My heart still raced. If all went well, I'd have some fantastic pictures. I got all I wanted and more. She sat on the edge of her nest as I moved away, defiant, majestic, protective, the way it should be.

The day remained calm as I dipped the paddle for ten hours before the sun started its slow descent into the lake and I beached. Before the teapot was empty, the day was gone, and the stars shone brightly.

The Big Dipper, Little Dipper, Aurora Borealis, and all the constellations came into focus. They were my traveling companions throughout the night. Even when stopping after five hours and sitting beside a glowing fire in the darkness, they watched. Their vigilance observed passing voyageurs, trappers, Indians, and all who came before them. I felt awed that the voyageurs could have stopped at this exact spot for their tea and pipes or slept under their canoes here. *What was it like then?* I asked myself, and then dozed.

My head jerked back upright after it dropped to my chest. There were no more thoughts of romanticism. The warmth of the fire was a distraction, and I needed to keep traveling as long as the lake was calm. Cold water in the face and a little running in place was a temporary elixir. By flashlight, I pushed into the darkness and groped northward. Soon a red glow appeared on the dark horizon. Its resemblance to a forest fire was startling as it got bigger and closer. For twenty minutes it burned until finally, a huge, reddish-orange moon peered over the water. Darkness could be a strange bedfellow.

Throughout the night I traveled. The burning moon finished its trajectory just as the sun rose to take its place. I had counted seven falling stars and had only one thing to wish for, food. That would come to pass shortly as I maneuvered into the mouth of the Saskatchewan River, racing a gathering wind. Over the last sixty hours, I had paddled fifty hours. However, things would hopefully normalize somewhat as the muddy water of Lake Winnipeg was now behind me.

The Bush

I passed a trailer court, a church, and the RCMP station before docking beneath a bridge next to two wooden boats. From the bridge, I could see very little. A long, black snake of a road weaved past a gas station, a large white building, and what looked like a hotel. Wearily walking the shoulder, I lamented my fading hope that there was more to Grand Rapids than this.

YOU ARE HERE was indicated with a red arrow on the directory map that showed me all I needed to know: the store, the post office, and the dam.

I was able to paddle close to the store and follow a Coke bottle strewn path to its doors. There was no sign, no advertisement. It was old, inside and out. But they did accept American traveler's checks. The few aisles provided food for a week, more than enough to reach the city of The Pas, only 100 miles away.

Upon returning, I noticed the two wooden boats were gone. Through months of association, I knew something was amiss, but I couldn't quite place it. *The life jacket!* It was there when I went for groceries and gone when I got back. Nothing could be done at this point, but it was very irksome. They could have taken more, like the watchdog tied to the front of the canoe.

Well into the morning, I cautiously traveled along the spillway and approached the huge Grand Rapids Dam. Not wanting to get too close, I pulled in next to a picnic table and took a short tour.

While half a dozen campers dotted the rest area, I skirted them and entered a large building which seemed to be a museum. Old photos lined the walls which showed the area before the dam was built. Centering one wall was a map of the foliage covering Manitoba.

151

In the center of the room was a large glass-enclosed counter. In it were tomahawks, rusted flintlock rifles, stone tools, arrowheads, and iron tools, all apparently found when the river was diverted to construct the dam. Next to this stood a well-constructed scale model of the dam and surrounding area. While I studied this, someone asked, "How far are you going?" It was a mid-thirties, short, dark-haired employee.

This led to a thirty-minute conversation that ended when I asked, "What's the easiest way around the dam?"

"Most people throw their canoe and gear in the back of my truck, and I drive them to the top," he answered. When I declined his offer, he helpfully traced the easiest route around the dam on the model, adding, "And that is not all that easy."

I laid my sleeping bag next to a picnic table, followed by a dry run over the lower part of the portage to plot a course to the road leading to the top of the dam. I was not impressed. It was dark when I returned and sat on the picnic table in the shadows of the dam. The area was well lit by strategically placed floodlights. I was slaphappy tired, dazed but not dead after being mobile for 48 hours. My body still perceived the rolling of the swells from the big lake as I zippered out the mosquitoes and slid into the down bag. I was going to sleep for a long time.

Six hours later I lay wide-awake though with little motive to get going as the wind was as bad as it had been all summer. After a light breakfast, I shouldered the canoe and started the portage. Apathy was irrelevant, for it didn't matter how long it took, I was stranded for now.

The wind created problems even on land, as I tried to ascend three long, steep flights of dew-covered stairs. Gusty crosswinds would lift the canoe off my shoulders and bounce me against the handrail. Eventually, I had to back down and sidestep up the steep, dew-slick, grassy slopes, keeping the canoe somewhat level and pointed into the cutting wind. Each of the three, fifty-foot tiers were a balancing act.

Topping the last tier, I labored across the open parking lot, went down and then back up a gully, crossed a muddy rock-strewn field, waded a knee-deep stream, squeezed through a long stretch of thick willows, and finally stood on the road leading to the top of the dam. The attendant was right; it hadn't been easy, and it wasn't yet complete. I gazed up the long, steep, rocky incline. *At least I was out of the wind.*

It was a methodical march, and I wasn't going to stop until I reached the top. The 120-pound beast drove me downward into the ground as it stabbed my shoulders. Finally, as the top was breached, a gale wind spun me in a half circle, back towards where I came from. Spray soared ten feet into the air as waves pounded the rock dike. Retreating just out of the wind I secured the canoe with a rope. If left on top, one good blast might send it airborne, coming to rest on the rocks 200 feet below.

With less surface area for the wind to catch, the packs were much easier to carry. For three days I camped at the upper end of the road, just out of the north wind. Then, on June 22nd, I was able to slide the canoe down 15 feet of jagged boulders to the water. Even though slide poles were jammed into strategic locations, deep, scraping sounds could be heard as sharp boulders bit into the bottom.

With the canoe floating from a tether, the packs were lowered one rock at a time. It was much too risky to have the heavy packs on one's back and maneuver across jagged, slippery rocks. With everything aboard and pent-up energy, I forged into Cedar Lake.

Lunch was at Lookout Point five hours later. Trees lay like pick-up sticks along the muddy shores, devastated when the dam reached its full potential eleven years ago. Ragged stumps, inches below the surface, awaited unsuspecting boaters. Firewood lay everywhere as I repeated the ritual for heating tea. While the small flames flickered, I hefted bigger pieces of wood toward the fire, throwing them as close as possible. A three-foot piece got an extra boost and resulted in a loud *thud*.

The canoe quivered as I turned to see a porthole where none should be. Walking to the canoe to inspect the damage, I cursed myself. A finger-size hole showed through the fiberglass. The wood planking behind it spread like a blooming rose. With a rounded rock, I tapped the flower flat. It was located high on the stern, inches above the water line. Since it wasn't the Titanic, repairs could wait.

Throughout the afternoon, mileage was hard won as the wind seemed to come from everywhere. It eventually settled from due-north; horizontal rain rode in on its gusts. Conditions deteriorated rapidly and shortly, I was shore-bound.

I spent hours walking the muddy beach and more reading beside the campfire. The walking turned to pacing, the hours into days. On the third evening, it was over. I was packing, hoping to travel until dark when a long, wooden boat passed. The motor soon died. Within minutes an inhospitable-looking man approached. In one fist was a rifle. The other held one of my paddles. "This yours?" he asked.

"Yah, where did you find it?" I said a bit astonished.

"In water, down shore," he said as he leaned it against a tree.

"Thanks for bringing it over," I said. As if not hearing me, he turned around and walked away, his green rain suit chafing between his legs. Gratefully I stored it in its rightful place, jammed between a pack and the canoe, not knowing I had even lost it.

I was able to put in five hours until darkness crept in. Facing me was ten miles of open water. This jaunt in the dark was not on the day's agenda so I docked until daylight, sleeping fitfully on a large flat rock.

By 5:00 in the morning, a south wind had developed. Instinctively I snapped the splash cover on. At first, the canoe bottomed out in shallow water, but then subsurface tree stumps were everywhere. The farther I went, the worse it was. The first wave that washed over the canoe caught me by surprise as it rolled over the splash cover. If it weren't for the cover, things would not have been good. However, there was no turning back into the wind. I was in for a long haul.

As another wave washed over the bow, Cedar Lake became worse than Lake Winnipeg. I knew I was one wave from disaster and longed for the added security of a stolen life jacket. It was *déjà vu*. It was speed-canoeing at its worst, and I wanted no part of it.

I was hanging in there and got attuned to the rhythm of the waves. It helped but didn't stop the occasional one that would almost roll me over. Cockiness finally displaced fear as I rounded a point and glided into a calm bay on Fort Island. More than happy to be there, I built a fire to wait for the sun to rise. The wind had whisked me across this ten-mile bay in less than two hours. I wondered what the rest of the day would bring.

By noon it was calm enough to make a dash to the shelter at the mouth of the Saskatchewan River. With the diminished tailwind, it was only an hour from Fort Island. Rounding the end of the island, I hoped to see where the Saskatchewan River flowed into Cedar Lake. This was not to be. Open water stretched to the horizon.

Completely baffled, I looked at the map and checked the

compass. The mouth of the river was supposed to be there. I landed back on the island and gazed in amazement. Checking my backtrack, all the bays, points, and islands matched the map. There wasn't a place on Cedar Lake where that amount of water was visible. Now north, east, and west showed boundless limits of water dotted by a few tiny islands. Then the situation became clear to me. It was simple enough to be embarrassing.

A purple, dotted line on the map extended miles to the east, swerved far to the north, ran miles westward, and then swung south to connect with the dam. Inside this area in small block letters was stamped "CEDAR LAKE RESERVOIR." What I was looking for was under water but still showed on the map. The dam had flooded over 2,000 square miles. Now the note an Indian told me at the dam made more sense. He said, "You'll probably never find the river. There used to be a couple of red ribbons tied to a tree near it, but they're probably gone by now."

Heading northwest toward a dot of land, I kept the mainland toward my left in case I needed a way out. This morning's folly would not be repeated. After traveling for hours, I came to an assortment of abandoned buildings. The map showed these remnants as the Cedar Lake First Nation. Knowing where I was, I now had a reference point.

Some of the old houses had water at their doorsteps; others showed high-water marks well up their clapboard siding. Apparently, this was still used as a stopping place, for fish guts were everywhere. The flies were atrocious as I ate lunch between the piles.

Keeping toward the west side of the reservoir, I kept as close to a northern route as possible. The water was mostly paddle-deep and through its clearness, I could see waterlogged trees crisscrossed along the bottom. Many still stood, standing guard over their comrades, bare, bleak, waiting to fall. As I swerved between these wooden sentries, a steady east wind arose. All day I traveled until a ten-foot wide stream flowing from the north appeared. It was my salvation, it had to be the Saskatchewan River. I followed it for an hour and found a tree-barren island. As I looked north, all that could be seen was water. This whole reservoir was one big current headed for the dam.

The day ended there as the skies had already begun to darken. It wasn't exactly an oasis, but looking around, I felt fortunate to be there. The island was a wide, long, high point of mud. Being miles from the mainland, I hoped a wind wouldn't arise during the night.

Rummaging through the food pack for supper didn't take long, as things were again dangerously low. I had bought enough food for seven days. The Pas was nowhere in sight. Today ended day eight. The wind and the weather were not my ally.

A light rain fell as I packed. Without breakfast and with constant map consultation, I followed the compass north. For twelve straight hours, I paddled without stopping, no lunch, and no land. What appeared at the end of the day was a foot-high strip of moss-covered mud. Washed against its banks were dead ducks and fish that told me something about my inability to catch a fish.

I camped at the end of the island on a wet, soggy, black bog that had a definite spring to it. I could stand and bounce on it like a waterbed. As I bounced, hope returned, for through the dusk across miles of water, I could see what looked like tiny, green trees on the horizon. In my mind, it had to be the north end of the reservoir.

The last of the Krusteaz pancake mix and syrup was used for breakfast. Four small boxes of Lipton Cup-a-Soup with a couple packets of instant-soup mix in each sat by themselves at the bottom of the food box. That was it!

By noon, I sat floating next to the flooded trees. Studying the map produced no coinciding landmarks. I had a choice to make; it was either east or west. Looking for anything that resembled a river, I started east. Ten miles produced nothing. I needed a plan. Facing east, I might as well have been standing on the edge of the Atlantic Ocean. The decision to backtrack to the northwest corner of the reservoir, heading west, allowed me to cover the entire northern boundary until I found the Saskatchewan River.

Searching for something to indicate the river, I traveled west for the rest of the day, backtracking along the north edge of the reservoir. There was nothing but flooded trees and muddy bars. I even kept an eye out for two red ribbons in a tree that were probably now gone. With daylight waning, I finally reached what was thought to be the corner of the reservoir. Home for the night was a muddy pimple split by a fallen tree.

Upon landing, Vagabond soared from the canoe to relieve himself after sixteen hours afloat. Setting the packs on the fallen tree, I removed the yoke from the canoe and rolled the closed cell pad over the ribs and planks. Laying the tent over the pad and fluffing the sleeping bag on top completed my nest. Without supper, I stored my mud-covered boots on the seat and crawled in.

When I awoke, Vagabond was curled at my feet, covered with mud. Usually, he would have gotten the boot, but instead I just repacked the sleeping gear and left, knowing I had a tenuous grasp on control. The food box was now down to two boxes of powdered soup, fishing was proving futile, a major river was lost, and I was still at least five days from The Pas. Adding to the dilemma, I had somehow lost the map. At least I had a plan; I headed east.

It took most of the day to get back to where I had camped the night before and another eight and a half hours for my luck to change. I noticed what looked like a road cut through the trees. With no land visible and only a wide aisle through the flooded foliage, I followed it, praying it wouldn't fade away. It did! My heart sank to an empty stomach as I sat looking at five miles of open water.

There was but one choice, straight north. The paddle just got heavier. It seemed hours before I neared the next tree line. I could see what appeared to be another opening and went straight for it. An hour of following a definite current yielded the defined banks of a river. Then there were pine and birch trees. I was never so glad to paddle against a current. Of course, it wasn't the Saskatchewan River; it was much too narrow. But it flowed from the northwest, and in that direction lay The Pas.

After four hours I stopped on a slight bank. My stomach roared from neglect as water heated four packets of tomato soup, not much after two days of not eating. From the lost map I remembered a river, a branch of the Saskatchewan called the Summerberry and felt I could be on it. That was encouraging. Even though hungry, mentally I felt much better knowing I had direction and was not adrift in a twilight zone.

As I slowly moved upstream against a strengthening current, the following day was intolerably hot. Fishing produced nothing and two long shots at ducks missed. This lifestyle was taking its toll. My strength was waning.

After twelve hours I took a much-needed break. Vagabond traveled the shore in search of food. Occasionally he'd find a dead fish and fall behind. Shortly before dark, I came to a houseboat on the other side of the river. With Vagabond back aboard, I made a beeline for it, knowing they'd ask me to stop for a beer or a bite to eat. "Hello! How far is it to The Pas?" I tried to shout in a graveled voice as I drew near.

The man on deck shouted behind him, "Hey, Herb! What's it to The Pas? Thirty miles?"

"Closer to 35," came a reply from deep within the boat.

Hovering, silently pleading, I said, "Okay, thanks," not allowing myself to ask for anything. Pride got in the way. The man gave a nonchalant "anytime" wave and took a mouthful of beer. As I moved away, my spirits were crushed.

And, boy, was I pissed! I fantasized that I should wait around the bend until dark, throw all their food and beer into the canoe, blow a half dozen holes in their fancy boat with the aught six, and head upriver.

But my predicament wasn't their problem. Still, 35 miles to The Pas was devastating. With all the hours I had put in, I was planning to be there by dark. *What a letdown!* Paddling far enough away to resist the temptation of going back and begging, I camped instead.

I hadn't been the only one to camp at that spot. An old campfire and a few papers lying about were mute evidence of past travelers. One of the sets of papers was a pamphlet published by the Canadian government, stating "Due to mercury poisoning in the lower Saskatchewan River, the water should not be taken internally. Potable water should be carried with you at all times." My thoughts turned to the dead fish and ducks seen along the reservoir and all the water I had taken internally over the last few weeks. My inability to catch any fish proved fortunate.

Not wanting to get going in the morning, I slept heavily. Fatigue and hunger dominated my body and mind. Still, I paddled, hour after hour. It wasn't worth the time or effort to stop and build a fire. Opening a foil envelope of soup, I dumped the dry powder into my mouth, tapping out every last speck from the envelope. It stuck to my teeth and congealed on the roof of my mouth. I had filled a plastic bottle with water from a tributary that morning and treated it with purification tablets. This highly chlorinated liquid was used to wash down the paste. After the last packet, my stomach pains eased slightly.

Finally, I came to a fork in the river. It widened and had to be the confluence with the Saskatchewan River. Hardly making more than a mile an hour against the current still put me 15 miles from The Pas and night was approaching. I had no intention of stopping. Maneuvering through 100 yards of sandbars, I crossed to the opposite shore. Mosquitoes rose in hordes, keeping me well away from the brushy banks. Stars slowly emerged into the wind-free night. If it weren't for the weakness, the hunger, the mosquitoes, and the current, it would have been a perfect evening to travel.

Hours passed as one stroke was followed by another and another. I was single-minded: The Pas. Peering and squinting into the darkness, I moved against the current. A thought came to me, *the transistor radio!* Between strokes, I'd grope through the pack until I found it near the bottom. It hadn't been used for a long time. As I spun the plastic dial, static crackled through the still night. I homed in, moving the dial back and forth in a minute arc. Then, it came in loud and clear, old time rock and roll.

At times I even found the strength to sing along. The little black box helped tremendously, lifting my spirits when they very much needed it. Finally, rounding a bend produced an encouraging sight. A red light blinked from the top of a radio tower miles away. It had to be The Pas. Shortly new disappointment set in. The radio station went off the air for the night, and all was quiet except for an occasional snore from Vagabond.

It was light and 5:30 in the morning when I pulled beneath the bridge at The Pas. Tying Vagabond to the canoe, I laid down next to it, arm over my closed eyes. I was spent, totally. I knew I couldn't lie there, and it was all I could do to get up. A week of hard paddling on boxes of dry soup had its drawbacks. Leaning against the canoe, I felt dizzy and it seemed my legs were ready to buckle. I almost vomited. Standing there swaying for a few minutes, I got my bearings and half-staggered to the bridge.

To the right lay a park. The city seemed to begin at its edge. To the left was an IGA grocery store backed by many small houses. I crossed the park and walked among the buildings. The city seemed lifeless. Only a police car crawled by, giving me the once-over. I walked up one deserted street and down another, but nothing was open. My legs ached. Even a candy bar would have helped. Then I saw a sign blink three blocks away.

I gratefully read from the window of Bill's Cafe & Bus Depot: Hours 4:00 A.M. to 12:00 P.M. Exhausted, I entered and sat at a corner table. The only other customer in the small restaurant was a police officer who the cook called Tom. The chef brought a menu and left. It contrasted sharply with my dirt-blackened hands. Even the creases were dirt-filled. Grime was packed under my fingernails though it

159

bothered me little as the cook returned to the kitchen with my order. It was a double order of pancakes and ham, a piece of cherry pie a la mode, and two glasses of milk. I could hardly get the words out to order since my voice was so dry, broken and hoarse.

While breakfast cooked, I went into the tiny bathroom to try and clean up. What looked out of the mirror above the sink wasn't pleasant. There was long, snarled, dirty hair, red eyes rimmed with big black circles, and a face sunk to the bone. It looked like it belonged on a deathbed.

Breakfast was at the table when I returned. The steaming pancakes drowned in syrup didn't last long. With Tom watching, I maintained a level of propriety. The pancakes were great, but the pie and ice cream were even more delicious. After two additional pieces and three more glasses of milk, I brought the meal to a conclusion with a large cup of sugar-laced tea, Lipton, of course.

I sat leaning my chair against the wall, relishing the moment. I knew I had to get up but for some reason didn't trust my legs. Getting them under me, I forced myself up and slowly, stiffly, made the short distance to the counter to pay the bill. While there, I bought six Oh Henry! candy bars and ate every one during the walk back to the canoe. The Pas seemed to be coming alive, but there wasn't much life left in my old stride.

Not two minutes were spent at the canoe when it struck. I fumbled, searching for the toilet paper but had to grab a book instead. Flying up the hill, legs pumping, I barely made the somewhat privacy beneath the bridge, Louis Lamour's book in hand. Damn, all those good pancakes, ham, and pie a la mode gone to waste. The Oh Henry!'s followed soon after! I should have known better. Now, half of Louie's book is gone beneath the bridge and without a page read.

Getting to the store, I was able to feed Vagabond and then lean back in the canoe for a two-hour nap. I awoke stiffly, not wanting to move. The sun hurt my eyes, and I was famished. After splashing river water over my face, I walked to the post office. A middle-aged man in blue thumbed through a stack of letters, occasionally sticking one between his ring and little finger. "That's about it," he said handing them to me. There were six letters.

Returning to the store, I bought two pounds of cherries, two ice cream bars, three cans of Pepsi, and five pounds of dog food. Disheveled Natives stood everywhere as I returned to the canoe; their disrepair had nothing on mine. Eating my sweets very slowly, I sat on the bank and read the six letters. It was the first news received in two months. It felt great.

The next stop was the police station. Climbing two flights of stairs in the recently constructed building, I stood before a long chest-high desk. "Can I help you?" asked an officer rising from behind a typewriter.

"Yes! Would it be safe to leave my canoe by the bridge overnight?" I asked.

"That's the worst possible place to leave anything in this town. There's a reservation across the river and a lot of theft goes on around there," he said.

"Is there a marina or boathouse anywhere I could keep it? I'll only be in town one night," I said in despair.

"Just a second," he said as he turned to talk to a man seated against the far wall. On his return, he stated, "The garage below is empty and if you want, you can carry your things up and keep them there, if they haven't already been stolen."

"That sounds great! Thanks a lot," I said with appreciation and returned to the canoe.

Wasting no time getting back, I was relieved to find everything in order. The garage was only 200 yards away, but it took nearly two hours just to get everything there. I was totally exhausted! With three strenuous efforts, the canoe was up on my bony shoulders. One sloppy effort got it off. Tying Vagabond to a tree at the police station and with a laundry bag over my shoulder, I went hotel hunting.

Skirting two toothless, glassy-eyed Natives on the front steps, I walked into the lobby. The husky clerk tossed three cans of beer onto the desk from a walk-in cooler. "Need a room?" he asked as he gave his fellow tribesmen change for their beer.

"Yes, I'd like one for tonight," I answered. He pushed a card and pen across the desk where I printed my name and brother's address, left the license plate number empty, and signed my name at the bottom. Seventeen dollars was exchanged for room number 29 at the top of the stairs.

Unlocking the door, I took two steps and sprawled onto the twin bed as the door slammed behind me. The thought of crawling between the clean white sheets was overwhelming. But there were still things to be done.

After losing $1.40 at the laundromat, I found a washer that worked. Then I stopped at the Western Union office where $500 awaited. Back at the laundromat, the washed clothes were thrown into a dryer while I tipped back against the wall in a plastic chair, lulled to sleep by its soothing monotony.

The silence woke me, not knowing where I was or how long I had slept. Not only were the clothes now dry, but they were also cold. Walking back to the hotel, the ninety-degree heat bore down upon me. Then I bathed. Cedar Lake Reservoir gunk clung to the high-water mark as the remaining dirty water whirled down the drain. A scissors was necessary to remove burrs and snarls from my hair before a comb could be run through it. Dressed in clean clothes, I left to find a theater.

Since none existed, the alternative was to eat. With eight pieces of chicken, a container of beans, coleslaw, bread, and French fries, I returned to the hotel. Only when the last piece of chicken was gone did I crawl between those luxurious white sheets.

Twelve hours of sleep on a full stomach was a great attitude adjuster. It was the best I had felt in weeks. After a T-bone breakfast, I stopped at police headquarters to thank them and tell them of my departure. After an hour of storytelling, I tackled the return portage, which took twenty minutes, canoe and all.

Everything was cached inside the canoe and covered with the splash cover. Vagabond was tied to the stern for visual protection. Then, it was time to do some quick grocery shopping. Wheeling a cart up and down the aisles, I gagged at the sight of the Lipton Cup-a-Soup section. At the end of the spree, I had three full boxes of groceries. I had no intention of running out of supplies again.

The two lightest boxes were carried on the first trip, set next to the canoe, and covered with a heavy pack to keep Vagabond at bay. His tail wagged gratefully as his teeth sank into a huge meaty bone I secured from the butcher. He lay down with a bone between his paws and went to work. Things looked well in hand, so I returned for the third box. I'd only be gone a few minutes.

Total chaos greeted me when I returned. Vagabond lay contented next to the canoe, head in paws. Then he saw me. In one fluid movement, he disappeared beneath the splash cover. I couldn't believe what I saw. Groceries were everywhere. Both boxes were annihilated. He ate two pounds of cookies, and one pound of peanut brittle. Then he chewed open a ten-pound bag of oatmeal, a 25-pound bag of flour, a five-pound sack of pancake mix, and a two-pound box of salt, washing it all down with a 32 oz.-bottle of maple syrup. His bone lay in the dirt untouched. It was an amazing accomplishment for just-under five minutes!

Amazement turned to fury in a heartbeat. I threw back the splash cover as he squirmed to escape between two packs. He gave a fearful *yelp* as I picked him up by the scruff, stuck his nose in the mess, slapped it slightly for emphasis, and explained in very simple terms what the problem was. On release, he wasted no time disappearing back beneath the splash cover. Still fuming, I completed the salvage operation and left for Cumberland House, eighty miles upstream.

In only a day I had returned to 14 hours on the paddle. Strength had returned rapidly. Skies were generally clear until early one morning when rain pelted the tent. Unzipping the door, I dashed to the canoe to cover the gear. By the time the gear was covered, the rain had quit. Looking forward to an extension of the last night's sleep, I crawled back inside the tent. Mosquitoes were everywhere; having left the tent door open for those few minutes was a grave mistake. The inside walls were covered with them. Dressing in a hurry, I stuffed the sleeping bag into its sack and rolled up the tent, mosquitoes and all, just to be rid of them. It took over an hour of traveling before the day started to lighten.

Not long after the sun rose, a green canoe swerved down the middle of the river. It turned my way and pulled broadside. "Hi, I'm Daniel," the occupant said, extending his hand.

I shook hands with the two-front-toothed fellow and said, "That's quite a load you're paddling." He explained that he was moving from Cumberland House, where he had been living with his uncle. The uncle had died three months before. Now the nephew was going to live in The Pas for a while. "You've got a big canoe to paddle there," I commented.

"Got to, just to hold all my stuff," he said, "plus some of my uncle's. I've got his radio here, his dishes, guns, and even his canoe. That's sure a nice-looking canoe you've got, and it doesn't even leak," he exclaimed while peering over the gunwale.

His craft was very old. The green canvas held numerous patches, and the inside was painted a dull gray. Water glistened in the bottom, and I would hate to have to portage it. "Yah," he said, "I have to wear these rubber boots over my moccasins just to keep my feet dry."

"Look at that!" he said, astonished, "My paddle is the same color as yours." We compared them, and it was true except that his was a foot shorter and half as wide at the blade. "Just cut it out of a spruce tree a couple of days ago and can't tell them apart." he continued, amazed at his ability. During this chit-chatting, I was losing hard-won ground to the Saskatchewan River and mentioned it. "Well, you're about halfway to Cumberland House, and it doesn't get any easier," he said.

Just above The Pas' ferry was a quarter-mile rapids. The landing area was a large flat rock, obviously well-used. Tangled fishing line and evidence of past campfires were everywhere. After portaging the canoe first, I swooned as I realized I wasn't fully recovered from my Lipton Cup-a-Soup diet.

Setting the canoe down, I noticed fresh blood splattered on the rocks and trail. Nobody was in the vicinity, so it must have come from Vagabond. He was a chore just to subdue as sugar still surged through him from misappropriated sweets. Once settled, I could see his paw was covered with blood from a cut across the pad. It was wide, long, and ugly. I washed it with soap and water, put a gauze pad over it, and then wrapped it with strips ripped from my only towel. With Vagabond tied to a tree so he wouldn't run and ruin the bandage, I returned for the packs.

Cursing the fragility of bottles, I set the packs next to the canoe. Vagabond wasn't lying down licking his wounds. He was thoroughly enjoying himself with a bloody bandage he would throw into the air, pounce on, shake vigorously, and then flip skyward again. *So much for a doctor-patient relationship!*

Before leaving, I took another clean gauze pad and re-bandaged Vagabond's wound. This time it was taped on. While paddling, I watched him closely and any chewing resulted in a tap with the paddle and a reprimand. It drove him nuts. Acceptance came until my back was turned.

Cumberland House was reached at 8:30 that evening. There was a man beaching a wooden boat, so I stopped next to him and asked about a place to camp for the night. "Just go to that clearing there," he replied.

"Is there anything open in town yet?" I asked.

"Yah, I'll show you but don't leave your gear there very long. Kids will haul it away."

A single-storied, rustic building greeted me as I entered town.

Looking fairly new, the bar wasn't crowded as I entered and sat at an empty table. Shortly a waitress arrived to take my order. Immediately I requested a bottle of Labatt Blue. "Did you want that doubled?" she asked.

"Doubled?" I questioned.

"Yah, everyone buys two drinks at a time, so they don't have to wait for the waitress," she explained.

Seeing her reasoning was sound, I said, "Okay, make it a double."

"You'll have to take off your hat if you want to drink here," she added.

"What?"

Annoyed by my ignorance, she repeated adamantly, "The law says you can't drink here with your hat on." I couldn't believe what I was hearing. It was either the beer or the hat. I held to my convictions for a time; she set my change on the table next to the hat and walked away.

I went to the restroom and learned some bad news. I thought I'd be going downstream on the Sturgeon-Weir River, but a guy was willing to bet $100 that it ran south, which meant I'd be going upstream all the way to Reindeer Lake. "Ask anyone around," the local said. I had no reason to doubt him. "Damn rough river too," he had to add. The messenger wasn't finished as he said the Saskatchewan River was too low to get into Cumberland Lake. "You'll have to go back down-river, portage around the rapids, and go up the Tearing River," he explained. *Not good news!*

Getting within spitting distance of Cumberland Lake didn't take long, and it glimmered in the early morning sun. The guy was right. I stood staring at 200 yards of mud and weeds. At least I had to try to get through before retreating to the Tearing.

The mud was wet, sticky, and deep. A trickle of water flowed in a narrow channel. Even though it was insufficient to float the canoe, by jerking, tugging, and pulling, I was able to get the outfit halfway. Then the trickle ended. There was only mud. From where I stood, I could see the whole of Cumberland Lake ringed with it and resolved to continue with the portage.

The heavy packs sunk me halfway to my knees before solidifying. Each step was an effort as I trudged toward the lake. Even the mosquitoes showed little mercy as I set the packs at the edge of the water. Then came the canoe. With a rope tied to the bow on one end and a loop wrapped around my shoulders on the other, I employed the "lean over and jerk a foot at a time" method. If I didn't have to stop and pull my foot out of the mud with each step, it would have been a much easier ordeal. After two hours of portaging, I floated in Cumberland Lake.

It rained day and night for 48 hours, and fishing finally produced an abundant harvest; soon I couldn't help but catch and release. The tent would be erected in the rain, taken down in the rain, packed wet in the morning, and was soaked when put up at night. Then on July 13th, it stopped. The sky cleared but a strong headwind persisted. I was only a half-day from Sturgeon Landing, a small settlement at the mouth of the Sturgeon-Weir River.

The half-day turned long as the wind held me under one mile per hour. By late evening I was at Sturgeon Landing, which looked more like a camp than a town. Tents were pitched along the bank, and five boats were anchored at the mouth of the river. An icehouse stood behind the dock. At its front, a Native kid stood next to three blocks of ice with a hose, washing sawdust from them. Ten people stood on the dock casting assorted lures into the river. Since this was too crowded for me, I camped on the other side of the river.

The following morning, three youthful paddlers crossed the river and greeted me. They were hunting for seagulls. After a short conversation, they returned to their leaky canoe, asking me for a return trip across the river.

"Thank you, mister," they shouted as they dashed toward their small village. I paddled to the base of the first rapids to see what I was in for. They appeared very shallow and very long.

Arriving back at the dock in front of Sturgeon Landing, it was a quiet morning. The store amounted to four shelves on a short wall stacked with staples, a pop cooler, and a glass-enclosed counter hindering small, sticky fingers from enjoying the candy bars it contained. A sign on the wall read We Do Not Lend Tools.

For a few minutes, I stood looking at the assorted pictures of northern pike caught in the area. They were impressive. Leaning against the counter were two Natives, drinking Pepsi as a morning pick-me-up while discussing outboard motors. There was little on the shelves I didn't already have except for two cans of Pepsi, twelve candy bars, and a strawberry roll that went into the larder. I headed for the canoe.

At the dock stood a retired businessman. "Yup, been coming

here from the states for the last twelve years now. My wife and I really enjoy it," he said. "That's a very bad river you plan on heading up," he warned. "The old trappers used to use it in the winter as a fur route, so I guess it could be done." he calculated. "You wouldn't catch me doing it though," he added. "I've flown over it."

I paddled as far as possible, which was not far from the village. Off came the shoes and socks as I got out and started pulling. It was shallow and rock-ridden. It took little time to realize my feet weren't going to tolerate this abuse. Again, well shod, I reluctantly stepped in, feeling the cold-water rush to soak the Red Wings inside and out.

It took four hard hours of walking and pulling up the rapids before reaching a three-foot high rock wall. A chute gushed through its center while water poured over rock ledges on both sides. Standing below one of these ledges, I pondered a route without portaging. The only way was to line the canoe up the chute. Pulling the lanyard produced nothing. While pondering strategy, the canoe floated to an eddy, from where it was then pulled beneath the ledge. It was filled with water in seconds. Vagabond was in belly-deep water while the packs floated. Everything was pulled out and stacked on a large rock in the middle of the river. Assuring him that I would return for him, Vagabond was placed on his own rock.

After struggling to escape the powerful force of the falls, most of the next day was spent battling more rapids. It resulted in covering only eight miles before reaching an irresistible place to camp. Unexcelled walleye fishing had been found. With a campfire crackling beside me later that night, I lay back on the large, warm rock. A belly full of walleye added to my comfort in the confines of the Sturgeon-Weir River.

After six hours, I reached an abandoned trapper's cabin along a stretch of calm water. I had to explore. A faint trail through knee-deep grass led past a rotted boat that would never see life again. Unusable trapping gear littered the place.

A pair of snowshoes lay across two rafters. They weren't much good. The frames were warped birch, and the webbing was frail string. I took them into the daylight and sat on the old overturned boat to study, knowing that someday I may need to construct a pair.

Taking my diary, I drew the image of a snowshoe on a back page. To this, I transferred every string of the old webbing. Each was numbered, stating whether it went over, under, or between when it crossed another string. It was not an easy job.

With my homework done, I examined the cabin's construction. I looked at the overhang, the notched corners, and the window, committing the construction to memory. Rounding the back corner of the cabin gave me a start. An aged, black bear hide hung from the back ridgepole, swaying in the breeze. I almost walked right into it. Flies abounded and it smelled like one would expect. Enough time had been spent examining the past. I returned to the present.

Traveling didn't improve, but I reached Amisk Lake on Sunday evening, July 18th, nonetheless. It was the end of the Lower Sturgeon-Weir River. Its course ran 25 miles and washed away 25 hours of travel time.

The next morning the tent was down, and everything was ready to go by seven o'clock. Instead of leaving, I walked a dirt road which led to a washed-out bridge that I had paddled under a quarter-mile downstream. A plaque next to the bridge told of gold that was discovered here in 1910, resulting in a town called Beaver City. It was a ghost town by 1918. When a light wind began to pick up, I knew not to linger; Amisk Lake was big enough to get rough, and it did.

Three hours and not much accomplished, I was blown ashore. The afternoon was spent waiting, but after a supper of bannock, peanut butter, and rice, the far shore of Amisk Lake was reached with no daylight to spare. Within a mile lay the Upper Sturgeon-Weir River.

Tucked between the shore and an island, I headed for the river, challenging the darkness. Soon I approached an empty dock. *Maybe an abandoned cabin,* I thought and tied the canoe to the peeled spruce pole landing.

Though nearly dark, a silver-sided building stood out in a wooded hollow. I went to the wooden door and knocked. It appeared no one occupied the dark building. The doorknob turned easily as I shouted, "Anybody here?" It was one, big, empty room. Dim light fanned to empty corners as the small flame of the Bic lighter swung in an arc. There was a table, a wood plank bed, and some trash strewn on the floor. Lighting a candle on the table, I read a dozen paper plates nailed to the wall. All had names, dates, weather, biggest fish, and how many. One read, "Wind-bound here for three days, rain all three days. Thank God for this cabin."

By other inscriptions, it seemed to be a government-maintained shelter cabin. The candle stub was limited so shortly I moved from reading the plates to checking under the bunk and in the corners, making sure there was nothing Vagabond could demolish. After confirmation I fell asleep almost instantly.

It was daylight and my nose itched. After exhaling a short, sharp breath, I noticed a feather floating in the air. I should have known better as I rolled over and sat up. Vagabond was busy tearing the last remnants of the down pillow to bits. Feathers were everywhere. It looked as if someone plucked a thousand geese.

I read the paper plates again in the daylight. There were some respectable fish caught, an 18-pound northern and a nine-pound walleye being the biggest. In addition, I noticed a few pamphlets, lying in a corner near the door. Each of the dozen small pieces of literature had a scuzzy looking gentleman on its front with a traditional felt hat resting above a full beard. They described different canoe routes throughout the area. Of the Upper Sturgeon-Weir, they stated: "Three days downstream, seven portages, the longest being 280 rods, and possible to do upstream." This could be important.

The shallow, weedy river mouth was easily recognized. I fished there for an hour before heading upstream four miles to Spruce Rapids. There on a tiny knoll rested a small cemetery. Most crosses were wood and hadn't long to stand. Picking up a pack, I started the 280-rod portage around Spruce Rapids.

It took all day to reach Scoop Rapids, where walleyes showed no tolerance for a yellow Canadian Minnow swimming through their domain. Now that was enough incentive to camp and seek out the big one. I was further persuaded by the black cloud mass rolling overhead.

Thunder soon boomed along the river valley as lightning slashed the sky. Rain pelted the land. Ten minutes later, it was over. As the storm moved eastward, the sun again shone through clean-smelling air, produced when cold rain washes over warm rocks. Pools of water lay on the surface of the rocks.

A flurry rose beneath my feet as a dozen small walleyes scurried through the small pools to regain the security of the river. Disbelief had abounded earlier when I read about Scoop Rapids in the brochure at the cabin. It stated that Scoop Rapids was so named because the weary traveler could stop here and scoop fish out with their hands. *Sure, maybe 100 years ago, but not anymore.* I set out to prove them wrong and failed. Though dancing like a drunk on the dance floor, I was able to maneuver over the wet, slippery rocks and corner two of them.

During the night another storm passed, but the sun was doing its best to dry the earth when I crawled out of the tent. Most of the morning was spent fishing, portaging, and fishing. The big one eluded me, and I gave up the cause for the sake of mileage.

By late afternoon I had traversed Loon Rapids, then fought a headwind to Birch Portage. The skid-pole portage disappearing over the hill made it easy to locate. It was about a half-mile over this portage, and the view from the other side was majestic. High pine-covered hills lined both sides of the long, narrow valley. The river was glassy and calm. On the right was a large meadow dwarfing a swaybacked log cabin teetering near its center. What a place for a cabin! Someone had good taste. I even felt a pang of envy. It took until 12:30 that evening to reach the end of the calm stretch of river. There I found a flat rock my size, threw the pad and bag down, and crawled in for the evening. Neither the twinkling stars nor the mosquitoes kept me awake.

It was not always wise to sleep on a rock. The half-inch pad and down bag offered only so much protection. I was a bit stiff and covered in bites. It was thirty miles to the next village of Pelican Narrows, but the calm day was spent lazily paddling and trolling. By evening, over 100 snaky northern pike had fallen to my prowess. One may have weighed in at five pounds. All were released.

After supper, I sat against a rock sipping a cup of hot tea. Feeling chipper, though already traveling twelve hours, I decided to cover the final eight miles to Pelican Narrows. It was calm and clear when I started across the large lake. Soon a motorized freight canoe pulled alongside me. It was a guide who worked this area. "Some pretty bad water on the Fond du Lac River. Best watch yourself," he warned as he pulled away. I also learned that the stores were closed on the weekends, which this was. Southend, the next village, was 100 miles beyond Pelican Narrows. The food box was very low, and though I didn't relish the thought of spending the weekend in Pelican Narrows, I didn't have much of a choice.

There was very little light left when I reached the other side of the lake. Passing a row of small reddish cabins, I rounded a rocky point. Twice I had to back off barely exposed rocks that grounded me to a halt, demonstrating severely limited visibility. I later learned that in a few short hours someone would find a body washed ashore on this narrow point. It was likely that I had passed within feet of it, not something a person would want to encounter in the darkness.

From the end of the point, the lights of Pelican Narrows shimmered through the darkness. It took forty minutes to reach them. Though it was well past midnight, the town seemed lively. People, mostly kids, strolled the dirt main street. Not having the least idea of what to do, I slowly followed the shoreline until reaching a long, wooden dock pointing to the Hudson's Bay Store. It sat atop a long sloping hill. Two teens sat on the front steps smoking cigarettes. I climbed the slope and ascended the wide, worn, wooden steps. Behind the glass door was a sign posting the days of the week. Following Saturday and Sunday was one word—Closed. Tonight was Friday.

I hopped off the plank sidewalk fronting the store and was going back to the canoe when I heard, "Hey, where you go?" A guy with his arm around a plump girl walked up to me. "I'm Lowlan, and she's my wife," he said. I introduced myself and we shook hands. "Let's sit on the beach and drink beer," Lowlan suggested. With little else to do, I agreed and the three of us walked to the beach where Lowlan immediately emptied his pockets. He came up with eight bottles of Labatt Blue and lined them up in front of him in the sand. He handed me one and took one for himself, while his wife helped herself.

The couple was well on their way. Lowlan described how he liked playing baseball. Then, he wanted to buy Vagabond. He'd get up every five minutes, walk over to the canoe and play with him. Sticking his arm between Vagabond's teeth, he would announce, "Look how friendly he is, honey. I'll buy him from you." He would then sit back down and say, "You my friend?"

"Yah, I'm your friend," I would reply for the umpteenth time. He dug into his front pocket and handed me something. It was a beaded headband.

"My wife made this, and I want to give it to you, my friend," he said. Taking it, I looked at it. It must have taken hours to make, as the look on his wife's face confirmed. It also told me something else as I tried to give it back to Lowlan. He wouldn't accept it. Finally, he took it, stuffed it into my shirt pocket, and said, "You my friend." What could I do?

A small island stood a stone's throw away, and I headed for it to get some semblance of privacy. It was a rock, thirty feet long and ten feet wide, supporting a small growth of willows on its south end. Next to the willows, I made my bed in the grass.

"Don't you splash me! Don't you dare splash me!" came a woman's voice. It was very close. I pushed onto one elbow and focused my eyes in the dawning sun. A guy and a husky woman were near the end of the island splashing water on each other.

"Oh, are you taking a nap?" the skinny man asked as he saw me for the first time. *Am I taking a nap?* Keeping my thoughts to myself, I just waved and lay back down until I saw them strolling along the beach wrapped in towels. Grabbing my bar of soap, I waded to my neck. Dunking was cold and refreshing after I soaped from head to foot. Decked out in clean clothes, I was ready to tour Pelican Narrows.

It was still early morning, and I had the whole day to waste. I walked to the RCMP station to find where the postmaster lived. What I got was a twenty-minute interrogation session. "Just like to know who's around in case anything goes ajar while you're here," he explained. With directions to a yellow house, he assured me that the postmaster wouldn't be home.

Proving he was right, I returned to the canoe, meeting Lowlan on the way. He was in a hurry but laughingly said, "I don't even remember leaving last night. I must have been drinking." Puffs of dust rose from Lowlan's feet as he hurriedly labored down the street. With little to do, I pushed the canoe into the water and toured the beach.

I followed the shoreline, looking at the houses. Glaring from a clear sky, the sun sent the mercury above ninety degrees. A man sanding an overturned boat yelled, "Come on up and have coffee." Grateful to pass a little time, I pulled in and followed him to his house. I was surprised. Most government houses on the First Nations were not impressive. They're cheap, prefabricated boxes to start with and the maintenance on them is usually very little. However, this one was different; it was just the opposite. The walls were richly paneled; a stereo console stood beneath a huge picture window overlooking the lake, and the modern furniture was neatly arranged. It was so clean I felt obligated to remove my boots.

We sat at the kitchen table, drinking coffee, talking about the United States. Since he planned on vacationing there next year, he was gathering as much information as possible about the country. The conversation turned to drinking in the village, and I found out why he had such a nice home. "I used to drink quite a bit, but I found out that I couldn't afford to drink and raise two kids like they should be raised," he said. "I had to change my life."

I was there for well over an hour and didn't want to overextend my welcome. So, I thanked him for the coffee and continued my tour along the shore.

Kids of all ages lined the shore. Many were in the water, enjoying the ninety-degree heat of summer. It seemed they made enough noise for hundreds. Going to the nearest island with trees, I set up camp. By eight o'clock all was quiet except for church bells. Then for an hour choir-sung hymns filtered through the village. This was followed by silence.

I had a good night's sleep with no urgency to get up. It was Sunday, July 25th, and still another day until anything opened. I passed the day playing the guitar, sharpening knives, fixing the yoke pads, going over maps, napping in the sun, and sewing my newly acquired, beaded headband onto my hat.

By morning I was the first one sitting on the steps of the store. People trickled in, lulling in the building's scant shade, avoiding the searing sun. At 9:30 the front doors opened, and people started in. I rose from the dirty, wooden steps and followed the crowd. The first stop was the post office window just past the main doors where I stood at the small counter, occasionally leaning over it so far, my forehead rested on the ornate metal-framed arch.

After twenty minutes someone approached from the back room. "I might have a package here. The name is Pushcar," I said to her. She looked around quizzically with that "I don't know what I'm doing" look, shrugging her shoulders.

"It's the small white one toward this side, next to the brown one," I said, recognizing my brother's handwriting. She handed it to me with a smile. On the way out I bought a box of chocolate-covered doughnuts and a quart of milk. Armed with breakfast, I returned to the canoe to read the news from home.

I almost finished the last of the twelve doughnuts when a voice behind me said, "Hey, are you Jerry Pushcar?"

"Yah," I said rising from the canoe seat.

"There's a girl back at the resort who wants to see you. She says she knows you," the local said.

A girl that knows me in Pelican Narrows? I doubted it. "What's her name?" I asked, puzzled.

173

"Barbara but they call her Bobby," he replied. I couldn't for the life of me remember anyone by that name.

"What does she look like?" I asked with curiosity.

"About *this* tall, blond hair, blue eyes," he said holding his hand flat at eye level. I was still perplexed. He gave me one last chance saying, "Her hair frizzles up all over her head, an Afro or whatever they call it." The bell rang.

"I think I know who she is now," I said.

"Will you stop at the resort before you leave?" he asked.

"Sure," I said, "I'll be there about noon."

He left saying, "OK, I'll tell her."

Barbara was good friends with Ray, a friend of mine from Biwabik. It was his loaned rifle that I slept with every night. I talked to her for a few minutes over a year ago. From what I understood at the time, she was a very avid outdoors person.

When I walked into the office, she was behind the desk, clad in blue jeans and t-shirt, Afro intact, talking into a radio microphone about someone at a hospital. "Well, hello there," she said putting the microphone down, "I thought I missed you. I was tempted to take a boat and go after you."

She invited me to an adjoining house where I sat at the kitchen table while she poured two whiskey waters. "I've been here since May 12th trying to get this place out of the hole," she remarked. "With the excellent fishing here, they should be clearing an easy thirty grand every summer." Getting up, she flipped over the Kris Kristofferson tape, and then returned to the table where we discussed our mutual friend and other acquaintances. Much of the time was spent learning about the area around Pelican Narrows.

After almost two hours, a delivery truck appeared outside the window. She had a business to run, and it seemed like a good time to excuse myself. "Here, take this with you," she said while slipping a huge sirloin steak into a bag filled with ice cubes. "That's about all I've got," she added while searching through her refrigerator. Unable to refuse her generous gift, I still felt guilty accepting it. She walked me to the canoe, snapped a few pictures, and said, "I'll send these to Ray. Take care of yourself and have a nice trip." I thanked her as she left and stuffed the steak deep within the food box, well out of the reach of Vagabond.

Still astonished by knowing someone here, I almost missed the green canoe that was freshly beached near mine. The deep canvas canoe reflected antique qualities. After a quick once-over, I entered the store and filled a small basket with necessities.

The two guys that owned the canoe couldn't be mistaken. One was at the counter squeezing an orange. He was my height, thin, and sunburned, trimmed with long blond hair, a headband, baggy pants, and woven rope belt. In the next aisle, I saw what had to be his companion. He was stocky, probably portaged the canoe, wore a light brown shirt, pants with suspenders, a red bandana, and like his partner, was sunburned. I passed him as he studied articles on the shelves, paid for my groceries, and returned to the canoe.

Shortly they appeared, each carrying a full paper sack. Our canoes lay twenty feet apart. "Hi," the stocky one said as he rummaged through a pack. With a spoon held high in triumph, I was invited to join them for ice cream and doughnuts. They introduced themselves as John and Tory. Both were from Minnesota, and both went to college forty miles from my hometown.

"Yes sir, we've been partying in Biwabik a few times," Tory proclaimed as he named six familiar establishments, all the while passing the pint of chocolate ice cream with the spoon. As we discussed our routes and found them similar, the donuts lay at our feet. They were going to Fort Chipewyan or Fort Resolution, depending on the length of the season. When an RCMP officer stopped to see how long they would be in Pelican Narrows, they were shifty. Later I found out they hadn't passed through customs when entering the country.

We stayed on the beach for the rest of the afternoon doing canoe repairs. Toward evening John suggested we buy a case of beer and paddle to an island to have a couple.

Approaching rapidly from the west were black clouds. Lightning boomed through the air, and a strong wind churned the water. We hurriedly got into our canoes and headed for the island a half-mile away.

As large drops of rain came in, John and Tory left, soon lost to the darkness. I followed. Water sprayed into the canoe as I struggled to keep the bow headed into the wind. Only when lightning split the sky and illuminated my path could I glimpse John and Tory. They were doing their best to reach the island rapidly; I went as hard as I could to try to keep stride with them. It was impossible to see any land in the darkness. But then, during one of the lightning strikes, I could see the beached, green canoe through the downpour.

With the tents up and the fire going, we lashed poles between trees and set their wide canoe across them to act as a roof. The rain had slowed to a hard drizzle. "That's the worst water I ever paddled in, and it scared the hell out of me," Tory confessed.

"How about some supper?" I suggested. "I've got a steak, cucumbers, and radishes." Tory volunteered a mess of potatoes and bread. Out came the pots and pans. Tory commandeered the responsibilities of head chef. He fried the potatoes and grilled the steak while John handled the greens. I gathered enough wood to last the evening. The aroma filled the campsite. When it was ready, Tory filled the plates. Nothing remained.

With the dishes done, we each found a dry spot under the canoe. Water dripped off the gunwales from the steady drizzle. Tory and I drank till sunrise. Four hours later, the three of us sat around the fire consuming a huge breakfast. The day grew hot, the wind continued to howl, and mosquitoes took refuge in whatever calm our camp could provide. I took leave of the fellows, saying, "I'll probably be seeing you somewhere along the way." I pushed off into a light fog.

Traveling the remainder of the day brought me to Wood Lake, a twenty-mile stretch of water running east to west. The wind had faded to nothing, and I opted to continue through the calm night, knowing how a light wind could devastate my travels on a lake this size for days. After a light supper, twilight shortly turned to darkness. Pulling my stocking hat over my ears, I slipped on a pair of gloves, placed the flashlight within easy reach, and then slid into the darkness.

Picking out a star to guide me westward, I cut through the night slowly and easily. I had all night. After three hours I noticed a campfire toward the south, blinking, spreading a warm glow upward into the surrounding pines. It didn't coincide with the star above the bow, but turning the canoe, I headed south.

Noiselessly the canoe approached the campfire using a stroke perfected over the miles. The dipping of the paddle couldn't be heard because it never left the water. On the return stroke, it was turned ninety degrees and sliced the water without sound as it was then spun for another forward stroke. Pure stealth!

"Come on up and have some raspberry pie, Jerry," came John's voice through the darkness, ending the covert operation still well away from the campfire. Their fire blazed atop a 15-foot cliff as I pulled next to their green canoe below. I made my way to the top of the cliff and sat next to the fire near John.

"Pretty rough ground you chose tonight," I mentioned to Tory as he jabbed the fire with a stick, sending sparks sailing into the night.

"It got dark and we couldn't be too choosy," he said as he picked up a ball of dough and pounded it with his fist. Satisfied with the beating, he lined a frying pan with the flattened flour mix, trimming the excess from around the top. In went a coffee can, filled with raspberries, juice and all. The excess dough was cut into strips and then weaved across the top.

"Just like downtown," Tory announced as he raked aside coals from the fire, set the pan on top, and covered it with a tin plate. Burying the concoction in hot embers, he predicted it would be ready in twenty short minutes as he stood and stretched.

While the pie cooked, we sat around the fire watching the Aurora Borealis swaying high above us. The lights moved in every direction as they changed from all shades of red, green, and white. It was a cosmic theater. When Tory announced that the pie was done, the spell was finally broken. Sliced into three sections, it was literally poured into three bowls.

"Hey, this is all right, Tory!" John cheered.

I gave him a compliment to the same effect out of kindness. Not that it was awful, I had just never tasted anything like it, though there were times not long ago I would have eaten the whole thing and wanted more. Admittedly he was at a decisive disadvantage as only flour and water were available for the crust since there were no sugar or eggs. A tinny taste, too, was transferred from his only appliances. I didn't comment as Tory said, "It would have been better had I had the right stuff for the crust. I can't figure out why it's so runny though." I kept my theories to myself. Thus is life in the bush.

As the fire burned down, John yawned heavily. I got up, saying it was late and had yet another twelve miles to go. I thanked them for the pie, bid them good night, and with strokes of stealth, vanished noiselessly into the night.

It was calm, cool, and moonless. Realigning the bow of the canoe with my guide-star, I again headed west. Stars seemed to fall from the northern lights as they streaked across the heavens. I was entertained with at least one every hour. By the time the seventh star fell, I was across Wood Lake.

The clear skies were replaced rapidly by gray clouds boiling over the treetops. Dawn was on its way as I squinted through the dim light, correlating my surroundings with where I ought to be on the map. From my current location, I could see the mouth of a small river a mile away that led to Frog Portage, the last leap before the legendary Churchill River. That could wait; twenty hours was enough for now. In addition, it had begun to drizzle.

Five hours later I rolled the wet tent and slid it into the nylon sack next to the aluminum poles. The earth seemed thoroughly saturated; it obviously poured through my oblivious sleep. Already the wind was robust, helping me appreciate the time spent on the water last night.

Traveling the mile to the mouth of the river, I found two cabins fronted by huge gardens. A handful of their wild potatoes would have been great for supper, but smoke curling skyward from one of the chimneys told a different story. The small creek wound through narrow lakes until I felt lost. The water shallowed to a foot and was layered with lily pads, making progress difficult. The creek rounded a point, emptying into a mile-long weed bed. This maze shrank into a narrow, winding channel terminating at Frog Portage.

Boy is this portage tucked away, I said to myself as I grabbed the old pole dock. A narrow-gauge track faded into the forest. Portaging the canoe, I followed the iron rail as it ran down, up, and along a flat. Again up, then down until ending at the Churchill River. There at the end of the tracks was a cart with a cradle just for a boat.

It made no sense to push that cart all the way back across the tracks, throw the packs on it, and then push it all the way back. It was just as easy to carry them. Although I had second thoughts halfway across, they vanished as soon as the packs were placed in the canoe and I was in the Churchill River.

Nobody Goes There

It felt good to feel the gentle pull of the current again, but I didn't indulge long; night approached. The smooth-landing rock slab on the island where I intended to spend the night held traces of countless aluminum boat bottoms. A trail led to a campsite cluttered with trash. The few birch trees were stripped clean of their paper bark to a height of seven feet, undoubtedly used to start fires. Bleeding sap oozed from deeply carved initials in two huge pines. Firewood didn't exist on this hallowed ground, seemingly used for eons. It had the unfortunate distinction of being situated in a perfect place during the evolution of the Churchill River, ruined with the passage of time and irresponsible campers.

Instead sunrise found me drifting down the Churchill, exuberant in its great northern-pike fishing. By noon, catch-and-release fishing had lost its glory. A long, calm stretch of water faced me, and a rumble sounded in the distance. It was Kettle Falls, five miles away.

Hugging the north shore, the rumble escalated as I traversed the deceptively calm water. Rising mist blanketed a faded rainbow as I ran a small chute, pulling ashore in a calm pool. It was here the portage started. It was short and downhill. Because the turbulence created by these falls deserved much respect, I decided to camp above them and take the short portage in the morning.

I walked along the falls after supper, enjoying their majesty. Far below, on an island, smoke curled through thick pine trees. On the beach stood a green canoe. *No raspberry pie for me tonight,* I thought, their company fleetingly missed.

Watching nature's raw strength usually put me in a reflective mood. A Native's words from the last town came to me. "They're putting in a 120-foot high dam on the Churchill. Pretty soon you'll be able to go all the way to Hudson Bay without a portage," he stated. The famed Churchill River with its miles of beauty, waterfalls, and hundreds of rapids, traveled for thousands of years, would be tamed. Its history would be drowned. In its place on the map would be a wide purple line meandering mile after mile. In the center would be stamped "CHURCHILL RIVER RESERVOIR."

Sleeping was a chore as slumber battled the roar of the falls. When I awoke, the sun was up, though not high enough yet to have vaporized the heavy dew. The short portage was completed before breakfast, while maps were studied in the warming sun. Confident that I could cover the 475 miles to Fort Chipewyan by freeze-up, the maps were stored, and I broke camp.

Whirlpools and eddies abounded beneath Kettle Falls. No smoke rose from the island as I passed. The green canoe was pulled onto the rocky shore and turned over. Continuing downstream, I reached the Reindeer River flowing into the Churchill from the north. It was here I would leave the Churchill.

Soon I came to Atik Falls. I saw no reason for it to be endowed with that title—it was more of a chute, one I was going to avoid either way. I never heard of anyone drowning on a portage.

Below the portage the river leveled, and by evening had widened into a lake. I could hear running water and gravitated toward it, seeking a campsite. A small creek tumbled down a five-foot falls, forming a deep pool before mingling with the Reindeer River. It exhibited excellent fish habitat. But there was a problem. The mosquitoes relentlessly attacked in droves. No time was wasted leveling a place for the tent. With a shot of Raid to the interior and a handful of GORP trail mix, I was in for the night.

Morning came cold. Peering out from beneath the sleeping bag revealed the tent blanketed with the "Locust of the North." A veritable hum arose as I disbursed them from the tent. When it subsided, I crawled out, stretching full length to face another day. It was a fine morning, clear and very crisp. The mosquitoes had vanished, lying dormant, awaiting the warming sun like a vampire waits for darkness.

That was fine with me as I went to the pool and started casting. In just a few minutes six walleyes flopped at my feet. After filleting them, I washed the twelve white strips of meat, laid them in two neat rows on a rock to drain, and then returned to my gear to break camp. With the tent down and packed, I started a fire, anticipating freshly fried fish.

With frying pan in hand, I was off to retrieve the catch. Astonishment turned to anger as the last fillet dangled from Vagabond's mouth. That, too, soon disappeared. He jumped at my articulation of the English language, heading for safer ground, two strides ahead of the frying pan.

I settled for a bowl of oats. With everything packed and ready to leave, I fruitlessly called for Vagabond. I called and called and called. Returning to the scene of the crime, I started a search from where I had seen him last. I was getting hoarse from calling. It was a great day to be canoeing, not looking for a dog.

Two hours later I found him, hunkered down behind the waterfall on a small island protected by a five-foot creek on each side. Lying in thick willows with his head across his paws, he watched me safely from behind his moat. I begged, pleaded, and apologized, all to no avail.

Finally, I'd had it, and in one great leap, I was on him. With soaked feet and Vagabond tucked under one arm, I pushed through the thick willows back to the canoe. After a quick bark, he did the dog-circle before lying down, and off we went into the morning made just for canoeing.

Feeling refreshed from the cold shower in the falls, I paddled all day before pulling into the portage at Steephill Rapids toward evening. There sat the cruising canoe. While John and Tory rested on a high cliff to the left, Vagabond bolted down the portage, followed by me with the canoe. Returning for the packs, I finished the portage, had supper, and returned over the trail to fish below the falls. Almost every cast produced a walleye from the swirling water at their base. There was nothing big, but it was fun.

It was getting dark as I returned to the canoe and climbed the rocks to the high cliff. John and Tory sat next to the fire watching their sourdough bread bake. "How's fishing?" Tory asked. I explained the situation while organizing the fishing gear.

With the fishing gear stashed, I picked up the guitar and tuned it. Tory got up, went to his pack, and brought out a flute. Sitting down cross-legged, he blew a few notes and told me to play something he could follow. I played the introduction to "Roll Over Beethoven." I heard no flute. Laughing in the background, John did a lame-armed jig and sang, "Yah, yah, yah, rock and roll." Without a word, Tory got up, returned the flute to its place and sat back down to watch his bread bake.

My tent was up for the night on the only flat, sandy spot I could find. "It's a nice night tonight. We're just going to sleep under the stars and rough it a little," John said. I bid them good night and drifted toward sleep. Within the hour there were rustling noises.

I heard Tory say, "Hurry up and get in here," followed by the *zip* of the door.

After a pause, John chuckled and exclaimed, "You must have it pretty rough at times by yourself. We haven't been wind-bound all summer."

"I've never seen a wind-bound train yet," I chided; they had taken the train around Lake Winnipeg. Another conversation was sparked about the fate of the Churchill. Silence followed, only to be rekindled by another question, and another. Tory gave out a long mournful moan. We took the hint and allowed the spark to die. There was mutual silence.

We were up two hours later. I was packed and ready to leave when Tory said to John, "You won't be talking for a week now. You talked about everything from here to Texas last night."

"Yeah, we sure did, and it felt good too. I really needed that," John responded.

I left them boiling their oats and slicing their sourdough bread.

It took most of the morning to get to Royal Lake where strong north winds churned the water to whitecaps. I didn't have the gumption to fight them. Behind the first island, I found an out-of-the-wind dip in a rock, tossed the pad and bag down, and rolled in for a nap.

When I sat up three hours later, the sun showed no pity. The north wind kept the mosquitoes at bay. Although I was groggy, cold spray from breaking waves alleviated most of that problem as I set forth into the whitecaps. The going was slow as I bounced north across Royal Lake. At its end, the water turned into a winding swampy river, offering welcome protection from the wind. On one of the bends, a boat was pulled into the weeds. Passing closely revealed clothes, fishing gear, and food inside. High on a faraway bluff were its owners. Two tiny figures were undoubtedly waiting for some type of big game to show beneath them. They had a commanding view of the surrounding territory for after paddling two hours, I could still see them at their post.

By the time I had reached Devils Rapids, the sun had crept behind the trees. I hovered below an island near the rapids' center, studying them. Water poured through on both sides of the island. Sheer rocks topped with scraggly pines lined both sides. Since the chute on the left seemed less precarious, I gave it a try. It was full steam, straight up the middle of the deluge. Then it was stopped dead, turned sideways, and thrust into a whirlpool. I dropped to my knees for stability, not prayer. It was time to study the other side.

It flowed fast, but if I could advance ten feet and cross twenty feet to a small pool, my chances of success were somewhat assured. Just as I had reached into the depths of my motivation, a motorboat pulled behind me. "Want some help upstream?" an occupant shouted. It was the two dots on the bluff.

"No, I think I'll try this side first. I already tried the other side and it was a bit too hard," I said.

"That's really fast, rough water you're going against," one of the men said. Inquiring about a portage, I learned that it started about a mile downstream. Standing now, the man explained to me exactly how he thought I should go about this. Pointing, he said, "You just back up, get a good start, and shoot right across to that pool there." "You just" are a funny two words when they pertain to someone else. I decided to try it since both of us couldn't be wrong.

Maneuvering to the calm behind the island, I dug in and gave it my all. The bow bounced into the rolling current and I heard, "Now, now! Paddle hard, real hard!" Keeping the bow pointed as straight into the onslaught as I could, the canoe still slammed into the adjacent rock wall with a jolting thud. Frantically finding a crevice in the rock face, I jammed the paddle into it and shoved with the muscles of many miles.

In one big thrust the canoe glided into the calm pool above. Both men were laughing and cheering. One was standing up clapping. I don't believe either expected me to make it. Soaring up the other side of the island, they waved in passing. Both were still laughing. Having bypassed the hurdle was enough. I made camp for the night.

The following day was August 3rd. It took all morning to reach Whitesand Dam. The quarter-mile portage around it was steep. I got to the top and who was there but John and Tory. "We're taking the day off here," John explained. The three of us sat around talking when two kids, loaded to the hilt, appeared at the end of the portage. They saw the three bearded white men and froze, afraid to approach closer.

For ten full minutes, they stood holding their gear, wide-eyed and confused before their father approached from behind. Ushering them to the end of the portage, he set his pack down and twenty horse outboard motor, then introduced himself as John. The man following him was Daniel. "There's the guy we showed how to get around the rapids," New John said motioning toward me, making no effort to suppress a laugh. Daniel spoke little English and only grunted in agreement occasionally. "Out moose hunting two weeks now and going back to Southend with nothing," he continued.

As load after load came over the portage, sweat dripped off John. Behind him came the two smaller kids and his wife, followed by a grown Saint Bernard, and Daniel muttering the few English words he knew. Lastly came the grandmother. Shuffling slowly, her back was bent while her gnarled hand wrapped around the top of a wooden cane. With an old, red scarf pulling back her white hair, a wrinkled face of many years was revealed. New John sat on the ground and announced, "Now only for that big boat."

Looking at Old John, I said, "Looks like he could use some help." While he agreed, Tory stayed behind, claiming barefoot feet.

The old, wide, canvas-covered behemoth was twenty-feet from bow to stern. John and I grabbed the front, Daniel and his father handled the rear. Halfway up the hill, New John called for a halt. "Daniel needs a rest," he proclaimed while wiping sweat off his brow. Leaning against the heavy-hulled ship, we all waited for the signal. The rest was brief. Meanwhile, Tory stood to the side taking pictures as we carried the craft to the water's edge. With the task complete, I wondered how it was usually accomplished.

New John was ready to leave. Now it was Daniel's turn to fume at his canine companion. He tugged, jerked, and kicked, but his Saint Bernard didn't feel up to another crowded boat ride. "You should have listened to me and shot that dog two years ago," John scolded impatiently. After much pulling, lifting, and short Cree phrases punctuated with English profanities, Daniel managed to get the dog aboard single-handed. With that accomplished, he jumped over the side to hold the boat steady while his elder affixed the engine. John stood on a "damn rock" that threatened the integrity of the canvas on his boat as he tightened the screws that held the engine to the transom.

"Now what would you do if that damn rock wasn't there?" I asked New John.

He thought for a few seconds and with new respect, laughingly said, "I'd get my boots full of water."

New John finally got everyone seated, squeezed in among their pile of gear. A sharp pull on the recoil starter brought the engine to life. With a huge smile and a wave, John twisted the throttle. The boat moved not ten feet and the engine died. "Son of a bitch," was all we heard as the starter was pulled until the engine responded. Again, there was a big smile and a wave as they headed for Southend. At full power, the bow never rose. I left shortly after, occasionally seeing the sun reflect off their boat. Before long, they were just a dot on the water.

By ten o'clock the next morning, I stood on the dock in New John's hometown, Southend. A small white community hall and half a dozen houses stood between the dock and the store. At the third house, a man stood in the front yard, balancing himself with one hand against the wall, urinating. He saw me coming and he walked over, pulling up his fly. He was in whiskey wonderland. "Hi, I'm David," he said with a slur and held out his hand. There was still an unmistakable drop of yellow liquid on a fingertip. I declined the handshake, saying I was in a hurry to get to the store. He followed me down the dirt road shouting accusations to the effect that I was a white man and too good to shake his hand.

The store was crowded with kids, inside and out. It seemed that each had a Coke or candy bar in hand. I purchased a few necessities and returned to the canoe, conscious of the many stares I received in the small, isolated community.

"Fresh eggs are coming in this afternoon," I announced to John and Tory as they pulled onto the beach twenty minutes after I did. John jumped out without acknowledging me and frantically searched through a pack, shuffling from one foot to the other. Toilet paper in hand, he anxiously scanned his surroundings. Spying a clump of trees behind the community center, he was off at a trot.

All he said waddling past was a muttering of "Jesus" under his breath. *Must have had raspberry pie again last night!* He could have at least said hi.

While waiting for the eggs, I questioned the locals about the Swan River, my intended route. Their responses weren't promising.

The opinions were universally something to the effect of, "Nobody goes there, real bad place, nobody goes there."

I'd heard enough. Fresh eggs weren't enough to keep me in Southend. I hadn't had them all summer, and I didn't need them now. Sitting in the shade on the back steps of the community center, John was reading a letter from home. Tory was stretched out in the sun on the grass, popping grapes in his mouth. "Enjoy your fresh eggs!" I shouted as I backed the canoe off the beach and headed north on Reindeer Lake.

Five hours later I floated in front of a sand beach with a rustic sign pounded into the sand. On it in bold yellow letters was stated TROUT CAMP. A man came down from one of the buildings just as I was about to leave. "What can I do for you?" he asked pleasantly. I explained I was just passing through and wondered what all the buildings were. "Well, I'll explain, but you might as well come up and have some coffee then, too," he offered. I got out, tied Vagabond to the thwart, and followed him to the cabin. Vagabond and a malamute were already getting to know each other.

"I'm Keith and this is my wife Mary," he said as we took seats around the kitchen table. They asked of my comings and goings, and he eventually turned to his wife and requested, "Mary, why don't you go and fix this man some supper?" She went into the kitchen as Keith continued, "A few hours earlier and you would have had fried chicken." About then, a man came into the room. He was introduced as a guide of their company and a furniture maker, to boot. He showed me one of the chairs he made with only an ax and a pocketknife. It was impressive.

"Seventy-five last year I made and fifty so far this year," he said proudly. Mary returned with a plate of two hamburgers, beans, potato salad, olives, and buttered bread. The chair inspection took a back seat to Mary's creation. It was impressive.

After supper, Keith got up and came back with a bottle of beer. "Thought I saw one stuck way back in the refrigerator," he said as he placed it in front of me. "Looks like you got the last one."

Before I got up to leave, we had discussed everything from here to New Orleans. It was almost ten o'clock when Keith brought out a huge map of Reindeer Lake. His finger traced Swan River. "That is a very tough row to hoe," he warned. "I don't know anyone from around here that goes in there during the summer."

As he walked me to the canoe, I asked him about a bunch of dogs I had seen on an island that day. "Watch out where you camp," he said. "They belong to a trapper and they're loose and mean when they're hungry, which is most of the time. They'd tear your camp apart pretty quick." It seemed like a reasonable thing to remember.

After circling a small island, now paranoid of ravaging dogs, John and Tory overtook me. Hearing about the great meal I had at Trout Camp, they had to one-up me. "Well, we had pork chops for supper with two of the nurses in Southend in their trailer," Tory gloated.

"I had a beer at Trout Camp," I said in retaliation. "The guy even gave me his last one."

"That's nothing," John said to balance the events, "he gave us his last two!" We laughed, and John said something about having to make some miles before winter; they pulled away. It was the last time I saw John and Tory.

Northern Pike, called Jackfish in Canada, are generally used as dog food. This one was shared.

The northern pike fishing on Reindeer Lake was excellent. Many 10- to 15-pounders were released the next few days. By midday, a southern breeze had developed. Ducking behind an island, I took out the tripod for my camera. Pulling two legs to full length, I turned it upside down and lashed it to the center of the yoke. The tent fly was then tied from the corner of one extended leg to the other. The bottom corners were fastened to the gunwales leaving enough slack to billow with the wind. Moving from behind the island, the sail immediately filled and away I went, faster than need be. A problem arose almost instantly. I couldn't see unless I stood up. I knew this was not going to work for long, but it was an experiment. It worked, and I'd perfect it later.

Rain set in for a week. In the seven rain-filled days and nights, I was able to reach Thompson Island, which lay completely burned. Between there and the forty miles to Swan River, there was an old cabin, tucked away on the backside of an island. As I passed, a strange feeling of sadness or perhaps pity for whoever lived there so long ago, so far away from anything, came upon me. It appeared so old, so useless, and so alone in its overgrown field. The old house beckoned me to stop. But then just as it had come, the strange feeling passed. This place was lonesome, and I was motivated. Turning my attention to what lay ahead, I fell again into steady rhythmic strokes, broken only twice with glances over my right shoulder.

Swan Bay looked like a thousand other bays on Reindeer Lake. I found it anyways. Camping at the mouth of Swan River gave me one last chance to change my route. Lake Athabasca could also be reached by a more northerly path, but I remembered that "nobody goes there" line that held a certain appeal to me.

Before darkness, I had time to pick blueberries. Greasing a pan, I lined it with dough. Into this went alternating layers of blueberries and sugar topped with thin dough saturated in butter. The edge around the rim was pinched and the top of the Dutch oven was put in place. Encased in coals, it was put off to the side to bake while I ate my usual supper of fish and fried potatoes.

The sweet odor of blueberry pie soon rose from the covered pan. Removing the lid revealed a golden-brown crust. With a dry pine twig, I gave it a poke. A stream of steam billowed, indicating that it was done. Setting it aside to cool, I brought out the map to the Swan River.

It didn't look bad on paper, a fairly straight shot and only 15 miles to Swan Lake. No rapids were shown, but that did little to stifle the planted seed of warning. Putting the map away, I placed half of the pie on a plate. It didn't have to be poured out. *Now that's what I call a pie,* I quoted smugly, *eat your heart out, Tory, wherever you are.*

It didn't take long to understand the river's reputation after I tried to portage the first set of rapids. It was useless as the surrounding land was choked with thick willows. Dragging the canoe around and over rocks was the only alternative. Traces of green paint were evident on some of the rocks at first, but above these traces there was no sign of humanity. It appeared John and Tory took one brief look at the Swan River and opted for the more northern route.

My feet ached from walking on slippery rocks. Twelve straight hours was enough. Swan Lake was nowhere in sight. I made my way up the bank and set up camp in a mosquito-infested muskeg swamp. The canoe was taking a beating. Two inches of water sloshed inside. Being tired enough to just sit after the twelve-hour campaign, there was little desire to start a fire and fix supper. The other half of the blueberry pie would do. It was stashed under the seat in a covered pan. When pulling the bow onto the bank, the invading water rushed to the stern. I watched in dread as the water immediately bloomed purple. To the rescue, I was too late. Removing the pan's cover revealed a toxic-looking blueberry soup. Sitting on the gunwale, batting hungry mosquitoes in the coming darkness, and being soaked to the waist, I drank the blueberry pie. It was little reward for a long, hard day.

Finishing the soggy crust, I studied the food pack. It was a good indication that it was getting light when you knew exactly what was in it and exactly how long it would last. There were three days' worth of flour, three pounds of oats, and four potatoes. There were many days until the next village.

Examining the map again over my morning rations of oats, I looked for some solace. There was none, and I willed the upper part of the river to relent but knew it wouldn't. It showed as a thin line meandering through swamps and eskers. I couldn't stew over it. First, I had to conquer the lower Swan River and get to Swan Lake.

Swan River. The locals say nobody goes there. I found out why!

Cold water filled my boots. *What a way to start a day.* I took my now familiar place in front of the bow and started walking and pulling, pulling and walking. In three hours I was there. It wasn't so bad, 15 hours of traveling at one mile an hour.

As I stood looking over the lake, there were no mosquitoes, forty mile-per-hour winds kept them at bay and churned the water. The small size of the lake kept the whitecaps short and choppy. I battled them for two hours to reach a small island where I planned to wait for calmer weather. As I unloaded the canoe, I recognized something was missing. It was the life jacket I had recently obtained in Southend. No doubt it dangled from a willow branch somewhere along the lower Swan River. There was also no doubt it was going to stay there. This wasn't a two-forward and one-back kind of country.

After a restful afternoon and a good night's sleep, I was ready to go. Heading for the upper Swan River, the canoe slid across the glassy lake, parting a low, clinging mist. It soon dissipated in the morning sun to reveal a clear calm day. The map showed the upper Swan River to be approximately twenty miles long, ending at Mullins Lake. There were long-walked, rough rapids but enough level, low-current stretches between them to justify the effort.

By early afternoon I came to a small lake paralleling the river. Following a short channel, I paddled to one end of the lake and let the wind blow me to the other, hoping to replenish my food supply. The large pond seemed void of fish, so I landed on a white sand beach enclosed in towering pines. It was at the foot of an esker, a beautiful, lonely spot. After a light lunch, Vagabond and I took a swim, the former reluctantly. After drying, I set out to pick blueberries. I'd pick a bunch, put them in the pail, and then take a few steps to another spot. Turning to empty a handful of berries, nothing remained in the pail but a deep blue stain. I had been robbed again. Vagabond lay nearby, nonchalant, eyes averted, purple drool dripping from his mouth. After a short discussion, he decided to pick his own.

With the berry pail full, I climbed the esker and followed a well-defined game trail across its top for two hours. Vagabond scouted ahead chasing anything that moved. I followed with the .30-06 and camera. The trail wound between two crystal clear lakes, 100 feet below. Chances were good that they had seen neither rod and reel.

As if things weren't hard enough, I decided to struggle that water-logged canoe onto my back. I went up the esker with it, followed its top for a half-mile, and then at a precarious angle, pushed through thick brush 100 feet down to the lake. I entered the water with great expectations of hooking a monster.

There was no monster; there was nothing. It was as shallow in the middle as it was at the shoreline. There was no inlet or outlet. It was a lens in the muskeg. In winter, it would freeze to the bottom, rendering it incapable of sustaining a fish population. Since this and the Swan River seemed to be devoid of fish, I longed for one of those huge northern fillets that were caught and released on Reindeer Lake. I also longed for the Swan River. Now I had to get back there.

Getting from the lake to the top of the esker was a major chore. The canoe rocked on my shoulders as I grasped willow shoots and thrust myself upward. It was slow, and I vowed to myself to always fish these out-of-the-way lakes from shore.

It was five o'clock before I completed the return journey. There was no reason to leave a campsite such as this so late. After supper I paddled around the small lake a few times, casting a red and white daredevil. Then the seemingly devoid Swan River produced two small northern pike. Both were a foot long, and my thumb and middle finger could encircle their girth. Even though they were pitiful, when boiled, Vagabond enjoyed them immensely.

The next morning I was off to an early start to cover the last ten miles to Mullen Lake. I felt that if I laid the fishing pole down, without touching it all day, there was no reason I couldn't reach the lake by evening. The Swan River held to form, as rapids after rapids flowed through mosquito-infested swamps. Hemmed in by thick willows, I could hear the bottom of the canoe being shredded. I frequently had to unload the canoe, pull it over unrelenting rocks, and then go back for the gear.

Vagabond didn't help matters. Struggling up the rapids, weaving between rocks, working for every inch, twice I looked back to see him sitting on a rock in the middle of the rapids, high and dry, watching me. I apparently had more concern for him than for the deserted life jacket, as I would secure the canoe, trudge all the way back and then retrace my steps with him under my arm. After the second incident, he was leashed to the thwart.

At times I would stumble into fast water up to my chest, grasping overgrown willows with one hand and pulling the canoe forward with the other. Other times I would lay poles over sharp rocks, providing a bumper over which to drag the canoe. A three-foot falls was exceptionally hard on the damaged craft, but I was ruthless in my pursuit of success.

Then came the beaver dams, one after another, after another. To pass them I had to stand on top of each dam and pull the bow up with a rope. I would then pull it forward until it sat precariously balanced. While it would attempt to slide backwards down the dam, I'd go to the stern and bail as much water as possible, then came the hard part. I would lift the entire back half of the canoe onto my shoulder, and once there, start shimmying it forward. A few different times I lost control of the canoe and let it slide off the dam.

More than once my spirits would lift as the river widened, making me think I was close to Mullen Lake. Shortly, there would be another beaver dam. I went over logs and under deadfalls. The feeling of misdirection teased my mind as I had been battling now for 16 hours and should have made the ten miles to the lake. All I could do was keep going, *as if I had a choice.*

Finally, I came to a high bank in the flat muskeg and decided to spend the night there. My back ached, and my stomach muscles throbbed due to the unconventional means of portaging the many beaver dams. I felt weary as I slid the tent pegs into the soft earth. Vagabond went off on a run as four grouse rose behind the tent. For his efforts, he was tied to a tree while I got the .30-06. I was in no mood to play around with the slingshot.

Supper was filling: grouse, one potato, a chunk of bannock, and blueberries. Sitting against a tree, I looked over the swamp. Little remained of the brilliant red sunset and the fire was a bowl of red embers. Vagabond lay contentedly chewing the remains of three grouse. It had been a very long day, and it took a lot out of me. I knew traveling this hard on this diet would run me into the ground. I just didn't know how long there was left of the Swan River. Rising with stiffness, I kicked dirt over the fire and crawled inside the tent.

I slept later than usual. Sore muscles were made loose again battling rapids, logs, and beaver dams. The canoe leaked badly. Since there were more rips than holes, a bailing session was necessary every twenty minutes. Some tears measured five-feet long. I could see no reason to try to fix them until reaching Mullen Lake.

As I neared its head, the river narrowed to a few feet, and ran fast and deep. At times I didn't think the canoe would squeeze by. Willows flogged my back as they crisscrossed like a spider web over the narrow channel. Chunks had to be sawed out of many deadfalls at least the width of the canoe to provide passage. Of course, there were also mosquitoes, hordes of them.

Blueberries, fish, and grouse became my summer staples.

Finally, the country started to open up. I knew the lake couldn't be far. I continued in waning but sure faith. My legs, from knees to ankles, were scraped and bruised from falling, stepping into deep rocky holes, and banging against fallen trees. It took still two more hours to reach Mullen Lake. It was a welcome sight. The last ten miles of the upper Swan River took 25 hours to navigate. For all my bullheadedness, I now understood. Just ask any Native in Southend. They won't tell you why, they'll just tell you "nobody goes there."

It was late when I left the outlet of Swan River, destined for an island a mile away. It took more than an hour to reach due to the cycle of bailing and paddling. Because the small island was covered with head-sized rocks, I had to rearrange them to establish a tent site. The wind had increased, and the smell of rain was close. I sat on the rocks rubbing Unguentine Ointment into my abused shins, studying a large, rotted tree directly behind the tent and hoping it wouldn't blow over tonight. Half of it was already lying on the island. Besides the round rocks, it was the only thing on this tiny island. I had pushed on it earlier and it seemed sturdy, but I had no trust in the limbless killer as it swayed ominously with the wind. Although I contemplated sawing it down, a heavy rain drove me inside before the idea could be acted upon.

Half-dreaming of being pinned beneath the tree, whittling an escape with my Buck knife, I sat upright with each loud, crack. More than once I peered out, eyeing the wooden sentry in the beam of the flashlight, predicting which way it would fall. Though each time reassured, sleep came sporadically.

Lightning strikes also crossed my mind. Being in the middle of a lake with that finger of death pointed into the heavens, lightning was probably the reason for its demise. During the night, the stopping of the rain relieved some of my anxiety. The wind was not as merciful.

I spent the next day on the island; the canoe needed fixing. Finally rolled over for inspection, it was a mess. Long jagged tears in the fiberglass peered back at me. But the biggest problem in fixing the fiberglass would be my lack of hardening compound. Desperately I squeezed the last drops into a can of resin. After mixing, it was applied to the worst damage and pre-cut patches of fiberglass cloth were smoothed over it. It was an ugly puzzle, but when finished, I was satisfied, considering the circumstances.

I wonder what's here; I explored while the patches dried. I was back within minutes. The fiberglass patches were checked after one hour, then two, then three. They weren't drying. It appeared the small amount of hardener was insufficient to create the needed reaction with the resin.

By morning, nothing had changed. The patches were as wet as

when they were applied. It was disappointing but would have to manage. Breakfast was a piece of fish. After consulting the map, I paddled to the shortest distance of land between Mullen Lake and Cains Lake. There was no trail, no portage, no reason for one.

A mile of tree-studded watery swamp separated the two lakes. It housed unlimited, featherless, small flying creatures. The packs were bad, but the canoe was most arduous. From being unrelentingly abused, the ribs and planking were saturated. It was about as heavy as it could get—my guess, 150 pounds, minimum. My fish diet didn't help matters. It seemed the lean meat was causing a variation of rabbit starvation due to my lack of other nutrients and variety.

Twice on the portage, my legs vanished in mud up to the crotch. Severely imbalanced, the canoe would follow gravity, nearly taking the side of my head with it. My legs didn't come out easily as the swamp compacted around it. When they did, they were soaked, black, and putrid; it was an odor not easily lost once caught.

It took four hours to portage the swamp into Cains Lake. Though my boots were soaked, I felt lucky not to have left one at the bottom of a sinkhole. If I had been wearing rubber slip-ons, there is no doubt I would now be barefoot. It had taken its toll on me. As I lay back looking at the sky on a small bluff overlooking Cain's Lake, my pants and boots reeked of swamp gas. An escalating wind could be heard through the pines. Through slit eyes, I could see them coming, black ugly clouds from the west. Soon lightning cracked across the lake as it boiled into whitecaps. It hit with a fury, a hard-pelting windblown rain. I didn't even move, staying spread eagled for what seemed like hours in the onslaught. After a full-clothed dunk to remove the swamp from my attire, I spent the night on the bluff.

Morning found me at the south end of Cain's Lake searching for a small creek. The map showed it flowed almost two miles into another small lake. From there it would be a short quarter-mile portage into Wollaston Lake. Miles and miles up the lake was food at Wollaston Post.

I found the creek. It made upper Swan River look good. There wasn't enough water to float the canoe, and as far as I could see, deadfalls clogged what little water there was. Still, I had to be sure. I made it 100 yards and came back running. Black flies attacked in swarms and unlike the fish, they were biting. Arms flailing, I fled to the canoe.

Vagabond was in terrible shape, too. He rubbed his paws over his eyes trying to relieve the plague that had descended upon him. The flesh around his eyes was bloody and swollen while his nose was bitten raw. Grabbing the canoe in stride, I headed for open water and relief. It only came when a light breeze forced them back to shore. Obviously, this was not going to be a pleasant portage.

I chose to chart a new portage where the map's contour lines were the closest together hoping the high ground would be drier and the black flies would be less competitive. Many are the times that man's hopes don't materialize. I came to accept this as I stood looking at the beginning of a three-mile route to Wollaston Lake. There was a steady incline that looked like a mountain of black pickup sticks. The endless carnage was the results of a major forest fire. Little was left standing. Above this black maze hung a hazy, gray cloud. It swirled like the Northern Lights and hummed like a Tibetan monk. They lay waiting.

I set a course toward the northwest. Two pairs of pants were mandatory along with heavy socks, a coat, and gloves. A stocking cap was pulled over my head as far as possible. With an ax I weaved through the maze, somewhat clearing a trail, blazing the few black trees left standing. The black flies were very proficient. An open mouth invited a coughing spasm as the dry devils lodged deep in the throat. Cutters and Deep Woods Off helped little as the miniature adversaries infiltrated my eyes, nose, and ears. One hand had to be constantly free to fan the face. This went on for hours until I had blazed the three-mile trail to Wollaston Lake. I didn't linger. It was back to the canoe, relief, and last night's camp.

Morning fog still clung to shadowed places when I reached the small bay where the trail started. I was saturated in insect repellent, and my stomach was protesting the breakfast of blueberries. The food box was again empty; better for portaging an optimist might say. I split the gear into loads for two quick trips instead of one heavy, slow one. I willed myself forward until the gear was at Wollaston Lake. It was over, back over, and back, covering the twelve miles in four hours.

Physically drained, I was drenched with sweat from walking with so much protective clothing. The clouds of black flies followed me everywhere; there was no escape. Searching for the positive, I looked no farther than the blueberries. In places, they lay like grapes in a vineyard, thanks to the forest fire. I didn't know how many more of them I could eat, but with a full bowl in my lap, I ate, tried to rest, and continued to eat. Then came the canoe.

The first half-mile was swamp with a few dwarfed pines. The walking was unyielding as my feet slid between the hummocks, helped by the oppressive weight on my shoulders. I forced my way to the burned area. After the canoe had been driven into my shoulders for more than an hour, I reached the scorched earth and jammed the bow between two narrowly spaced blackened trees for a rest. One fell over and the canoe hit the ground. With a sigh, I just stood looking at it while being bombarded with black flies. It was a gruesome state. What could possibly justify their existence but to torture some unfortunate victim? Even under the canoe, they would congregate in such numbers as to create a high decibel drone; they continued to bombard from every angle. It has been said that they have driven men mad. I cannot contest that.

After a short nap, I groggily grabbed the gunwale, lifting the canoe to my knees. Trying to roll it onto my shoulders, I couldn't find the strength. A second attempt failed. I sat down for a short rest, collecting my thoughts. *This has to be done,* I told myself, *you've done it hundreds of times before.* Another attempt was successful but just barely. Extending despite the weight, I moved wearily forward.

It got worse. The amount of time I could keep the craft on my bare-boned shoulders grew progressively shorter. The yoke dug in with an awful vengeance. Tree over black-fallen tree I hurdled. The higher they lay, the worse they were. Time crawled. I forced myself to last seven minutes at a go. With nothing on which to rest the canoe, each time it was dumped, I had grave doubts I would get it back up again. Never was it rolled up on the first attempt and seldom on the second. So, it went for four hours.

I collapsed in the moss at the edge of Wollaston Lake. *God, I'm tired.* I was tired from the portage. Tired from the flies. And tired from malnutrition. I just lay there dreaming of things I'd buy at Wollaston Post; ice cream, chocolate chip cookies, steak, cucumbers, radishes, caramels, the list was endless. Vagabond lay beside me twitching, dreaming his own dreams, probably of bones and bitches. I don't know how long I lay there, but it was long enough that the swamp had soaked through to my back. Yet, I still needed to find a place to spend the night, preferably where there was no soot, swamps, or swarms. Reluctantly I loaded the canoe and pushed off into Wollaston Lake.

It was two hours before I found a spot below rock cliffs in a small patch of scrub pines. With a piece of cold fish in hand, I sat in a blueberry patch and had supper. Too tired to raise the tent, I dragged my bag beneath a small rock ledge, laid it on a thick blanket of moss, pulled it over my head, and slept.

For 13 hours I did not stir. When I did, I was activated in slow motion. I put on a pair of warm, dry, wool socks. It was the first time my feet were dry since being introduced to the Swan River nine days ago, which meant nine days to travel thirty miles. But I became a better person for it. Consequently, I don't tell people to go to hell anymore; I tell them to go to Swan River.

Freeze-Up

The pendulum swung. A light wind was at my back and I set sail. Though bailing constantly, the breeze pushed me 25 miles. Vagabond even seemed to enjoy it as he lay high and dry on a log platform erected especially for him. It was bug-free for now, though many bites were scratched into bloody scabs.

After six hours, I passed a camp tucked into the end of a bay. Smoke rose from one of the five tents. Well past the camp, sailing northward, I heard someone yell. I looked back and could see three men motioning for me to come back. One pinpointed me through a pair of binoculars. Thinking they needed help, I collapsed the sail and turned back into the wind.

Soon one left in a motorized canoe so I saved my strength and waited. Within minutes we drifted gunwale to gunwale. There was an invitation to supper and a cot for sleeping. They were having steak and he mentioned the cot had a mattress on it. How could I be tortured so? I could almost taste the steak. I wondered if they had ketchup. My mind seesawed as the tailwind blew and I wanted to get to Wollaston Post. The matter was settled when he mentioned they had been wind-bound for the last five days. With a pang of regret, I declined dinner, thanking him for the offer. The sail was reset, and teeth were clenched until enough miles passed to eradicate any option of heading back south.

I made it ten miles closer to Wollaston Post. The wind died as the day darkened. For supper, I sat leaning against a tree popping bite-sized pieces of ketchup-dipped steak into my mouth. It was just more blueberries and dry baked fish, but in my delirium, I could have been tricked. I ate my fill and went to bed.

Relaxing after a twenty-hour day on Wollaston Lake, Canada.

The sun was nowhere near rising when I left the following morning. The wind had done a turnabout and already pushed whitecaps across the water. The closer I got to Wollaston Post, the worse it became. The canoe was really bobbing, but the only way I wasn't going to get there was if I swamped. When the shoreline turned to litter, I knew it couldn't be much farther. Rounding a windblown point, I looked to the end of a small, calm bay. There stood Wollaston Post.

Boats were tied along the dock. A film of gas and oil covering the water released a pungent odor. Maneuvering past the dock onto the muddy shoreline, I walked uphill past a pile of oil drums, skirted a stack of telephone poles, and entered the local store.

It was small and ill stocked. There was no hardware, nothing to repair the canoe, not even duct tape. A Bee Gees album played over the PA. I knew better than to shop on an empty stomach and I was highly qualified for that description. So, for $4.80 I bought a pint of strawberry revel ice cream, a package of six pecan rolls, and a pound of butter. With these, I returned to the canoe to formulate a list fit for a king.

Sitting on a rusted oil drum, I buttered a pecan roll. When I bit into it, the parched white frosting cracked, and dry crumbs rolled to my lap. Turning it over revealed hairy, green mold clinging to the

200

bottom. Scraping it off, I added more butter, and then washed it down with strawberry revel ice cream.

While force-feeding myself I watched a young girl with a coffee pot walk to the end of the dock. She fluttered the top of the water with a hand to form an opening in the film of oil and dunked the pot. Holding it with both hands, she retraced her steps. *What a breakfast, moldy rolls and oily coffee.* Throwing the near-empty ice cream carton and three rolls to Vagabond, I went shopping.

The same music played as I took one of the six carts and guided it through the small store. The dreams I had on the shore of Wollaston Lake slowly vanished. At the checkout line before me stood ten pounds of oats, ten pounds of potatoes, two cartons of eggs, five pounds of sugar, 25 pounds of flour, a small block of cheese, and a bag of chocolate chips. There was not much for frills, but for where I was, what could I expect? There would be no more dreams.

While a lady bagged the basics, I talked to the manager about getting something to repair the canoe. "I think you might be out of luck," he said, "unless Bill Bends has some left from fiberglassing his boat last fall." Bill lived on the other side of the bay. I packed my groceries and was off to find Bill Bends.

He was AWOL. I sat in the canoe holding onto their dock while talking to his teenage son, explaining my predicament. Vagabond was anxiously trying to get out and see what their strange-looking goats would do when he chased them. Bill's son said that all they had left were a few pieces of cloth, and I was welcome to them. Cloth was not the problem. I needed the resin and hardener. I graciously declined his offer and was on my way.

At the end of the bay, a gale wind blew, sending spray high off a rocky point. I went as far as possible and set up camp. There was garbage everywhere. To make matters worse, every half hour a large boat would stop 100 yards offshore, near the mouth of the bay. Barrel after barrel of debris was dumped into the water and quickly came ashore with the wind. It contained mostly fish entrails and bones. It stank like hell. I walked the shoreline a short way, and found it covered everything. Obviously, that was where their garbage also ended up as cans and bottles littered the shore. Among all this were hundreds of seagulls, many too fat to fly.

I set up camp well inland. A steady drizzle fell most of the day as I took apart my dilapidated, plywood food box and reinforced it with one-by-two-foot strips ripped from discarded fish boxes. With the task completed, I sat next to the fire, watching a three-pound chocolate chip cookie bake. What an aroma to have to share with garbage and guts!

Sleep came hard as Vagabond set up a constant vigilance, warning me of every creature that came for the free feed. With little sleep, I left early and traveled all day. Another six hours brought me to Snowshoe Island at the north end of Wollaston Lake, just ten miles from the mouth of the Fond Du Lac River. I needed a break after the Swan River episode and decided to spend a day on the island. Besides, it was raining, I was dry, and intended to stay that way.

I did nothing but read all day and sleep all night. There were no pangs of guilt. The following dawn was colder than usual, so I pulled the sleeping bag over my head for extra warmth and slept a few more hours. Daylight revealed a drooping tent. I unzipped the door and peered out. Everything was covered with snow. It was only the 27th of August. Clad in Fruit of the Looms, I slipped on my boots and dashed to the canoe. Out came the wool pants, wool shirt, gloves, and hat. With the dash back to the tent, I felt the excitement of the first snowfall, the changing of the seasons, and the goosebumps.

I broke camp with new zeal. I was rested, and the world felt fresh. Already the morning sun was turning the early snow into slush. A few lingering bits clung to shadowed places in the canoe, but soon they would join the water sloshing in the bottom. The ten-mile dash to the Fond Du Lac River seemed effortless. Drifting at its mouth, I studied its intricacies on the map. There appeared to be many rapids, which translated into many portages with the heavy canoe. But I wouldn't want it any other way. I was going downstream.

The days grew easy, shooting many minor rapids and making quick miles with the current. On two occasions, I took healthy sprays in the face. The water ran down the front of me and entered the garbage bags inside my boots that were supposed to keep my feet dry.

140 miles from the village of Stoney Rapids I stopped early, two hours before sunset. For supper, I fried fish in an unaccustomed way, with butter. It was a luxury, as were the trout that were browning.

Tea and cold trout were breakfast at 5:00 A.M. It looked to be a sunny day as I shook frost off the tent and packed it. Not a cloud could be seen in the deep blue sky. Only a few diehard mosquitoes ventured into the chill, and it was a comfort knowing their days of domination were ending. The morning was spent gliding through some fast whitewater. By noon I stopped at two old cabins perched on a high bench. It looked as if neither had been used for some time. Six small dog houses lay to one side. Sloping toward the river were piles of moose and caribou antlers weathered white by many summer suns. After lunch on a doghouse, I was at the first portage of the Fond Du Lac River by midday.

The portage was easily spotted by the well-worn trail that wound beside the rocky rapids. The sun had vanished, replaced by high gray clouds. My strength was returning post-Swan River; I hoisted the canoe on the first try but rolling it onto my shoulders was still an effort. I changed into felt-lined Sorrel pack boots, as my hiking boots exhausted their usefulness. Tying the laces of the Red Wings together, I hung them over a limb at the end of the portage thinking maybe someone would come along and find some use for them. The toes in both boots were worn through and keeping my feet dry was nearly impossible. $75 boots, *ha!* They didn't last one season.

Later that afternoon, I shot the Fleet Rapids and went over Redbank Falls. Although I expected to portage both, neither were very difficult; finding a place to camp was. Blackened trees and burned earth lay in all directions. It may have been a continuation of the Wollaston Lake fire, or it may have been caused by a separate lightning strike. Either way, the results were the same.

A flock of Canada geese flew overhead, belching arrhythmic calls to their navigator as he led them south on their yearly migration, the long *V*-formation deviating little. Trees had turned golden and frost coated the ground each morning. The seasons were in transition. I enjoyed the crisp, fall mornings. Just the smell in the air was rewarding. It made a person feel alive, energetic, and confident.

That's how I felt when I entered Thompson Rapids. It ended with an attitude adjustment. Normally I wouldn't have made the attempt, especially in the canoe's condition, but after a normal shoreline reconnaissance, my confidence was persuasive. A slight misjudgment of the current's strength meant that the canoe wasn't allowed to enter the rapids where it was optimal. Sucked in, I was facing ejection. All I could do was keep the craft straight and face the frightening facts. My stomach dropped and rebounded to expel the air from my lungs as I flew through a chute and dropped four feet. Water poured over the gunwales, and a whirlpool spun me around, spitting the canoe over a ledge sideways. Landing hard below the ledge, the downstream gunwale submerged and bobbed back up, pouring in more water. Vagabond didn't grasp the delicacy of the situation as he shot up, looking for an escape route. The canoe teetered with an inch of freeboard. I still felt alive, energetic, but with renewed confidence, angled toward shore.

Throwing the floating packs ashore, I bailed the canoe enough to roll it over. Repacked, it was an easy stretch of river to the next turbulence. The rumbling could be heard a long way away. It was Manitou Falls. The word *Manitou* in Cree means God. In mine, it means *portage*.

I pulled onto a flat rock above the falls. Vagabond jumped out and busied himself with old campfire tidbits. Walking to the edge of the falls revealed boiling water. I jumped across a five-foot chasm above for a better vantage. Vagabond recognized it was no place to slip and wanted nothing to do with the leap. The river poured into a rock cavern and disappeared until coming out at the bottom of the falls. In its innocence, it looked like a water slide at an amusement park. I am not that naive or adventurous.

It wasn't a long portage nor was it hard. Burned trees lay across the trail, but they posed no great obstacle. With the short jaunt finished, I left not knowing that this was only the upper part of the falls. It was a quick trip to the lower falls as the water between them moved at a rapid pace. Respecting its force, I stopped below a fifty-foot sandbank well before the rising mist. Getting everything to the top of the sand cliff was a chore, but once there it was an easy walk to the pools beneath the falls. I found that many grayling congregated there.

The following morning, I shot the Brinks and Brass Rapids, and then was helped by a tailwind down the 32 miles to Burr Falls. Playing it safe, I stopped early and looked for a portage but couldn't find one. The trail could have been on the other side of the falls, but from my vantage point I could see no portage landing. I walked to the bottom of the falls and saw no sign of a trail. So, over very high, very rocky, very rough terrain, I made one. It took four hours to transport everything across the tree-fallen, makeshift trace. When completed, the two hours before darkness allowed just enough time to reach the day's destination, Black Lake.

Arctic grayling provided many tasty meals along the cold northern waters.

Black Lake First Nation glistened in the morning sun as I landed next to a dock. The 15-mile paddle across Black Lake was a good early-morning stimulant. Wide awake, I walked into a small store and bought two cans of Coke. Two Natives lounging against the counter informed me I couldn't get to Stoney Rapids on the river. "You can try but nobody gonna see you no more," one of them said. Asked if he had ever been through there, he said, "I been here fifty years and don't know nobody who has." The store owner came in, and I squeezed what information I could out of him.

"I don't know," was the usual response though he strongly advised me to take a truck to Stoney Rapids. "That's the way everyone that comes through here goes. Nobody goes down that way," he warned. Those last five brutal words caught my attention. It was *déjà vu*.

You would think I would have listened. I found out quickly that since nobody went there, nobody had made portages. The first half-mile of my endeavor to portage followed a foot-wide, rock-strewn ledge below a large rock cliff. Well below flowed the river. It was a successful balancing act until my foot slipped.

To keep from catapulting, I dumped the canoe. It landed squarely on the side of my knee, rolled off, slid twenty feet, and came to rest against a pine tree. Lucky it didn't keep going. Even treating it gingerly, I could feel the swelling commence. Although knees aren't meant to have 150 pounds drop upon them, nothing seemed to be seriously damaged. Sliding to the canoe, I maneuvered it back onto my shoulders, limped up the slope, and continued along the ledge. I negotiated the pass and hobbled to the base of the first falls. Returning for the packs, the swelling slowed my time considerably. After I dropped the last pack next to the canoe, a good place was found to set up camp. There I could lick my wounds.

The bruise was nasty. I noted that it ran from knee to ankle as I nursed it in the morning light. As a result, my enthusiasm was low as I lined and portaged the mile and a half to Elizabeth Falls in eight hours. Needing to get the canoe beyond the falls before dark pumped a surge of adrenaline through my veins.

There was no scouting the trail. *Throw the canoe on your shoulders and start off.* It was steep and strewn with rocks, trees, and bushes. It was also three miles long, and it was dark when I tossed my opponent, the canoe, from my shoulders beneath Elizabeth Falls. I then had to return for my gear.

Zigzagging through the woods in daylight, over an uncharted three-mile route is one thing. Getting back in near-total darkness is another. I felt the urge to run, to finish ASAP, but knowing the consequences, I set a slow pace. Then it started to rain. Using a lighter, I followed its glow to a birch tree. I cut a stout branch, smoothed it, and whittled it to a point. Pulling loose birch bark off the tree, I skewered sections until there was enough packed bark nestled halfway-down on the stick. Pushing a piece back to the end of the branch, I lit it. The oil-rich bark flamed up, lighting my way. When a piece was close to extinguished or ready to fall off, another piece would be slid up to keep the torch lighted. When the pieces ran low, another tree was found, then another, and another. It took a long time to reach camp that night.

A strong wind whipped the rain all night and throughout the morning. When it slowed, I broke camp and brought the packs across the three miles to the canoe. With the gear again consolidated, I looked across a five-mile stretch of open water to the next rapids. The wind churned it white. It was a good time to pick blueberries.

I could tell that the berry harvest for this year was coming to a close as frost was beginning to take its toll on the crop. I finished last night's pickings for breakfast. The morning was clear, cool, and very windy. In a traveling disposition, I bucked the strong wind toward Woodcock Rapids, picking my way through the turbulent water, paddling and portaging when necessary. There was no sign of habitation. The water was fast and dangerous. By evening, one portage separated me from Stoney Lake.

The portage in the morning was hard, worse than any on this stretch from Black Lake. The canoe went first. It was a long, hard haul, but exited beneath a waterfall. I was rewarded with the sight of a dock. Limping to it, I set the canoe down and turned my attention to two cabins in the background. A motorboat was tied to the dock and smoke rose from one of the cabins. No one seemed to be around, so I sat down for a few minutes before returning for the packs.

"Where the hell did you come from?" asked one of the three men walking straight toward me from the smoking cabin. They didn't look friendly as they descended upon me.

"I'm just portaging through," I said.

"Nobody goes through here. I've never seen anyone do it. Never even expected anyone could do it!" one in a white t-shirt exclaimed. "I'm John Franey from New Brighton," he said extending his hand. "This is Jim, and this is Lee," he introduced his partners. Being friendlier than I thought, John offered, "Come on up and have some coffee." I managed to work the invitation into my schedule.

After two cups of Irish coffee, finishing their chocolate cake, and two hours of conversation, I excused myself to portage the packs. By then, both Jim and John lay flat on their beds, sick.

The packs took a few hours, but upon my return, I shared lunch with Lee. Jim and John were in the same condition. While eating, Lee stated that last year a 400,000-acre forest fire raged through this area. "Lucky we've still got the cabin," he said. It was a beautiful spot below the waterfalls, but everywhere a person looked across Stoney Lake was blackened. It had to be disheartening. It was early afternoon when I left, wishing John and Jim luck with their health. The village of Stoney Rapids lay past Stoney Lake, then a few miles down the Fond Du Lac River. It was a good place to finish for the day.

Seldom did it seem that the wind ever blew as the current flowed. It tried to hold me back for four hours until I reached the head of a two-mile-long section of rapids. At its end was the village. There was nothing that could be done there tonight. I set up camp and would face the rapids in the morning.

When morning arrived, Vagabond was gone. I walked a mile upstream to five old houses. No Vagabond. I walked the two miles to Stoney Rapids, combed every street, and walked back. No Vagabond. Checking the five old houses again produced nothing. The nine-mile hike with a sore knee before breakfast was not appreciated. With hostility focused on the dog, I packed the gear and shot the rapids.

The rapids were easy. The first stop was the store. Armed with two cans of Coke and three Hershey bars, I roamed the few streets looking for Vagabond. Few people ventured out this early; it was nine o'clock. Opening one of the candy bars, I was surprised to find that it was white chocolate. A bite revealed that it had merely reached its shelf life, scummy whiteness coated its exterior. Head back as I chased the ageless chocolate with Coke like it was medicine, who should trot down the road, dog on each side, contented as could be, but Vagabond. I could swear he was smiling. I wasn't. The harem faced instant dissolution as Vagabond was escorted to the canoe and detained.

With that problem finally resolved, it was time to return to the store and resupply the food box. There were no potatoes in the village, and the smallest sack of flour was 25 pounds. Fresh fruits or vegetables didn't exist. But, in the cart were six tubes of contact cement. With these, hopefully, the fiberglass cloth could be saturated and temporary hull patches fashioned.

I tried a small patch immediately. Drying for four hours, the results looked positive. With the rest of the glue, I patched what I could and returned to the store to see if there was anything I had missed. There was nothing.

Upon leaving the store, I was invited to a party. There was one stipulation; I would have to supply the beer. That involved chartering an airplane for $180 to fly to Uranium City to purchase it. That seemed like desperation drinking to me, and I politely declined.

At the canoe, the patches were dry and seemed to have potential. An airplane swooped low overhead and put down on the dirt runway. People seemed to attack it from every direction. Box after box was unloaded as people greedily grabbed what was theirs and dashed to the security of their homes. Me, I crossed the river for my own security.

I was at the store when they opened at 9:30 and monopolized the last twelve tubes of contact cement. Back across the river, I used them all. They lay drying in the warming sun as I leaned against a birch tree playing "Apache" on the guitar, wondering if Tory could follow it with his flute.

"Hello there" came a voice from the river, breaking my concentration. He had no motor and took me by surprise. After introducing himself, he said that he was out checking his fishnets. "Here, have these," he offered as he handed me two fresh trout and a bottle of beer. "We don't get much live music around here," he said while sitting back down in his old, weathered, rowboat. Grabbing his faded oars, he bid me a nice day and then crossed the river to town. It was the first and last time I was ever paid for my musical abilities. *How kind!* I don't know how long he had been sitting there. Maybe he just felt sorry for me.

Shortly after, disaster hit my insides. The *A, B, C, D*'s of suffering appeared: appetite loss, bad stomach cramps, chills, and diarrhea. It literally put me down. Pity was now bestowed upon John and Jim, who had been laid out flatter than fillets when I left two days ago.

I crawled out of the tent for the umpteenth time 24 hours later. It was noon. Two hours of travel the day before had been a struggle, so I pulled ashore to camp. I wearily set up the tent and fixed a meal, then crawled in. The next thing I knew the sun was shining. I didn't know if I slept two hours into evening or twelve into morning. Seeing the position of the sun, I found it was the latter.

The long rest regained much of my strength though motivation was lacking. I still had the chills, unable to get warm. It took eight cups of sugar-laced tea and hugging a roaring fire before I was ready. Then, I sentenced myself to eight straight no-nonsense hours of paddling before stopping for a quick afternoon lunch. While gathering firewood, I found two iron ax heads lying in the forest. They were still sharp and serviceable. Their presence baffled me, as they seemed unused. With hand-carved birch handles, they would split a lot of firewood this winter. I appreciated saving the few extra dollars they would have cost for my funds were fading fast.

Four more hours brought me to a vacated shack. It was a mess. It appeared a bear knocked in the door and rearranged the interior. Garbage and rusted tools were scattered everywhere. But the roof seemed sound and with some tinfoil and baling wire, the wood stove was made operational. The mattress on the wooden bunk had seen some hard living. Mice scurried in fear. It wasn't much, but it would keep me dry from the weather that had developed an hour ago.

It took time to get used to the pattering of tiny mice feet. Vagabond couldn't be kept inside, I'd never get any rest. Sleep finally came around midnight. I awoke with a jolt. The ground shook and a roaring rumble rolled through the cabin. Heart pounding, rifle in hand, I jumped off the old mattress and got outside before the place collapsed in the quake. What I saw was not expected. Thirty feet away was a tugboat under full power, pushing two barges, slowly struggling up this wilderness river to resupply the store at Stoney Rapids.

The trembling slowly faded, as did the rain. By morning only an increasing wind tarnished a glorious "second-summer" day. The wind seemed to want to hold me in check, and the current offered little resistance to it. I fought the headwind for two twelve-hour days before reaching another village. It was Fond Du Lac.

While sitting on the beach eating a sugar-filled supper, six Natives approached but held their distance. There was finger pointing at the canoe and much discussion in Cree before the group dissipated. One remained. He seemed to be the eldest, and he approached to shake hands. Shortly, he was relating his experiences and describing the area around Fond Du Lac. At his request, I produced a map, and he showed me all the places he'd been and all the places I shouldn't go, one being the stretch of falls and rapids between Black Lake First Nation and Stoney Lake. I didn't mention that I had just covered that stretch of water. He said he was waiting for two weeks until going to his trapping cabin for the winter.

He also spoke of the plight of Native heritage and lifestyle in the bush. "Forty years ago, no jobs in summer at all. Now plenty but nobody wants to work, too much welfare," he said. "I still trap. I have to," he added. "Still run dogs too. Got two Ski-Doos at home, but dogs don't need parts every week to run."

His eyes seemed to mist as he spoke of his 25-year old grandson. "Took him on the trapline for the first-time last winter. We stopped for tea and he tried to build fire out of green wood. He is 25 and can't even build fire." He spoke of his age and mentioned he was glad he wouldn't be around many more years to witness the plight of his people. He walked away as if the world weighed heavily upon him.

Seven hours downstream and I was on Lake Athabasca. It was impressive: extremely large and filled crystal clear, the shoreline was lined with gold as the white birch and poplar prepared to shed their leaves for another season. The fishing was great. Many trout were caught as I glided on fifty feet of invisible water. It almost produced vertigo seeing a trout straight below at the end of the line at such depths. Struggling through the clearness, most would be released as they broke the surface. Then, in the midst of this dream "the big one" hit.

Each time he went in the right direction, I would let him drag the canoe with. I released the drag on the reel, knowing this would be a long fight and he needed to tire out. Most of the line screamed out. I repeatedly pulled and reeled, only to lose all my efforts in a matter of seconds with each escape attempt. For twenty minutes we fought before the unseen beast weakened. He made desperate runs as I headed for shore and solid footing, preparing to literally land him. Water sprayed as he flew through the surface in a final attempt to expel the hook. Still he fought as I grabbed the wire leader and slid him over the rocks. The fish was huge, well over twenty pounds. Trout would be served for breakfast, lunch, and dinner for many days. The fillets were massive.

I was still bloated in the morning and skipped breakfast. The weather stayed calm and clear. I decided to portage at the base of Cracking Stone Peninsula, heading toward Uranium City. Two miles before the portage I stopped to make a lunch. While the bannock baked, a truck stopped on a narrow dirt road that skirted the lake. Three kids in their late teens charged in my direction through the brush. I backed toward the canoe and rifle. "Where you coming from?" one asked as they reached the fire.

"I started in New Orleans," I replied.

"Oh, is that on the other side of the lake?" another asked. He was surprised when I explained where New Orleans was located. They were just three kids out for a ride. We talked for a few more minutes before they trudged back through the woods to the old Ford. One boy's departing words were, "I've traveled all over Canada, and there's sure not many left like you."

The portage led to Beaverlodge Lake. I reached it during the supper hour. Surveying the scene were many boats and numerous picnickers in a party mood, curious about my presence here. Most were inquisitive about how the canoe and gear were going to get across the peninsula. "On my back," I explained more than once. Many offers were extended to put everything in the back of the truck and drive me to town. "You'll be across to Martin Lake in less than 15 minutes." Declining, I arranged things for portaging.

Shuffling everything across the dusty road took four hours. It would not have been bad if it didn't start so severely skyward. As it was nonstop over the road, I was happy to set down the canoe. It had lost no weight. Back on the water at dusk, the first island beckoned.

Once one got over that initial cold each morning, it was a glorious time of the year to travel. But even those mornings one could grow accustomed to. I took my time, enjoying the weather and acting like winter wasn't coming this year. After eight miles in the early morning, I slid into a small marina-type area.

The city still slept as the early morning sun warmed its buildings. There was a small hotel open. From its lobby, I called my sister to see how things were going. I was also broke and needing a transfer. It took 15 attempts to reach an operator. When she rang the Western Union number, the line was busy. I kept trying. After 45 minutes a familiar voice said the money would be in tomorrow. Following a twenty-minute update, I went to the grocery store to gaze at what I couldn't afford.

There was little for me to do in Uranium City with the few dollars I had. So, with a dozen cookies and two used books, I returned to the canoe, heading for the nearest island, camp, and leisure.

I was at the steps of the bank by ten o'clock the following morning. There was nothing. After browsing through the Hudson's Bay Store, I sat in the hotel bar with a glass of water for a moderate amount of time and then returned to the bank. Still nothing. Checking again after a trip through a small hardware store and another glass of water at the bar produced no results. The bank closed so I went to have one more shot of water at the bar. On this trip, I met a man named Pete, who told me he gave two white guys in a green canoe a ride to a place called Morris Point. Apparently, John and Tory hadn't been wind-bound yet.

I spent the night on the island base camp and was the first customer to enter the bank in the morning. It was disappointing. Sitting in Uranium City's poor attempt at a park, I read until noon where after I, again, confirmed "nothing." Another four hours of reading led to the same conclusion. It was beyond irritating. Days were shortening and water freezing up. I called my sister and she started calling around.

"Call the office in Duluth, Minnesota," they told her. Duluth said to call the office in Missouri. Eventually she found who to call at the Western Union office regarding a cancellation of services and then went through her banker. They would teletype the money to

Regina, who would then telephone it to Uranium City. With that hope, I went to the Hudson's Bay Store and bought a 26-cent can of dog food and two pieces of bubble gum with my last thirty cents. I was now, officially a vagrant. That could be the life for those seeking the sanctuary of the wilderness.

Again, the teller shook his head as I walked through the front door. He must have seen enough of me by then. I told him that Western Union was canceled, and it was coming in from Regina by phone. "Well then, they have probably tried, but the electricity or phone lines to town are down this afternoon." It was another lost day.

The idle days grew long. On the bank steps, I lobbed stones at an empty beer bottle. A lady approached saying she was from the newspaper. She had a small notebook and pencil in hand. "Could I have your name? Where did you come from? Where you going? How many miles?" I answered her short questions with short answers. Without any interest, this seemed to be a real chore for her. With neither a smile nor a thank you she just closed her notebook and walked away.

I knew I was in luck as soon as I walked into the bank the next day. The teller was smiling. "It came in first thing this morning," he gleamed. "I never knew who you were. Why didn't you tell me?" he said. I had to mull that over a few times, wondering what difference it would have made. "Come on back here," he said energetically, and I followed him into an office. There was a huge map hanging on the wall behind his desk and upon request, I traced my route through Canada and across Alaska. Then a lady came in and asked question after question, after question, until finally, finally, I was able to put my hands on that money. The man and woman told me to have a great trip as I walked out the bank door, hopefully for the last time.

I thought to myself in disbelief, *five days! Five wasted days it took to get that money here.* I entered the Hudson's Bay Store. I left $150 behind, but I couldn't complain. In one of the bags was enough fiberglass cloth and resin to recover the entire canoe.

By the time everything was packed, Friday was well on its way. After devouring a barbequed chicken and two pounds of grapes for supper, I walked to the bar to say goodbye to the bartender who so graciously kept me hydrated during my stay. He wasn't working so I sat at a table and ordered a beer.

Within minutes a man approached the table and asked if he could sit down. He introduced himself as Matthew Yooya, owner of the Stoney Rapids Hotel, still under construction. "I saw you in Stoney Rapids a few days ago but never got the chance to talk to you," he said. "Most people in Stoney Rapids wouldn't talk to you because they thought you were a boogieman." I gave a chuckle, but the guy was dead serious. When I think back on it, few did talk to me except the elder trapper. "I believe it's very historical that you came through here, and the town should remember that," Matthew said as one of his associates sat down. His name was Fred, and Fred was not sober.

"You must be getting paid for doing this," Fred kept repeating. "Why else would you bust your ass like that?" After eight explanations, I managed to get the subject changed.

"How much radiation is in the area from the uranium mines around here?" I asked.

"Well," Fred drooled, "I had my house checked last summer, and it was twenty times more than the safe level. Twenty times, twenty times, twenty times." He kept repeating it as if he couldn't comprehend it. Then Fred started crying. Tears rolled down his cheeks as he explained how his 19-year old son turned into a policeman and how he loved him and didn't want him to leave home and on and on through big sobs.

Matthew suddenly remembered an important meeting he was late for and stood up to leave saying, "If you ever get this way again, you'll have free room and board at my hotel in Stoney Rapids for as long as you like." We shook hands and there I sat with slobbering, sobbing Freddy.

It was embarrassing but Fred settled down, finished his drink, and left. Soon his replacement appeared in the form of his daughter. She wanted to take me home and feed me a moose steak. I could see other plans in her face, too, and she turned angry when I repeatedly refused. Dejected, she left to sit with another girl a few tables away.

I noticed a guy sitting next to the wall staring at me. Getting up, he talked to the waitress. A moment later she stood before me saying, "You'll have to leave." Surprised, I asked why. "You can't come in here wearing a knife." That was understandable. Picking up my change, I bought a newspaper with it and walked out the door. It was an interesting thirty minutes.

The mile walk to the canoe was pleasant in the late evening. At camp there was barely enough light to read the three-page local newspaper. Behind the want ads on the back page was a small box in the bottom, right-hand corner. It read: "Gerry Pushcar, from New Orleans, is passing through on a 6,000-mile canoe trip to Nome, Alaska." I wasn't from New Orleans, my name was misspelled, and the mileage was 3,000 miles short. So much for a historical passage!

But historical refers to the past and I needed to think about the reality of my present. It was the 25th of September, and winter was not far away. Each morning became darker as fall approached. I left my island base camp at Uranium City heading west instead of back south to the portage. Crossing Martin Lake, I went through a narrows to Clinch Lake, followed a meager river for a mile, and then was obstructed by a logjam.

I pulled the bow ashore and explored the rest of the river on foot. There was one more log jam, two small waterfalls, and a mile through the brush without a trail. When I returned, the stern of the canoe was filled with water. There was no sense in going on with the craft in such a state. The canoe would be fiberglassed right where it was, seeing as it made more sense to carry the fiberglass *on the canoe* than in the pack, anyways. Furthermore, the poles and plywood floor that had kept my feet out of the water, which percolated through the leaks could then be abandoned.

Pulled up, turned over, and dried before a huge log fire, the canoe was made ready. I pulled off long strips and patches of hardened fiberglass that clung weakly to the hull. Most were old patches from last winter's stay at Williams. It was a big job and sweat oozed as I took a rasp and smoothed the bottom. When all was ready, on went two 15-foot long patches. While these dried, I carved and affixed a birch handle to the bigger of the two ax heads found on the Fond Du Lac River. When the fiberglass dried, a second coat of resin was applied, thus ending another day.

The portage wasn't pleasant without a trail. I dropped the canoe for a rest near where a one-lane dirt road crossed the small creek on a very narrow bridge. Soon a small car stopped, and two blue-clad nuns jumped out. "Where are you going, son?" one asked in a voice that only one who had taken vows could have. I answered all their questions, and they decided I had guardian angels watching over me. They promised to pray for me, waved goodbye, and shouted a blessing from the Lord over the car's engine.

After returning for the packs, I reached the end of the portage at a small inlet called Bushell and paddled into it. No water seeped between the planking for the first time since my introduction to Swan

River six weeks ago. Past the calm inlet, Lake Athabasca was churned white. I would have to wait. It was twelve hours before the canoe could be slid off the smooth, weathered rock where I waited. I pointed west.

Days and the traveling season continued to dwindle. For 22 miles I followed the north shore, keeping a vigilant eye on the planking, looking for any leaks. There were none. After a quick supper, the lake remained calm. Priming my body with a pot of tea, I hoped to continue throughout the night. But, like a shade drawn over a window, the setting sun seemed to pull dark clouds across the blue sky. With their darkness came lightning. I stretched it to the limit, knowing when the swells were bad, a strong wind was not far behind.

It didn't take the swells long to develop nor the wind to howl across their tops, forming spraying whitecaps. Trees bent backwards as lightning cracked the sky like a fragile eggshell. Only when the rain came did I enter the tent, glad I had landed when I did.

By morning the wind had diminished but was far from calm. For two days progress was marginal as I struggled against it and its ally, the rain, until they defeated me at Spring Point. Being stranded gave me time to study the map. I located my position approximately eighty miles northeast of Fort Chipewyan. My bones told me it was time to start looking for a place to spend the winter. A location 35 miles north of Fort Chipewyan looked as if it might have potential. It was October 1st.

Clinging to the north shore, I hoped the south wind would be merciful as my path was totally exposed to it. Sometime mid-morning a twenty-gallon barrel that lay washed ashore caught my eye. It needed investigating. Since both ends were attached and contained little rust, I could immediately envision a use for it. Cached in the bow, my basic heating problem was solved for the coming winter.

By noon the south wind had become a problem. The shoreline was shallow, and my intuition urged me to beach. I happened to be in a fortunate place, for 200 feet away were the remains of a massive building. Its wreck was strewn over the ground, a testimony to the strength of the winds coming across the lake. Even though creosoted three-by-six-inch floorboards still supported a huge diesel engine, there were no walls or roof. I scouted the area and found three two-by-sixes that weren't rotted. With these, I fashioned a doorframe, and finding a sheet of three-quarter-inch plywood, made a door to fit. No hinges were to be found, but I did find a broken-handled hammer. My intuition was correct; the wind now had a definite howl to it. I was going nowhere.

Into the fire the hammerhead went while I searched a birch grove for an appropriate handle. After a bit of whittling with the Buck knife, a new handle was then coaxed into the head. It was put to work pulling and straightening nails for my winter home.

The pile of swerving, shanked nails piled up, but I needed a home for the night. Four empty 55-gallon barrels were stood upright and maneuvered to form a small rectangle. I covered the top and three sides with plywood torn from the surrounding willows to form an improvised lean-to with a flat roof. When finished, I was out of the wind and out of daylight.

Sometime during the night, the wind doubled, threatening to return the plywood to the willows. By morning the only thing anchoring the roof was a foot of snow. It covered everything inside and out. I didn't know what the wind-chill factor was for twenty-degree temps and forty-mile per hour winds, but I could vouch for the fact that getting dressed in it held little comfort.

I kicked through the powder looking for plywood reinforcements as the roof had developed a definite bow in it. Blinding snow bit my face while I struggled to shore up my hobo camp. I needed heat. Finding a topless barrel, I vented the bottom using three shots from the .30-06. Tipping it up, it was then pushed as close to my dwelling as I dared and a roaring fire was started within. Inside the cubby, a sheet of plywood was pulled across the side, leaving the only exit blocked by the stove. The barrel roared and belched in the opening as ninety percent of its heat followed the smoke into the storm. The other ten percent was cherished as I huddled close, book in hand, listening to the wind scream and watching a world turn white.

It wasn't the best, but it was better than what was going on around me. The wind did its best to reach me but only succeeded when I ventured out to refill the stove with wood—cruelly often. It crossed my mind that this wouldn't be a bad place to spend the winter. With all the available materials, it wouldn't take much to build a comfortable place. *I might not have any choice,* I pondered, looking past the wood stove. But there was still a lot of open water and already I could see the bottom of the food box. It blew all day and night.

By morning it had lessened. The swells were a respectable size when I pushed the canoe straight into them. They were just as respectable when they swamped me three hours later. Drying out gave me time to work on the stove. With ax and hammer, I chiseled the door opening. Wanderlust hit and so I hiked four miles down the beach, returning with two spruce hens for supper.

Lake Athabasca was stingy, allowing little travelable time. Only two hours into the next morning it became rough and I sought refuge. Back paddling hard right, I angled toward shore. As I dug hard a sudden, excruciating pain shot up my back. I couldn't straighten, and it was all I could do was to paddle one handed to the nearest shore. I was a ship without a rudder and expected no mercy from the swells. With my nose bent over the thwart, I managed to keep some semblance of control moving toward shore. There was an old cabin in my peripheral vision, a quarter-mile up the beach. All I wanted was to be on land.

Finally, the canoe beached with a thud. As the swells tried to force the canoe sideways, I struggled to get out. Just a few lame jerks on the bow were all I could muster to slide it up the beach. The only real security was a rope tied to a tree. If the storm blew up, there would be trouble for me. Any change in my posture almost sent me to my knees. Like an old man with a canoe-paddle cane, I shuffled toward the cabin.

The door to the one-room shack opened easily with either my hand or my head. A wooden plank bed stood in one corner. I sat, hunched over, on its edge. It took a long, long time to lie down and get my legs up.

As the day wore on, I began to experiment. Through pain and error, I realized that by keeping my back rigid and rolling off the bed to my knees, I could stand and take small steps, though I was still bent at an odd angle from the waist up. Any deviation from this position had disastrous results. This way I was at least able to get to the canoe and food box. It took another full day before the paralyzing twitch was reduced to a tolerable level for work, longer before it became comfortable.

Back out, I gingerly traveled five hours to Fiddler's Point before feeling a strain. Not wanting a repeat performance, I sought land immediately. I pondered my predicament. The temperature seldom

218

rose above freezing now and Fort Chipewyan was still 45 miles away. It seemed unreachable, as the constant, pounding swells blocked my efforts for days at a time.

The break allowed the pain to improve from a sharp twinge to a dull ache, allowing enough mobility and dexterity to finish and re-stow the wood stove in the canoe. By evening, the darker it got, the calmer it became. I couldn't afford to sleep. Few swells disturbed the temperate water by the time the canoe was loaded. Dressed warmly, I launched the canoe and followed the haunting shoreline throughout the night. Little seemed alive in the blackness. Only paddling kept the occasional shiver at bay until building a fire ten hours later.

The sky lightened as I huddled next to the fire, sipping tea. Soon the sun would rise, giving light but little warmth. I couldn't linger for there was no trusting the calmness. Shore ice had developed overnight, and I followed it for eight straight hours, racing nature's wintry grasp. I knew the end of my second season of travel was near. A strengthening bitter breeze confirmed this as the canoe's worn, wooden keel skipped across frozen mud, bringing the canoe to a halt. Before me lay Fort Chipewyan.

I trudged along a frozen path to a road with urgency. Condensation steamed upward with each breath. Having been left tied to the canoe, Vagabond barked at the breach of contract. My stomach moaned in protest as I passed the Athabascan Cafe and entered the Hudson's Bay Store. Hunger could wait. What I needed now were enough supplies to survive a Canadian winter in the bush.

Like most bush stores, it was not lavish but rather stocked with essentials. It didn't take long to fill the shopping cart. The wheels skidded more than rolled, bearings straining under the massive load as the wire wagon screeched toward the checkout counter. The clerk was quiet and efficient. The boxes piled up. After these were carried to the canoe, I returned to the back door for 200 pounds of flour, 50 pounds of sugar, and 100 pounds of potatoes. It was a joy to dump that last fifty-pound sack into the canoe and even more of a joy to sit inside the Athabascan Cafe, waiting to be served.

The two hamburgers and a Coke hardly caused a slight pacification to hunger, but darkness was fast approaching. I went to the counter, paid the bill, and ordered two cups of tea to-go. The owner didn't speak English as a first language. "Tuga in tea?" The man asked in a rapid tongue. I didn't understand him and as I wrinkled my brow, he repeated, "Tuga in tea, you want tuga in tea?" His frustrations and my embarrassment showed as he slammed a sugar bowl in front of me and pumped his finger at it saying, "Tuga, tuga, tuga, tuga, tuga! You want tuga in tea?" He smiled widely as I understood and watched as I stirred a teaspoon of tuga into each cup.

Steam curled around the plastic lids confining the tea to their Styrofoam containers on the floor of the canoe, as I paddled south to the nearest island. The gathering darkness only allowed enough time to collect an armload of firewood. I was tired as I lay beside the open fire, snug in a down sleeping bag, watching the Aurora Borealis pulsate above. A huge orange moon had stealthily risen to dwarf the lights of Fort Chipewyan beneath it.

As the fire snapped, Vagabond's eyes would open and focus on a rising ember only to lazily shut again as the spark disappeared into the night. I thought of the freezing nights and the snow which would soon enclose this land. Shimmering, shattered, shore ice already reached outward around this island. It was well into October, and I needed some place to spend the winter. I thought of the shelter I would build, tucked away in a cove of pine trees, hidden in its warmth while the cold wind whistled outside.

I awoke to Vagabond's alarming growls shattering the stillness. I groped for the rifle while worming out of the sleeping bag. It was a frightening way to be awakened. Only a few glowing coals lay in the sandy hearth, but in the moonlight, I could see movement at my winter supplies. Shouting and shooting into the dark produced immediate results as a creature struggled down the shore, followed by puffs of white clouds. I gave chase, but the invader's speed increased rapidly. Then it was over.

I stood cursing into the night as a white dust settled around my legs. At my feet lay an empty, torn, fifty-pound flour sack. With a swift kick, I sent it farther down the beach, and then followed the white trail back to the canoe to assess the damage. *Just the sack of flour.* I was thankful. To prevent further animal atrocities, I carried the many pounds of provisions to the campfire.

Traces of light and fading stars seeped over the towering timber around me as I opened my eyes. Something had again awakened me. I rolled over and looked directly into the back end of a huge dog that was alarmingly close. The mongrel's head was buried deep into my winter supplies. My hand inched toward the firewood pile and curled around a piece of firewood.

With a mighty yell, I leapt up swinging. The bludgeon sliced the frigid air, then sent vibrations soaring through my arms as it struck solid rock. Blaspheming followed the pilfering cur as it bounded toward the security of the tall pines. A two-pound bag of prized walnuts flopped in its drooling jaws. The commotion woke Vagabond, and he concluded the episode with five brutal minutes of barking.

Thoughts of sleep now became an exercise in futility, so I pulled on icy boots and eliminated the morning's cold by carrying everything to the canoe. As the coffee pot perked merrily, I stowed the last pack and sat down to a wholesome breakfast. The morning star was neutralized by the daylight, and tiny people could be seen moving near the Athabascan Cafe. It entered my mind to cross to the mainland and luxuriate in its warmth with a steaming cup of tea before me, but the ice crunching beneath the canoe conveyed a decisive warning. Freeze-up was near.

The silt-laden waters of the Slave River slid beneath the hull as the bow lazily bobbed forward. The once golden birch trees were now skeletal digits clawing the blue sky. Only the brown, withered leaves of the willows clung with their stems of life. But these were not sought. I was looking for pines, tall, straight, and off the beaten path. I had a general idea where I was going, Flett Lake, 36 miles north. It looked good on the map, being six miles off the Slave River, hopefully out of society's way.

The day was long. By its end, nature had lost its beauty. I became more and more aware of the brown river, the brown trees, the drab sky, the hunger, and the tired arms. Even though I was traveling downstream, pushing 1,000 pounds against a strong headwind for thirty miles had taken its toll. Flett Lake lay six miles to the east at the head of a small creek. It would have to wait until morning. Snow that had fallen in the last two hours blanketed the ground. The earth no longer held enough heat to melt it. Kicking it aside, I performed the long-practiced ritual of making camp.

Pings were heard as I opened my eyes to a blinding sun glaring off the white snow. The empty coffee pot caught droplets of melting snow that would again leave the branches naked. Even the snow on the ground might disappear in the warming air. I crawled out of the sleeping bag and stretched. The beauty of nature had returned.

The distance to Flett Lake was more time-consuming than difficult. Sitting silently at its outlet, I leaned on the paddle, braced gunwale to gunwale, and peered into a wall of weeds. A shallow channel twisted through the ever-narrowing marsh, dotted with cattails until fanning into open water. The first thing I saw while gazing across Flett Lake was a sign nailed crookedly to a tree. Block letters said GILLIGAN'S ISLAND.

Behind the tilted sign stood two white wall-tents glistening in the morning sun. Smoke rose from their stovepipes. Two arms parted the doors of one tent and then disappeared as a stream of water arched through the morning air. Not wanting to intrude on their privacy, I crossed the lake and re-entered the creek that fed Flett Lake. Within a half-mile, on top of a twenty-foot bank, I found a collection of cabin logs among an immense forest. Here I would spend the winter. It was October 10, 1976.

Ten days and $9.36 provided sufficient shelter to combat the minus fifty-degree days.

Flett Lake

I studied the ground over a cup of tea. Something surged through me. Maybe it was a basic instinct, or the feeling of finally being home, or just the challenge of the situation. Whatever it was, it produced motivation.

The first thing was the foundation. *Just obliterate the low willow bush, remove a little dirt here, and fill in a little there.* It didn't take long. When the area was level, I assembled my two-foot folding saw, checked the edge on the ax, and then waded into the forest. By darkness the foundation was snuggled into the earth, and the walls were on their way up. The five-ax handle-length green logs would provide roughly 144 square feet of living space, more than adequate for its intended purpose.

It went fast. After four days of work, I sat atop the twelve-tiered wall and rolled the last saddle-notched log into place. The plastic window, four millimeters thick, was installed, and the prefab plywood door swung inward on old boot-leather hinges. Hopping from my perch, I landed on the dirt floor, shielded from a biting wind that had driven ugly gray clouds across the sky. Using a tarp, I fashioned a shelter deep in the northwest corner of the cabin and rolled the twenty-gallon barrel stove in front of it. With my back to the wall and feet to the warmth of the barrel, I watched as swirling snowflakes slowly eradicated the last vestiges of summer.

By morning, the silence was absolute. The tarp sagged precariously, and a dome of snow arched over the top of the now cold stove. The sun held no more warmth than the moon. A loud crack echoed through the stillness as pressure caused the thickening river ice to scream in relief. I emerged into a white world. There was a foot of snow in my living room.

The wind finally died after four days. I was willing to gamble on one more trip to town, calculating that supplies were easier moved on water than on foot. I packed for a week and slid the canoe across thinning ice to an open sliver of water at midstream. This watery thread would soon disappear under a blanket of white.

I shifted all the weight to the stern of the canoe, not to be denied by the ice. This raised the bow enough so the canoe could glide on top of the ice wherever there wasn't open water. Every time ice was reached, I'd make my way to the front and cautiously bob up and down until the ice beneath the canoe broke free. Thus, the process was repeated for almost a mile. It took hours to reach open water in Flett Lake. My mettle was challenged, for getting back could be difficult. I knew the Slave River would at least be open, so if nothing else, I would make a small sled and pull the supplies over the last six miles with my dog team—Vagabond and me.

Though fringed with ice, the stretch across Flett Lake posed no problem. The people at Gilligan's Island waved as I passed. One shouted, "When you coming back?"

"In a couple of days," I shouted back.

"Hope you make it before the creek freezes," someone else shouted. With a wave, I entered the creek that connected Flett Lake to the Slave River.

It was open in the middle, and I followed the ice-free lane to the Slave River. It was dark when I camped at the junction and dark when I started upstream in the calm morning. Visibility was near zero. What the darkness didn't obliterate, a heavy, cold fog did. I hugged the shore, listening to the shattering of shore ice as my wake would lift and deposit it elsewhere in many small pieces. By noon the fog had lifted, but I fought the current all day. By evening only 23 miles had been logged, seven miles short of town.

It was well below freezing the next morning. A light wind didn't help matters. Enough shore ice had formed that there was a noticeable difference from the day before. I knew I couldn't linger. Stopping only occasionally to run in place, warming my feet, I reached the frozen muddy landing by 11:30 A.M. Although there was nothing at the post office, the postman said a message awaited me at the Hudson's Bay Store. Curiosity took hold and I went there immediately.

It was a box, a birthday present from my brother and sister. It contained a .22-magnum rifle with a $130 price tag still hanging from the trigger guard. In my circumstances, it was an exquisite gift. It was much appreciated and proved much more appropriate than the .30-06. As soon as possible, I called both Tom and Terry to thank them and after a thirty-minute talk with each, finished my winter shopping.

I needed lighting for the winter and decided on an economical kerosene lamp. When I went to the warehouse, the worker said the five-gallon cans were buried, and he didn't have the time to dig one out. "Use fuel oil. It works just as good," the lazy, red-eyed man said. Trusting that it would, I bought five gallons, along with a small radio, and all the walnuts in town. Between portages from store to canoe, someone had stolen one of my paddles and a 25-pound sack of flour.

I explained this to an RCMP officer who was standing in the street waiting for me. "Could I see your ID?" he asked as he shrugged his shoulders in reply to my loss. It meant little to him, but for me, being paddle-less would put me in a predicament. It was like stealing a horse in the Old West 100 years earlier, or at least like depriving someone of their saddle.

I knew he could do little about it as I took out my wallet and handed him my Minnesota driver's license. He glanced at the closely-shaven image and then at me saying, "You used to be a handsome fellow, at one time." We stood in the middle of the street talking about hunting and fishing for at least thirty minutes before he left, saying, "Maybe we'll be up there this winter. We like to check on guys like you on occasion."

It was already late in the day. The wind had picked up, but what I thought of the most were the creeks on both sides of Flett Lake. I left without a spare paddle. Within a mile, I came to an old man struggling to get his antiquated, wooden boat into the river. The water had gone down and left the boat twenty feet from the water. I pulled ashore and between the two of us, it still took 15 minutes of rocking and pushing before it floated.

No words were exchanged. The man didn't know any English, and I didn't know any Cree. He gave me a big smile and waved as I left. I didn't get far. The wind had churned the river white and darkness wasn't far away. I pulled onto a large rock, climbed into the sleeping bag, and waited for morning.

The wind was tolerable as morning arrived, and it took all the daylight hours plus two to reach the unfinished cabin. It was much easier getting back than I had anticipated. Upon reaching the creeks of Flett Lake, I found the high winds of last night had raised the water and broken the ice. Some had floated into the Slave River, and some was blown ashore. It was a clear shot to the cabin. I felt very, very fortunate. The cabin would impress few, but I was glad to be there.

An interior view of my five-ax length square log cabin before moss chinking.

Over the next few days, I busied myself with filling in the gable ends, then notching and setting the rafters. Perpendicular to the rafters and on top of them, poles were laid to form the roof with forty per side; it was an endless task. By the time the last one was in place, the river in front of the cabin was frozen from bank to bank, creating a mile-long ice rink any lad would have envied. Being without skates, I instead installed the stovepipe, much to Vagabond's delight.

With the stove hooked up, Vagabond gravitated toward the heat. He quickly grew too comfortable with it. After cooking pancakes one morning, I smelled something burning. Vagabond lay against the stove, curled comfortably against the hot barrel, smoldering in his sleep. "Get away from there!" I shouted as five gallons of drinking water descended upon him.

Through a cloud of steam, Vagabond rose like a drowned demon. With a vicious shake, he showered the cabin. With a scornful stare, he headed for a corner, shook again, turned two circles, and lay down. There was no trust left in his eyes as they followed my every

226

move. Only two pancakes could restore his trust in me as I brushed the black, kinked hair from his once white coat.

After breakfast, I cut many armloads of wood, packed a lunch, picked up the rifle, and started walking. My excuse was to get away from cabin building, though itchy feet were a greater motivator.

Following the creek upstream, I circled another small lake and was back by dark with two spruce hens and two rabbits. Cleaning up after supper, I sat on the dirt floor, leaning into a corner of the cabin. Bright stars peered through the roof poles. All was quiet except the occasional pop of burning pine in the stove. With each *crack,* a shower of sparks was sent up the pipe to mingle with the stars.

It could have been emotions or maybe the stars lined up just right between the roof poles, but whatever it was I picked up the guitar and wrote a song, "I Still Love You":

I gave you my heart,
You tore it all apart.
We even took those vows;
You broke them anyhow.
What can I do now?
I still love you!

I saw you yesterday;
You turned and walked away.
Our child was in your hand;
He'll never understand,
Until he's a man—
My little Dan.

So, I'm sitting at home,
Drinking all alone,
Staring at the glass,
Crying about the past.
It should have lasted forever,
Because I loved you.
I still love you!
I still love you!

And with that I sheathed my country music career along with the guitar and went to bed.

Breaths of the warmer seasons gave it one last go. The temperature rose enough to melt most of the existing snow, but it did nothing to the frozen rivers. Using it to my advantage, I slit open garbage bags and tacked them on the outside of the roof poles. Around the roof's perimeter, I constructed a 16-inch high ledge, creating essentially a tub on the roof. In this I dumped bag after bag of "Canadian cotton", moss, for insulation. The uses for this plant are limited only by one's imagination. When finished, there was a 16-inch mantle of moss over my winter home.

Laying poles over the new, natural shingles, I heard the unmistakable *whomp, whomp, whomp* of a helicopter. It came right up the small river and it was quite intimidating to see the big Bell 47 hovering at my doorstep. "Mr. Pushcar how are things going?" came a voice over a loudspeaker.

"Just fine," I shouted. *They can't hear me.* I don't know why I bothered to answer over the beat of the rotors. After I waved them an O.K. sign, they disappeared over the treetops. What a splash of reality! Society could find me if it wanted.

The weather quickly fell toward winter. While the short daylight hours passed swiftly, the temperature plummeted. One evening I turned my attention to reading. Filling the new lamp with fuel oil, I touched a match to the wick, sliding the globe into its three-pronged support. Turned up high, the lamp illuminated the dark cabin only seconds before the cold glass literally exploded. Cold glass plus burning fumes don't mix.

Scrabbled back together, the creased and torn mantle belched black soot like a coal-fired locomotive. After an hour, moss that dangled between the roof poles resembled black stalactites. Nose blows turned black, and the light faded as soot coated everything. Something had to be done to maximize function, even though it "worked just as good as kerosene."

Finding a dozen, identical-diameter tin cans, I removed both ends and duct taped them together to form a long tube. This was forced through a hole in the roof and hung an inch above the lamp's mantle, drawing the black soot outdoors. Far from pretty, it worked.

The weather kept me indoors where idle solitude crept in and captured one's emotions. At the midnight hour on a sleepless night, my past boiled to the surface. It struck me, of all things in the form of a poem, and I wrote "I'm Sorry":

228

Maybe your mother is right,
A loner will take to flight,
And lead your emotions astray,
Only to return another day.

But your feelings are your own,
Though your mother's I can't condone.
For she feels we should part,
Your decision was from your heart.

So, all and all, I can't complain,
The love we had will be unchanged.
But our lives are so different I had to choose,
Between the way God made me and you.

So again, the day came, and I went away,
To follow the streams that lead me astray.
Over calm lakes with mountains above,
To leave behind the ones I love.

And as the fire flickers in the dark night,
I stare to its depth in lonely plight
And as the stars fall from the sky,
I'll wish you happiness till the day I die.

So too, ended the one brief interlude of my life, in a dark lonely
cabin in Northern Saskatchewan, where I was a poet.

The stove was not airtight, which caused it to run out of fuel
during the day and more importantly, at night. To remedy this, I cut
a slot in the stovepipe, flattened a tin can, and created a damper. By
sliding the flattened peach-can damper in and out of the slot, I could
somewhat control the blaze. With the make-do damper and the right
combination of wood, stoking operations were cut to once during the
night, though the fire was usually left to go out and rekindled in the
morning.

No matter how much the little stove tried, though, its efficiency
was curtailed by the air that seeped in between the wall logs. This
became more and more a priority item as the day's highs got farther

and farther from 32 degrees. The snow that once was, melted in a single day and saturated the moss. Two days later it froze. *So much for insulation.* Now it had to be chopped free with the ax and set next to the stove to thaw. Instead of returning it to the roof, I took the thawed moss and stuffed it between the logs, all around the cabin. Chinking the cracks took all of two days but made a remarkable difference in my living conditions.

My next standard of living improvement was the outhouse. It was ten steps behind the cabin and three feet down. A shovel would have helped, especially after getting through the first frozen foot. With the help of boiling water, ax, hammer, and frying pan, I chiseled it down. Over this was built a miniature log crib complete with log top. Dirt from the hole was packed around the outside of the crib, and its main utility was complete. Gathering the tops of the trees used for cabin logs, I placed them tepee-like over the structure to form a windbreak. With a little ax work, I cut the inside branches to produce a very comfortable cubby.

Plumbing was included with construction costs of the cabin.

Next, I turned my attention to interior decorating. No curtains were hung, for I saw no reason to deprive myself of what little sun there was. I made a bin for firewood, two shelves, two plywood-topped tables, and a chair salvaged from an 18-inch diameter stump. Then came the bed.

It was three-feet by seven-feet and built into a corner. The base consisted of a short pole tacked knee-high to the wall on one side, and on the other short side a pole spanned from the adjacent wall to a corner post that ran from floor to ceiling. Seven-foot poles spanned the two short ones. Between them three-foot wrist-size poles were laid giving slats upon which to lay. I added another layer of poles along the perimeter of the slats to retain them, and this crude box was filled with pine boughs to form a mattress of sorts. Covered with a camouflaged blanket, it looked great. Lying on it proved firm but much better than sleeping on the dirt floor with the occasional shrew.

Finally, the cabin was complete. It took ten days to erect, including the outhouse. The biggest construction expenses were the sections of stovepipe, pushing the bill to $9.36, including tax. If need be, I probably could have worked around that, but it didn't matter. I had a home for the winter.

Not exactly a feather bed, but functional.

Asleep on my new bed, a whip-like crack awoke me. My home was cold. I fumbled for the flashlight inside the sleeping bag. The only way to assure its function in the cold was by sleeping with it. *Crack!* Again, the ice echoed as I dashed to the stove, stoked it, and crawled back inside the down bag. The ice seemed to crack on a regular schedule while it formed. Soon it would thicken into silence.

With the cabin warmed slightly, I quickly dressed and hastened to the only truly warm spot, next to the stove. After a leisurely breakfast, I portaged the canoe for the final time of the year. I had left two of the wall logs extending four feet past the end of the cabin. On these, upside down, the canoe was placed for the winter.

With the canoe situated, I concentrated on the woodpile. For days I made my way farther and farther from the cabin in search of standing, dead, dry trees. They were felled, cut into lengths of manageable weight, and carried to the cabin. There they were cut into wood-stove length pieces. After being split, they were moved inside to the woodbin and stacked in anticipation of the very cold winter nights sure to come. I didn't veer from this objective until there was a cord of dry spruce inside and a cord of green birch outside. It was almost dark when I brought the last armful of spruce inside to fill out the cord.

Lighting the lamp, I then opened the stove's flue to get enough heat to cook supper. It was to be a skinny pike that I had caught through the ice a week ago. I floured the two fillets and stepped back as they spit fire upon entering the hot grease. On the back burner, rice boiled merrily. Flipping the fillets, I noticed black bits of ash appearing on them. Bewildered, I looked up to see the roof on fire.

Flames reached skyward as blackened moss sifted between the roof poles. With the water bucket, I was out the door and up the crisscrossed joints where the wall logs met in the corner. The water doused the flames but handful after handful of smoldering moss had to be thrown to the ground. When the crisis was over, a six-foot circle of black-charred roof poles lay before me. It didn't take long for the fire marshal to see what had happened. Moss had slid against the hot stovepipe and ignited. It was fortunate it didn't happen when I was sleeping.

Supper had to be changed as the still steaming rice lay across the floor in front of the tipped-over pan. The longed-for fish floated to the top of the black-soot sludge in the frying pan. *Vagabond won't mind.* I tossed them and settled for a loaf of day-old bannock, crawling into bed with a book, vowing to make needed repairs in the morning.

It was fixed before breakfast. Constructing a two-foot square box from scrap boards, I nailed it to the roof poles around the stovepipe, filling the box with sand taken from beneath the ice. Thawed moss was then placed around the outside of the box, covering the blackened poles. Life resumed at its normal pace.

It was already Halloween. I hadn't seen 15 degrees for a week, but very little snow showed on the ground. Since the woodbin was full to the ceiling, and the cabin was as clean as it was going to get, Halloween seemed like a good day to scout the area.

After two cups of tea, Vagabond and I started out heading upstream. Within two miles, we came to a narrow set of rapids with two small, frozen waterfalls. From there, a trail, possibly a snowmachine trail, wound four miles to another lake. Stopping here for supper, Vagabond's ears stood on end as howling wolves echoed across the lake. The spine-chilling chorus, coupled with the coming darkness, flamed phobias that dated back millennia. With these in mind and a quickened pace, it was still well after dark before we had covered the six miles back to the cabin.

The following day turned remarkably warm, almost fifty degrees. To supplement food supplies, I set a dozen rabbit snares on trails around the cabin. Checked late in the evening, there wasn't a drop of snow left or a rabbit snared. Near the last snare, I flushed a spruce hen that refused to tree. It ran along the ground just out of rifle range in the thick brush. *Finally, I was in luck!* Its wings rustled as if it had flushed and I thought it treed. *I'm going to get a shot!* I followed the sound of the wings until they stopped. Preparing to shoot I moved forward and found it already caught—it had run right into one of my snares; supper was obtained.

Although the only radio station I could get was broadcasting the U.S. Presidential elections the next day, I had more important things to do. Armed with the ax, I roamed the woods searching for birch saplings suitable for snowshoes. With six found, I returned to the cabin and whittled them to size for future soaking and bending. With that accomplished, I settled as comfortably as possible into the stump-chair and opened *Trumpets to Arms* by Bruce Lancaster. I started the first chapter for the fourth time. It was my only book.

Wanderlust never left. It was a welcome antidote to boredom. I had found a new lake on a hike the week before and had to explore its boundaries. With a stomach full of oats, a small sack on my back, and Vagabond tied to a tree in front of the cabin, I was off with the .22 magnum.

I kept close to shore where I trusted the ice was thicker, and boot skated around the perimeter of the eight-square-mile sheet of mirrored-ice for three hours. This brought me to a rundown log cabin, a good place for lunch as my stomach growled and my shins ached from this unaccustomed mode of travel.

Since the cabin had a three-foot hole in the roof, there was plenty of fresh air for lunch. Utensils and rusted traps lay scattered near a rusted stove. A bed lined the back wall, and a table stood near the door. It was smaller than my cabin. The last recorded witness of occupancy, printed in pencil on the log wall, was from April 1976, just last spring. Brushing green beef jerky from the table, I sat down for a quick lunch, wanting to cover the miles home before dark. The twenty-mile jaunt temporarily satisfied my wandering spirit. It didn't last long.

Two days later I was back at the trapline shack. The last two miles I followed a snowmachine trail directly to the cabin, cutting off miles from skating around the lake. Peering inside the cabin, it was obvious someone with ambition had been there. The place had been cleaned, new bedding was placed over the old mattress, and a new stove sat where the rusted one had been. There was even an attempt to fix the gaping hole in the roof. Feeling like a trespasser, I closed the door and skidded across a short section of frozen lake to follow the trail home.

Though darkness crept in quickly, this time I didn't quicken my pace. It was a small game hunter's paradise. Spruce hens perched obliviously in the pines, as white rabbits dashed from cover to cover, their ghostly forms prominent in the snowless forest. It was a cruel quirk of nature to be camouflaged for snows that didn't come. Even the ptarmigan appeared as white fireworks in the dim light, spreading throughout the trees. Shortly the rifle sights were lost to darkness. Since the game bag was full, I quickened the pace home.

As a result, the next week was one of leisure. Hunting, reading, solitaire, and guitar playing occupied much of my time. The wood-freezer out back contained enough small game to last a month, but soon enough the wood-boxed bed needed tending. Pine needles lay in piles underneath, forcing bare-branched springs into a role they couldn't satisfy. After two hours of cutting and hauling fresh pine boughs, the mattress returned to its original condition.

Since the heat had dried the dirt enough to create a dust cloud with every step, the floor also needed attention. Again, I turned to the indispensable pine boughs, weaving them over the floor, keeping them well away from the stove. It appeared that these two features would require monthly maintenance.

By November 16, the snow came to stay. There would be no more belated warm days. Even knowing it was to be a long winter, my mind frequently flashed ahead to the coming summer. I thought about the route, and mulled gear. One piece that was surely needed would be a backup paddle. As none were available at the store, I'd have to make one.

Placing a seven-foot log in the homemade sawbucks, I sawed parallel three-inch deep cuts, six inches apart, perpendicularly down one side of the log. Then with the ax, the blocks were knocked out, producing a flattened surface. The log was flipped, and the process repeated on the opposite side. This produced a rough board. Tracing my paddle's profile on this, it was hewn to the line, then streamlined to the desired thickness. Abandoning the ax, the sheath knife took lead on the finishing touches. It took much whittling and scraping, but the final product was rewarding. It was then lashed to a straight, stout pole to prevent twisting as it cured over the long winter.

An unfortunate result of the long winter was the way I had to wash my clothes. I arose early to complete the dastardly chore. While the clothes and a bar of soap were thrown into a bucket, I made a washing machine by roughing out another two-foot board. Cuts were made across one flattened face at half-inch intervals. Every other half-inch section was notched out, producing a rugged, riffled washboard. Armed with this, I attacked the laundry vigorously. The socks, shirts, and pants each got one stretch on the board. The underwear got two. When all was finished, a hole was chopped in the ice for the rinse cycle. From the frigid waters, they were transported inside the cabin and hung on a line with split-stick clothespins. Everything appeared clean except the underwear—that had seen whiter days.

Knowing too much housework is not healthy it was again time for a walk. I was at the line shack well before noon, and it appeared nobody had been there since my last visit. After a light lunch, I decided to follow a southerly trail, ending across from Gilligan's

Island. The white canvas tents blended well with the wintry shoreline. Near them, six howling dogs danced to the scent of a stranger. I had already walked 16 miles and had a few more to go. Not lingering, I set my course for home.

Shortly, probably alerted by the dogs, a snowmachine left Gilligan's Island and headed directly toward me. "Where you going?" a man asked as he stopped next to me and dismounted the mechanical dog.

"I was out for a walk and am now headed home," I answered. We shook hands and he introduced himself as Raymond Cardinal. After talking about trapping for ten minutes, he offered me a ride home where we could continue the discussion in depth.

After inviting my first visitor in, the first person I had talked to in a month, I got the fire going while he gave the place a once-over. During tea, we discussed the area, trapping, and the history of his line shack. "You should hunt squirrels here," Ray said. "They pay $1.25 apiece for them at the Bay, and I'll sell them for you. You won't have to buy a license," he added. The Bay was shorthand for the Hudson's Bay Store. That sounded like a great idea. *Money and something to do!* Hopefully it would stabilize my dwindling finances. "I'll stop by tomorrow and show you how we set snares for squirrels," Ray stated as he ducked and went out the plywood door. The sound of his snowmachine soon faded into silence.

Ray and his brother Happy stopped by two days later. They brought a squirrel hide stretched on a board to demonstrate the procedure. It seemed simple enough. "All last year our family got only 100 of them," Happy said. In my mind's eye, $125 was $125.

I was up early, motivated to start a squirrel line. Ambitiously I readied myself, eager on the first day of employment. Through my wanderings, I knew a dozen excellent areas among the tall pines, untapped, renewable resources unseen by man's eye for centuries, wealth just waiting. Sugarplums danced in my head.

I checked these areas and came home with six. The sugarplums were gone. Skinning them was an easy matter, but boards on which to stretch and dry skins were another concern. Instead of taking two hours to mill a tree into a single board, the plywood tabletop provided eight excellent boards, ready-made. With the skins stretched and left to dry, I started to replace the tabletop.

Ray and Happy stopped by three days later and were surprised at my 24-squirrel tally. They were headed for the line shack to string their winter trapline and couldn't stay long. While they were here, we tried one of Happy's .22 shorts in the .22 Magnum rifle. It seemed compatible so Happy offered me four boxes of shells until I could get to town and buy him replacements. It would be a substantial savings, as shorts were $.85 a box, compared to $5.50 a box for magnums.

Thanksgiving arrived windy, snowy, and cold; it was a good day to stay close to home. I started transcribing my diaries over a pot of tea and spent the afternoon working on the woodpile. Since it was the traditional American feast-day, I too conducted a celebration, here in the Canadian bush. Instead of rice and squirrel, or rice and rabbit, or rice and spruce hen, or rice and fish, I opened a can of Klik. It was a blend of ground animal parts that was Canada's answer to America's Spam.

Out came my best. The table was set without linen. Fresh buttery rolls were replaced by bannock, cranberry sauce by a tin can of fruit cocktail. Steam rose from the pan of rice. *Just like hot apple pie,* I thought. But, even in my strongest imagination, I had a hard time believing that the jelly-encased block of "meat" was turkey. Its presence dominated the center of my best—and only—plate and quivered every time I bumped the table. Thankful for what I had, I ate my fill.

The day after Thanksgiving marked my 27th birthday. At minus twenty degrees it was just another day of wood cutting and squirrel hunting. My treat would have been nothing in normal circumstances. The Grey Cup football game was broadcast, static free, on my single-station radio. Though I didn't know a single player or either team, it was a welcome diversion. It turned out to be an exciting event, with Edmonton beating Saskatchewan in the final twenty seconds by a score of 23 to 20.

After the game, I took Vagabond squirrel hunting across the frozen river. He'd see one and chased it from tree to tree, continually barking until it scampered into its winter hole in the ground. Vagabond would give a desperate leap at nothing. Then the dirt would fly until he'd hear another chatter and off he'd go. This process was much repeated until we went home empty-handed. Vagabond sat in front of the cabin listening to the squirrels across the river while I cut wood until dusk. Every few minutes he turned, sadly looking at me for a few seconds and then turn back to stare across the river, longing for another hunt. I think we differed in our opinions of *effective* hunting.

My way of hunting continued as winter came in earnest. The first winter front plummeted temperatures to 42 degrees below zero and had little trouble seeping through the cabin walls. I awoke to an ice-covered beard as the inside and outside temperatures equalized. The five-gallon water bucket was a solid block of ice. Even after fixing breakfast, most of the cabin's warmth centered around the stove. Not two steps away from it, fogged breath would rise to the ridgepole. Not wanting to hug the stovepipe all day, I donned my warmest clothes, stoked the stove, and went squirrel hunting.

Freeze-dried snow crunched beneath my feet as I walked from one barren squirrel area to the next. At the end of the normal line, I logged another three miles, hating to admit defeat. The cold never relented as ice hung tusk-like from my beard. By the time I retraced my steps back to the cabin, it was dark. Any heat gained during the day slowly faded; the mercury peaked at 32 degrees below before its downward slide. I hadn't seen one living creature over the 16-mile trek. Maybe that should have told me something—most animals are smart enough to stay in their dens or cabins in these conditions.

No gushing blast of heat escaped as I opened the cabin door. Lighting the lamp, I noticed I had left the rubber camera cable release on the table. It shattered into seven useless pieces when I picked it up. Now I knew it was cold as I started the stove and fixed supper. Afterward I lounged in bed, cozy in the down sleeping bag, reading. *Not now,* I prayed from beneath the warmth as my bowels began to stir. Procrastination lasted three chapters, no more. Then it was me, Charmin, and forty-some below.

Temperatures refused to moderate as December appeared with its short daylight hours. Firewood disappeared rapidly, necessitating excursions increasingly farther from the cabin to find dry, dead wood. One morning a treasure was found a quarter-mile across the river. Seven tall, dead, standing pines were studded in a fifty-foot ring. These were downed, cut to 15-foot lengths, and carried to the cabin before lunch. By dusk, they were cut to stove length, split, and stacked. I hoped they would last two weeks.

Thirty minutes of light remained, so I set off to check two squirrel hot spots. I lined up a shot but pulling the trigger produced nothing. The shell jammed in the chamber and working the bolt proved futile. Returning to the cabin, I sat at the table and played gunsmith.

With the muzzle toward the ridgepole, I repeatedly worked the bolt and pulled the trigger. The shell wouldn't fire or eject. Even tapping and prying with the knife-tip was unsuccessful. Running out of tricks, I levered the bolt forward, pressing into the shell, and again pulled the trigger. There was a flash and tiny bark fragments drifted down. A hole appeared in a roof pole as the gunshot echoed throughout the small room. Cordite fumes filled the air.

It appeared to be a "warm-gun, cold-weather" situation produced by condensation freezing the shell and firing pin. Working on it near the stove thawed the breech and returned it to firing condition. It was taken apart, hung from the ridgepole to dry, and then sprayed with WD-40 for future use.

While the rifle heated, so did the outside temperature. With it came the snow. It fell for three days nonstop. Bright and early the following day I was off. It was already zero degrees and too warm for the down parka, so I dressed in layers. Even so, I sweated breaking trail in the deep snow. I thought, *snowshoes sure would be nice.* I should have finished them.

I trudged to the end of the trapline and followed a ridge northwest. From the ridge, I took a compass reading and picked a bearing to where the cabin should be, navigating the shortcut in the coming darkness. Soon the compass had to be read by match light. I stayed the course through thick willows, tall pines, and knee-deep snow. When it was over, I stood on the edge of my creek, 100 yards from the cabin.

The cabin had hardly come up to temperature when a snowmachine stopped on the ice below. Tea water was on before there was a knock on the door. Invited in, the stranger introduced himself as George, "Ray and Happy's brother." While I poured two cups, he explained that Ray was at the dentist in Fort McMurray. "We were drinking a little last weekend and got into a little scrap," he said. "I hit him in the jaw and knocked a few teeth loose so I'm checking his traps while he's down there."

How brotherly, I thought.

He continued with, "It's one of those times when you get drunk and don't know what you're doing and you're sorry for it the next day."

Then we talked about the bad rapids on the Slave River, followed by the inevitable subject of trapping. From there George told of his attempt at bootlegging in Fort Chipewyan. "Drank the damn stuff before I could sell it," he explained. "Then I had to go buy some from Joe to keep drinking. It just wasn't worth it."

George was the type that sure could tell a good story; he talked about his friend named Fred. "Crazy Fred" were the exact words he used. "He's the only one that can get lost in Fort Chipewyan," he stated. "He broke into the Hudson's Bay Store four times; stole a few candy bars and a pack of cigarettes. They finally got a little tired of him after he broke into the post office last year and put him in jail for six months. He said he stopped to get his mail, and they were closed so he just broke in and got it."

The tea was gone, and George was storied out. He stiffly rose from the guest stump and with a heavy limp, half-stepped toward the door. When asked about it, he said he broke it in a fight last year.

"They hauled me to the hospital and gave me a shot of something that put my head higher than the moon. I was laughing and chasing nurses in my wheelchair, really having a good time. Then they sent me home. Boy, no matter how much I drink, I never felt like that," he concluded.

George ducked under and limped over the log threshold and said, good night. I felt we'd get along well together, but also thought I made the right choice to spend the winter in these circumstances instead of Fort Chipewyan's.

The days leading up to Christmas were spent reading, writing, cutting wood, and walking the 16-mile squirrel line daily. Christmas was no different. While the world celebrated, I sat by myself in a cold, dusty one-room cabin in the middle of nowhere. Just like old prospectors, trappers, and even priests, I followed the path of my choosing. There were no qualms, just longings. I picked up the harmonica and played "The First Noel." Thus ended Christmas.

Two days after Christmas, I had returned home after a six-hour walk in deep snow at twenty degrees below zero. Hardly had I made it through the door when Ray stopped on his way through to check his trapline. It was a short visit and he did not look healthy.

Framed in his beaver hat, his face showed signs of abuse. His nose and cheeks were bruised, and empty spaces showed between his swollen lips. He had two teeth pulled on the bottom and one on top, all in front. I asked him how he felt, and he replied, "Not so good." They had been forced to wait until the swelling went down and just yesterday pulled the teeth. It did nothing for his smile.

New Year's passed, as Christmas had. The only thing it brought was a ten-day, minus forty-degree spree. Neither the wind nor the Cardinals moved, nor anything else. I'd take the occasional walk knowing I was the only thing moving in my environment. Hoarfrost glistened from every tree branch in the blinding sun, steam rose from water forced to the surface by the oppressive weight of thickening ice. It was a silent world broken only by my booted steps on crystalline snow.

Even with these walks, keeping busy became a chore. On the 9th of January, I tried in vain to connect with the Super Bowl on the little radio. In the five fleeting seconds of reception I did manage to hear that the Raiders led the Vikings 16 to 0 before the announcers faded back into static.

Another washday was soon upon me. This one was not for my clothes, however, but for me. Heating two buckets of water, one was used for the armpits up and the other from the armpits down. My union suit was in bad shape. The crotch was gone, and both legs were split down the inseam. Cut open and laid flat, they would have made great curtains for the window, but the ridicule would be hard to bear. I just slipped them into the wood stove.

Mid-January a thaw set in. Temperatures soared to 25 above. It felt like spring. Squirrel hunting was great, but the rifle wasn't. The day started out well with four kills out of four shots, but then things changed. I missed six in a row from less than thirty feet. A squirrel's head was about the size of a silver dollar and I just didn't miss shots like that, never mind six in a row.

After four shots at a black knot in a poplar tree, a six-inch pattern was produced that I could not comprehend. It must have been the result of shooting shells not intended for the rifle. Either way it was a depressing sight, as my livelihood was now at stake. To make the gun even less functional, the casing would split with each shot, expanding so much it had to be pried from the chamber. If I weren't so dependent on it, I would have sold it to Ray.

The warm weather held for a week, spurring a total devotion to squirrel hunting. No daylight was wasted in this endeavor. As the temperature cooled, I planned for a trip into town. The .22 shorts were gone, and some supplies were getting low. The day before leaving, I thoroughly cleaned the cabin, cut a generous amount of wood, and buried 150 squirrel skins behind the cabin in a stout wooden box.

It was well before daylight when I closed the door and wired it shut. Leaving Vagabond with a pat on the head and three days' worth of food, I descended the hill and started across the ice toward town. Vagabond didn't know whether to bark or eat. There was just a hint of light above the trees after I crossed Flett Lake and passed the Cardinals' camp. Only a thin wisp of smoke rose from the chimney of an unlit tent. The hard snow surface crunched beneath my feet as the heat wave of last week succumbed to twenty below temperatures. The noise sent the dogs into a barking frenzy, but no one appeared.

I continued along the tree-lined creek to the Slave River singing all the John Denver tunes I could remember. When that was accomplished, I switched to Johnny Rivers. They accompanied me two miles along the Slave River, rewarding me with a hoarse throat. With only 28 miles to go, I followed the main snowmachine trail along the river toward town. Five miles farther somebody on a snowmachine going in the opposite direction stopped long enough to tell me, "You're a whole long way from town, but it's a nice day for a walk."

With their empty encouragement, I followed the trail down the river, through tall, barren willows, over a rise of land, then back to the river. As the miles grew, so did the soreness on the inside of my thighs. The heavy Sorrels were not made for walking distances. They had lost their bounce by the time another snowmachine passed, disappearing around a bend as he headed for town. The guy didn't even wave. As the day progressed, the weather warmed.

It must have been close to zero degrees. Finally, though miles away, the radio tower appeared above the treetops. I kept walking with my down coat thrown over one shoulder and the sun setting over the other. Eventually, the river widened, and Lake Athabasca stretched to the horizon before me. To the left, the lighted buildings of Fort Chipewyan were in sight. It was another hour, almost dark, and ten minutes before five o'clock when I ascended the steps of the post office. It took just under ten hours to walk the 36 miles, *not a bad pace*. With three letters and a box under arm, I stopped at the store for a bag of Almond Crunch cookies and a can of fruit cocktail. With supper in my pack, I went to the only place in town with a room to rent.

It was a large trailer. In my allotted section there were four tiny bedrooms. For $14 a night, there were no interior doors to be had, not on the bathroom or the bedrooms. The choice was mine, but since I had the place to myself, I really didn't care.

After settling in I walked to the Athabascan Cafe for a cup of tea. Ray was walking out as I went in. When I told hm how I got to town, he responded in disbelief, "You walked all the way in? I leave at noon tomorrow and can give you a ride back," he said. I told him I would be ready.

After tea, I returned to the trailer for a hot, invigorating shower. It wasn't hot for long as the pipes soon turned cold. Sitting at the only table drying my hair, the door flew open and four men trampled in. They were in their forties and had just flown in from Edmonton. The whiskey bottle was opened before they were unpacked. I had a drink with them before two excused themselves, complaining of a rough day at their offices and a long flight to get here. I dug as deep as possible but found no sympathy. Having not seen a movie in over a year, I finished my drink, thanked my hosts, and headed for the cinema.

It was terrible. The picture was out of focus, and the sound was distorted. Since all the chairs were on a single, level plane, when someone in the front row moved, it created a chain reaction of movement that rippled all the way to the back row, where I happened to be seated. Kids ran rampant. The neck-wrenching experience lasted four hours including intermission and numerous breakdowns. It was eleven o'clock when I walked back into the trailer. One of the guys snored on the ragged couch. The empty whiskey bottle stood trophy-like, dominating the tabletop. Passing it, I flopped down on the bed. It had been a long day.

I slept two hours before waking in a sweat. The office personnel had cranked up the heat to seventy degrees for the city folk. Covered by only a sheet, I sweated until morning. Four snoring men left little silence as I packed my few things, went to the post office, and mailed my camera for repairs. Grocery shopping took no time and with little to do, I sat in a booth at the cafe and waited for Ray.

Many cups of tea later Ray arrived. We loaded the sled and headed for Flett Lake, me sitting behind him on the snowmachine. Things went smoothly as we glided across the white frozen crust. Occasionally a watery rooster tail trailed us as we sailed across seeping overflow. Four miles from the Cardinals' camp, the machine dropped 18 inches into a pocket of water. Gunning it, Ray sprayed water everywhere. We almost made it before the machine tipped.

Ray leapt to safety, landing on his dry feet, leaving me to go down with the ship. With windmill arms and flailing legs, I skidded on my butt across the water-covered ice while attempting to stand. Ice water filled my Sorrels, soaked my down mittens, and seeped through my wool pants. Ray was laughing much too hard to be of any assistance. Wet, but back on my feet, I helped him tip the machine up and pull it out, and we were on our way. Every few minutes I would hear a chuckle from up front, and Ray would shake his head. It was the first time I had heard him laugh.

Shortly we pulled up next to the tiny cabin at the Cardinals' place. Ray's mother was there along with his sister, girlfriend, and a cousin. While I dried my feet, Ray's mother fixed bannock and potatoes. The tea was delicious, the potatoes just right, and the bannock, if tried next to mine, would have embarrassed me. After an hour, Ray offered me a ride home. I was getting comfortable, but it was best that I left. Without incident, Ray pulled up below the cabin and we carried everything in. He had to check his trapline, so he left immediately after one last gibe—something about a duck with a broken wing trying to fly out of a pool of water. Halfway down the hill, he was still chuckling.

As Ray's taillight disappeared around the river bend, my attention turned to Vagabond. It would be an understatement to say he was glad to see me. Unleashed, he couldn't jump on me enough. After he was fed, and the cabin warmed, I read the news from home and then opened the package. There were clothes, treats, more soap than I'd ever use, and enough books to span the winter. Leaving everything on the table, I climbed into bed with a book called *Grizzly*, knowing tonight I wouldn't be sweating. It was four o'clock in the morning when the lamp ran dry.

Sweat was not a concern as I occasionally woke with a cold head. Condensation clouded my frosted face as I forced myself from the warm sleeping bag to start the stove. The sun had been up for hours. Apparently, one warm night in the five-star trailer had spoiled me. Then I looked at the thermometer. It was 52 degrees below zero.

Long johns were no match for those temperatures. I hustled to the cold stove, crisscrossing dry kindling on the dead ashes. Wanting quick heat, I took an empty can and half-filled it with fuel oil. It poured like a slush puppy. Holding a lighter under the can until it liquefied, I drenched the kindling, dropped a burning match inside, and stepped back. Nothing happened. Covered in goosebumps, I impatiently waited for the roar. A shiver ran through my bones as I peered inside. The match lay burning on top of a piece of oil-soaked kindling. Ceaseless shivers began, and a tingling developed in my fingers.

Grizzly was torn in half at the bookmark, and the already-read pages were carefully layered over the dying match. A corner flared and spread. Birch bark was placed over this and covered with more dry kindling. It flamed a few seconds, filling the room with a comfortable crackling. Soon a cherry-red spot began to grow on the side of the stove near the air vent. Since it would not do to ignite the cabin again, I had to be careful not to over-heat the barrel.

Round and round I turned like a rotisserie in front of the warming stove, trying to warm both sides of me. It was impossible. It was either one side or the other. After stoking the stove with logs, I chose the other and heated my backside to nearly its ignition point. Icicles still dropped from my beard as I dashed to the cold sleeping bag. Burrowing deep, I waited for the cabin to warm.

It never did exceed Sorrel and wool shirt temperatures but opening the front door did create a phenomenon. It appeared the world was afire as the inside and outside atmospheres collided, creating a dense cloudbank rolling toward the little stove. This was repeated throughout the day as I'd enter a frigid world, split two logs to heat my domain, then enter the much warmer cabin for two cups of tea. This process was continued until dark when the high of forty below reversed direction.

The cold weather held for days, but eventually I had to get out. It was 25 below when I left to check on the 16-mile line. *I'll pack the trail if nothing else.* And, I did pack the trail and nothing else. Nothing stirred, though it did cure my wanderlust for a few more frigid days. Cabin fever meant that soon the wood in the inside bin again reached the ceiling. It was guaranteed warmth, practically money in the bank. The latter, I did not want to think about.

February brought a lot of snow. Ray stopped-in one evening to tell me the price of squirrels had dropped from $1.25 to $.75 apiece. Dispirited, I wondered if all this walking was worthwhile. It had taken a devastating toll on my now smooth-soled Sorrels. The rubber on the sides was cracked and worn through, and three patches had to be sewn on each boot to keep the snow out. Since I couldn't afford sixty dollars for a new pair, they'd have to do.

Inspired by lengthening days and softened weather, the hunt

continued. Day after day I'd leave at first light, trudge through deep snow all day, and be lucky to be back by dark. Then the standard chores: *chip out the hole in the ice, carry water, fix supper, skin and stretch the day's catch.* I needed a change, a vacation. So, for two days I did virtually nothing. Then, with a pack on my back, I was gone before daylight.

As the sun slowly rose, I walked four miles into higher country, following a ridge for three miles before dropping down into a pine-covered valley where I stopped for lunch. After hunting the valley, I headed east for three miles and came to a long, frozen lagoon that extended into Flett Lake. A ribbon, made by a snowmachine split the inlet, heading toward the Cardinals' camp. I followed the ribbon in that direction.

It wasn't long before the bobbing light of a snowmachine rounded a point and raced toward me. Stepping off the trail, it stopped beside me, and a girl hopped off the sled's runners. It was Ray's younger sister Molly and their father Joe. Joe didn't speak English, so Molly did the talking.

She said her father had shot two moose ten miles away, and they were going to butcher them and bring them home. Looking at my pack, she asked, "How many squirrels you get?" I told her I got 13 today and had a total of 225. "Ooowee," she replied, "that's lots." When her father said something in Cree, Molly jumped back on the runners. They were off and disappeared into the fading light. There seemed to me to be a certain twinkle in her eyes and a very friendly smile on her face as she waved goodbye. *This cabin lifestyle, messing with my imagination,* I reasoned. Since I was still ten miles from home, I couldn't dwell on it.

The following morning, I again slid on my worn boots in the darkness of the cabin. *I must be half-crazy or a glutton for punishment.* I'd usually leave before daylight, walk twelve hours, and get home well after dark, hungry as a spring bear. Then I'd get up and do the same thing the next day, all for seven or eight dollars. It was a very difficult way to make a living. The scary thing was that I enjoyed it. It was still dark when I closed the door.

Like it or not, I soon had three days off without pay; strong winds were pushing a storm. It gave me time to overtake a backlog of chores that weren't crucial to daily life, so they never seemed to get done; things like sewing missing buttons, darning holes in socks, tightening loose handles, and sharpening dull knives. The tasks never seemed to end.

It was mid-February before the weather calmed and I was back on the prowl, beginning with a good ten-dollar day. Leaving my main trail, I took a shortcut in order to reach home before dark. This brought me to the trail that ran between the Cardinals' and my territory. Two sets of small moccasin tracks went in each direction on the trail, indicating possible visitors during my absence. I followed the tracks to the cabin door.

Swinging from the ridgepole of my cabin was a white package. Sliding the looped rope off over the pole, I brought the package inside. A note fell to the dirt floor as I crossed it to light the lamp. On the postcard sized scrap of paper was printed:

Dear Sir,

We came here to visit you, but you were not home. We brought you some moose meat. I wonder if you will like it and if you want some more meat, you can come and get some more. We are coming to visit you on Wed.

Signed,
Molly & Marlene

Thinking it a very considerate gesture, I wasted no time cutting a thick steak from the five-pound block of meat. The last time I had a piece of good, red meat was with John and Tory, sitting under a rain-drenched canoe on Cemetery Island eight months ago. The steak covered the bottom of the ten-inch pan and curled up the sides. It sizzled away as I mixed a batch of bannock and started a pan of rice. The aroma filling the cabin tested my self-control. Finally, without restraint, I completed the feast. It was all I could do to finish.

Contented, I rocked back on the stump, picking my teeth with a sliver of wood, remembering the twinkle in Molly's eyes when I met her on the trail with her father. *Could that have anything to do with the moose meat?* I wondered. Maybe it was just coincidence, but today happened to be February 14, Valentine's Day.

Staying home the next day, I arranged my life for visitors by washing my spoon and two cups, baking bread, taking a bath, and raking the floor. The weather was an absurd forty above, causing water to run off the roof. 52 degrees below seemed a lifetime away.

When Wednesday arrived, the cousins made their entrance at noon. After hushed voices and a light knock, I invited them in. As they shyly stood next to the woodpile, I asked if they'd like to sit down. Awkwardly, they took the few steps to the bed and sat down. I stationed myself on the stump. Marlene was blushingly shy, and Molly had little to say at first. Because I am near the bottom rung of the conversationalist ladder, the first half-hour was strained. All I could think of were questions about them and the area.

Finally, our tongues loosened. "How big is that city called Minnesota you come from?" Marlene asked. I told her it was a state, kind of like Saskatchewan or Alberta. That seemed to be the turning point. Now it was their turn to ask questions and did they ever. They had to know all about my family, friends, their ages, and what Minnesota was like. It dawned on me that these girls had probably never been fifty miles outside of Fort Chipewyan.

"How often you wash your floor?" Marlene even wanted to know. She immediately flushed with embarrassment having realized it was dirt.

"You'll have to bring your scrub brush over next time and clean it for me," I teased.

"Oh you," she said as the redness deepened. I refilled their two teacups many times as they tried to teach me words in the Cree language. Though I proved incompetent at Cree, I did pick up information about my furs. Only a few weeks remained to squirrel hunt.

"Next month it warms up and they turn black inside and are no good to sell," Molly stated. Her father had 110 already. "44 which I shot," she beamed.

Molly then turned the conversation towards, what I suspected was, the real reason she was there, "Whatsa matter you? How come you never come down to visit?" I offered a lame excuse, and she ended the subject with, "You better pretty soon or my mother will get mad and come over here and get you." That, I didn't need to hear, and I promised to visit soon.

It was already getting dark when they said they had to go. "I saw a big black bear yesterday in the woods between our camps and he really looked hungry," I chided. That got their attention and earned me the privilege of walking them home.

I walked three-quarter-stride behind the two moccasin-clad women. Marlene was a junior in high school, and Molly was three years older. They gabbed all the way, enough to scare any bear. "How come you spent Christmas and New Year's out here all by yourself?" Molly wanted to know.

"I didn't have any place else to go," I replied.

"You should have come to our house!"

Feeling safe within a mile from their camp, they assured me I had walked them far enough. Then Molly asked if I had liked the moose meat. After receiving a positive response, she responded, "We only brought a little last time because we didn't know if you'd like it. We'll come the same time Monday and bring lots of it." As we said our goodbyes standing on the ice in the dark, a dim square of light showed from their cabin just a mile away. While they walked down the snowmachine trail, Ray's scoped .22 rifle was slung over Molly's shoulder with little Marlene following close behind.

The next two days were dedicated to squirrel hunting. On the 20th, I ate a huge breakfast and sipped tea for two hours, planning to cut wood all morning and hunt all afternoon. While I was out front "returning tea to nature," I heard female voices at the bottom of the hill. Bow-legged, I moved to the back of the cabin. Molly and Marlene had come to visit.

"It's too nice out and nothing to do at home," Molly lamented. After sharing the traditional cup of tea inside, Molly picked up the guitar and strummed a few chords. Although shy about singing, she sounded good once motivated. "This one reminds me of you," she said as she sang "Blue Eyes Crying in the Rain." Failing to get me to sing, they both attacked my love life. Marlene wanted to know if I had any girlfriends.

"How come you're not married?" prodded Molly.

Having no good answer, I replied, "No one ever asked me to."

Then Marlene whispered something in Molly's ear—

"You ask him."

"No, you!" Marlene replied

Molly defied, "No, I'm not going to ask him."

"Well, you're the one that wants to marry him!" Marlene piped a little louder than I believed she had intended. Molly's face flushed in the ensuing silence. Me, I feigned hearing loss and busied myself with the teapot.

As her embarrassment faded, Molly asked, "Do you have any pictures here?" The only pictures I had were in a magazine that my brother had sent. There were half a dozen pictures and four or five pages of script done by the editor of the *Water, Woods, and Wildlife,* a magazine in Minnesota.

"Are you going to keep these?" Molly inquired.

"Yah, I've been using pages out of it to start fires in the morning," I kidded.

"Oh, no, no!" she cried, "I'll take them," and she did.

By evening a snowmachine stopped below the hill and a knock sounded on the door. It was Molly's older sister, coming to give them a ride home. She stayed for half an hour before the three left, all crowding onto the seat. "Watch out for that bear!" I called after them. Waving, they headed for home.

The next three days I covered many miles, hunting hard until I ran out of shells. This necessitated another trip into town. I allowed one day of rest and relaxation before the long walk. During my recuperation the cousins stopped by, driving Joe's snowmachine. They wanted to borrow books for a few days, and I told them to take whichever ones they wanted. When I mentioned to Molly that I was walking to town in the morning, she replied, "For what, to find a girl?" There sure seemed to be some zip in the little woman.

"Well, it's pretty hard to say what I'll be finding in town," I said with raised eyebrows and a coy smile. She thanked me for the books and left.

Since the days were getting longer, I waited until some light showed before leaving. Little activity surrounded the Cardinals' camp. Only the dogs acknowledged my passage. The temperature had dropped drastically so any slush had frozen, making the walk more tolerable. Carrying a walking stick, I stopped occasionally to send an ice chunk arching into the treetops with my flawed golf swing. Nothing stirred, not even the wind.

Halfway to town I abandoned the birch club and focused my energy on the trail. Not one snowmachine was seen throughout the day as I tacked on mile after mile. As I approached the outskirts of Fort Chipewyan, a dead dog lay beside the tree-lined trail, its role in life reduced to carrion. Even though it was 5:20 when I reached the post office, I could see Bill through the dirty window still sorting mail. Tapping the window, I was able to conduct business through the back door where he handed me two letters and a box containing my repaired camera. Then, I was off to the trailer.

With my money in the cash drawer I was informed that the

sewer line and water pipes were frozen. "But," the manager added, "you can shower in the small cabin behind the trailer."

There was no heat in the cabin. Until I turned the stiff faucet handle a six-inch icicle dangled from the chrome showerhead. Like snorts from a raging bull, two blasts of air sounded and then, amazingly, water spurted out. I undressed in a cloud of steam and dashed under the hot water.

Only when the water cooled did I dive back into my clothes. White frost formed on the walls as I pulled on my stocking hat. I shuddered at the thought of being buck naked and wet at twenty degrees below as I hustled back to the heat of the trailer. I chose the same room as last visit. With my hair somewhat dry, I walked to the makeshift theater and watched the weekly movie.

I did my shopping early in the morning, getting a good start on the 36-mile walk. On my feet were a new pair of cheap imitation-leather boots with gum soles, on sale for $9.99—about the price of my cabin. On my back was a 75-pound pack. Its weight included my old boots that I dared not throw away.

Halfway home I set the pack down to rest. Hardly had I gotten situated when a snowmachine stopped. "Hop on, I'll get you to the Cardinals' camp," said a young Native man. Putting my pack into the towed-behind sled, I had barely mounted the runners before we were off. It was my lucky day.

To the young, velocity is a virtue. I was able to confirm this as we accelerated down the river, contacted a large heave in the ice, and became airborne. The sled flipped in midair. I bounced twice before rolling to a stop. Through a spinning world, I saw my pack with $500 worth of newly repaired camera equipment whiz by. The area above my knee was already in pain before I skidded to a stop. "Are you hurt? Machine has too much power!" he said, wide-eyed. I reloaded the sled and got back on.

True to virtue, the kid's speed still knew no boundaries. He threw me once more before reaching the Cardinals' camp, but being my lucky day, I landed in soft snow. I thanked him and left before he could offer me a ride home, limping across Flett Lake.

Slow Thaw

Before long, March 1st came in sunny and warm. I couldn't take being holed-up anymore. Grabbing the rifle, I was off. After a long day's hunt and a good catch, I walked behind the cabin to gather kindling to start the evening fire. Little moccasin prints abounded, and my name was scratched into the snow in a dozen different places. With my arms full of dry pine branches, I rounded the side of the cabin and faced an elaborate work of graffiti. At eye level, etched deep into a large poplar tree was "M.C. + J.P."

Now that gave me something to think about as I attacked a huge pan of fried ptarmigan and bannock. My thoughts were altered by the sound of approaching snowmachines. Walking to the bank, I saw headlights scanning the trees as they advanced along the bumpy trail. Back inside I did a quick clean, and within minutes the machines were stopped and silent. Voices replaced their mufflers.

After a resounding knock, George was the first to enter. "How you doing, Jerry, old buddy?" he said with a wink. Behind him entered his girlfriend, Irene, an Eskimo from a village at the mouth of the Mackenzie River, a guy I hadn't met before named Edward, and Molly. George sat on the edge of the bed, unzipped his coat, and took out a bottle of Seagram's VO whiskey, almost empty.

"Have a drink with us there, buddy," George said waving the bottle. My chipped porcelain cup was half-filled with water, then topped with VO. Taking a small sip, I passed the cup to George. He clumsily passed it to Irene, then a brief stop at Molly, who, as a non-drinker, declined, before it was shuffled to Edward, and returned to me. George picked up the guitar and filled the room with a bluegrass Cree melody. After two songs the party was ready to move to Ray's cabin.

"Come on and have a drink at Ray's!" everyone pleaded, except Edward. I skeptically climbed on the machine behind George. We were off into the night in an instant.

Ray and Leona sat at the table reading *True Detective* magazines as we entered. After George's warm welcome, Leona poured tea. The VO cup was already blended when the two girls entered behind Edward. He was covered with snow, having been the third person on a small machine. Edward sat at the table with Ray and Leona as cards were dealt. While George and Irene sat on the bed, I sat to one side with Molly. George's grunted snores soon dominated the conversation. Ray turned up the volume on the Charlie Pride tape in compensation.

After one round of the cup, the bottle was reduced to one amber swallow. Everyone, except Edward, agreed that I should have the honor of finishing it—and I did. George snored on.

As there were only two chairs in the cabin, Edward knelt at the table, playing cards. When he dropped two cards and picked them up, I instinctively looked down and noticed his half-smoked cigarette burning into the dry wooden floorboards. Trying to be friendly, I picked it up and handed it to him. He took it without thanks, smoked it, and then nonchalantly returned it to the combustible floor. I don't know if Edward didn't like me or if it was just because I was sitting next to Molly.

The card game continued for an hour until Leona suggested we continue the journey. She shook and shoved George, rousing him to a sitting position. Bobbing and weaving at the edge of the bed, he dazedly oriented himself, took careful aim at the exit, and plunged into the cold, night air. The machines soon came to life, as did George.

Edward insisted on riding with Irene and Molly, so my fate was in the hands of George. Following Irene's machine, things must have seemed dull to George—to relieve his boredom, he would pull his machine ahead until the shroud of his nudged the rear of the machine in front of him. Pinning the throttle, he'd send the machines along at a lively clip. When the girls screamed loud enough, he'd slack off and have a good laugh.

Molly perched on the last few inches of the seat, clinging to a delighted Edward for dear life. I suggested to George that maybe I should drive as he closed the gap again, sending the scream-laden machine faster down the trail. At that moment the ski on Irene's machine clipped a tree, spinning it sideways in the trail. George swerved to the right, missed Molly by inches, and came to an abrupt stop at the base of a poplar tree. All went flying.

"What the hell you trying to do, kill me!" George screamed unjustly. Irene retaliated with unladylike comments of her own before we all gathered around the Ski-Doo to assess the damage.

The cracked cowling left plenty of yellow paint on the poplar and a buckled ski pointed skyward. A two-foot strip of bark dangled from its twisted tip. George's bouncing weight failed to alleviate the ski problem, so we continued on at a much slower pace.

Dismounting in front of my cabin, I waved goodbye to the somber caravan. It was nearly midnight. With the temperature at 45 degrees, I hated to go in, but the sky seemed to convey a warm morning. In addition, I had things that needed to be done tomorrow. On the way up the bank, I wondered what George was going to tell his father; he had just bought the now-crippled machine new that morning.

The snow was vanishing fast. Leaving before daylight, I walked the 21-mile extended line for the last time, retrieving the few lynx snares I had set over the winter. I resigned myself to the fact that it was a very poor year for lynx. That I had left abundant breeding stock was little consolation. The squirrels were a different story. The season's tally stood at 424.

Soon after returning home from the 21-mile hike, Molly came by and told me that Ray was going to town tomorrow and, "Offered to sell your squirrels for you." Seeing as how I had no Canadian trapping license, I more than welcomed the opportunity. At last month's rate, my depleted bank account would raise about $400. Since the balance had slid well below the thousand-dollar mark and Nome lay many months away, his kind offer was a much-needed boost.

I was up before the sun's rays pierced the forest with the intention of forever preserving my winter's hunt in the archives of photographic history. For over an hour, I sat on the stump, stringing squirrel hides onto quarter-inch nylon rope. With the hides strung onto two ropes, I tied them between two trees, one tier above the other. Then, with the camera set and the hides neatly arranged, I wound the self-timer and dashed back for a "hunter-and-his-prey" photo.

As winter waned, it was time to take my winter's catch into Fort Chipewyan.

I had time for only two pictures before a steady drone betrayed a fast-approaching snowmachine. With controlled panic, I destroyed any evidence of the scene. I'd feel very foolish if Ray, or any trapper, caught me in this vain position, for one lynx skin was worth more than my entire winter's catch. Molly and Marlene trapped squirrels, ten-year-old boys trapped squirrels, but 27-year-olds who were supposedly at home in the bush didn't trap squirrels. Sometimes one had to be humble.

I managed to get the hides into the pack before Ray's smiling face showed above the bank. "Ready?" he asked as I threw two letters in with the squirrels and shut down the stove. The first stop was the Cardinals' camp for a cup of tea with Molly and her mother while Happy and Ray packed the sled. With that chore complete, we started for town.

Ray and Irene rode the machine, Happy stood on the sled runners, and the "Great White Hunter" reclined in the sled's basket with his feet propped on his winter's catch.

Our small troupe moved slowly toward Fort Chipewyan with the little Ski-Doo Elan pulling more than it should have. We halted three times during the two-hour trek, twice due to the operation rolling on its side and once midway for tea. Passing homes on the bank above the frozen river and climbing the hill where I docked the canoe, we navigated the main street past the Athabascan Cafe. Amazingly, the same room was available at the same trailer. The trip sure beat walking!

Things were going well, and I was in high spirits. I received a box from my brother, did my shopping, and scrimped for a shirt and pair of jeans for the summer's travels. Then I met Ray. We were in the middle of Main Street when he informed me, "I just sold your skins. The guy I usually sell to is out of town, so I had to sell to someone else."

"What kind of price did you get?" I asked with greedy expectations. He pulled out a roll of bills wrapped in paper and bound with a rubber band.

"Hundred twenty," he said as he handed me the compact bundle.

"What?" I uttered, feeling my face redden.

"The guy said it was late in the season and that's all he'd give me for them," Ray explained.

I felt cheated, ripped off and kicked between the pockets. "The receipts right there with it. I gotta go to the Bay. See you later," came Ray's fading voice. Then, he was gone.

The sun shone brightly as I stood alone in ankle-deep mud on the main thoroughfare of Fort Chipewyan holding a few ragged pieces of Canadian money in one hand and a small piece of white paper in the other. I was not happy and could not think of enough names to call that flea-infested fur buyer, though I tried my damnedest.

I had a hard time coming to terms with the thought of all those hard-earned skins piled neatly on his floor. I could hear him gloating, "What a deal I made with that fool! Easiest 300 bucks of my life!" I wasn't much happier with Ray, for he seemed little concerned with my interests. In my barely-controlled rage, I even envisioned a $300 split between Ray and his friendly fur buyer. As I shoved the bills to the bottom of my pocket and headed back to the trailer, the many torn pieces of the receipt blew across the muddy street.

I decided to watch a double feature that evening to rid my mind of misfortune. On the way to the theater I calculated my winter's profit. It seemed there wasn't any. I had walked 1,500 miles through deep snow without snowshoes, eradicated $100 worth of ammunition, and spent untold hours skinning, fleshing, and stretching flea-infested squirrels. It seemed it was time to change professions.

The movies weren't worth watching when I had watched them three years earlier, and they hadn't improved with age. On the way back to the trailer, I met Ray and Irene walking hand in hand along the road. "We'll be leaving first thing in the morning," Ray remarked. That was fine, I was ready to leave at any time.

Morning arrived crisp and clear. With everything packed, I was more than ready to return to Flett Lake. Half-frozen mud crunched beneath my feet as I walked to meet Ray at the Athabascan Cafe. I chose a booth facing the front door to watch the comings and goings of Fort Chipewyan. There were plenty of comings and goings, but there was no Ray. By noon I could drink no more tea and walked to the post office.

There stood Ray and Happy. Blood ran freely from Ray's mouth and nose. "I'll get that skinny little son of a bitch," he vowed while smearing the flowing mess across his shirtsleeve. Apparently, Ray had been drinking through the night. When he entered the Hudson's Bay Store to cash a check, the clerk wouldn't cash it, saying Ray was too drunk. In the midst of Ray's rebellion, the clerk hit him. Meanwhile, another clerk and the manager came to the aid of their comrade. Someone clubbed Ray with a two-by-four, and the three unceremoniously dumped Ray out the back door.

Ray was convinced he needed some coffee so Happy and I guided him to a booth at the cafe. The waiter brought a pot of coffee and enough napkins to wash Ray's crusting face. Only a trickle of blood remained dripping from Ray's nose when an RCMP officer approached our booth. "Do you have any white gloves?" he said directly to Ray.

Ray became a model of innocence as he remarked, "White gloves, just these." He threw a pair of dirty, white cotton gloves onto the table-top.

"Open your coat," the officer instructed Ray. Ray complied and was lightly frisked. I was sitting on Ray's right and watched the proceedings. From my angle, I could see into Ray's coat. Under his left armpit there appeared to be many fingers that belonged to a pair of white leather gloves. I sipped my coffee, minding my own business. "You that American that's staying at Flett Lake?" he asked me.

I answered, "Yes."

"Were you here when this happened?" he asked.

I replied, "No."

He turned to Happy and asked, "How about you Happy?" Happy remarked that he knew nothing about it. The RCMP officer turned and left. The tension seemed to leave with him as Ray rezipped his coat.

"You were lucky," I said to him.

He looked me right in the eye with great misunderstanding on his face and grunted, "Huh?" I poked him under his left arm. He gave me a broad smile, got up, and enthusiastically roused, "Let's go find something to drink!" It appeared I wouldn't be getting home today. Maybe Ray did have a friendly fur buyer.

As Happy went his way, Ray went chasing the bottle; I went back to the room. Darkness arrived. At least that was one thing a person could depend on around here. It was a warm evening, so I thought I'd walk to the other end of town to see the Cardinals' house in the city. "Where you going?" someone shouted as a snowmachine stopped next to me. He introduced himself as "Charlie." When I told him, he stated, "We just came from there and nobody's home. They're at my sister's house, having a party. Hop on. I'll have you there in just a few minutes." Those few minutes were just what I feared. But it was Friday night and I didn't have to work in the morning.

The next morning, I walked to the edge of the lake where a crowd was gathered. Sometime during the early morning, a concession stand had been erected. It appeared the town was having a Spring Carnival. On the lake, mushers were harnessing dog teams for the start of a race, and a cameraman milled through the crowd interviewing people. It looked like most of the townspeople showed up, many congregated at the concession stand. Soon the dog teams were on the trail and wouldn't be back for an hour. I decided to walk the two miles to the Cardinals' home because I needed to get back to Flett Lake.

I found no such luck once there. I hoisted my empty pack, vowed to find Ray in the morning, and started down the trail to the trailer hotel. *Patience,* I told myself as I walked. A small Ski-Doo pulled next to me, and one of the riders said, "Where you going, Jerry?" I had no idea who it was, but the two of them were in quite a stupor.

"Back to the hotel," I answered.

They staggered off the machine and one of them was able to slur, "Help us finish this beer and we'll give you a ride there." It took no time at all for the bottle was already empty.

I had my Duluth Pack with me, and the one named Ed said, "Jerry, you sit in the middle and I'll wear your pack and hang on behind you." I relinquished my pack and the crowded little Ski-Doo putted toward downtown.

"We lost your buddy!" I shouted to the driver before we had made it 100 yards.

He half-turned and said, "Yah!" and kept going.

"He's got my pack with him!" I yelled over the engine noise. He kept going. When I looked back, Ed was in a staggering run, waving his arms and yelling. We drove on. At last, we stopped at the hotel and I got off. "What about your buddy back there?" I asked.

"Who?" he asked through clouded eyes.

"The guy that fell off back there," I pleaded. Not concerned about old Eddy, I wanted my pack back.

"I don't know," he slurred and away he went having noticed two girls walking down the street. I walked back down the trail for the third time that day looking for my pack and Ed. Both had disappeared.

This weekend must have been the biggest celebration of the year because when I returned to my room, a Fort Chipewyan social was in progress. "Have a beer!" a guy called Tom greeted me with one. *So much for the idea of relaxing with a good book.* For the next twelve hours, booze and broads seemed the focus of the town.

I left soon after, spending the evening at the restaurant drinking tea. When I returned to the hotel, the party was over, but the partiers hadn't left. There were no empty beds. Kicking aside a few beer bottles, I rolled out my sleeping bag on the hard floor.

After three hours of harassment the next morning, I took a shot of whiskey to appease my roommates. Just about then Happy arrived and was convinced to have a few chugs on the bottle, too. From there we stopped at his friend's place to retrieve my lost Duluth Pack. There, another party smoldered. Happy wasn't much of a drinker, and a few more shots did little to right his equilibrium.

Three dogs sprinted from Happy's sled as we left the house. The mongrels had torn open the canvas and from what I could see, ripped open my sack of flour and eaten most of my butter. Happy said a few choice words, tied the tarp back up, and off we went.

On the way home many were the times that I tapped Happy on the shoulder and shouted, "The sled's tipped again!" And, many were the times that he would address it indifferently. Fortunately, everything was securely tied in a canvas sled bag or we would have returned home with an empty sled. Happy was apparently eager to return to the bush.

It was dusk when we pulled in front of my home on the hill. We undid the ropes that secured our load to the sled, and Happy groaned as the canvas was pulled back. A look of dismay spread across his face. My flour, sugar, oatmeal, and Crisco oil were a heterogeneous mess. With a couple dozen eggs and a few more miles, I would have had months' worth of cookie dough. My misfortune wasn't Happy's concern, however. The remnants of a cardboard box and broken, empty suitcase was. They had contained his girlfriend's wardrobe.

We did what we could, but it wasn't much. When we finished separating our load, two piles lay on the ice. One contained the remains of my groceries; the other, mutilated clothing. With a sigh, Happy stuffed the goo-impregnated clothes under the tarp, threw the broken suitcase on top, and lashed everything down. We bid each other good night and Happy headed for camp. I hoped his girlfriend was forgiving; he only had a few short miles to think of one grand explanation.

I was weary. Through all my visiting, I hadn't eaten since Friday afternoon and here it was Sunday night. What was left of my groceries I dumped on the table. After eating a pound of cheese and half a box of crackers, I crawled into the cold sleeping bag planning to emerge only when forced by hunger, nature, or the stove. So ended the Fur Rendezvous of '76.

I awoke famished twelve hours later. Gratified by a huge breakfast, I salvaged the remaining groceries. Careful rationing would be pertinent until the rivers opened. With the mangled groceries arranged, the cabin received a thorough cleaning. The finishing touch was the installation of wall-to-wall "cardboard carpeting" to keep the dusty dirt floor where it belonged.

The following day I hit the trail, rested and charging full-bore. By three o'clock I was back with four rabbits for the stew pot. Tracks indicated two small-footed people visited while I was gone, no doubt female. By dusk, the chores were done, and I was reclined on the bough bed reading a relaxing Western. The flickering yellow light from the kerosene lamp rolled across the pages as a gentle breeze found its way down the bean-can chimney. I stirred from my daze when I thought I heard voices. I sat unmoving, all concentration directed to my ears. There was no mistake, the voices were getting nearer. Suspiciously, they were from behind the cabin. With rifle in hand, I snuck into the near-darkness.

"Oh, we're tired," puffing red-faced Molly said, as she trudged toward the cabin. Marlene dragged behind in no better condition. "We followed your tracks this afternoon all the way to the top of that big hill, and then way, way, around, shouting and shouting, but we never saw you," Molly lamented.

Marlene stammered, "Boy, that was a long way! We were tired, and it was getting dark, and we were almost lost, and really scared." Her voice trailed off as Molly gave her a disapproving glance. They limped in for a cup of tea, not knowing how fortunate they were. I had walked only half the usual distance that day.

Molly, Marlene, and I walked abreast through the darkness covering Flett Lake. It was a slow pace with little talking, very unusual. Across the lake, a snowmachine came to life, and soon a bobbing light approached. It was Joe looking for his daughter and niece. After a few things were said in Cree, the two girls somberly boarded the machine. Joe didn't seem happy. As the red-tailed Ski-Doo faded across Flett Lake, I turned and walked home.

March slowly came to an end. In the two weeks since Molly and Marlene's trek, I had written 200 pages of manuscript, doing little else except daily chores. Days were growing longer, and winter breakup seemed an endless tease. I was restless. For relief, I packed a lunch and left before dawn on a twenty-mile jaunt, confident there would be no followers.

It was hours after dark when I passed in front of the Cardinals' camp. Their dogs filled the night with a chorus of excited rapture. A lone figure emerged from the unlit tent and invited me in for coffee. It was Sam, one of Joe's friends. Explaining that the whole family had gone to town, he was left by himself. We entered the dark tent, warmed by a glowing stove.

Sam resumed his task from prior to my arrival, struggling with the cap to a Coleman lantern, while I directed a flashlight on the project. No matter how hard he pounded the refill cap, it wouldn't turn. Through two cups of coffee he fought, finally throwing the lantern into a corner with disgust. Cursing his lost pliers, he settled for the soft glow of a candle.

I reclined into three layers of black bear hides and questioned Sam about trapping lynx. As moonlight filtered through the many burn holes in the tent's roof, candled shadows played against the water-stained canvas walls.

Sam placed a number 3 Victor trap on the pine bough floor as the square tin stove snapped a command, sending a shower of glowing sparks into the night air. Outlining a cubby with his finger, he explained the use of stepping sticks as a few of the hotter embers settled on the tent, adding to the multitude of holes. "You put meat in can and leave it near stove. In two weeks, add perfume and put here," he explained while pointing to the back of the make-believe cubby. It took some explaining in his broken English before I realized the perfume wasn't manufactured by Estee Lauder but came from between a beaver's back legs.

Much to my dismay, Sam drifted from trapping to bragging about his most harrowing firefighting days. "Couple of years ago a helicopter and water bomber crash," he said. "Everyone died. Before that, dumb Indian walk into propeller. No more head," he continued shaking his head. "Then tree fall on another Indian's head and he die." I told Sam it sounded like dangerous work, but he replied, "No, no, not for me. Me cook." Pointing to his chest, he said, "Up at four o'clock and cook for fifty men." But there were drawbacks. "They make me wear this real bright orange coat. Can't hide or sleep no place no more."

Sam conveyed that he was by himself because Joe and his family had to attend a funeral. "The guy died of headaches," Sam said. When I asked if it was a brain tumor, he said he didn't know what that was, but explained that the deceased was drinking when his wife hit him over the head with a whiskey bottle. He went on his trapline the next day and complained to his partner about a headache. "Next day, dead," Sam said summing it up. I couldn't argue with that prognosis.

After some time, Sam ended his long-ago adventure tales from the fast and turbulent waters of the Mackenzie River with two huge yawns. I would have liked to have heard more about the river trip, but those universal good night signs couldn't be ignored. I thanked Sam for his hospitality and stepped into the cool April air. It was past midnight and the moon had vanished. Descending the bank, I started on the crusty, white trail home. Sam had already extinguished the candle.

April brought an abundance of warmth. Already the river in front of the cabin revealed a watery chasm. A fire was needed only for cooking as winter relaxed its grip on the Northland. The smell of life-giving spring was in the air. As fear of freezing slackened, my caution would be renewed. I descended the riverbank with the water bucket, and chips flew as the ax bit the thinning ice. Beckoning a few feet away was the torrent of open water. There was no apparent reason to chop through ice when all that was necessary to fill the bucket was a little light-footedness.

The reason became abruptly apparent as I crashed through and sank to the bottom. I stopped with a gentle thud as air bubbles streamed toward the halo a foot above my head. Current brushed my face as I followed the bubbles to the surface. Despite the shore-side ice scraping my armpits, I gave two good kicks, got a leg on top of the ice, and rolled out, grateful to be wearing blue jeans and a t-shirt, not winter-wear. Breathing came in gasps as I dashed for the warmth of the cabin. A towel and a change of clothes removed any evidence of my lazy indiscretion. When the shivers subsided, I retrieved the water bucket that had stopped twenty feet past my new water hole. Receiving a worse fate, the ax lay in a watery grave beneath the ice, for only future archeologists to recover. I had no intention of going after it.

With the matter of water access resolved, I set out to disarm and recover two lynx snares at the end of my fruitless trapline. I expected nothing in them and that was what I got. It was dark when I passed the Cardinals' cabin and without snowshoes, my body was weary from walking twenty miles in soft wet snow. I made plenty of noise in passing, and the dogs eagerly responded.

As the tent flaps flew open, "Come on up, Jerry!" echoed across the lake. It wasn't long before a cup of coffee was at my feet and a bowl of steaming moose stew was in my lap. Everyone in the tent seemed to watch me eat. The assembled crew included Joe, Mrs. Cardinal, George, Irene, Ray, Leona, Tom, Sam, Happy, Molly, Marlene, Alphonse, and Willey. The small tent was crowded. I stayed for the whole two-and-a-half-hour, Cree-talking, coffee-drinking spree. I didn't understand half of what was said but laughter abounded. Finally, George gave me a ride home, though Molly offered her services as well. It was a full day but not quite over. I drank so much coffee that sleep evaded me for hours, even in my exhaustion.

Snow turned to rain as the spring days warmed and lengthened. I read a book a day and quietly neglected my writing. Wanderlust had its grip on me and wouldn't let go. Thankfully Ray stopped early one morning and said, "My dad says you can hunt muskrats along the river, if you want to." It was a welcome change, a break from boredom, a new occupation.

Vagabond left shortly after Ray did that morning. Calling throughout the day was in vain. Just hours before dark, I started a search upstream. The six-mile walk produced nothing. Darkness neared. As I approached the cabin, I could see a faint outline moving toward me, well down the trail in the Cardinals' direction. It would take a few steps, stop, scan its surroundings, and then proceed in this cautious manner. Slipping behind a tree, I set an ambush. Slowly it neared. Every so often a clanging metallic sound could be heard. I had no idea what that could be until it came into view. "Just where have you been?" echoed between the riverbanks as I jumped from my blind. Vagabond leapt straight up, landed in a low crouch, and began slinking on his belly along the ice to lay his head against my feet. "I should leave this thing on you and teach you a lesson," I said as I pushed down the weak spring of a small muskrat trap he acquired sometime during the day.

Although there was no way a trap that size could hurt him, his melodrama made it appear that his leg was shattered, and he wouldn't last the night. Managing to push open the door, he curled up in his favorite spot next to the stove. I fixed him a plate of food, hoping the pain wasn't too excessive for him to get it down. It was gone in two minutes. In another few minutes, he was snoring. Ah, the joy of being home! By morning Vagabond's recuperation was complete, though he made a wide circle around the trap dangling from the sawbuck.

It was the middle of April and a 100-yard stretch of open water lay in front of the cabin, just enough for a short, canoe-based muskrat hunt. I pushed the canoe in and got three. The cruise the next day got five. Ray stopped in that afternoon with a few letters and a package containing an assortment of Easter tidings from my family. One letter was an invitation to my ten-year high school class reunion. The other contained my bank statement confirming that I was worth $595.

As rotting ice succumbed to open water, the muskrat tally slowly increased. Early morning and late evening hunts produced more skins than my stretching boards could handle, so down came the writing table. No guilt pains arose as I cut it into four tapered boards, for a pen hadn't touched my hand in a month. Besides, the bank statement provided a logical justification. At this point in my life, stretching boards were more important.

Departure was getting close. My guess was within a month. A day of preparation was set aside to avoid any last-minute delays. While things to be mailed home filled a small box, things not essential to the trip were discarded near the empty woodbox. The food box was taken apart, re-glued, and re-nailed. Clothing was sewn, and buttons re-attached. I was ready in just two hours.

Now I could concentrate on *Wilderness Man,* by Lovat Dickson. Chapter Two was interrupted by the whine of a chainsaw. I went out the door to see Joe and his friend Willey slowly making their way toward me, both swinging hatchets. Behind them was Ray with a chainsaw, followed by Molly and Marlene acting as the cleanup crew. The procession marched through my front yard. Since it was hard getting by the river in front of the cabin, the Cardinal Council had voted to develop a bypass. It was the bush version of eminent domain. I went inside, got my gloves, and gave them a hand.

When the trail was fully punched through, the crew lined up for a picture. Marlene hid her face, but I snapped a solo of her sitting on a log soon after. With the click of the shutter, she jerked her head up like a startled whitetail deer, turned beet red with eyes verging on tears, and then dashed for the underbrush. Molly had a good laugh and then moved in. She gave me an addressed picture of herself, tormenting me until I promised to write her this summer. With her mission accomplished, she rejoined the crew as they headed home.

Muskrat hunting drew to a standstill. The boards lay empty. After a cruise through my hunting grounds proved futile, I beached the canoe on the edge of the still solid lake and crossed to the Cardinals' camp for a visit. Since it was washday, everyone was busy. I drifted from one tent to another drinking coffee, visiting, and taking pictures. An invitation to supper introduced me to fried beaver tail and dried muskrat, which I found surprisingly edible.

Toward evening Joe vanished and later returned with two otters and a beaver. His six-year-old grandson and I watched the proceedings as Joe commenced to skin and stretch them. Little Tom's sly eyes weren't overly interested in what was going on. Instead they were riveted on me. His glancing looks took in every inch of me but never once caught my eyes. It seemed a thorough investigation. Joe finished his fur preparations, little Tom had caught an eyeful and disappeared, and I wanted to get back to the canoe before dark. Mrs. Cardinal kept me well fed, giving me a sack containing dried muskrat and beaver tail, and Molly escorted me to the waiting canoe.

Company was scarce for some time after that. The temperature had soared, making the remaining ice on Flett Lake dangerously rotted. Not wanting to stay home on one such eighty-degree day, I wandered toward company.

The distance doubled due to ice conditions, as I followed the safety of the wooded shoreline. I didn't care. It was the type of blue-sky day made for walking. Halfway along the lake, the thick trees parted to reveal a low grassy knoll. Behind this was a crude log cage protected by a huge bear trap chained to a poplar tree. It was sprung, but still looked wicked with the double-spring trap armed with eight jagged teeth welded to its jaws. It must have weighed forty pounds and was identical to the kind the immortalized mountain men of the Rockies could set by hand. What an opportunity for instant, legendary fame! I pushed, squeezed, jumped, and screamed trying to reset it, finally realizing that legends didn't come *that* easily. It was time to move on.

Keeping to high ground, I climbed a rocky hill that overlooked the Cardinals' camp. Dotting the clearing were three canvas tents and a log cabin standing nearly complete after three years of work. Happy's little cabin lay tucked to one side. Hammering echoed across the lake as I could see Ray, Happy, and Joe working on the roof.

Descending the hill, I reached the outskirts of their camp when something broke from cover. It was little Tom, fumbling with his pants on the run. As he approached the first tent, I heard the little camp crier herald, "Manni-ow's coming! Manni-ow is here! That Manni-ow's coming again!" Everyone came out from their tents to observe my approach. Work stopped at the cabin, and it seemed I provided a perfect excuse for a tea break.

After two cups, Molly's mother said, "Come, I show you." Three beavers lay in front of the tent, and I received lessons in skinning, fleshing, and stretching beaver hides. Before Mrs. Cardinal finished the last beaver, the tent flaps flew open and Joe sprang out quicker than an old man should be able.

One hand held a shotgun, while the other covered his mouth. *Olee, olee, olee,* Joe honked, then emptied his shotgun. Eight more shots bellowed from near the cabin. An undisturbed flock of geese lazily disappeared over the tree line as Joe mumbled something in Cree, jammed fresh shells into the shotgun, and returned to finish his coffee. I wondered how often this ritual was carried out. My curiosity was satisfied within minutes.

Since it was getting late, and I had no intention of tromping through the woods after dark, I gathered myself. "When you come back?" Molly's mother asked between goose-brigades.

"Maybe in a few days," I managed to say.

Hastily, Molly interjected, "How about tomorrow?" I explained that I had much to do tomorrow but would try to make it the following day.

This excuse was accepted, and I said goodbye, trod across many empty shotgun shells, and started the long walk home. Still no goose simmered in the pot atop the Cardinals' wood stove.

During the night a strong wind arose. Tall pines swayed, and ice piled high along the shores. By morning Flett Lake was open. It was just as well, for my interests swayed to a more important matter—leaving. My total muskrat count rested at 48, not bad for a half-mile of river. Now all I had to do was find some way to sell them.

My neck hairs stiffened mid thought as I contemplated the much-needed dollars I would receive from the muskrat skins at breakfast. All peacefulness was sucked from the cabin as I heard a loud *whomp, whomp, whomp,* hovering above the moss roof. The timing was eerie, paranoia hit. "You can't hunt, trap, or take employment of any kind while you're in this country," the customs officer's stern warning a year or so ago flashed through my adrenalin-filled mind. With subdued panic, the furs flew into my empty food box. Stretching boards were jammed on top, and the whole affair vanished beneath the bed.

From the doorway, I watched as the second RCMP officer hit the ground below the hovering helicopter. They ducked as they advanced with hands on their hats, while their machine rose and disappeared beyond the trees. Nervously I met them at the top of the hill. Where I came from, authorities didn't seek out a person without a reason, and especially not by helicopter. A death in the family came first to mind. Confiscation, jail, and fines due to illegally taking furs came second. However, something wasn't right—they were smiling. "Hi," the older one said as he introduced himself and his partner. As we shook hands, he explained they stopped in to visit while their pilot checked on the fishing a little north of here. Strained hospitality invited them in for tea.

Soon the conversation focused on canoeing from New Orleans to Fort Chipewyan. It dominated the next half-hour until a hum in the distance drew near. "Thanks for the tea and make sure you check in with us before you take off," the older officer said as they started down the hill to meet their approaching transportation. They boarded the hovering craft and lifted straight up. "Have a good trip this summer, Jerry," boomed over the microphone. Then, they were gone. No hassles, no prying questions, nothing, just a friendly social visit to see how I was doing. How I wished the rest of the world was like that!

Shortly after they left, my red canoe's hull skimmed the shallow shoreline of the now open Flett Lake. No water appeared inside, proving my patch job adequate. Halfway across the lake, I pulled ashore. Ray had stashed his father's homemade canoe here a week earlier, stopped by ice on the lake. I couldn't resist a tour in an authentic Cree canoe.

Joe told me earlier that he had made the ten-foot craft three years earlier out of native spruce, covered it with canvas, and completed the job with dark green paint. It was light on portages and used mostly for muskrat hunting in the surrounding lakes. I rolled the frail-looking craft onto its rounded bottom and effortlessly slid it into the murky water. It had no keel.

It rocked slightly as I put one foot in the center and rocked exponentially more out of control as the other foot followed. In a split second the world flipped on end. When it righted itself, I stood next to it, drenched, muddy, and humbled. A person would think that after paddling some 6,000 miles he'd be able to handle such a little boat. I tied the bow of the incompetent creation to the stern of a real canoe and prepared for a second attempt toward the Cardinals' village. Only then did I notice Ray. He was standing on the shore, laughing hysterically.

"I just came up to get my dad's canoe," he said as I pulled ashore. I explained that I was just bringing it to their camp when he suggested that I should jump in again and wash the mud off my pants. I offered Ray a ride home in the main boat, but he declined, and pushed off in his dad's canoe with hardly a ripple. As we headed toward their camp with me in pursuit, I knew he was showing off.

While we walked the path to the tent where tea and cherry pie were being served, chickens ran to-and-fro. My muddy pants and overall wetness didn't go unnoticed. The crowd there thought it was hilarious when I told them about Joe's canoe. I knew if I didn't tell them Ray would and it was best to get the story straight from the start. After an hour near the stove, I strayed toward the roof project on the new cabin. I met Joe at the tent coming up the trail for coffee. "Good house," he declared as we passed. I agreed and went for a closer look. As I neared the cabin, I heard laughter behind me, and plenty of it. Undoubtedly Joe had reached the tent.

"You take this when you go," Molly's mother said to me after I returned to the tent. She filled my coffee cup and set a cherry pie covered in plastic wrap next to it. "You stay here another year maybe?" she asked as the cup filled. I tried to explain that I had to finish this trip and had almost 3,000 miles yet to paddle. Thinking about it for a few seconds, she concluded, "Good, good, you go finish, and then you come back." What could I say?

After a meat and bannock supper, Molly and Marlene wanted to canoe to a high rocky point three miles west of their cabin site. Since I had no pressing engagements, Molly settled in the seat at the bow, while Marlene sat on the floor in the center, and I took the stern.

A strong, tailwind blew us across the small lake and through a long slough in record time. Climbing to the summit offered a panoramic view. Molly and I sat next to a small fire talking while Marlene bobbed among the rocks writing her name and date in white chalk on any surface big, flat, and smooth enough to accept her scribbling. The sun teetered on the treetops, Marlene ran out of chalk, and the fire turned to ashes. As the time to leave became apparent, Molly pointed to my arm and said, "Gee, look how big your veins are."

As if on cue, Marlene grabbed my hand, jerked it to her nose, and took a good whiff. "How come it smells so funny?" she asked. I replied, jokingly, that I had just finished going to the bathroom; she turned as red as a ripe apple.

The trip back was slow. Before long, Marlene started squirming and complaining about the seat of her pants being wet. Apparently, the patchwork wasn't as good as originally thought. Anyway, my sympathetic heart was busy pouring all it had into making headway against a very stiff wind. I strained against it, dropped the girls off, and headed home. Tomorrow I planned to paddle into town and sell my muskrat hides.

By 10:00 A.M. I had packed what little I needed and headed out. The small creek to the river was ice-free, but the Slave River was a huge, ragged floe which posed no immediate threat, and I skirted them until camping at dark. I pulled into the muddy dock at Fort

Chipewyan just after noon. It was May 1st. There would be no partying escapade this time. Selling the muskrats was a priority.

An invisible oppression escaped the house as the door opened to my knock. The guy standing there had all the attributes of a crook. He was short, fat, sweaty, beady eyed, and smoked a cigar. I entered the haze-filled home to witness thousands of hides piled in every room. I showed him Joe's authorization note, license, and the 48 hides. He looked at every hide for less than a second and tossed each into a pile he described as, "Damaged." "Best I can do is $98," he said throwing the last one in with the others.

"Just two days ago the price was almost five dollars a skin!" I snapped.

"Look!" he bellowed, "I'm busy, either take the $98 or get out."

Dislike seeped through my pores as we both knew I had to take the money for there was nowhere else to go. "Do you think I can get more for them at the Bay?" I asked in total honest innocence. It was the wrong question.

He viciously cocked his short fat leg, kicked the pile of my hides across the floor, and threw the empty pack on top of them. "Take the Goddamn things out of here and see!" he screamed, red-faced.

Kicking the hides back across the floor, I took the $98, and left, leaving the door wide open. *That guy really needs some fresh air,* I thought as I wandered away. After a few calming cups of tea at the cafe, I was ready to head back.

Progress was impossible, hardly making it a mile. Ice clogged the river as far as the eye could see; the only available landing spot was a huge flat rock. Camp was made immediately. The huge, jagged ice field was quite a sight. Throughout the night the constant grinding of icebergs battling for position filled the air. By morning, many open paths had developed in the kaleidoscope of ice. Into one of these leads, I maneuvered the canoe. It was not a good choice. Within two miles I was surrounded by ice.

Open water had all but disappeared. House-sized blocks of ice bobbed like whales grinding a path to Great Slave Lake. Maneuverability and courage grew limited as jagged ice blocks sandwiched the frail Old Town and squeezed. I pushed, pried, and prayed to save the craft and me from a pulverized end. A rib cracked, and water seeped in. There was little I could do except ride it out and hope for the best.

The best arrived, and I made the best of it. It was four tense hours later. With a spellbound leap, I stepped ashore and pulled the battered boat up behind me. I was very displeased with what nature did to my fiberglass repairs. Looking up and down the white clogged river, I knew I had no justifiable complaint.

By morning a northerly gale had pushed the ice on Lake Athabasca to its southern shore and allowed the Slave River to clear itself of ice. That same gale made my morning, afternoon, and night difficult as I battled toward home. It was dark and near midnight when I reached the Cardinals. I was tired, hungry, and slightly sore from a six-month layover. I also didn't argue when a voice in the dark called, "Sleep in Ambrose's tent tonight if you want."

"Get up, Pushcar! It's already eight o'clock," George yelled into the tent. Fresh eggs and coffee waited at the kitchen table. Hardly was my cup of coffee finished when, then and there, it was decided that my tent should be put up next to the cabin and my remaining time should be spent with the Cardinals. I came up with excuses, but the Cardinal Council had voted without me again.

We secured the rest of my gear and brought it to their camp. With my coaching, a rubble of poles, ropes, and nylon was finally turned into a tent by Molly and Marlene. It was one of the stipulations of my changing residency. With that accomplished, they pitched their tent next to mine.

While my sleeping bag was being shaken out, a motorboat docked. Happy jumped out with a blood-soaked bandage wrapped around his hand and dashed for the cabin. Everyone rushed in behind him. By the time I got there, the bandage was off, revealing raw meat and gouges across his knuckles. Apparently, Happy was coming from town when his outboard motor quit. He removed the cover, pull-started it, and while putting the cover back on, raked his knuckles across the spinning flywheel. He had already lost a considerable amount of blood and couldn't get the wound to stop bleeding.

Mrs. Cardinal left immediately and soon returned chewing some sort of leaves. She mixed the pulp with lard, put the concoction wherever Happy's hand bled, and re-wrapped it. "See this finger," Happy said to me as his mother finished the bandaging. "I hit it with a hatchet when I was little. Although it was only hanging on by a little flesh, Mom sewed it back on. Pretty good, huh?" he said as he wiggled the doglegged finger. The bleeding soon stopped, and the crisis was over. Within the hour Happy was back in the boat headed for town to see if stitches would be necessary.

With Happy gone, everyone sat down to a moose and bannock lunch. After this, a blanket was laid on the ground, and the five women in camp held a leg-wrestling contest. There was much giggling and laughing. When it was over, it was the guys' turn. George was the current camp champ, and I, though inexperienced, was the only contender.

We lay on our backs, hips together, facing in opposite directions, then lifted our inside legs three consecutive times to Molly's count. On the third lift, we locked ankles and pulled. The champ won the first two rounds while issuing explicit instructions on how to improve my losing technique.

On the next round, I hooked George high on the ankle and gave it all I had. His body rolled over mine, teetered momentarily on its feet, and then came to rest a few feet away in a sitting position. "Jesus Christ, Manni-ow, I think you got it!" George exclaimed to a laughing audience. The contest was to go five rounds, the winner needing three victories. Fortunately, the former camp champ was a graceful loser.

After a late supper, George suggested an evening muskrat hunt in my canoe. I was all for it, so we grabbed our .22's and pushed off. We paddled, and George did the shooting when a muskrat would appear. After three misses he suggested we head northwest across a shallow marsh. After much pushing and pulling, we came to a small creek carrying almost enough water to float the canoe. As we took a lay of the land George whispered, "There's a bear." He was right.

My eyes rarely left the black beast as I inched the canoe along. George loaded his rifle to the hilt with .22 shorts. At fifty yards he shot once, twice, thrice. Nothing happened; the bear didn't even move. Then it stood on its hind legs and raked the willows growing along the bank. It looked huge. When George fired again, there was a dull *plop* and a spine-chilling roar as the brute dropped to all fours and tore through the underbrush. Then, all was quiet. We waited. As it got dark, a low moan could be heard from deep within the forest, followed by another and another. When there were no more, George wanted to move in.

This is crazy, this is crazy, echoed in my head as we beached where we first spotted the bear, checking for any signs of blood. There was none. A two-inch willow bent horizontally two feet above the ground had been hit three times. Separating ourselves thirty feet, we penetrated the forest.

White knuckles encircled my Buck knife as I had little faith in our small bullets. Despite knowing what a wounded bear was capable of doing, we stalked deeper into the woods. This was no squirrel hunt. George silently got my attention and pointed to a black mound fifty feet ahead. We approached cautiously; I had my Buck knife drawn. My only consolation was that I knew I could run faster than George!

The bear lay unmoving. George poked it once with his rifle barrel, ready to leap, and then again. We were grateful there was no response. The huge bear had succumbed to a pea-size piece of lead that had penetrated its lungs.

As we waddled toward the canoe George supported the front of the bear while I assisted from the rear. Although I was all for cleaning it in the field to lightening the load, George wanted to get home before dark. So, with much effort, we set the beast in the canoe and off we went.

The first mile wasn't easy, as the extra weight forced the canoe to the muddy bottom. We reached deeper water and then camp in the oncoming darkness.

After a pot of coffee and almost an hour of glorified hunting tales, we skinned, gutted, and quartered the animal aided only by the light of a lantern. George got the hide and credit for his prowess with a rifle. Nothing was said about missed shots and muskrats. The meat went into the Cardinals' larder, allowing George to flesh the hide in the morning.

He scraped the hide over and over with a chiseled tool made from the leg bone of a moose. "Damn stinking, bear!" he wailed with every other stroke. While George wavered between admiring his new rug and lamenting the amount of work required to turn it into something useful, Molly and I hauled water and cut firewood. Before long, the scraper found itself on the ground and the scrapee found himself on a duck hunt. Heading toward my cabin, I was again in the stern of my canoe with the marksman riding shotgun.

Ba-room! the shotgun continually spoke as we crossed the lake and headed up the creek. By the time we reached the cabin, the only things in the bottom of the canoe were empty shotgun shells. As we gazed at the tiny, bare cabin, I told George he could have it, including everything inside. "I'll put a wood floor in it and move in next month," he said, eyeing the cabin's potential.

I took one last look around the bleak log enclosure. In certain places, the sun's rays penetrated the walls from spaces where the moss chinking had dried, shrunk, and fallen away. The pole bed, with its useless pile of dry brown needles, clung to the wall in the corner. Without the pad and blanket covering it, bare branches reached upward like broken springs. The kerosene lamp with its roadmap mantle sat on the lopsided table, dangling above hung the soot-covered bean can chimney. Even the cold, rusted barrel stove, which had tried vainly to radiate warmth at fifty below, now looked pitiful. Sap oozed from the stump like an infected wound. It was worn smooth from months of service. From this day forward, this place would hold many unforgettable memories. I closed the door to George's cabin and walked away.

The following day Mr. and Mrs. Cardinal returned from a trip to town. Evidently, it was quite an event. Everyone, but for me, was talking at once and happiness abounded. The boat was loaded to the gunwales, and everyone pitched in to transport the goods to the cabin. If I hadn't known any better, I'd have said that they hadn't seen each other in months. *I could have sworn they'd only left yesterday!*

Days passed rapidly. Most definitely, May 9th was a day to remember. It was my first attempt at eating boiled moose nose followed by huge black bear steaks and bannock. For over a week now, three meals a day, I had eaten nothing but wild meat and bannock. The cramps had gotten bad. Sneaking into my tent and eating some *Manni-ow* food helped things return to normal.

It was eight o'clock when I entered the cabin on the morning of the 12th. Molly's mother was in an uproar. "Look at crooked house already. I put pan on table and water run out. No good. Crooked!" she fumed as she waved a spatula. Joe sat patiently at the table sipping his coffee. He said something in Cree, and the conversation ended. After finishing his coffee, he walked quietly to the washbasin, lathered his face, shaved, and then lathered his balding head. When he turned to face Mrs. Cardinal, she broke into a roaring laugh.

Soon the day arrived for the men to depart on their spring muskrat hunt. While George and I emptied a fishnet, Leon, Ray, Alphonse, Willie, and Joe packed for a two-week trip north of Flett Lake. Before the net was emptied, the three canoes were packed and ready to go. After carrying the tub of fish to the cabin, George handed me a beaver and a half-dozen muskrats. "Hold them up high," he said as he snapped pictures with his Polaroid, giving me one and his mother two for the family photo box.

After photos everyone walked to the water's edge where the hunters were boarding their canoes. Two canoes were already in the water when Joe came up to me, looked me square in the eye, and said, thank you. He turned quickly and boarded his canoe. I didn't know why he would have said that. If anything, I should have been the one thanking him. The three crafts moved into the lake.

"So long, Manni-ow!" George shouted as he raised his paddle in salute from the stern.

I responded with a wave, "See you, bear hunter." It had been fun.

The rest of the day was quiet with the men gone. Molly and I spent a few more hours carrying water and expanding the woodpile. Then I played cards with the five women left behind. After a huge supper, Molly's mother presented me with two loaves of raisin bannock, pictures of their family, and a pair of beautifully beaded, moose-hide moccasins trimmed with beaver fur. They were going-away presents, since I was leaving in the morning.

It was well into the night when Molly walked me to my tent. It seemed like just yesterday when I first saw her sparkling eyes. There wasn't much to say. "You'll never come back here, will you?" she asked as we reached the tent.

There was no sense in lying. "No," I said, "I doubt it."

She seemed to be searching for something to say. All that could be said was, "Goodbye then, Jerry," her voice broke and she turned, running to the cabin door. For an instant, there was a spew of light and then total darkness. I walked to the bank and sat with my back against a tree. For hours I sat there, just thinking and listening to the crickets.

Just a faint light showed in the eastern sky. There was no sense in delaying things. Rising from my niche against the tree, I broke camp and loaded the canoe. It was then that I noticed "Molly" carved into the front of my guitar, just above the sound hole. I felt a pang of regret as I looked back at the darkened cabin and then stowed the guitar next to a pack. When I looked again, one of the curtains was pulled back. I pushed off and glided the canoe across Flett Lake. The Gilligan's Island sign soon vanished in the morning fog. It was Friday, May 13th, 4:06 A.M.

On the Road Again

It took me a few days to get my head right again, but I guess life moves on, just as the Slave River does. I went swiftly past the mouth of the Peace River, heading for a place called Fort Fitzgerald. Logging thirty miles a day posed no problem in the spring meltwater. By the evening of the third day, I was camped on the edge of the tiny settlement. It is the gateway to what are said to be some of the most treacherous rapids in Canada. They went for 16 miles.

Awaking early the next morning, I waited until a reasonable breakfast hour before trying to find someone to talk to about this formidable stretch. The first four doors I knocked on produced no response. I detoured the fifth and final house in the row because of two nasty-looking dogs chained to the steps.

My map showed that a gravel road paralleled the rapids down to a town called Fort Smith below them. From all the terrifying stories I heard about these rapids, I decided this road would make a great portage trail. Another factor encouraging that decision was the presence of three white memorial crosses gleaming in the morning sun near the head of the rapids. It took little imagination to realize their purpose.

The portage wasn't just a stroll down a gravel road. I wasn't in shape after the long winter. By midday, I had everything ferried to the three-mile mark and broke for lunch. After downing a cold can of corn, I was ready to shuttle everything another five miles before dark. I stashed the packs next to the road, hoisted the canoe, and with Vagabond beside me, plodded down the wide gravel trail.

I didn't get far before a car stopped. In the front seat were two younger men and an elderly woman. "It's a long way to Fort Smith with that thing on your back," the driver said, "want a ride?" I politely declined as I set the canoe on the gravel and answered the usual questions. "There's a guy in town that knows these rapids really well," the one named Don said. "His name is Jacques Van Kyke and he kayaks through them every so often. If you talk to him, take a few portages, and be very careful, I'm sure you could make it through." I liked the sound of that plan, so after stashing the canoe, I hopped into the back seat with Vagabond and we thundered down the dirt road to meet Jacques.

Don was a schoolteacher, and his passenger Tim was an unemployed dentist. The lady was Don's aunt, who was seeing the countryside before going to the airport. Don made one stipulation before giving me a ride. I'd at least have to spend the night with him and his family. After I agreed, Tim held up an Oreo cookie and asked if I cared for one.

Before I could speak, Vagabond sprang into action. He knocked the cookie out of Tim's hand, and leapt over the seat to retrieve it. Somehow the cookie fell between the aunt's legs. Of course, Vagabond had no propriety or intention of giving it up. After a few shrieks, the car was stopped, and the cookie found. With everything under control, Vagabond was delivered to the back seat. Again, we were underway. No more Oreos were offered.

Fort Smith wasn't far away by wheel. While Don brought his aunt to the airport, I lounged under a hot shower. By the time I had finished, Don had a supper of caribou ribs and potatoes already on the table. Two hours of adventure tales followed before I crawled between two clean, sweet-smelling sheets. That was a first in many, many months.

Arrangements had been made for me to meet Jacques. Noon the next day found me sitting at his kitchen table. The homesteader came in from feeding his chickens and fixed a lunch of cold cuts, cheese, ice cream, and tea. After this, maps and aerial photos of the rapids appeared. "It can be done all right, but you have to be awfully, awfully careful," he warned. He went on to explain that a few years ago two Germans came here to challenge the rapids. "One managed to make it to shore," he said, "the other and the canoe were never found." I left with renewed confidence and a weight lifted from my shoulders—approximately 350 pounds spread out over 13 miles.

Throughout the rest of the afternoon, I helped a friend of Don's pick roots for birch bark baskets and then empty his fishnet below the appropriately named "Rapids of the Drowned." Don did everything but beg me to accompany him to a prayer meeting after we ate. For every reason he had for my going, I had two for not attending. When it was over, Don took a thorough whipping in cribbage, getting me back to the canoe with plenty of daylight to plan my next move. With a wave, Don was down the dirt road.

I sat on a log in the settling dust, listening to the roar of the water below me. *Well*, I thought, *I might as well see what's down there.* I took a dry run and it was steep and clogged with thick willows. Droves of mosquitoes were there to meet me. At the bottom, I had to literally ax a path to get to the edge of the river. But luck was with me, as I had descended to a spot of relative calm between massive rapids.

After the climb back up, the canoe came down first. There was no way I could get it down on my shoulders. It went down keel to the ground as I swerved it through the thick willows. One hand held the canoe in check while the other swatted mosquitoes and grasped trees. The packs were much easier, with gravity almost too helpful.

With everything packed, I started upstream, wanting to get to the base of the upper rapids. It would allow me as much distance as possible to get to the other side. Jacques had said the easiest portages would be there.

Everything was straightforward as I started across. Small whirlpools spun under the canoe as I slid downstream increasingly fast. While the roar of the water was never not present, it continued to grow as I was stroked toward destruction. Then, I was released from the river's grip as the current slackened into an eddy. I weaved the canoe among numerous rocks while just fifty yards away, muddy, foam-tipped haystacks danced to the river's tune. It was time to find a portage.

Ok Jacques, where are they? I searched for any indication of a portage. None existed. Throughout the day I found not an inkling of one. So, I made my own. Taking my time and studying each set of rapids from above or on shore, I followed my intuition. *Paddle when you can and portage when you must.* After many portages, this method allowed my passage, including the infamous "Rapids of the Drowned" section, without incident. After a short portage around Fort Smith's sewage plant, it was over. Canada's worst lay behind me. Now it was an uninterrupted downstream river run all the way to Great Slave Lake.

Out came a book because it was time for the river to do some of the work. With a dime store Western, I lay back against a rolled-up coat and ruddered just enough to keep the craft on course. It was a relaxing evening, and just as the strong, silent hero was about to save the buxom blonde's family ranch from two dozen hired guns, dusk fell. I swerved toward one of the few rock outcrops along the muddy banks and made a hurried camp. Supper in the darkness was brief.

Early the next morning a rare sight appeared thirty feet away on the muddy bank; a sprawling moose calf nursed from its mother. The shutter clicked twice before the cow was off at a run, leaving the calf stranded. The wobbly-legged, little thing tumbled and stumbled trying to keep up. Twice it slid from the muddy bank into the water. The third time the toddler hit the water, it decided to stay there. I maneuvered close to it; the mother was nowhere in sight.

Vagabond turned circles in excitement, barking at the injustice of it being just out of reach, a few leaps from shore. The shutter continued snapping as I held one eye to the viewfinder and the other toward the vicinity of the mother's disappearance. I expected the trees to part at any moment as the rage-filled monstrosity made an entrance. The fledgling giant lay in the water with only its head exposed. While its nostrils opened then closed with each hard breath, its brown, innocent eyes gazed straight ahead.

I couldn't tell if it was floating or standing on the bottom. I leapt from shore to rocks off shore and coaxed it to dry land with a paddle. It was a chore as the youngster was already no lightweight. Once out of the water, it folded its spindly legs beneath its body and lay its head down, seemingly content waiting for its mother's return. I continued on, having no desire to meet her.

The days passed quietly as I drifted, paddled, and read. I was informed by two boaters that Great Slave Lake was still jammed with ice so there was no rush to cover the remaining eighty miles to it.

One afternoon I was called to sit upon a fallen log. I had just finished and broken through the tree line, returning while juggling a diminished roll of toilet paper, when not ten steps away a black bear seemed to be doing the same thing—heading for my canoe. Our eyes locked in indecision; neither moved. Nostrils quivered as the black bear and I instinctively identified motives. My heart raced as seconds passed.

I broke the spell with a whistle. A white, nap-dazed, swivel-head appeared over the gunwale. There was a great *woof!* from the canoe, and immediately, the bear disappeared in a flurry as vicious growls from Vagabond became land-based. Grabbing the leash-struggling killer, I maneuvered him back into the canoe, where his state of slumber resumed within a mile's travel.

As we drifted, Vagabond slept. My mind wearied from reading, but my body refused sleep due to inactivity. I couldn't go on like this. With a glass of Tang for breakfast, I set a goal for Fort Resolution and went to work.

By 11:00 P.M. I was at the mouth of the Slave River, having not left the canoe since the glass of Tang that morning. My hindquarters were rheumatic, and I knew deep sleep would not be a problem. Before me stretched a mile of clear, calm, blue water that fronted miles of broken, conglomerated ice. The temperature seemed to drop twenty degrees as I glided the canoe into Great Slave Lake. Shortly, Fort Resolution was in sight. I beached on the rocky shore and pitched the tent in a soft square of sand. Town could wait until morning.

Up early after a long night's sleep, the ice pack loomed ominously close, idly awaiting its windblown destination. After a short paddle to the boat landing, a boardwalk snaked across mud and tundra to a collection of buildings. The rough-sawn pine flexed in the permafrost mud as my weight moved across the boards.

My first stop was a place called Hunter's General Store. I inquired about the location of the post office. "At the Bay" came the abrupt reply. Upon further questioning and more vague answers, I learned that it was, "Down the street, way at the other end of town." Way at the other end of town meant three blocks along the boardwalk. The first thing I saw on entering the Bay was a sign stating "Jerry Pushcar, Please Contact the Local RCMP."

I followed the clerk's instructions to the local office. There I rang the doorbell numerous times until finally, a puffy-eyed, uniformed sleeper turned the lock, opened the door, and questioned my presence. Things were quickly resolved. Apparently, I had left a small sack of odds and ends at Don's house, and he gave it to the RCMP at Fort Smith. Arrangements had been made to send it ahead to Fort Simpson where it would be available to me upon request. I had no idea of the package's contents, but the gesture was appreciated.

Back at the Bay, I stood before the caged post office window. The girl behind the counter gave me a knowing glance. With her assumed telepathy, she scanned through a stack of envelopes and handed me one. As I handed it back, she explained that she thought I was from a scientific research party. After giving her a few clues, including first and last name, her telepathy homed in on my sister's envelope. Soon I was at the checkout counter cashing one of the two $100 money orders.

It was almost noon and I needed to do some grocery shopping, but not on an empty stomach. After a leisurely lunch that consisted of two bags of taco-flavored chips, two Cokes, two Eat-More candy bars, one bag of Kraft caramels, and two banana popsicles, I hit the aisles. No junk food was purchased, only healthy natural essentials. There was nothing to keep me in this village so, on a sugar-high, I dipped the paddle and swiftly took off.

For four hard hours, I fought a headwind as the shoreline slowly slid by. Then, all was quiet. Not a breeze stirred the mirrored surface. Soon the paddle stretched idly across the wooden gunwales, and I leaned back against a jacketed-pillow and dozed.

When I awoke, the sun blazed my sleep-laden eyes. Grogginess struggled to retain its lingering hold on my waking mind. Like the voyager of old, I dipped the paddle, tipped the blade to the sky, and drank as water slid off the handle. Most of it went down my neck so I switched to my cup. With the grogginess gone, I got my bearings and continued west along the southern shore. Within the hour, I met the ice.

The ice barrier lay like a mosaic, a crumpled, white blanket extending miles before me. There was nothing to do but wait until a wind from the south provided an avenue along the shore. I beached on the narrow gravel shoreline. Extending from the lake's perimeter to the tree line lay 200 feet of bare-barked, crisscrossed trees of every size and shape. They were like pick-up sticks, only on a much grander scale. I was fortunate, for just to my right were two huge logs, crossed at their ends, forming an inverted *V*. Beneath lay a bed of sand, just big enough to house the tent.

It was a cozy campsite. Firewood was unlimited as pines reached skyward behind me. Tons of ice noisily grated against the shore in the increasing north wind. As my campfire crackled, I was snug between the knee-high logs. Vagabond's reassuring barks drifted down the coast as he futilely pursued a weasel through the wooden maze. There was no telling how long the wait would be. I nestled in along the shore of the forlorn Great Slave Lake. Retreat became blocked by ice; there was no visible water. More than 100 miles across this rolling ice mass lay the mouth of the Mackenzie River.

With one quick look at sunrise, I decided to sleep late. Ice still extended to the horizon. Noon found me on a hike five miles down the shoreline to an abandoned campsite. A ripped, brown, Eddie Bauer jacket lay discarded next to a long-dead campfire. Its shell was haggard, but I knew a use for it. After walking back to camp, I took my knife and carefully slit the inner seam of my sleeping bag. I then cut open the coat and stuffed the prime goose down into the bag where cold spots had developed over the years from hard use. This added insulation was then secured in place by a row of overhand stitches.

My attention was split between the last of the stitching and the weather. Dark, ugly clouds had mounted the white ice and were rapidly displacing blue sky. With them came yet more wind and a cold rain. The north wind's winter bite swept through the ice field before pounding the shore. My biggest concern was that the wind would force the ice high along the shore, my house ending up an igloo. For two days I kept constant vigilance, leaving the tent zipper open just enough to witness the slightest movement. All the while I was cocooned, one hand exposed to the chilled air holding a book. Bottle cap size pieces of butterscotch lolled in my mouth as the paragraphs slid by. Vagabond slept at my feet, out of the weather. Restlessness grew and sleep was hard to come by.

Early the next morning, I systematically pounded the inside of the canoe with the ax handle, trying to remove some of the caked-on Slave River mud from its outside. I had to hurry since the ice had moved out, exposing a mile-wide ribbon of open water. Within two hours the canoe again bumped the edge of the ice pack. I should have stayed where I was.

It was another two rainy days before a strong southerly gale bent the pines. The ice vanished into a thin, white line on the horizon, a margin between water and sky. Dusk was setting in, but it mattered little as daylight by this time extended for twenty hours. It was June 1st and leaving a place called Dawson Point, I was geared up to make miles.

As I traveled through the dim-lit night, the cold twilight kept the mosquitoes on shore. The sun rose, and I continued throughout the day, stopping every five hours or so for a quick cup of tea. Deep ice-filled bays kept me on edge as I crossed their mouths. Bobbing in the cold water for a half a dozen hours with an offshore wind and miles of rotting ice between me and the nearest land was not pleasant. More than once my heart quickened as a sudden gust made the canoe sideslip. If anything happened during these crossings, survival was not expected.

I had reached the far side of another bay and was again traveling without stress, two steps from land. A light offshore wind had developed, and I could see small whitecaps miles out. For hours I clung to the shore in the protection of the pines before rounding a small point. There, a short way up the beach stood a slanted, weather-beaten shack. A huge, fiberglass, fishing boat rode the light swells, anchored near a path to the dwelling. "Hey, come on up!" someone yelled from the doorway as I passed. Three men appeared. Pulling in, I was introduced to Ernie, Willey, and Napoleon. In that order, they appeared half-drunk, drunk, and obliterated.

I followed them into the drafty, one-room shack wondering what I got myself into. The first thing on their agenda was to fix a house drink for their guest. It was cold tea, sugar, and a healthy shot of Vodka, strong enough that it took most of an hour to consume. In that same time, they managed to find the bottom of a newly opened "fifth". Most of the conversation during my short stay revolved around the pros and cons of going nine miles out into the lake to check their fishnets. Finally, it was decided that when the willows in front of camp quit moving, it would be safe to go out.

When I left, I left alone. Napoleon was at Waterloo, Willey was throwing up in the willows, and Ernie sat in the only chair with his chin on his chest. Closing the door behind me, I started down the muddy path to the canoe. Behind me, in front of the shanty, the willow branches lay motionless, almost as if they too, were sedated.

The Village of Buffalo River lay 16 miles down the shore and that was to be reached before camping. Through the calmness, it took five hours to get there; it was five o'clock in the morning when I arrived at the mouth of the river leading to town. It had been 44 hours since I had last slept, and Dawson Point lay well over seventy miles behind me. I needed rest.

After six hours of sleep, I headed upriver for two miles to the Village of Buffalo River. A light rain started and became a downpour. By the time I returned to camp with a few needed groceries, I was drenched. For two days I waited for the sky to bleed out. When it did, it didn't last long. In the lull, I dashed thirty miles west, just past Hay River, where it really let loose. For ten straight hours it poured, pelting the nylon tent with fury, before a blue sky crept over the lake. Without delay, the final thirty miles were logged, and I crossed the mouth of the Mackenzie River three miles to Beacon Point at the tip of Big Island. From there I could see and feel a current drawing everything northwest into a funnel, siphoned 1,000 miles north to the Arctic Ocean.

The Mackenzie River flowing to the Arctic Ocean

From my camp at the mouth, it appeared that the Mackenzie had sucked all the ice from Great Slave Lake. There was none in sight and I was not complaining. I followed this watery jet stream for fifty miles as it flowed past Fort Providence, crossed the length of Mills Lake, and re-entered the river. It remained tolerable, and soon I pulled up to a steep, mud bank in front of Fort Simpson. I tied the canoe to a metal rod protruding from the cut bank, put the splash cover on, and toured the town. It didn't take long.

I sat on top of the bank tossing rocks into the muddy water when someone behind me said "Hi." He introduced himself as Bob, a local guide, and was curious about my presence there. While discussing the local bear population we heard the beginning of drums. They were faint, but definitely drums. "Come on, let's go," Bob said; off we went. On the door of a long, white building was a sign that said Drum Dance Tonight.

We entered the dimly lit building filled with cigarette smoke. A three-beat symphony pulsated throughout, augmented by traditional Native lyrics. Vibrations rolled through the floor joists as nearly 100 feet stomped in unison to the pounding drums. The bodies danced in a shadowed circle, each united by their hands on the waist of the person in front of them. *What a sight!* Watching for twenty minutes, I suddenly noticed a heavy-duty female looking straight at me. As she started across the floor on a dead course, I knew deep in my heart it was time to check the canoe.

The canoe was fine, and Vagabond received 15 minutes of attention before I returned to the gathering. While the dance continued, people entered and left the circle at will. An elderly man brought me a folding chair. Thanking him, I set it next to the wall, so I could rock onto its back legs. I was comfortable, banging the back of my head slightly against the wall as I rocked to the beat of the drums. I watched for some time, when before I recognized what was happening, I was yanked out of the chair and dragged onto the dance floor.

An old, veiny hand pulled mine until the hobbled and toothless lady brought me to her spot. "Come, come, I teach," was communicated and we blended into the circle. I felt awkward, self-conscious, and totally out of place as I followed my tutor round and round. She held nothing back as she pounded her left foot three times and then responded with her right. Finally, my escort tired. After walking me back to my seat, she lit a cigarette and said, "Good, good, hey?" With polite enthusiasm, I tried to praise the fun of it all as she clapped her hands and gave a satisfied, hearty laugh before swaying back across the dance floor with a halo of cigarette smoke trailing her old silver hair.

"You must have more Indian blood in you than me," Bob said, still squatted in the same spot I last saw him. "This thing will go on well into the night," he said, "how about some food?" That sounded like a great idea, so I followed him to his house and sat down for a meal of Arctic Char, jerky, and bear lard spread over homemade bread as if it were butter. We ate our fill until Bob said he had had enough. He plopped onto a couch saying, "Sleep anywhere you want," and I chose an overstuffed chair. Three hours later, after writing Bob a thank you note, I was back in the canoe flowing with the Mackenzie River. At this time of the year the sun never sets, and I paddled in sublime peace; only the slight dip of the paddle sounded and even the drums were silent.

I didn't feel troubled by the amount of sleep I received, and I made up for some as the canoe drifted. The day was calm and sunny. Soon the Nahanni Mountains came into view and I was hailed ashore. There stood the most disheveled character I had ever seen. His clothes were ragged and filthy as were his hair and beard. Everything about him was unsightly. "Come on up to my camp for tea," he suggested with an English accent.

I had reservations but followed him along a narrow inlet to a nicely hung tarp fronted by a smoldering campfire. Beneath the tarp lay a worn sleeping bag with a wooden box at its foot. He rummaged through this near-empty box and said, "Damn, you wouldn't have any bags, would you? It seems I've run out." I didn't, but asked if he drank coffee, and he replied that he did but it had been a while. So I returned to the canoe for the jar of instant coffee crystals. "Bring your own cup, would you? I only have one!" he shouted as I walked down the path.

The guy was friendly enough as he filled the two cups with hot water. He was 37 years old, came over from Wales, England six years ago, prospected in the Nahanni Mountains and had seen better times. "Got enough money for a few provisions and a little gas for my rig there," he said, nodding at a new 22-foot Petersboro square-stern canoe with a new 15 horse outboard. "Cost me $1,800 and broke me, but it'll get me back in," he said with satisfaction.

For three hours I learned the finer points of gold mining while the coffee crystals faded. The man seemed sick with gold fever, it dominated his being. Along with the fever, he also had the shakes. If I drank as much coffee as he, the whole canoe would be shaking. His appetite for the brown brew seemed insatiable. As I excused myself on the pretense of following my own dream, he was still going on and on about the next big strike. Though I did take my porcelain cup, I left the jar of instant next to the fire. If he noticed the much-diminished coffee container, he didn't mention it. I couldn't ridicule the guy, for there were times in my own life when I could have challenged his condition, if not surpassed it.

Days and nights fused as the constant daylight enabled me to travel at will. One evening the canoe clung to a small eddy below Rocher qui Trempe à L'eau, a mountain of smooth, greenish-gray rock situated on the east bank of the Mackenzie. It reached hundreds of feet skyward and terminated somewhere deep below the river. An impulse to climb was felt, but the tire of 110 miles in 34 hours impeded the initiative that it would have required.

By mid-June, I was already halfway down the Mackenzie. The current had increased slightly and when the weather cooperated, miles came easily. The water sped between high, steep, muddy banks topped with green towering pines, many hanging over the tops of the banks like bangs on someone's forehead. Ten hours of pulling the blade one day got me into Fort Norman just before midnight.

Although everything was closed, the inhabitants walked the dusty streets, still reveling in the midnight sun after a long winter. Taking the tour, I noted tepees erected beside framed houses, giving credence to contrasting lifestyles. A voice interrupted my photographing one of these contradictions; "Are you paddling a red canoe down the river?" It was an RCMP officer. After I acknowledged that fact, he casually added to his statement, "Someone reported a red canoe floating down the river with nobody in it." Not much was needed to solve that mystery. The canoe hadn't floated away, and so even in the middle of nowhere, it appeared it was difficult to nap on the job without being noticed.

The town of Norman Wells came and went sometime during the early morning. All appeared dead except for huge concrete fingers belching flames and black smoke into the morning sky, the price paid for refined oil. Even the huge, fiercely black rain clouds approaching from the north surely wouldn't dampen those fiery fingers. I stopped across from Rader Island and hunkered down for the watery onslaught.

I was not disappointed. The downpour subsided three days later. I crawled out of the tent and started a fire in the aftermath. Rader Island was enveloped in a thick fog and steady mist. While the fire intensified, the wet tent and damp sleeping bag were stuffed under the splash cover. After a hot meal, I paddled ten hours. The mist and rain brought me to rapids.

The high water had softened them, leveling the turbulence far below the surface. Fast-rolling water and many swirling whirlpools spoke of what lay at their depths. High on the west bank stood a monument to an RCMP officer who lost his life here. Ten miles below the rapids, I stopped at Donnelly River for a cup of tea. Forty miles and eight hours after that, I reached Fort Good Hope.

It was still early morning when I slid the canoe onto the beach in front of the village. Construction materials were piled high along the shore. Skirting these, I passed a church and stopped at the store. It was closed, and a routine tour followed. The homes were predominantly log cabins, but judging by the contents on the beach, they would soon be replaced by government box houses. A faint smell of urine permeated the town as the summer sun melted winter's waste.

My wanderings brought me to a graveyard. Most of the 100 or so graves were marked with plain, white, unnamed crosses. Behind the church was the sole, well-kept grave. Like a sentinel, a large, black marble marker watched over the remains of the priest and his brother who founded the church; they had died in 1864.

An assemblage of mosquitoes drove me from this congregation. They were no better at the store as I sat on a wooden bench in a steady mist, waiting for the doors to open. A constant, two-handed battery held the blood suckers at bay until nine o'clock when the manager arrived to start the day's business. There was little to choose from, and even at that, it cost me twenty dollars. With the tiny box of groceries under my arm, I skirted the construction materials, boarded the canoe, and followed the current.

The next three days weren't pleasant; everything, day and night, was done in the steady rain. Even Vagabond was contentious. Constant headwind and whitecaps cut mileage in half. Hordes of mosquitoes greeted me every time I set foot on shore. There would be no more reports of empty red canoes floating down the Mackenzie, as every mile was now an effort. On the fourth day from Fort Good Hope, a patch of blue showed momentarily. Watching it through the rain, it slid across the sky and vanished, just a splash of hope on a dark canvas.

Gray dominated and there was no sign of the rain fading. The troop slowly moved through the wet gloom of the muddy Mackenzie. On July 1st, I was forty miles from the village of Arctic Red River. A few miles below it I would leave this river and travel west over tributaries into the Richardson Mountains and into Alaska. Maybe the sun was shining in the United States, but here it had rained heavily now for twelve straight days. Everything was damp, my spirits included.

When I awoke on the evening of the second, after sleeping through a slightly-improved afternoon, it was cold. Finally, the rain had quit; now it was snowing. Supper was a handful of raisins, a piece of cold fish, and a candy bar. I left in the windblown snow just before midnight. By morning, the temperature had risen. This was verified as windblown sleet overtook snow. The few degrees did nothing for my wet, tennis shoe-clad feet.

Many times, I wished I had my Sorrels, but alas, they were waiting for me at the post office in Fort Yukon, on the other side of the mountains. Well past its prime, my ripped rain gear offered only slight protection. The wetness, the headwinds, the rain, and the sleep patterns—it was all wearing on me. All I wanted was to find a big, flat rock, lie on my back with arms spread, and soak in the sun. Instead, I pulled onto the bank after seven hours and stepped into ankle-deep mud, twenty miles short of Arctic Red River.

Shivers ran through me as I put the coffee cup to my lips. Wet warmth soothed my shriveled hands as they cradled the steaming porcelain. Leaning against a tree offered trivial protection in the near-freezing elements. The hard-earned fire hissed, and ringlets appeared in my cup as rain dripped off my hat brim; rain was the only sound.

Hollowness enveloped me as the glowing embers beneath the fiery flames mesmerized me and my malaise. It took two hours of just sitting to steel myself. Even then I was loath to leave. A lighter shade of gray indicated morning; Arctic Red River was just down the way.

It took eight hours of wet, windy paddling to reach the village. From the time I docked to the time I reached the door of the store, a mere 100 yards, it was made obvious which natural resource was most abundant in this village of 85—mud. The store stood at the top of a meek knoll, and I struggled all the way up. When I got there, it was closed.

Desperation set in. I stood in the downpour, drenched to the skin. I knocked on the closest door. The guy who appeared was big, not quite as tall as my paddle, but as wide as the doorway that framed him. "Yah, what do ya want?" he growled through the opened door.

"Could you tell me when the store opens?" I asked.

"It don't till I open it," he said with finality. "I seen you out there struggling an hour ago. Most people got enough sense to quit in this weather. It's been raining without a letup now for 18 days. Come on in," he said, stepping aside. He didn't have to ask twice, not that he would have anyway, so I slid through the doorway into the warmth of the room. It felt great, as did the hot coffee. In return, I listened as he poured out his isolated stress.

First, he explained how he acquired the store manager's job. "I worked for these guys in 15 different stores in the last ten years. Then they dump me in this hole." He also told of his close association with the villagers. He was unkind; "Ain't a one of them worth a shit. I got no use for any of 'em. All they know is how to play poker." His meandering bluster continued, "Here's how smart they are. They fired one of the teachers because he lied on his application. Said he finished eighth grade and he only finished seventh. That was after he taught school here for ten years. No wonder they're all dumb."

Next, he demonstrated the high esteem in which the villagers held him. "The first three months I was here they called me Timapace. I didn't mind much. It's a nice flowing name. Every day I'd walk down the path, or someone would walk by and holler, 'Hi Timapace!' I'd wave and smile and get along real good with everyone. Then one day two drunks got in a fight out front and my name came up a couple of times. It was 'You S.O.B. Timapace!' or 'You goddamn Timapace!' or something like that. Didn't take long to realize that they ain't talking about me but about some guy making babies. I kicked both their asses to hell and back, and word got round real quick. That was the end of that."

His respect for his fellow man in Arctic Red River never wavered as he continued his epic. "Lazy thieving bastards is what they are. All summer long I cut and haul wood, so they can shop in comfort come winter. And what do they do? They steal firewood off the pile out back. About two years ago there were real nice boardwalks all over town. Come winter, they pulled them up and burned them. Now they scream cause it's all mud."

"Anyway, this wood stealing went on and on, all winter, and I got pissed. I got this little cannon in back that uses black powder, and so one day I drilled a two-inch hole down a log, packed it full of black powder, plugged it, put a little X on it, and laid it on top of the woodpile. It took a couple of days, but it disappeared. That night, old Benny came running out of his house in his drawers screaming, 'Fire!' Burnt the house right to the ground. Never figured him for it, but he still says that the stove just blew up. He's still living with his mother." Once he controlled his malicious laughter, he finally acquiesced; "Come on, I'll open the store for you."

As I browsed around the nearly vacant one-room store, my

damp pants clung to me. I could only buy the meager essentials, spending 25 of my 31 dollars. The next place to spend the other six dollars was hundreds of miles away, across a mountain range. I envisioned starving as I slid the six lonely dollars back into my wet wallet. The food box would be far from bulging; already my stomach rumbled. I thanked my host and stepped out into the rain. I began sliding my way down the knoll and turned to wave at the "Village Factor." He waved, shook his head, and closed the door. The mud oozed over the tops of my tennis shoes.

The skies held nothing back as I pitched the tent in front of Arctic Red River on a desolate grassy spot surrounded by mud. The bag was wet from constant exposure, but I had no choice but to use it. Since the nylon door faced the village, I could see the smoke curling out of the warm houses. Even in my deprivation, sleep was managed in the thirty-degree wet bag, but not much. It came in spurts of varied longevity.

The last spurt revealed silence, and nothing beat against the tent. Poking my head out, I found a sky that was half-blue. It had been weeks since seeing the sun. I was out the door, packed, and on my way in minutes. What a joy to paddle again without the cumbersome rubber raincoat, without the moistening feet, without angels crying! A continuously strong headwind prevented any great accumulation of miles, but I reached the Peel River, went against its current for five miles, and camped across the river from a place called Little Village. It consisted of four ragged tents and three barking dogs.

The mountains beckoned me far in the distance as I challenged the Peel River's current in the morning, looking for Husky Channel, which would lead to the Rat River. Without a doubt, I was ready to leave this Mackenzie Delta, with its mud, its willows, brown silt-laden water, and endless mosquitoes. While dreaming of crystal-clear mountain streams, a skiff pulled next to the canoe and offered a tow. After a negative reply, I gazed at the assemblage; on it, a man, woman, ten kids, seven dogs, and mounds of equipment was heaped. On top of all that, he wanted to tow me. "That's quite a load you've got," I indicated with a nod of my head.

He explained that he was going to Fort McPherson to work for the rest of the summer because he needed some spending money. The current was destroying my morning's work as we sat side-by-side, but I departed with a fresh whitefish, though little knowledge of the Rat River. He summed it up with conviction as he said, "Going to get pretty rough, I guess."

Across the Husky Channel, about 25 miles, posed no problem. A small winding creek flowed from the channel into the Rat River. As the crow flies it was two and a half miles, by water, it was five hours and a good place to camp for the night. Morning brought clear blue skies.

I was at the western edge of the Mackenzie Delta and anxious to start the trek up the corridor that wound into the mountains, culminating at Summit Lake. If I had known what lay ahead, I would have not been so eager to start this fresh slice of hell. In theory, my upstream run on the Rat River was a brief 52 miles. Instead, its introduction was nine hours in cold, waist-deep water. I pulled the canoe, unable to paddle the torrent.

My garb for the McDougall Pass, a high corridor between the Mackenzie and Yukon Rivers.

Cold to the bone after this opening round, I climbed up a 600-foot vantage point to rejuvenate my numbed legs. What I saw at the top, through my mosquito-net covered head, was anything but inviting. Isolated patches of ice and snow clung defiantly in shadowed crevices along the valley walls. The frothing river lay like a white, frayed rope meandering along the valley floor, hemmed in by scrub pines and thick willows. Seemingly all the mosquitoes in Canada entered the country through this corridor, swarming in gray clouds. The view made the Swan River look complacent.

As I towed the canoe, the skies were blue and cool, though only my shoulders and head benefited. Hours piled up; miles did not. At the end of the day, I reached deep, fast water below one of the hundreds of sets of rapids. I held the bow of the canoe in an endless tug of war against the current. I was exhausted and stuck, the laborious walking and glacial waters having taken their toll. Fast water surrounded me. My body shivered, and I began to lose. Springing off the bottom, I reached across the canoe and grabbed the far gunwale, using my last energy to shimmy in. I rolled in with gallons of water as the current swept us downstream in victory. Hours of hard-won progress sped by before I could wrest control. It was time to camp and regroup.

Usually things looked better after a good night's sleep, but the following morning, July 9th, I battled through the deepest part of the Rat River. Throughout that day and the next, 23 hours were logged in the frigid water. Many were the times that I had to get out and let the sun restore my frozen legs. Meanwhile, the water remained fast and deep, with thick willows lining each bank, confining me to the waterway.

It began to abate, as the farther into the mountains I was drawn, the shallower the water became. This benefit was offset by the rush being much colder, but I would take that trade. My spirits were high with new-found headway. Though the canoe was losing its confrontation with the river rocks, and food quantities were low, a few days' worth at most, I figured I'd be at Summit Lake in another long day, and salvation at the village of Old Crow only 200 miles downstream. Nothing worse crossed my mind.

On the morning of the 11th, I sat by the fire sipping hot tea, waiting for the sun to top the mountain peaks. It was easier to wade into the cold current under its presence. I pondered my state while waiting, my whitewater-walking wardrobe humoring me. A ragged, canvas bucket hat clung to my head with a mosquito head net dangling from its brim; neck to waist was a heavy wool shirt with its sleeves terminating at gloved hands; around my waist clung blue-jean cutoffs, protruding from them were well-worn, once-white long underwear; they ended at wool socks, covered with ragged, blue sneakers whose vital spark had long since extinguished. Each step produced a *plop*, as the soles no longer adhered to the uppers.

Dressed to pull the canoe 52 miles up the Rat River to reach Summit Lake, high in the Richardson Mountains.

Soon they were cremated under my last pan of potatoes, their ashes strewn by a gentle mountain breeze filtering down the Rat River valley. The gentle mountain breeze soon morphed into a straight-down-the-pipe gale. After eight hours, I had to get out. The wind-chill had devastating effects. For four hours I sat next to a blazing fire, wrapped in the tent tarp, sipping coffee, my back to the wind. Then, back into the frigid water.

If there had been any flat water, there would be whitecaps to impede my progress, anyways, I reassured myself. I rounded another winding bend in the river. Looking up, I couldn't believe it. There on top of a low bank, stood a cabin. I scampered up the bank behind Vagabond, .30-06 in hand, knowing he would want first dibs at any creature not expecting company. All was clear as I slowly pushed open the door with the rifle barrel.

It was an empty trapper's cabin, used only in the winter.

Littering the dirt floor was garbage, the source of a rank smell. Not even a stove was in existence. Long, coarse, brown hairs caught on a sliver of wood suggested that a bear may have dined here at one time. Above the cabin door in crude letters was carved BEAR CREEK CABIN. I found the creek on the map, a small tributary, and a rough relation to Summit Lake showed they were separated by only twelve miles. Freshly motivated, I put in another seven hours and ended a 15-hour day. Surely, I'd be at Summit Lake tomorrow.

Surely, Summit Lake tomorrow, I mocked after twelve hard hours of pulling the next day. Exhaustion was upon me. My meager staples no longer offset my energy output. The roomy food box now held just two pounds of oats, two days' flour, one can of Klik, very little sugar, a handful of coffee, and a dash of salt. In addition, no fish in the endless rapids and no game along its banks could be found. Making do with what I had, surely, I'd be at Summit Lake tomorrow.

No Summit Lake, I agonized after ten cold hours; it was nowhere in sight. Ice now covered the ground beneath the willows. The river had narrowed to twenty feet, but the walking was just as hard. Mrs. Cardinal's beautifully beaded moccasins weren't made for this type of abuse, but they were all I had. Vowing over and over to never make another prediction, I waded up the crystal-clear water that flowed from lofty mountain peaks.

Luck intervened. I reached two small pools at a fork in the Rat River that produced fishing at its finest. Arctic grayling and trout responded to every cast. Eating my fill many times, I spent a day and a night plundering that glory hole, insatiable hunger temporarily abated. When it was time to leave, I chose the fork with the most water, assuming that was the best route. I was wrong. After two hours the compass confirmed my growing suspicion. Finally at the base of the mountain, I decided the best way to orient myself was from a vantage point. Abandoning the canoe, I climbed.

Mountains obscure distance, and hours later I finally reached the jutting rock, high above the valley floor. Just the view was worth the ascent. I spread the map before me and sorted out the lakes and creeks dotting the valley. From this, I was able to pinpoint my exact location. While the canoe was on Fish Creek, it should have been on Rat Creek. Summit Lake lay seven miles up the pass from the fishing hole at the forks. The cabin at Bear Creek lay five miles downstream from the forks. Comprehension came hard. If correct, it had taken almost three days, 29 hours of travel, to cover the five miles from the

Bear Creek cabin to the forks. This was not good.

My vantage from which to plot a course to Summit Lake, standing in the background.

After retracing my steps to the forks, I put in another shift of world-class fishing. I stocked up, knowing the food box needed replenishment, and started up Rat Creek. Almost immediately there was a four-foot waterfall; this rock ledge had a direct bearing on my choosing the wrong fork and losing half of a day. Above the falls, nothing changed.

I endlessly pulled the canoe until a beaver dam blocked my passage. Behind it was smooth, glassy water, a sight not seen for fifty miles. It was a welcome view, even if it was only two canoe-widths wide. Ogilvie Lake was reached well into the night, where at its edge I set the tent on soft, spongy moss and had a 14-hour, wake-free rest. In the morning Ogilvie and Long Lakes were crossed. From Long Lake, a small creek flowed out of a small, unnamed lake. On the other side of this, the water ended. Then, only a half-mile of tundra separated me from Summit Lake and the Yukon watershed.

Relative to pulling the canoe, I carried the packs across the bog with ease, especially the food one. Then came the waterlogged beast. Before shouldering it, I flipped it over and inspected it. *Damn Rat River shredded it,* I assessed.

I gave it twenty minutes to drain, then, knowing it would get no lighter, positioned for the lift. I gave it my all, and it took every bit. Rolling it to my shoulders was anything but smooth. I sank into the tundra. The unlevel ground caused a staggering dance as I fought for balance on the unforgiving hummocks. The canoe's weight was oppressive in my present state, but nothing atop my emaciated frame would stop me from reaching Summit Lake. I moved laboriously through the maze, though careful not to stumble and drop the canoe. If I were forced to raise its weight again it would be devastating. One foot after another, after another, after another, until finally, the canoe was dropped unceremoniously at the edge of the spongy tundra.

I had reached Summit Lake. It was grandiose, a dream in my barely-lucid state. I had covered 7,000 miles in the last two and a half years, and this was the most imposing place I had ever been. The lake was completely calm. Flowers resembling cotton balls grew in profusion and contrasted sharply with the purple mountains rising all around. Scattered, stunted pines spotted the base of the mountains, and huge white clouds floated across the clear blue sky. I imagined them as dumplings, bobbing in the chicken soup I wished I had. Instead, in this pristine setting, I used the last of my flour and settled for a fluffy loaf of bannock and the last piece of cold fish. By noon the next day, I was ready to descend the mountains.

Summit Lake, a milepost of sorts. From here,
everything now flowed to the Bering Sea.

The Long Descent

The Bering Sea was on my mind as I crossed Summit Lake. The sea lay 1,500 miles away, all downstream, and I was satisfied that my chances of reaching Nome were still good. Only a mile long, the outlet of Summit Lake consisted of deadfalls, shallow water, thick willows, and dozens of places where the canoe was wider than the winding creek; it didn't matter, I had momentum. Three hours of very physical maneuvering brought me to the Little Bell River. It was shallow, rocky, and extremely adept at gashing fiberglass; if the canoe had been less waterlogged and wasn't carrying gallons of water, the river might have been easily navigated. As it was, there was no sense in trying to fix the hull until deeper water was reached.

That only came to pass once entering the Bell River. After a few hours of un-hindered floating, I noticed a moose antler propped on a sandy bend of the west bank. It appeared to have something written on it. Close scrutiny revealed this message:

July 16, 1977,

Ubanke from Inuvik, NWT,
Passed here while traveling to Tanana, Alaska,

Have a nice trip,
Klaus

Camping next to the graffitied moose antler, I wondered how the guy had gotten here. I knew where he didn't come from, the Rat River. *Probably a fly in,* I guessed. There was little doubt we would meet soon; the note was dated yesterday.

The following morning, I sorted the canoe's worst slashes and applied to them what fiberglass I had. It was very, very far from covering them all. It was also very, very far before I could get any more. There was a slight chance of obtaining some in Old Crow, but six dollars wouldn't go far. My best hope was Fort Yukon, 400 miles away. Coupled with an empty food box, I knew a long campaign remained.

The resin on the fiberglass was dry by mid-afternoon. Within an hour of leaving, water seeping through the canoe soaked my now beadless moccasins. The beaver trim had disintegrated days ago. The few rapids that the Bell River sported produced no difficulty, but survival between its banks did.

For over an hour, a mother goose performed the fabricated injury ritual of waterfowl-parenting, driving her goslings down-river well in front of the canoe. Time after time the .22 spoke, but the shorts coming from the magnum barrel sought their own destination. Then I got a break. The troupe went for cover in deep grass above the muddy shoreline, and Vagabond and I were right behind them as they quickly scattered. For fifty yards, I brandished the paddle, primitively hunting supper. It was like scything hay while on the run. When it was over, I got two, two more escaped, and Vagabond secured another two.

He had every intention of keeping them, but after my partner and I settled our differences, I took a six-hour break to boil and then roast the four small geese. Frying was out of the question, as grease hadn't been had in this household for quite some time. I ate the meat off the eight small legs, and Vagabond devoured everything else. A cup of coffee put the finishing touches on our caveman feast. Even though I felt full, I knew the nutritional content of the lean legs was small.

A quick downpour quenched the remains of the fire, and a double rainbow escorted me for a few bends downstream. For seven hours I paddled and bailed down the Bell River. After a quick rest, maneuvers were continued for six more hours, bringing me to the mouth of Watery Creek. The day's tally amounted to fifty miles in 24 hours, in which eight moose and one brown bear were sighted. The tent was immediately occupied, as nourishment from the goslings was long gone.

Soon three northern pike went from Watery Creek onto a board and were baked for breakfast. In my malnourished state it was getting hard to get out of bed and get motivated. Only a teaspoon of coffee and not much more sugar remained in the food box. After a twenty-mile dash to Eagle River, I built a small fire and savored the last cup.

The terrain had changed drastically since leaving Summit Lake. No more majestic peaks could be seen as I traveled throughout the bright night and well into morning. The water widened and deepened as it wound between looming, green pine-forests. By noon, the Bell River had reached and become the famed Porcupine River. This called for the end to another 24-hour pilgrimage at the first spot level enough to house the tent. After a supper of cold fish, freshly harvested onion grass, and sugar water, sleep came easily and stayed that way. It was as bright as day when I awoke at midnight.

Making my way to the river, I splashed cold water over my face with cupped hands, trying to drown out the weariness. From my kneeling perch next to the river I noticed tracks in the mud; they lead past the canoe. The pads alone were as long as my foot and twice as wide, not including the toes and claws. Recognizing they weren't there when I beached the canoe, a shiver shot through me. The tent was but twenty feet away. *Where was my watch dog, Vagabond! Probably sleeping.* It may have been just as well. Nothing was damaged. Sometimes it paid to have an empty food box.

Discarded caribou antlers littered the shore as I made my way down the Porcupine toward the settlement of Old Crow. It was less than ninety miles away, and I sure looked forward to spending my last six dollars there. Though the paddle became heavier, hours and hours were piling up. Breaks consisted of baked fish and onion grass. Even the sugar was gone.

After traveling all night, it was late morning when I passed Rat Indian Creek. A bright orange tarp sat conspicuously a mile below its mouth. I could see movement under the tarp ahead as curling, white smoke rose lazily to mingle with the morning air. I angled closer to shore. Soon, the smell of coffee reached me. A red-bearded white man and two Natives came into view; they sat on logs situated around a fire, sipping from cups. I was directly in front of them now, hoping a hail for coffee would reach across the water. After nonchalantly waving, the bearded man then returned his attention to the fire.

While the smell of coffee faded, the current carried me away. Then, they were behind me, almost out of view. My empty stomach rumbled in protest. Indecision set in. White smoke from the white man's fire seemed to create a Christian halo over the campsite as I looked over my shoulder. *Maybe after all these years the missionaries were working on the wrong race,* I mumbled in my disappointment. Old Crow was still a long way away. With much disparagement aimed at myself, I turned the canoe around. Hunger had a nasty habit of displacing pride.

Thoughts flowed through my mind as I conceived ways to beg with dignity. I settled on a direct approach. Starting off with hi, I got right to the point. "You wouldn't happen to have any flour you'd like to sell, would you? It seems I ran out a couple of days ago." They were surely doing better than I was right now. I didn't know what six bucks of flour looked like, but I was willing to find out.

"Sure, but sit down and have a cup of coffee," the bearded man said while handing me a steaming cup. Sitting on a log next to him for two torturous hours and two cups of coffee, I listened to him talk nonstop about his cameras and the work he was doing here as an archeologist. Then I had to tour the dig site and see all the bits and pieces that were found. It was interesting for a while, but only after another hour did something of more interest approach, the mess tent.

The inside was a beautiful sight. These guys had more food than I'd eaten since leaving New Orleans. After stuffing a little flour, a few tea bags, a stick of butter, a can of soup, a tin of sardines, and two eggs into a sack, he handed it to me saying, "We have a camp just outside of Old Crow. Could you give them this food list? We're running low on a few things." I said yes, eager to return the favor, and he handed me a folded piece of paper. Declining any money, he mumbled something about, "Government-funded anyway." They were all back around the fire by the time I pushed off. I made it around one bend, beached the canoe, and pigged out.

A light rain set in before I reached the bottom of the teapot, so I repacked the cooking gear and moved on. The rain increased steadily, and by the time it peaked, I was under the protection of a long-neglected cabin. Most of the chinking between the logs was missing, but the floor was solid, and the roof only leaked on one side. By rummaging through discarded materials outside, I was able to fit together something resembling a stove. While rain pelted the sod roof, Vagabond and I, our stomachs refreshingly half full, were able to enjoy a warm, relaxing evening.

When I awoke the next morning, the steady rain convinced me

to spend the day huddled next to the makeshift stove. The layover did wonders for my mind and body. I was rejuvenated and ready to go. For eleven nonstop hours, I traveled through the night until reaching Lords Creek in a slight drizzle. It was 35 miles from the archaeology site and still 35 miles from Old Crow. After a five-hour tea break in which I ate the remains of my food, I was ready to tackle the miles to Old Crow. I left in earnest, but only a few miles downstream the skies started to clear and I came upon another encampment.

A man named Bill Smith introduced himself after beckoning, "Come on in and have some baked fish!" Behind him stood a dirty wall tent, a couple of dogs, and a Native lady whom he introduced as his wife. She flashed a smile as we exchanged greetings and before I knew it, there was a bowl of hot stew on my lap and a cup of coffee in my hand. Whitefish and bread were sandwiched between two grill grates and propped next to the fire. Then Bill got to talking.

Hidden behind his bush clothes and shaggy head, was remarkable intelligence. He was an attorney, working on Native land claims and, "Giving the Queen of England a hard time." He believed that since the Natives of Old Crow never signed a treaty, they owned the land from the mountains to the U.S. border, then north all the way to the ocean. Of course, the Queen didn't agree, but that had not discouraged him. Turning to woods lore, he spoke of dog sleds, caribou herds, roots to eat, medicinal willow bark, sap to draw out infection, fish drying, getting oil from fish guts, and the famed Hudson's Bay Company.

After three hours, he slowed down considerably, which was too bad, since I was quite interested. He beamed as he showed me the pullover caribou parka his wife made, and the hand-crank sewing machine she used to make it. Then, he asked his wife to, "Clean out her cache and get a bunch of odds and ends together for this man. He's got a long way to go, and we're breaking camp in a few days so there's no sense in us carrying it out."

Mrs. Smith piled surplus tins and small bags in front of the tent while Bill reached deep within his reservoir to give me a step-by-step lesson on making pemmican. He was pounding a small hammer against a rock, beating an invisible piece of jerky to a pulp, when Mrs. Smith let us know that the cache was cleaned out. Setting the hammer aside, Bill went to the pile of goods and stuffed the cast away items into a sack. A two-pound box of sugar certainly caught my eye. It was a tattered box with 47 Cents stamped on its top. Bill and his wife exchanged a few words in Athabascan, and he replied, "She says it's from her mother. It may be a little hard since it's from 1936."

Bill followed me to the canoe as I led the way, gunnysack dangling over my shoulder. "I wouldn't mind spending a couple of weeks out in the bush with you some winter," I said as I put the sack in the empty food box.

"Well, if you're going to go through all that trouble, you might as well plan on the whole winter," he invited. It was a tempting thought as I thanked him and headed for the archaeologist's headquarters in Old Crow.

It was an hour before midnight when I landed in front of their tents. The camp was almost lifeless. Walking into the mess hall, I found a dishwasher and told him that I had a note for Ken. Ken was alerted, and I shortly handed him the scrap of paper. "Too bad you didn't come a few hours earlier," he taunted, "we had a big steak feast." Before turning for the door, he added, "There might be some coffee left in the pot."

No steam rose as I filled a Styrofoam cup. Carnation powdered-cream clotted as I stirred it into the cold brew. *Maybe it needs a good shot of 1936 sugar,* I thought, as I watched people come and go. No one said so much as hello. While dishes clanked in the kitchen, I dazedly swished cold coffee grounds around the bottom of the cup. The lights went out and a door slammed somewhere out back. A dog barked far down the shore. I debated whether to camp or go into Old Crow. Sitting alone among the six long, mess tables in the huge empty tent, I knew I didn't belong. Finishing the last of my swill, the foam cup made a soft, hollow *thud* as it hit the wooden table. Before it rocked to a rest, I was out the door.

Old Crow was a quaint little village. I pulled in front of the store early the next morning and beached next to a 15-foot aluminum canoe. Observing the gear inside it, I guessed that it belonged to Klaus, author of the moose-horn message from days before. My first stop was the Bay, to see how hungry the 300 miles to Fort Yukon were going to be. As I passed cookies, candy, potato chips, and ice cream, complete control was maintained. It was just as well for I had no Louis Lamour books, saw no bridges, and wasn't going to repeat sins of the past.

Instead, I stood at the counter with five pounds of flour, two pounds of oats, one pound of margarine, and a small box of tea bags. *14 cents in case of emergency,* I mused on my remaining change. I was lucky that my costs didn't include a fine; a mere interrogation, lecture, and warning from the game warden about my uncased gun and no fishing license sufficed, as I bit my lip and apologized. His high-decibel reprimand was penalty enough.

As my rations were being bagged and the game warden interrogated me, a guy waited behind me to pay for a map and groceries. I thought it could have been Klaus. Just as I was leaving the store for my appointment with the customs office, the guy grinned at me.

"Went through the same thing this morning with the game warden." Klaus introduced himself and explained that he had immigrated from Germany to the bush four years ago because, "There is no wilderness left in Germany." He also confirmed my suspicion that he didn't drag up the Rat River, "I flew into Bell River and have had pretty much enough of this canoeing since then." He complained that his dapper, clean-shaven appearance and Hush Puppy shoes confirmed that he was cut from a different bolt of cloth than the locals, too.

Since Old Crow was the last Canadian town before reaching the border with Alaska, I hoped the customs office would return the $370 that I had paid upon entering the country; supposedly it was to be returned upon leaving. Paperwork followed the official's check and double-check of everything listed on the customs entry form, and then disappointment. It would take months to obtain the refund. In my backwoods mind, I gave the money to them when I came in and they should give it back to me when I left. But governments just weren't that simple. *Maybe it was best,* I thought, as I left Old Crow, for there was no doubt in my mind that I would need that money if and when I reached Nome.

It was a great day, clear, warm, and windless. I took it easy, drifting, napping, playing the guitar, and occasionally paddling. Sometime during the night, I arrived at Foster's Cabin, twenty miles downstream. Here I fixed a lean supper, took a couple of hours off, and then was back in the canoe. Not a breeze stirred as the sun beat down.

Lightly snoring, Vagabond lay on top of the Duluth Pack, soaking up the warm rays. Suddenly he woke with an itch behind his ear and sat up to scratch it. Naturally, his body followed the sloping contour of the pack, and he rolled into the cold Porcupine River. Within the hour, Vagabond set himself up for another dunking. *Some dogs just don't learn.*

Well into the day, I reached the abandoned remains of Rampart House where Klaus's red tent stood out against the few remaining gray, weathered, windowless buildings. "Come on in for coffee!" he shouted as I neared. Vagabond was in his usual precarious spot and came to life when he heard Klaus's voice. Excitedly clamoring from one end of the canoe to the other, he tried to get ashore without getting his feet wet. The canoe had just entered ten feet of thick, brown slime, a barrier between open water and shore. Vagabond's whining and yapping ended in a dramatic leap to what he mistook for dry land. With all the grace, beauty, and poise that a Samoyed can muster, he flew through the air, legs churning, and then sank as he broke through the surface.

If his dignity was dampened, it wasn't evident, and he dog-paddled through the slime to gain solid footing. Once reconnected with terra firma he shook heartily, and then dashed for Klaus. The pup was already sitting next to Klaus, content in all his attention, when I beached in the slime and jumped out. The coffee was hot, so I took a seat next to the fire and Klaus and I got to know each other better. When the pot was gone, I pitched my tent next to his and called it a night.

Klaus left after breakfast while I toured the long-abandoned buildings. They were interesting but very little had been left behind. With my curiosity satisfied, I soon followed Klaus.

Our paths crossed again a day and a half later at what appeared to be an abandoned school. Wet books, papers, typewriters, and records lay scattered throughout the long, low structure. A rusting barrel stove with cast iron fittings that had been once used as a heat source sat crumbling. In front of the building, empty barrels lay everywhere. Many sheets of plywood appeared to have been taken by the wind until they stopped, interwoven with the willows. While Klaus took a nap, I used one of these sheets to make a new food box. There wasn't much to put in it, but a little foresight never hurt. Fort Yukon was not many days away.

Klaus's nap ended with my pounding the food box together. Rubbing the sleep from his eyes, he went to work building himself a sail to catch a steady tailwind that had arisen. While lashing a pole to his canoe, he said, "You have to show me how to make that bread in a frying pan."

"Maybe," I said without conviction, "it's kind of a secret recipe." It took years to develop and nothing short of torture, or a well-timed question while short on food, would cause me to divulge it. Klaus finished rigging the sail, pushed off into the breeze, and with a huge smile called, "See you in Fort Yukon!" Setting the new box in the canoe, I filled it with odds and ends from the pack. Klaus was soon out of sight. Then, I got to work, matching Klaus' ambition.

After cutting two crossbars from saplings, I lashed them to a mast, which was then lashed to the yoke. Nylon ropes from the top of the mast to the stern and bow held the mast rigid. Next, I tied the tent fly to the crossbars, leaving plenty of slack to catch the wind. It was precarious until I was able to orient the canoe with the wind, then, the sail filled, and the canoe surged ahead, momentum stabilizing the operation.

At times, a gust would cause the end of the lower crossbar to dip into the water, reminding me that maybe this wasn't such a good idea. The lack of stability was further exaggerated whenever I stood on the seat, the only way I was able to aim the canoe. Soon Klaus came back into view. I maneuvered beside him and lay back against my coat. With embellished ease, I'd occasionally use the paddle as a rudder. He seemed surprised to see me as I breezed by effortlessly. Picking up his paddle, Klaus tried in vain to compensate for his inferior sail.

"Now that really pisses me off!" he moaned between strokes.

I waved and parroted his taunt, "See you in Fort Yukon!"

It was late when I stopped for the night at a place called Sherman House. Klaus pulled in three hours later. Only one of the deserted cabins looked like it would stand through the night, and only just, but I set up camp in it. Klaus wanted nothing to do with it. "No telling who or what might be lurking around yet," he explained, "besides, I'm a little superstitious." He set his tent up well away from the old haunts.

Emerging from the old cabin early, I made enough noise to awaken Klaus, wishing I had a few chains to shake around his tent. After breakfast, we packed and left together. There was no wind and we kept a close pace throughout the ten-hour day, bringing us to the mouth of the Sheenick River, where a tiny log cabin overlooked the Porcupine River.

The small log structure seemed to have been built recently so

Klaus had no superstitious qualms. He must have been unaccustomed to ten-hour days as he walked right up to the door, sleeping bag in hand. Inside there was nothing but a small stove and two rough wooden beds. The floor was dirt and Klaus's six-foot frame hit the ridgepole. Because the logs weren't peeled, it was obviously a hurry-up job, probably a line shack for a winter trapper. We chose our respective bunks and called it a day.

Under an oppressive noon sun, breakfast was served. As waves of heat shimmered off the water, I decided to spend the rest of the day here and travel during the cooler hours of the evening. Klaus agreed it was a good idea, so after washing his clothes, he channeled his energies into creating a huge pot of soup. German style, he said. While I watched, he dumped three different flavors of soup mix, canned peas, canned tomatoes, old mushrooms, stale rice, six different spices, and moldy beans into the pot. Who knows what else was slipped into his secret recipe when my attention was diverted. With the mixture concocted, it was placed on the back of the stove for four hours, until it was, "Done to perfection."

When mess call was announced, two bowls were filled by a coffee-can scoop. Klaus couldn't eat it, I wouldn't, and Vagabond shouldn't have. Within the hour, he was sick. After a healthy loaf of bannock, we traveled throughout the night, spent the day under the coolness of the pines, traveled another night, and by mid-morning were facing the muddy waters of the Yukon River. It was August 5th.

"So, this is the mighty Yukon of Alaska," I said to Klaus in amazement.

"How are we going to paddle up that!" Klaus asked, Fort Yukon lay one and a half miles upstream. He was exasperated to have come this far only to face defeat. Whirlpools swirled by in the muddy water, huge volumes rolling past on the 1,200-mile way to the ocean.

"We don't have much choice," I instructed, "keep the front of your canoe straight into the current, do not get turned sideways."

"Ok, I'll follow you." His meek reply revealed little confidence.

Although it was hard, it couldn't compete with parts of the Mississippi. A fish wheel creaked in the current as I inched around it. Falling behind, Klaus paddled frantically. It was well over an hour before I reached a small eddy at the edge of town. Klaus was nowhere in sight. I unpacked the canoe, emptied gallons of water, and waited and waited.

As I started to think that Klaus may not have gotten around the fish wheel, he appeared, inching his way along the bank. He was drenched in sweat when he landed, but also exhilarated at his conquest, "Man, oh man, I didn't think I could do anything like that!"

"We can go back and do it again if you'd like," I teased. He declined.

Klaus went to the nearest store, and I proceeded to the post office. Two large boxes awaited me, one from my brother and the other from my sister. It had been three and a half months since I had heard from home and what welcome news it was. There was a menagerie of goodies; food for thought and stomach, clean pants, socks with heels and toes, and best of all, a new pair of boots. I immediately removed what was left of Mrs. Cardinal's slippers, put on a new pair of wool socks and slid into the felt-lined Sorrels.

Even though it was over eighty degrees and they were good to thirty below, and my feet had been wet for almost three months, they felt great. *Let 'em laugh,* I mumbled as I knotted the laces, cramming as much junk food into my system all the while. I carried the remaining treasures to the canoe and stashed them in the food box, before donating the remains of my prized slippers to the river. I felt bad for abusing such a gift.

At the riverbank I read the mail. My euphoria was shattered by the final letter, one that stated, "Your money is in Fairbanks. Do you want it mailed to Fort Yukon?" My sister had sent $500 through RCA Alaskan Telegraph with explicit instructions to send the money to Fort Yukon; I was not happy when I called them. To make things worse, they refused to put it on a plane or wire it, insisting they had to mail it. Today was Friday, so the earliest I could expect it was late Monday.

I had just traveled up one side of a mountain range and down the other, and here I sat with 14 cents in my pocket. I couldn't afford to sit for three days doing nothing. The canoe needed fiberglassing and Nome sat well over 1,500 miles away; it was August, and paddling season had less than three months remaining. There was but one solution. Grabbing the green ammo box, I headed back to town.

It took some searching, but I found a store owner who would give me a $100 loan against the $1,200 worth of camera equipment that I left as collateral. It irked me to the core, but I didn't know what else to do. Then, I had to turn around and give him back most of the one hundred-dollar bill, as he owned the only store that sold fiberglass.

When I returned to the river, Klaus was stretched out in someone's skiff, sound asleep. With gloved hands, I started right in at the bottom of the canoe. Long, ragged sections of fiberglass pulled off, releasing trapped pockets of water. In some places, the damage was four layers thick. It took hours to scrape and pry off the loose pieces. Exposed to the hot sun, it would be dry enough to re-fiberglass tomorrow. Then, I'd be back in business.

Stuffing the shredded fiberglass into a 55-gallon barrel trash can, I heard, "Where you boys from?" from a customs officer standing behind me.

"We just came in from Canada," I said.

"Thought so. Let's see what you've got there," he demanded and walked over to my gear. Klaus slept on. "Open that pack there and empty it," he said, pointing to the dog pack. There was nothing in it but a few books and clothes. He said nothing about my rifles or fishing gear. "He with you?" he asked nodding at the snoring German.

"Sort of," I replied and shouted, "Klaus! Hey, Klaus!" I went over and shook him awake. "Someone has a few words for you," I said as he rubbed his eyes in a stupor under the burning sun. The officer apparently didn't approve of Klaus's accent for his gear was more completely scrutinized. After the final inspection, the guy hopped into his pickup, and I asked if he'd give me a ride to the store.

"I suppose," he snorted; I regretted asking the favor instantly. Not a word was exchanged until he pulled to a stop a half-mile from the store. "This is as far as I go," he said and left me standing in a cloud of dust. The store closed in five minutes. I didn't make it. Either my track days were over, or they closed early.

I chose the latter and walked back to the canoe where Klaus had been struggling with a Pabst Blue Ribbon for the last hour. "It tastes like fermented water. Wish I had some good German beer!" he said as he threw the empty into the trash barrel and headed for his tent.

"Where you going?" I asked as he crawled in.

It sounded like he said, "To sleep," as the zipper completed its arch.

It's only nine o'clock, I internally protested. We only put in thirty hours of paddling to get here, and while I ripped fiberglass off the canoe, he had a five-hour nap, and *now* he wanted to sleep *more?*

Maybe the can of Pabst Blue Ribbon made him sick; either way it seemed I'd have to tour the town by myself.

I had met a red-haired Irishman named Ron earlier at the post office, and since I was feeling social but there were no bars in Fort Yukon, I decided to take him up on his invitation for a drink in the evening. "Long, low, log cabin across from the liquor store," were his directions. They were accurate. The place didn't seem to have many moons left in it. Knocking on the loose door, I heard, "Come on in!" Ron and two others sat around an old cable-spool table drinking beer. A kerosene lamp, settled neatly in the spool's center hole, cast a ghostly light around the unfurnished room. "Grab a six-pack off the porch there," someone called. I set the cans on the spool, settled on a wooden box, and introductions were made.

A three-hour debate of local history and trapping methods followed. Ron told one of the stories. It gave tribute to the great ingenuity and adaptive skills of the local peoples. Seemingly, time after time the liquor store was broken into, and a substantial amount of bottled liquids were relocated to a more practical location. Finally, the city-owned store had had enough. Welders and heavy metal were brought in, and every opening was affixed with iron bars. The problem was solved for a few months. Then, it happened again. It was briefly a mystery as all the enveloping steel was still intact. But the city had underestimated their patrons' perseverance—in the back wall was a new entrance, fabricated at the clever blade of a chainsaw.

The next morning, I felt the canoe had dried enough to start the repair work. It took only a few hours to cover and shouldn't be long to dry in the hot sun. With little else to do, I lay back on the warm grass, waiting on fate to decide the afternoon.

It came in the form of a boat carrying four people and six dogs. "Come over and see my beautiful dogs!" a woman with a can of beer in her hand yelled to me. The two kids left toward town while the man emptied the boat; I walked over. "Half-wolf," she said with pride, "we used to keep them up by Beaver, but passersby came in and tore up all the floorboards looking for gold or something," She was clearly drunk, judging by her wavering focus.

"Drifters, just like you," she spat, the topic turning for the worse, "then you steal all our supplies and when we stop there when it's fifty below there's nothing there because drifters like you steal everything," she continued, maliciousness building in her soul. "Then the whole place was burned to the ground last winter by drifters, just like you!" She said as she reached her crescendo.

I could feel a redness creeping into my face. "How do you know it wasn't some local people?" I tried to say with civility.

"They just wouldn't do anything like that," she retorted.

She was working up quite a lather, and I countered against my better judgement. "From what I've heard, people around here will steal anything that isn't bolted down. Even the police told me this is the home of the best river pirates on the Yukon." It didn't seem to be the right thing to say.

She threw her half-empty beer can against the bank and screamed, "You goddamn drifters come around here thinking you can do whatever you please! You son-of-a bitches steal and burn cabins!" She was thoroughly upset, and worse, was getting out of the boat. Her embarrassed husband intercepted her and calmed her, promising that I had nothing to do with it. She calmed, Dr. Jekyll reemerging from Mr. Hyde, and started talking about her dogs again.

"Want a beer?" she asked as nicely as could be.

"No thanks," I said and returned to the canoe.

Klaus was standing wide-eyed on the bank behind me, probably thinking, "Maybe Germany wasn't so bad after all."

When the wolf-woman left, Klaus and I cleaned up messes we hadn't made around our campsite, a sign of goodwill. Everything went into the 55-gallon trash barrel. Within the hour, four kids with .22's strolled down the bank. They stopped at the trash barrel, threw everything that would float into the river and opened fire. When their missed targets disappeared in the current, they shouldered their weapons and headed back toward town.

We headed in the same direction. Klaus, with a touch of homesickness, said, "Let's go find a phone." We found that there was a pay phone at the airport. It was a long walk in hot Sorrels and when we arrived, everything was locked.

Pulling on the third and final door, a voice behind us said, "What's up, fellas?" We explained that we just wanted to use the phone. "What for? Why this phone?" came his probing questions in a rude tone. After a long, hard look at us, the guard let us in. Although Klaus tried for almost an hour, no one answered at his home in Inuvik and the operator wouldn't place a collect call from Alaska to Germany. Finally, he gave up.

Walking back, we passed the Sourdough Inn. The remnants of a party lay in the path, a balloon, snared by its own string. The night was dark, but I was sure that if Klaus had seen it, he would've stepped on it. But he didn't, I did. The *bang!* echoed into the still night air, my hands clasped my chest, a gasping moan expelled from deep within me, and my legs buckled in a sensational stagger.

I watched Klaus from the corner of my eye, his jaw dropped, and his face turned white. He stood frozen. A barely audible noise came from him in German. Staggering a few more steps, I stood up with a grin. Realizing the crisis had passed, Klaus fully regained his German language once again. With blood returning to his face, he said, "Damn you, I thought you got shot! I was ready to run behind that car there." We had a good laugh and found two more balloons. Klaus got to them first.

Except for a little general clean up, Sunday was one of rest. Monday came in hot. My feet were drenched in sweat by the time I picked up my money and camera equipment. At the store I shopped thriftily, for my few hundred dollars had to get me all the way to Nome. It didn't take long to purchase the needed groceries and fill the new food box. Four small patches were also applied to the canoe to finish the repair job.

Klaus had purchased a used three-and-a-half-horse motor at a great discount and used Ron's toolbox to craft a two-by-four motor mount for the back of his canoe. After four hours, it was time for a test run. Thirty minutes of pulling the starter and precise adjustments passed before the engine sputtered to life.

"Go upstream in case you have to paddle back!" I shouted to Klaus as he pulled away. He waved acknowledgment and was off with a smile.

An hour later, he silently pulled in, the motor resting on the floor of the canoe. "Motor mount broke and almost lost the whole thing," Klaus explained as I pulled the bow ashore. Not to be defeated, he spent the next three hours rebuilding with a four-by-four.

Soon both canoes were in fine shape, and Klaus was anxious to get going. After shaking hands and exchanging addresses, he cranked his "great savings" and was off to his original destination, Tanana. As noise from the little engine faded, Klaus was gone. I left shortly after.

It was August 9th and the Bering Sea lay 1,200 miles away. The locals said it should be no problem. Even though the current was in my favor, as I pushed off, I was concerned that I might end up in a long, dead-end slough. Fort Yukon is situated in the middle of the Yukon Flats. Here the river valley bulges many miles wide and is intersected by hundreds of channels and sloughs. *Keep the main current under the canoe,* I told myself. The small town of Beaver lay 100 miles downstream. With the way I advanced in this current, it shouldn't take long to get there.

With Canada well behind me, it was good to be back in the United States and with the Yukon River stretched far in front. Since leaving Fort Yukon, I had traveled seventy miles in eleven hours. It was great traveling again with a watertight canoe. As I was relishing this phenomenal occurrence, a small aluminum boat pulled beside me. Holding gunwales, the man introduced himself as Jay, a trapper and fisherman from the area, born and raised in Ely, Minnesota, close to my hometown. We drifted toward Beaver for almost an hour, just reminiscing. When I mentioned my run-in with the wolf-lady, he stated flat-out that she was, "Full of bullshit." However, he added a warning, "The village did get drunk last summer and run a bunch of canoeists out of there with shotguns." As we parted, Jay wished me luck, saying that I was about twenty miles from Beaver. A light rain came up after about four more hours, and it looked like it would get worse. Although Beaver was close, it could wait until morning.

In less than an hour back on the river, I was at the muddy bank in front of Beaver. Tied there was a battered, red and blue kayak, and next to the store and post office stood a tiny yellow tent. The owner of the kayak, leaning against the white wooden flagpole, introduced himself as Satch. Two elder ladies sat on the wooden steps of the log store peering our way.

"Did a guy named Klaus stop here?" I asked Satch.

"Him no stop. Go right by," he said laughingly in his heavily saturated Japanese accent. Then, for forty minutes I smiled and bobbed my head, trying to decipher his terminology. Satch was fixing a pot of coffee on a small butane stove when a kid of maybe seven years walked up.

He asked without pause, "Are you one of those robbers?"

Frustrated and teasing, I grabbed him, threw him over my shoulder, and said, "Yeah, I rob little kids and feed them to my dog!" I headed for Vagabond holding the brainwashed little squirmer. His screams didn't end until I set him down and he got out of reach. The kid stuck out his tongue and laughingly ran to the safety of the elders on the steps.

As I entered the store, the four old eyes stared at me. The kid had vanished. I needed nothing from the store, more than anything curiosity had drawn me inside. Four candy bars satisfied my interest. On the way out, I noticed a blue wheelbarrow next to the store. On it was taped a sign saying Do Not Remove—U.S. Mail Truck. As far as post office vehicles were concerned, that had to be at the bottom of the totem pole.

The little boy, "Puppy Chow", was sitting on my food box, awaiting my return. "Take me to Stevens Village," he begged as I got ready to leave. I gave him a candy bar and explained that there wasn't enough room for him. He agreed to stay and pushed me off with a wave. As I drifted down the Yukon, I noted the darkness. Days were getting shorter. I was losing the sun to winter at a rate of six minutes a day.

Stevens Village was passed without stopping, and I planned to travel throughout the night. Hugging the north bank, I hoped to avoid any nighttime traffic. A few boats roared by, but then it seemed I had the river to myself. Since the current had slackened considerably, I didn't foresee any danger in the dark. In silence, the blackness engulfed me for hours before a faint gray showed on the horizon. With the gray came a faint hum that broke the silence. It grew with the minutes as a boat was nearing. Soon a noise louder than the outboard could be heard. It was the music of Alice Cooper.

While the bass notes reverberated across the water, I lit a match to mark my location in hopes they wouldn't pass too close and swamp me. It drew them like a magnet.

"Got any pot?" one of the two asked as they pulled beside me.

"No, I don't," I answered.

"Damn, how about some coffee then?" the smaller one said.

When I replied sure, he pumped up his Coleman stove, dipped his pot in the Yukon, and in 15 minutes we had what he called, "Fresh coffee." Both guys were twenty and said they had just come in from fighting forest fires. One of them had already had quite an adventurous life by the time he was 17. His accomplishments totaled three arrests, two weeks in solitary confinement, burning out on acid, contracting the clap four times, and getting his girlfriend pregnant, twice. "Been slowing down these last couple of years though," he explained as he changed tapes to Doctor Hook.

"Want a drink?" the guy in the stern asked. "We got a case of whiskey and ten cases of beer under that tarp there." I stuck to fresh coffee. They had a little information about Klaus. "Yah, we saw him. He was about twenty miles down from here. The lower unit went out on his motor, so he gave us all his gas and went on paddling." When the coffee was gone, we parted.

"Sure you don't have any pot?" came a final plea. With a shake of my head, they started their motor. Doctor Hook soon faded up the Yukon.

We had drifted almost to the Alaska pipeline bridge. Looming ominously before me, it was silhouetted against the early morning sky. Pulling ashore, I wanted to inspect this silver tongue that slurped oil until rich men's appetites were full. Since it still wasn't quite daylight, I sat beneath the bridge, drinking tea. Within the hour I was able to climb the steep bank to the road. If anything looked alien in this vast land, this was it. Anywhere within reach, there were names, dates, and towns scribbled on the naked concrete. It appeared all fifty states were represented. I didn't like it and didn't linger, for to me, the pipeline symbolized an irreversible change that would make Alaska like the other states, confined by rules and regulations, harnessed, broken.

I traveled throughout the day, slept when normal people do, and floated a full morning, before I arrived in Rampart. The two-story building used for the store was old. It was locked, so I sat on the river-view side in the shade, on a rickety, graying wooden bench, deciding whether to linger or leave. There was just enough breeze to keep the mosquitoes at bay, but I thought that if I was just sitting, I could be doing the same thing in the canoe. I made to leave, but banging behind the building drew my attention.

Upon investigating, I found a chicken-necked, skinny-armed guy beating on an outboard motor part. "Be with you in a minute," he said with an Alaskan drawl, "which is two past your limit." It seemed he was having trouble with his hand-eye coordination. Finally, he gave up on the project, grabbed his beer, and retired to the bench in front of the store. Small talk followed. He asked if I needed anything from the store only after his empty beer can was tossed, bouncing off the rim of the trash barrel. Without grace, he removed the padlock and we entered the old building.

As we walked over the badly warped floorboards, he entered a floor-to-ceiling cage of alcohol and retrieved a six-pack of beer while I gathered a few groceries. A short, stocky man entered and downed two beers while cursing at the skinny manager. Apparently, they

316

weren't the best of friends. The stocky guy soon turned his vindictiveness toward me, and within minutes I was challenged to an arm-wrestling match.

"Ain't no one up and down this Yukon River ever beat me," he said as we took our respective places at the waist-high wooden counter. "Just 'cause you paddled some little boat down here from Fort Yukon don't make you tough," he mocked. We locked hands and he said to the manager, "You say go, Jack." For thirty seconds our arms didn't waver. Sweat developed between our palms. He started going down before recovering.

"He's cheating, he's cheating you!" Jack yelled to me. Sure enough, the guy had his loose hand hooked over the edge of the counter, pulling for extra leverage.

"You keep out of this, you skinny son of a bitch," he threatened and broke the grip. "You're pretty good but I'll beat you after this beer," he vowed. When the beer was empty, he said he had to go somewhere but would be right back.

"Good riddance, you bastard!" Jack hollered, the door slamming shut.

"What do I owe you for the groceries?" I asked Jack.

"Huh? Oh, you paid for those long time ago," he said. I told him a couple of times that they weren't paid for, but he kept repeating, "Yah, yah, they're all paid for. Don't worry about it." So, I didn't. Maybe the competition was payment enough.

Walking back to the canoe, I met a man named Paul, who swore he was going to give me a great deal on some smoked salmon, "Just nine dollars a pound!" He showed me his huge smokehouse where hundreds of salmon strips slowly cured. It was torture; I could taste them in the air. However, I couldn't see spending the little money I had on such a delicacy. Fortunately, things were negotiable. He walked away with a slightly used .22 magnum rifle for fifty dollars and a bag of smoked salmon. It was an ideal transaction. He thought he got a good deal, and I knew I did, too.

It was 35 miles to the rapids that marked the nearing confluence of the Yukon and Tanana Rivers. The mileage was quickly completed, taking a three-hour break only once there. The rapids were just wrinkles in the water, and I shot them at dusk, traveled all night, met the Tanana River, and pulled into the town of Tanana just before noon.

After spending fifty dollars at the store, I was told that, "Klaus

317

came in early this morning, sold his canoe and broken motor for next to nothing, and was on the first plane out of here." The manager continued, "Couldn't have been more than 15 minutes ago that it took off." It would have been nice to see Klaus again. *Another time, another place,* I thought.

I passed the outskirts of Tanana near shore. From the bank, a girl in a buckskin dress asked if I wanted a cup of coffee. I had put in a lot of hours and could use one. Tying the canoe to a stump, I followed her to a small camper trailer. She was a bit on the heavier side, and if the hair on her legs were trees, she had quite a forest. A true hippie. At least it was combed.

Another girl was at the trailer, and they introduced themselves as Joyce and Suzie, both from Minnesota. Coming down the Yukon from Dawson by canoe in 29 days, they were trying to find a ride to Nenana, up the Tanana toward Fairbanks. There they planned to winter in a tepee while supporting themselves on what they could sew. It sounded like a rough life and I would have told them so, but Satch arrived.

"Hi, hi, we meet again," Satch said smiling from ear to ear. Then, he turned to the ladies and announced, "I, Satch, come from way up Lake Bennett." He was cordially invited for coffee and within the hour he volunteered to prepare supper.

Satch produced two mason jars packed with fish, encrusted in a thick, salt brine. The fish was fried and set next to a pan of rice. Then I pitched in a loaf of bannock, and everyone served themselves. It looked appetizing, but its appearance was very deceptive. Midway through the meal, everyone was looking for the water jug. "My, my, forgot to wash away salt," Satch said apologetically. Apparently, the fish went straight from the mason jars to the frying pan.

After the meal, three quarts of Hawaiian Punch, and two huge pots of tea hardly quenched our thirst. I announced I was headed for bed, having chatted by the fire long enough. I'd been up for 41 hours with three-quarters of that in the canoe. Joyce said there was a couch inside for one of us, and the floor for the other. Not wanting to be bothered, I slept under a tall tree, fifty feet from the trailer.

When one arose, everyone did. Susie had had a problem during the night. She explained, "I drank so much last night that I had to get up to relieve myself. But—it was so cold, and I kept putting it off, until I had no choice. If I had a different pot, I would have used it—" she trailed off, looking at the same pot from which our breakfast coffee had been poured.

Wondering what she was going to do in the tepee come winter, I couldn't help but tease, "Yah, the coffee does taste a little funny this morning." She reddened slightly. Shortly after the last cup was downed, we parted ways. The two women went to town looking for a ride and Satch stayed on the beach.

I went 35 miles down-river and took a nap, until a fierce wind whipped through the willows, rocked the canoe, and awoke me. Traveling was rough, the gusts reversing the current. I bobbed, weaved, and worked between combers for two days to reach the village of Ruby. Although there was little there, at a small store I was able to purchase a dozen eggs and a tomato. Then, it was back into the headwind. At night the wind would lessen slightly, but by morning, the tent would be snapping in its wake. Even with the wind, each day held enough heat to conjure a sweat, though the nights held a definite chill. Mileage was severely hampered by these conditions, and only after three long days was I able to reach Galena. It was three o'clock in the morning.

The town of Galena was a landmark of sorts, signifying that Nome was less than 1,000 miles away. Even though it was dark, somewhere there was a rowdy crowd. I could hear it all the way at the beach where I docked. It was Saturday night and a bar called Hobo's was packed. Drifting between people at the long wooden bar, I read the many names carved into its rough, worn top. Somehow, I got between two guys arguing about whose sheath knife was sharper. As their volume escalated, they suddenly displayed them for comparison, wanting me to be the judge.

When six o'clock rolled around, the bartender started escorting people to the door saying they'd been closed since five o'clock. The half-sipped beer sitting at my elbow vanished, only to be replaced with a fresh one. "Take it for the road," the bartender said, nodding toward the door. It was a clever way to persuade patrons to leave. Hobo's was officially closed. The sun was almost to the treetops when the door closed behind me. I followed the gravel street to the canoe, shoved off and left Galena behind me.

At noon a sandbar beckoned and I beached the canoe. With feet on the gunwales and a coat behind me, I lay back and slept. The sun seeped between my eyelids four hours later, and within minutes I was revived and nearly ready to go. *Where's my hat!* I looked through every pack in vein, knowing that I had it on when I started the nap.

The only thing that I could think of was that it slid off my head and was now drifting away in the current of the Yukon.

It had been family to me. Beginning with my 1,200-mile journey to Hudson Bay years before this trip, it had been with me through so much. It was with when I left New Orleans on the Mississippi, surviving each time I swamped going north; across Superior, Winnipeg, Cedar, Wollaston, Great Slave, and Summit Lakes; and it had traversed the St. Croix, Winnipeg, Swan, Fond du Lac, Slave, Mackenzie, and Rat Rivers. I mourned its passing and thought about these places, and the countless others in between. I imaged my hat would rest on a lonely sand beach in some faraway village, still adorned with its beautifully beaded moose hide headband and Molly and Marlene's signatures. Now, it was gone.

As I left the sandbar, the river was windless. It took most of the day's light to reach Koyukuk. I didn't stop for I needed nothing, and the summer was slipping away. When the river's course took a sharp dogleg to the south, I stopped for a quick supper and was back in the canoe before the full moon rose. After three hours I drifted past many boats anchored in front of Nulato. Glittering on the beach in the rays of the moon were many broken bottles. A floodlight could be seen in the village, and the steady groan of heavy equipment broke the otherwise still night. If it had been daylight, I may have stopped, but a pungent smell around the harbor combined with darkness compelled me to continue.

As the moon began to faint in the brightening sky, I could see shore enough to find a suitable place to rest. The cool night had thoroughly chilled me. After gathering six armloads of wood, I stretched out beside a blazing fire, alternating sleep with refueling, leaving only once I ran out of wood.

After a few calisthenics thawed my blood, an all-day paddle to the village of Kaltag kept it warm. The people were very friendly as I was invited to coffee before Vagabond was even leashed. Following a man to his home, I noticed numerous log dwellings being replaced by government prefabs. They were out of place among the quaint, old, log dwellings. To me, the wooden boxes held no appeal. Entering one fortified my opinion.

When the coffee was poured, and pilot biscuits set on the table, a problem arose—the guy talked less than I did. But, over an awkward cup, I did learn that there was a shortcut to the ocean from here. A trail started from Kaltag and went to the Unalakleet River, which flowed into the sea. "You'll cut many miles off your journey," the man said. It was true, but I didn't relish portaging across sixty miles of tundra on a dog sled trail.

The shopping spree in Kaltag came to nil. The things I needed most, Crisco, batteries, and camera film were nonexistent. Even pop and candy were hard to find, for the fall barge had yet to arrive. It was just as well, for my wallet was thinning. After a half hour talk with the manager of the Co-op, he walked me to the canoe. He told me, "Some canoes were shot at up on the Koyukuk River a couple of weeks ago. It seemed the Natives there resented the whites for taking their land." There was warning in his voice.

It was September 1st and I was an hour out of Kaltag; the Bering Sea waited 500 miles downriver. 700 miles down the Yukon, both day and night, I was getting travel-worn. After seven straight hours, I dozed for two in front of a warming fire, then resumed into the night. The moon cast an opaque light through the overcast skies. Well into the darkest part of morning, I could smell a fish camp was near. Permeating the air were competing stenches, dog dung and drying fish.

Shortly an illuminated wall-tent came into view. The dogs picked up my scent and warned their master. Joining in with a howl of my own, the dogs went wild. The chorus echoed across the river and the tent flaps flew open. A figure lighted the dogs with a lantern held high. Its rays flickered off a rifle in his other hand. The dogs grew quiet in their master's presence. I slid by noiselessly as the dogs took a verbal thrashing. Light faded from the surrounding trees as it was encompassed by the tent. Silence prevailed. Drifting past the fish camp, sans souci, I again lifted my head toward the moon and called out in the night. The effect was instantaneous.

When warmth came into the day, I took a four-hour break and then traveled until darkness drove me ashore. Clouds had shrouded the Yukon and groping in total darkness could have had dire consequences. The next morning, I came across the remnant of a vanishing tradition. It was a huge smokehouse, twenty-by-forty-feet at the base and almost 15 feet to the arched ceiling. Many years of ash lined the pits and the dirt floor. Although the skeletal frame was constructed of poles, what was most impressive was that the outer skin was made entirely of birch bark.

A quick stop was had at the store in the village of Grayling, and

Anvik was reached eight hours later, the last three in the rain. I beached beneath a log cabin, tied Vagabond under a thick spruce, and dashed up a steep bank to the store. It was typical of the others found along the Yukon; pop, candy, and chips for the kids, basics for the adults. With a Coke, a bag of potato chips, and treats for Vagabond, I dashed back to the dryness beneath the pine. Vagabond welcomed the treats and begged for more. A few drops escaped the layered branches as I leaned against the tree's trunk sharing a bag of chips with Vagabond. In a gulch with a bridge above me, I was preparing to build a fire when someone on the other side of the ravine started waving his arms and calling for my attention. I left the bag of chips with my partner, crossed the Anvik Bridge, and stopped at the first house on the right. There, Tom Woods welcomed me with a hot cup of coffee.

I got to know Tom and his friend Richard, and we played poker until six in the morning. The wind and rain pounded the small cabin the entire time. By 10:00 A.M. snores came from the beds. Pacing the floor, I wanted to leave. There was no letup in the weather. If anything, it got worse. The day dragged on and on. Even a book couldn't alleviate the restlessness. Every twenty minutes I found myself looking out the window to the sky

Rain still dripped off the eaves the next morning, but the wind had blown itself out. While Tom still slept, I closed the door behind me, greeted Vagabond, and launched the canoe, not leaving it for the next ten hours. By evening a heavy fog replaced the steady rain. The dark hours were again passed bedded next to an open fire, and the first hint of light found me well on my way. Holy Cross was passed by noon, and evening found me looking into huge, black, clouds. They were surely rain-filled. The river flowed generally west from here to the ocean and black, rolling clouds, split by long bands of lightning spread from me to the horizon. It was going to get nasty.

Heavy drops speckled the water as I pulled ashore. The ground shook, the sky rumbled, and the clouds opened. Looking for a heavily boughed tree to get under, I noticed a roof, barely visible through the trees at the top of a small slope. Rain started in sheets and lightning spoke directly above me as I dashed up the incline. My pants snapped in the wind as pinpricks stung my face. I was drenched before reaching the small cabin.

Grateful there was a generous overhang on the front of the building and noticing the back of the storm creep over the horizon, I simply planned to wait it out. As it passed, a boat arrived, and a guy got out. Seeing Vagabond and me, he sprinted up the hill toward us and his cabin. A long-barreled .44 Magnum was on his hip, and his disposition wasn't one of amusement. "What the hell you want here?" he said in a vicious tone. Explaining my intention, I offered to leave. I almost felt like one of those "goddamn drifters." His eyes went to the padlock and unbroken windows. After giving me the once-over, he relaxed, and offered, "Well, as long as you are here, you might as well have some coffee."

Over two cups of coffee, he explained to me that people had been breaking into cabins along the river and stealing whatever they wanted. No longer could places go unguarded. Things had changed and not for the better. The storm waned, so after thanking him for his hospitality, I apologized for trespassing and walked out into the steady drizzle. Following me out, he locked the door and escorted me off his property.

While I spent the night across the river, the rain never ceased. My faith in modern nylon tents diminished, cursing that it never dried in perpetual humidity. It was natural that everything capable of absorbing moisture did so. I needed a place to dry out. I spotted that place six hours later, a log cabin nestled into the side of a hill.

Though there were no windows and the door stood wide open, apprehension abounded. The beachfront was cattails and a band of mud cratered by the pelting rain. I sunk near to my boot tops and sloshed to firmer ground. It didn't slow Vagabond in the least. The cabin was bare except for a few wooden bunks and a rusted sheet metal stove. It was well put together, with a large overhang in front that was perfect for sitting under to get out of a storm, but I had other ideas.

After starting the stove that hadn't seen a fire in a long time, I began to revolve next to it, slowly drying out. I arranged the tent and sleeping bag over a bunk for the same purpose. There was something unusual about the cabin. Most of the logs had holes in them that had been plugged with wooden pegs. Later I learned that a dozen guys built a raft at Lake Bennett and floated down the Yukon one summer. National Geographic did a story on it, including a documentary. Reaching this far before winter intervened, they made the cabin from their raft. It wouldn't be long before winter would interfere with my plans, too.

After preparing a huge supper, I stoked the stove, blew out the candle, and settled into one of the hard, wooden bunks that I moved close to the stove. Dim, flickering firelight escaped the rusted stove top to cast shadows across the dark logs. Other than the dancing firelight, there was total darkness in the windowless cabin. Wind and rain tried futilely to pierce the log walls and my warm security. For now, there was nothing more I wanted. I slept contentedly.

I awoke in the fetal position. It was pitch-black, and the stove was cold. Patting the floor with my hand, I found a match and lit the candle. I quickly re-kindled the fire, wanting to get going before daylight. To accelerate things, I set the coffee pot directly on the flaming logs inside the stove and was rewarded with richly smoked coffee by the time the dry gear was repacked. With the last cup downed and grayness creeping through the cabin's open door, I was ready to go, hoping to make the next village before the fall wind arose again as I knew it would.

When I landed last night, nothing had been available for securing the canoe, so I sank the paddle blade deep into the mud and used it for a dead-man. Now, I couldn't get it out. Back and forth I worked it until it snapped. It was my last paddle, and so too had become family. I was sad and angry at myself. With much coaxing, I was able to break the sticky tension and pull the trapped blade from the mud.

Felling a tree and making another crossed my mind. Instead, I produced a twisted lawn chair from behind the cabin. With a file, I patiently scribed two breaks in the aluminum tubing until a twelve-inch section was free. Into this I pounded the blade on one end and the shaft on the other, keeping the handle and blade as parallel as possible. It wasn't pretty, but a good day's work with it confirmed its adequacy, a day that got me to the muddy beach of Russian Mission. Whitecaps rolled up the river as I made my final approach.

"Don't stop there, too muddy. Better over there," a bent-backed guy said pointing to a spot that looked all the same to me. He introduced himself as Mike Gleskak and said he had just come down to the beach during one of the few lulls in the weather. "Come up and have coffee with me," he directed. I stashed the ungainly paddle and didn't hesitate to follow.

I followed Mike to a small, log cabin, taking a step to every two of his aged strides. Skirting a deep puddle, we entered the cabin through a leaning porch and sat at a table. Mike introduced me to a guy named Mark, who was also canoeing the Yukon. Left with a partially paralyzed arm from a stab wound, Mike asked Mark to pump the lantern. "Got into a drunken fight last April," Mike explained, "cut most of the muscle in my arm."

After coffee, Mark prepared fish, rice, and beans for supper, while Mike turned on the one-station black-and-white TV for the nightly news. It seemed strange in this faraway place, to be sitting in an ancient cabin, watching television. Maybe it was just that I hadn't seen one in over a year. When sports were over, Mike flipped it off before retiring and said, "Bring your stuff up and wait out the weather."

Before rolling my sleeping gear out on the dirty wooden floor, I went to the canoe to make sure Vagabond was situated for the night. Mark left behind me for his girlfriend's house. With everything set for the evening, I stood on the porch taking in a few last gulps of clean air. Inside it was dry, but also there resided the pungent, sulfuric odor of raw sewage.

The weather did nothing but worsen. After a breakfast of coffee and biscuits, Mark and I donned our raincoats and spent the morning nailing together a fuel oil stand from old two-by-fours and bent, rusty nails. After lunch, we installed new-to-him oil and wood stoves in the small cabin. Mike seemed pleased with our work and not at all annoyed at the weather that held us in Russian Mission.

Just before dark, I ran down to feed Vagabond and make sure he had a dry spot to spend the night. Whitecaps still pounded the beach as the stiff wind blew relentlessly, the rain coming in sheets with no sign of change.

I was greeted by the wind and rain and devastation the following morning. Mike was returning from the beach as I mounted the porch when he called up to me. "Those guys told me dogs killed your dog last night."

I made Mike repeat himself, his news couldn't register. It still didn't until I got to the riverbank. Vagabond lay next to the canoe covered in mud. His leash was still attached and wrapped around his leg, he hadn't had a chance. He was dead. Kneeling in the mud, I stared at him, and the sky, and the river. I cut the leash, cradled him in my arms, and carried him down the beach to a rock outcrop at the edge of town. Here I buried him in a shallow grave, covered with rocks. There would be no more traveling companions. I would go it alone.

I spent the day cleaning the .30-06, splitting wood, and going through the motions. Mike found out whose dog killed Vagabond and that evening I went for a visit. The wife was the only one home. She knew why I was there and was obviously nervous. "Our dog was loose last night, but it didn't look like it was in a fight," she said but refused to show it to me. "I found him on the other side of town, so I doubt if it could have been him," weak excuses came one after another. A dog could run from one end of the village to the other in ten seconds; I didn't buy it.

"If I ever see that dog loose again, I'm going to shoot it," I told her, "and I just might anyway," before the door was slammed.

I went to the home of the tribal chief. "Come on in," came a faint voice answering my knock. I entered the room and peered through a thick cloud of smoke that clung to the ceiling. At a round table sat eight men, each with a stack of bills before them. Each set of hands held a fan of cards.

"Is Norman here?" I asked.

"What can I do for you?" answered a guy dressed in double knits.

"I suppose you heard about my dog?" I asked.

"Yah," his answer was short.

"What are you going to do about it?" I wanted satisfaction.

"Nothing, you should have brought him up and tied him next to the house." I glared at him. Unfriendly thoughts came to mind, but silence prevailed. He made an apology, but I couldn't hear it through the door.

Whitecaps still blanketed the river. All I wanted to do was get out of Russian Mission and make miles toward my destination. Instead I cut and split wood for an entire day, providing for Mike's long winter ahead. After supper, Mike's cousin Pete came over and invited us to his house for some strong home brew. Mark was at his girlfriend's, but I was up for the challenge. "Some of the best stuff in town," he claimed, putting a carrot in front of the horse.

The carrot was ineffective. I couldn't finish a glass of the concoction, but those two old-timers sure whooped it up; I got plenty of stories about the good old days. After three hours Mike had had enough, and I guided him home through the unlit pathways without a flashlight. When I got him inside, we sat at the table for an hour until I ushered him to bed. Even after I closed the valve on the old Coleman lantern, sleep evaded Mike. He accented a slurred rendition of an ancient Eskimo song with giggling, his cacophony resonating the old, dry cabin logs. Then came "Oh, oh—" and I thought Mike may have overdone things, causing a heart attack. I was already half out of the sleeping bag when the evening came to an end with "—oh, am I drunk." There was one more giggle followed by silence.

September was half-gone and still the weather held me at Russian Mission. Mark showed up after breakfast, and we did Mike's fall cleaning. Although there were many things I would have gladly taken to the dump, Mike kept a sharp eye on his belongings. "Oh, hang that up there. I may need it someday," and, "store that in the cache, it'll come in handy," were some of the many instructions coming from the kitchen table. Next came a job that called for the flip of a coin and which might relieve the odor that dominated Mike's domain. If I had a two-headed coin in my pocket, I would have had no hesitancy using it.

Apparently, the government came into the village last summer and put plumbing in everyone's house, no matter what. Since Mike's home, up until recently, was heated with a small wood stove, when the temperature plummeted to fifty below zero, some areas of the old cabin didn't receive much heat; the corner where they placed the toilet and sink for instance. Naturally the pipes froze. Nevertheless, Mike kept using the toilet, too hobbled to go out in the night. Its capacity had been reached long ago, and its contents were in the late stages of fermentation. The coin was flipped and Mark's color paled as he looked for a scoop. I found him an empty coffee can; it was the least I could do. Even though he gagged throughout, he completed the job.

While that went on, I worked out in the wind and rain, hauling gravel in a wheelbarrow to fill the pool in front of Mike's door. Then I went in and shaved for the first time since leaving Minnesota, some 18 months ago. Mark had already left for his girlfriend's house, so I couldn't congratulate him on the quality of his work. It smelled as if he had done a good job.

It was September 17th. The weather had finally changed. No rain fell from the dreary sky, and the wind lay dormant. It was all I needed to pack my gear. Mike advised me to stay. It had been 18 days of high wind and rain; he predicted more as he dug through a newly cleaned closet. "Here, you might need this," he said, handing me a paddle. Since there was no denying that fact, I accepted it with gratitude. He walked me to the canoe.

"It's going to be lonesome here when you leave," he said as we shook hands. After thanking him for his hospitality, I left him standing on the beach. We exchanged waves, and I felt sorry for the old-timer, he was lonely. I said a final farewell to Vagabond as I passed the small mound of rocks at the edge of town and continued into a gathering wind.

Mike was right; within twenty minutes the rain started. Shortly after, whitecaps battered the canoe. During the first three hours, I struggled to attain two miles. The next three hours were no better. The last three hours of my day convinced me that I was wasting my time. What had been accomplished in nine hours I could usually do in two, weather permitting. But at least I wasn't stagnant, I was moving toward a goal.

All the next day I inched my way down this wind tunnel they call the Lower Yukon. By evening I reached an abandoned settlement called Ohogany. Five cabins in different stages of decomposition stood in a small clearing. Like teeth on a saw, they all slanted in the same direction. It seemed a good place to see if the storm would last through the night.

Set back at the base of a hill, dotted with white crosses, stood a church. The door was open, so I peered inside. It was remarkably well kept. The altar, podium, candlesticks, and benches all appeared to be handmade. People probably came here to pray for the repose of the souls marked by the crosses on the hillside. I closed the church door and made myself as comfortable as possible in one of the dilapidated shacks. It was much lonelier without Vagabond curled at my feet.

The elements confined me most of the next day, but I managed to slip in three hours before dark. With the sky looking better than it had in a month, hope surged through me. Throughout the night the tent was pelted as the sky shook away remnants of the storm. By morning it had cleared, bringing frost-covered land that, combined with the condensing daylight hours, made Nome slip a little farther away.

Four strong hours brought me to Marshall. After a dash to the store, I was on my way. The Yukon was changing, not just its colors, but its topography too. Trees were replaced by tundra, the land flattened, the river widened, and the current became much slower. While flocks of geese were leaving, I descended on the Yukon Delta.

The stay at Russian Mission had allowed me to accumulate much pent-up energy. With Marshall behind me, I put that energy to good use. By dark, I managed 25 miles in the sluggish river. Supper was three pilot biscuits and an orange. So was breakfast. Reveille arrived at 7:30, I was on the water by 7:45, with the sun rising by 8:30. I paddled with a sense of urgency.

Condensation rose in the chilly air as I pulled into Pilot Station, having covered twenty miles by 12:30. "Where you going?" asked one of the four Natives who met me at the beach.

When I told them, another replied, "Not in that thing you're not." They all had a good laugh. I was going to tell them where I had come from and see their response, but my delivery was ruined by an invitation for coffee. After an hour of coffee, crackers, and conversation, I went to the store and did what little shopping I could afford. With tiny Pilot Station behind me, I covered 15 miles in the remaining light. By morning the wind had erupted. A three-hour head-to-head battle with it turned me into a futilitarian.

A considerable amount of water had splashed over the gunwales, and I needed to get ashore. There was nothing but mud. As it oozed over my boot tops, I trudged up a slight rise. Climbing to its peak, I looked in all directions. Nothing could be seen but flat tundra lying unaffected in the cold howling wind. There was no firewood here or anywhere along the mud-ridden banks, and little hope of raising the tent in the driving wind.

I was a cork in the ocean, looking around at the rolling nothingness. I found a depression, not mentally but in the tundra, which I lined with the tent, threw the sleeping bag on top, and crawled in like a goose in a nest. The wind blanketed me and this desolate land. Stretched prone on the damp tundra, I waited on the wind less than 100 miles from the ocean.

I had to get out of the dimple. At the very first sign of light, I pushed the canoe back into the river. The wind was at my back, *finally*. Needing to make the most of it, I breezed right past Mountain Village. By afternoon, things were going too well my way. The wind at my back was now a gale. I found myself looking over my shoulder, wondering if the next wave was going to roll over the stern.

Of course, a fresh driving rain didn't help, but the worst part of the predicament I found myself in was that I couldn't land. The shore had turned into a cut bank. Atop it was a foot of soil, but between it and me was solid ice, Alaska's permafrost. Water would spray 15 feet into the air as waves rolled into the ice cliff with an upward crash. The ice bank continued as far as I could see.

The farther I was blown, the worse things became. In turn, waves began to fall into the canoe, and it was accumulating. Surging ahead at a terrific speed, surfing brown, white-topped waves, I hoped one wouldn't slam me into the unforgiving shore. The rain increased, and I didn't dare abandon the paddle to don the raincoat. There was nothing I could do but ride the wind and hope for the best.

For hours I teetered in limbo. Then came a small point of land. It was more of a jog in the ice, and I knew only one chance at landing would be had. If I was blown past it there would be no turning back. Maneuvering dangerously close to the break, I rode high on a wave until I could wait no longer. I paddled hard left and then ruddered hard right. The wave broke as the canoe and I were literally dumped into a small pool on the downwind side of the mud and ice point. There was little to break the wind, but there was enough. Waves continued to crash onto the point as I scrambled for cover. I couldn't deny that I was glad to be on shore, even the muddy bank felt like salvation. Even better was a corrugated tin building hidden on top of the tundra behind the point. *Things were going my way.*

The building was a smokehouse made of loose, galvanized tin that slapped against its frail wooden frame, the wind trying in vain to level it. It stood alone in this sea of grass and tundra. Poking my head through the door, the odor of the dark, smoke-impregnated interior was strong. Rain dripped constantly through the roof and puddled on the muddy floor. The fire pit was put to use immediately, and it soon emitted little heat and a lot of smoke. For its intended purpose, it worked well, for mine not as much.

No imagination was needed to know what I smelled like after standing inside the unventilated smokehouse throughout the afternoon, trying to dry out. I had to leave for fresh air at regular intervals. By evening the rain had slackened, but the loose siding still fluttered in the stubborn wind. Before darkness invaded, I hung the tent fly over the oily, soot-blackened poles used to hang fish to divert most of the rain. Beneath this I laid three scavenged boards, found on the wet tundra which, when butted together, formed a mattress. Crawling into the sleeping bag, I watched the coming darkness and tried to sleep.

Faint light penetrated the darkness of the smokehouse through its many cracks. I stepped outside into the freshness of the morning. While I cleaned my nostrils, black snot flew to the tundra. I felt dirty inside and out. My mouth and throat were parched, but you take the good dry with the bad. Scanning my surroundings, it was a forbidding and unforgiving place. No trees grew here, just tundra and flowing yellow grass. The muddy water had risen two feet overnight. The wind still showed a presence and a light rain fell. Getting as far away from the smokehouse as possible was my plan for the day, I couldn't spend another moment here.

As I challenged the increasing headwind, rain seeped through the split seams of my rain gear. After three hours, the permafrost began to fade into more coastal environs. Again, the wind was threatening my existence, and a few leaning cabins on the bank beckoned salvation. I trudged through tall, wet grass to the sturdiest of them. Its door lay where it had fallen off rusted hinges. A once white flagpole swayed to the tune of the wind at the end of a long, ingrown path.

Inside, an ornate cook stove, its oven door flopped down like a tongue, greeted me from across the single room, its once glamorous, green porcelain facade now shattered by many bullet holes. Many of the shelves that blanketed the walls had succumbed to gravity. A mound of paper lay beneath an overturned box, receipts from this old store in a place once known as Fish Village.

One of the legible documents was made out to Andrew Westdahl from the former tenant of this building, Alstrom Trading Company. The 1955 prices in this barren land were:

50 lbs. Sugar - $11.50
16 lbs. Coffee - $24.00
10 lbs. Potatoes - $2.00
9 lbs. Oats - $1.75
6 lbs. Rice - $2.00
6 lbs. Lard - $3.50
2 lbs. Butter - $2.60
1 lbs. Tea - $1.75
12 Traps - $12.00
6 Flashlight Batteries - $0.90

These wet shreds of the past held no use in fire making, but by shaving slivers off a fallen shelf I was able to bring the bullet-ridden stove to life. Fully stoked, it provided little heat in this drafty, door-less place. Even though I stuffed rags into the broken windowpanes, it only changed the pitch of the whistling wind. Even so, it was a five-star hotel compared to the smokehouse.

Throughout the day I shaved, read, and constantly checked the weather. By evening, it was no better. Even the weasel that shared this place called it a day. With a few sweeps of my arm, I cleared the top of a frail table and lay down. I would wait to see what morning would bring to my desolate refuge.

There was no sound when I opened my eyes. Just a hint of gray pierced the old store, giving everything an eerie, hidden look. I saw no reason to start the stove and try to cook, especially when the weather was cooperating. All I did was leave.

Studying the map in the growing light, the Yukon Delta reminded me of an octopus, tentacles branching toward the sea. The tentacle I wanted was the northernmost, which started at a place called Havaksarah, an estimated seven hours from the store at Fish Village.

I didn't find a place called Havaksarah but after seven hours did find a channel flowing northward. After another eight hours, I stopped. Not because I was sick of the rain that had started four hours earlier, but because three cabins sat on the bank in a deserted place marked Joe Sherman Village, defying the odds of nature. Fifteen straight hours was enough. It was dark, and I was, once again, wet.

Very little remained of Joe Sherman Village. In another lifetime there would be nothing. Other cabins lay flat, awaiting burial. A very old barrel stove was scrounged along with enough pipe to get the stack through the rusted roof jack of the best cabin. They were probably thrown out before I was born.

Soon the old barrel came to life; light seeping through rust holes in its sides and flames shooting up the stovepipe demonstrated this. I kept the fire small as it warmed and livened the old place, but only slightly. Again, food was getting low. One can of Campbell's tomato soup and a few handfuls of oats remained. After a two-course meal, I curled up next to the leaky stove.

By daylight, the wind had awoken me. While the cabin creaked and moaned under its constant pressure, I pleaded with it to stand tall for another day. I dashed to the canoe, making sure it was secured. It was no weather to be prancing around in long johns, for from the cabin doorway, I looked back at my tracks in the accumulating snow. A full-scale blizzard was in progress.

Visibility neared zero as I foraged the surroundings for firewood, and I was going nowhere. Although the storm kept me rooted, by evening, patches of blue appeared between the cold, snow-filled clouds. I took this as an omen, for it had been raining or snowing for the last 26 days.

There was no blue in the morning sky, but I made it to Kotlik, the last village before reaching the ocean, in four and a half hours. At the store I bought $25 in necessities, but 35mm film was nonexistent. At the post office I wanted to send what exposed film I had to my brother, but the person at the window didn't know how to send registered mail. Then, while looking through maps at the city office, I got a break. The clerk knew of one camera in Kotlik and it belonged to a minister at the Protestant Church.

The road to the church was lined with deep mud and pools that could support fish. After kicking the goo from my cleated boots, I knocked on the door. Though I was *kind-of* Catholic, I presented my plea to Jim. It worked. He gave me a twenty-exposure roll from the refrigerator, and I donated one of my few remaining five-dollar bills.

I thanked him and was about to leave when he asked where I had come from. The long answer got an instant invitation to a spaghetti and moose-meatball dinner. I told him many tales stretching all the way back to New Orleans. When it was over, he invited me to stay the night in a converted van behind the church. I didn't decline. It was heavenly compared to the places I had inhabited during the last month. It didn't even leak.

After I got situated in the van, he invited me to the game room that was open for two hours each evening for the village's kids. Together we set up a ping-pong and foosball table. Before the kids dribbled in, he challenged me to a game of foosball. Forgive me, Lord, but the reverend was literally raked over the coals.

As the kids arrived for their night of socializing, he dared them to challenge me. I took them all on, turning each and every one away defeated. The victories piled up; all those hours I spent in my misspent youth were finally paying off. At closing time I walked away undefeated. I was at the top of my game, only—I wished I could have played someone who didn't have to stand on a box to play.

Jim and I cleaned the room after the kids left. From there, we moved to the huge sauna where he taught me how to lose at backgammon. For three straight hours, sweat, dirt, and smoke poured from me. The moisture was replaced by tumblers of homemade root beer. A bucket of ice-cold water over the head finished the evening before I crawled into a bed at 3:00 A.M.

By 5:30 A.M. my biological bell rang. By six o'clock I was in the canoe. It was cold, and I don't know what possessed me to leave that converted van with clean sheets and a heater after only two and a half hours of bliss. By eight o'clock the last waters of the Yukon River slid beneath the canoe.

I sat in awe facing my next opponent. This one wasn't standing on a box. Before me stood the final obstacle—400 miles of ocean.

Traveling past the mouth of the Yukon River,
it was a dash against winter to reach Nome.

Homestretch

The tide was out, and I was very wary about following the channel, as it continued far into the ocean. I was now on the Bering Sea, and across Norton Bay lay Nome. Although huge sandbars kept me from nearing the coast, by following paddle deep water for three hours, I managed to get where I wanted to be, a few strokes from solid land.

It took a full day to reach Point Romanoff. The wind had stayed calm, but the temperature was well below freezing. Fresh water was in short supply, but by breaking through the ice on tundra potholes, I was able to meet my demand. After supper I became comfortable next to a roaring fire, only to wake two hours later, curled in a ball next to a pile of ashes. An amber glow reflected off the red canoe from the moon's radiant light and a star-filled sky. I didn't linger for I knew what light winds on big waters do, and these were big waters. I made the most of the calm night.

The three-quarter moon was still visible when daylight arrived. By my rough calculations, I judged that I was nearing the St. Michael Channel. Stuart Island would protect me from the ocean for a few miles. Ahead of me and set back on the tundra a short way, stood a lantern-lit tent with sparks streaming from a rusted tin chimney. I debated whether to stop or not. I didn't feel comfortable walking up to someone's tent and announcing my presence, but it never hurt to be sociable.

"Hello!" I hollered through the thin white canvas, "is anybody here?"

"Come in for coffee!" came a reply. As I pulled back the flap and entered, two Eskimo men were pulling on their boots, getting ready

335

to go hunting. After a cup of coffee, one said, "Go ahead sleep here where it's warm if you want. We go hunting before it gets too light." The warmth of the tent was making me drowsy and it must have showed; long hours in the cold were taking a toll. When I awoke almost two hours later, I scarcely remembered the fading sound of their outboard motor.

Paddling through the channel revived me enough to follow the coast all day until dark. I wanted to continue into the night, but clouds hid the moon and the darkness was complete. It was too risky. By morning the wind remained calm, though rolling swells pounded the shore. A heavy frost provided a base coat for the snow that had begun to paint the earth white. Thin wafers of ice careened off the canoe as I proceeded, to be smashed against the beach. Freeze up was dangerously close.

Seals popped up everywhere as I pulled onto the beach of Tolstoy Point for lunch break. On the bank there seemed to be miles of frost-covered blackberries trying to stay above the falling snow. A handful provided a cold treat. I had my fill. They didn't stand a chance in the increasing snow.

Minutes after leaving it was made clear to me that I was trespassing, for strolling along the beach was a brown bear checking its holdings. I held my ground from deep water and shot it four times, hoping the pictures weren't blurred from my constant bobbing in the swells.

I much preferred the snow to the drenching rains and felt lucky to get another full day's travel in. By evening I was looking for a campsite. Through the flakes a black sand beach with a rocky backstop looked inviting. There were piles of driftwood for the night's fire, so I topped a swell and rode it in. When the bow struck the coarse sand, I jumped out and pulled the canoe as far from the surf as possible. I went in search for straight poles, to be used to roll the loaded craft well away from the ocean. They weren't hard to find in the tangle of driftwood piled against the backstop. Returning to the canoe with a bark-less pole over each shoulder, I nonchalantly looked up, not liking what I didn't see. It was the canoe, not where I had left it.

What I saw sent a shock through the depths of my stomach. The frail red craft was on its way toward Russia with the afternoon tide. Throwing my burden aside, I was at the water's edge in several bounds. Every possible recovery option raced through my mind as I cursed myself for my apparent carelessness. Everything I owned was inching farther and farther away. I could only see one possible solution, and it was a dreadful one.

As snowflakes floated down, I fumbled at the buttons of my wool shirt, starting a pile of clothing behind me that grew with each passing moment. My eyes were riveted to the canoe while my fingers whizzed through the routine. When ragged pants topped the pile, I slowly waded in with only my union suit to combat the searing water.

Transparent razors glanced off my knees as I advanced. The water deepened. A shiver ran through me as it passed my navel, and I stuttered, an *oooh* escaping my lips as I glided into the breaststroke, taking pains to keep my head above water. From this vantage point, the water seemed much clearer. The cold water gripped my chest. Breaths came in rapid succession. My jaw started to palpitate. The distance closed as I pumped my arms and legs, forcing my seizing muscles forward. The canoe appeared mystic at eye level, almost as if it were floating on glass. Finally, my hand touched the gunwale. On the way out, I thought about boarding the canoe, but knew if I didn't succeed, things would be infinitely worse. With one hand on the canoe, I started in. The beach beckoned 100 yards away.

Progress was slow but definite as I pulled the canoe from a side-stroke. The plan to keep my head dry proved futile as swells washed over me. The distance to the beach closed and by the time my feet touched bottom my hair was frozen. While snow continued to fall, I pulled the canoe onto the poles and above the waterline, then dashed to the driftwood pile for anything that would burn. *Where was my body fat when I needed it?* I groaned, shivering out of control.

The driftwood pile produced a small piece of birch bark and a handful of dry twigs. Fanning away the snow, I made my hearth. The frozen-stiff union suit crackled in protest as I ran to the canoe for matches. The fire makings were arranged next to the driftwood, so wood would be on hand. With shaking hands, I dropped the first two matches. The third came to life and was laid on the birch bark. With relief, flames erupted.

I stiffly rummaged through the woodpile, joints frozen like the Tin Man, and soon a roaring blaze lit the beach. By alternating front and back toward the fire, I was able to return the frozen union suit to limp wetness and work it off. A naked race through the snow brought my dry clothes back to the fire where I hurriedly dressed. Floating into the rising flames were heavy snowflakes.

The fire burned throughout the night to dry my only union suit. It was a very broken sleep schedule as refueling was required every few hours. By daybreak there was hypothermic fatigue and little motivation to leave. I nursed cups of tea to stay awake. Eventually, the union suit was done to perfection, stiff, gray, and filthy from the night's smoke, but it was dry. At this stage, that was all that mattered. Its stiffness chafed against my skin as I packed to leave, but a ten-and-a-half-hour day worked it back into the smoothness to which I was accustomed.

After a scant supper, I sat back and watched seals bobbing in the surf just offshore. Two of them were together and kept rolling over and over on the surface. I didn't know what to make of it. I guessed they were either playing or newly married. When darkness arrived, a beacon blinked far down the coast. It had to be the village of Unalakleet, still miles away.

Darkness brought wind, and the snow no longer fell in a graceful fashion. Twice during the night, I had to move the canoe to higher ground as rising swells seemed to want back what they had once taken. Morning brought huge white breakers that speckled the horizon, but I was able to travel as the wind had shifted to an offshore direction.

It howled above me as I hugged the protective shore. It took nine labor-filled hours to reach the Unalakleet River with its village on the other side. To get there, I'd be exposed to the river's strong current and the strong winds pushing it. Both led directly into the ocean. Unable to sit waiting when food was so near, I started across.

It wasn't a smart decision, but I made it. A few watery surges breached the gunwales, and I knew luck was being pushed. Finally, with the canoe on land and tethered, a ten-minute walk brought me to the local store. Here I purchased a week's worth of groceries. That left just thirty dollars and 300 miles of ocean to contend with. "Been in the bush a while, huh?" the grocery clerk asked as I picked up my small bag to leave, "I can smell it on you."

Must be the union suit, I thought.

Blinding snow swirled in an east wind as I walked back to the canoe and feasted on two Hostess cherry pies and a can of Coke. "Just go up the river a bit," had been the simple direction on how to get to the boat landing. I tried to, and struggled, and struggled, but I could make no headway against the current and strong, snowy wind.

Landing almost proved disastrous. I could go no farther so I docked in someone's front yard. Pulling the canoe well away from the river, I walked to the nearest house and knocked.

A little elderly lady introduced herself as Mary Barr and opened the door to the small house. "Would you mind if I put my tent up in front of your house for the night?" I asked as she squinted at me in the dimly lit porch.

"Sure, sure, go ahead," she said. "But it's so windy there. You should put it way back." Thanking her, I went to unroll the tent on the blanket of snow.

As I stood with my back to the wind and shook the nylon tent so that the wind would unfold it, a boat pulled ashore behind me. A lone man jumped out and tried to pull his heavy craft out of the angry river without luck. After rolling a rock over the flapping tent, I was able to help him secure the boat well above the water's reach. Introducing himself as Joel Oyaumick, he offered me a night's lodging at his mother's house. One glance at the tent dancing in the wind was plenty convincing.

While rolling the tent back up, Mary Barr and her friend Martha ventured out to see where I had come from. "I must see that canoe," Mary said. They both walked over and gave it a thorough examination. At one-point Mary laid into it with her foot to test its durability. Upon their return, I mentioned that Joel offered me a place to spend the night, and they volunteered to guide me to the right house.

"Just a stone's throw away," she said. She wasn't willing to dally. "Let's go! It's too cold out here for me." Mary pulled her collar tight against her neck. Through the snow, I followed them to Joel's mother's house.

I scrutinized my surroundings from the kitchen table. *Well-kept house,* I thought. A glass of orange juice in front of me was constantly refilled. For a full half-hour, I was questioned before Mary and Martha got up to leave.

"Where did you stay last night?" Mary asked while hovering near the door. As I described the area with the little creek running through it, she recognized it immediately, saying, "Oh, that's my land claim!" She obviously had another question but was apprehensive to ask it.

Finally, she blurted, "How old are you anyway?"

"Fifty-one," I replied as seriously as I could.

Waters Beneath My Feet

"Oh! Well you sure don't look that old," she said in surprise.

"Well, I found the fountain of youth where I camped last night. You better hang on to that place." For a moment there was belief in her eyes before she broke into a roaring laugh. "I'm really 27," I admitted after a moment.

With their curiosity satisfied, the two ladies were out the door. The smell of moose steaks drifted through the house. Joel said they would be ready when I had finished a hot shower.

By morning the weather was unchanged. Throughout the day I read and listened to a baseball game on the radio. One of Joel's sisters arrived in the evening and fixed a huge supper of steaks, corn, peas, potatoes, and homemade bread. Shortly after, his mother returned from their upriver camp, herded the family together, and marched them off to church. Upon returning she immediately went to the freezer and produced a huge bowl of something she called Eskimo ice cream. It was a mixture of frozen fish, berries, and seal oil.

Joel's oldest sister, a teacher, brought out an Atlas. "Hard to believe," she kept saying as I drew a pencil line from New Orleans, across the continent, and then along the coast to Unalakleet. "My students will really enjoy this," she said upon leaving. People slowly drifted to bed. Me, I couldn't help but finish the last of the Eskimo ice cream.

I was up at daylight the following morning and ready to leave when Mrs. Oyaumick came from a bedroom and demanded, "Where do you think you're going without breakfast?" Soon, before me were three eggs, toast, and a steaming cup of coffee. "What else would you like?" she asked.

Boy, a guy could get used to this, I thought, as I explained to her that she had already done more than enough for me. There are not many people left who will take in a stranger like that. Growing up here, she probably had been through many hardships of her own and could relate to my humble situation.

Her family trickled into the kitchen one by one and each was fed in turn. Throughout her continuous cooking, we had an interesting discussion about living off the land. It ended with a situation that happened here just two weeks ago. A man left with the intention of walking to Shaktoolik, thirty miles up the coast. He hadn't been seen since. Although both air and ground search and rescuers covered the area, only his windbreaker was found. They had seen seven bears from the air and feared the worst. The general opinion of the outcome

340

wasn't encouraging.

The Oyaumick family was fed and off to their various destinations by nine o'clock. After thanking Mrs. Oyaumick and accepting a thermos of hot coffee, I followed suit.

It was Columbus Day, and it was calm. Though the wind rested, swells still pounded the beach. I rode one onto the sands twelve miles from Unalakleet for a lunch break. When it was over, I had a problem. Twice I tried to mount the breaking swells, and twice I was deposited on the beach with six inches of water inside the canoe. Because it was a pleasant place to camp, I didn't force the issue.

Though there remained no breeze, it took three attempts to conquer the breaking swells the following morning. The sun's rare appearance a few hours later seemed to have a calming effect upon the ocean. It was just as well, for throughout the day, sheer rock cliffs observed my passage. Near midday two Eskimos guided their boat next to mine and asked if I had seen any whales. The only whales I had ever seen were at the St. Paul Zoo, and I didn't believe these were the ones they were interested in, so I just said no. They looked slightly dejected and upon leaving, one said. "Hope you have a gun. There are lots of bears around. Killer whales during the day and killer bears during the night." It made one think.

The rock-faced cliffs finally gave way to miles of sandy beach. Here, I ended the day. I could see the lights of Shaktoolik in the cold night from where I huddled in my sleeping bag next to a blazing fire. A six-hour dash against a rising wind in the morning got me to the village. Bear tracks, big and small, were abundant on the soft, sandy beach. Walking up to the abandoned buildings, I noticed that there was not a soul around.

Doubt entered my mind about seeing the lights last night. This place seemed to have been abandoned for years. Confusion was averted when a Honda three-wheeler came down the beach.

"What are you doing here?" the man demanded. His huge bulk looked ridiculous on the small three-wheeled vehicle. When I said I thought there were people in Shaktoolik, his response was again skepticism directed at me, "Just where did you come from?"

"New Orleans," I said.

"Is that on the East coast?" the man wanted to know.

"No, it's over toward Mexico more," I explained.

"Got a passport?" he persisted.

I'd never seen a blond-haired, blue-eyed Mexican, but I just said no.

When he finished his investigation, he introduced himself as the local minister and explained that the town was moved two miles down the coast years back because of flooding problems.

"I have to go now," he said abruptly and putted off down the beach on his little three-wheeler. His wide form above the little machine looked more ridiculous from behind. How I wished I could have pulled my camera out before he disappeared down the beach.

Eight kids ran to the canoe the moment it landed in new-Shaktoolik and bombarded me with questions. "What's your name! What's your name!" they shouted.

They weren't satisfied until I said, "Jesse James."

"Where you from, Jesse! Where you from, Jesse!" they all asked at once. And so it was, question after question, until I vanished into the store.

The only money spent was to mail eight rolls of film to my brother in Minnesota. *Jesse's wallet's sure getting flat,* I anxiously thought. Seeing how there were no banks in town, I walked back to the canoe with every intention of leaving. Before I could, I met Dan Savetilik.

He was burning old papers behind the school where he worked, and a casual conversation turned into an invitation to supper. "I'll be back here in ten minutes, and we'll go up to the house," he said and walked back into the school. I sat on the gunwale and waited.

"Welcome, welcome, welcome to our house!" Dan's wife said with glee, "Sit down and have tea before supper." She was one of the most cheerful people I met along the journey. Their daughter and two adopted children arrived shortly, and a chicken dinner with all the trimmings was served. Dan and I discussed the troubles of the world as the dishes were being done. Then, the family was off to church.

While the service was conducted, I checked the canoe, toured the town, and leaned against a telephone pole to watch a dozen kids play baseball under a dim streetlight. When I saw a light return in Dan's house, I left the ongoing game and knocked on their door. "Oh, we thought you got lost," Dan's wife said with concern, though I couldn't conceive it in a town with one short road and 150 people. Again, tea was served, after which everyone went to their respective bedrooms for the night.

Early to bed and early to rise were the habits demonstrated by the head of the family. After two cups of coffee at breakfast with Dan, he was off to work, and I plied my trade.

Standing by the canoe, I jumped from foot to foot, clapping my hands together, waiting for enough light to depart. Condensation rose from my lungs, to be whisked away by the stiff breeze. It wasn't the first and surely not the last time I would long for my warm winter clothes waiting patiently at the Nome post office. Winter was making its presence felt. Finally, the cliffs of Cape Denbigh peered through the gathering light and I started out.

Both the Shaktoolik River and the area where the river fanned into the ocean were clogged with ice. For four hours sheets of it popped, cracked, and shattered beneath the canoe. Upon reaching clear saltwater, I turned ninety degrees to the right and headed out beneath the near-vertical rock faces of the cape.

The wind was no longer a breeze. As the high cliffs loomed above, it didn't take long to realize that I was committed to something that could greatly overtax my abilities. The further I advanced toward the cape's southern point, the worse the seas became. It might as well have been Cape Horn. There was no place to land, as the jagged cliffs ran deep into the sea, and I couldn't turn back in the mounting swells. To lose to them would mean being slammed against the cliffs, the swells' mere rebounds now rocking the already teetering canoe. This was no place for my craft.

When I neared the northern point, the end of the cape, I worked my jaw like a ventriloquist and their dummy, trying to loosen the muscles that threatened to lock. Absolute concentration was needed as the cape split the rolling water, sending chaotic waves in unpredictable directions, the wind churning their tops white. Fierce swells smashed the cliffs and sent water twenty feet skyward.

Entering the turbulent apex, a huge, rolling, white wave picked up the front half of the canoe and slammed the bow down into the trough. Recovering, I rolled my hips and the canoe over the crest of the next. Finally finding my timing, I was able to quarter into them, hoping the next wave wouldn't be The Rogue. Fully exposed to the last of the cape, I faced a blast of wind. Swells at my back pushed me into it for 200 yards. Then, in the midst of the tempest, the rock wall opened to reveal a sandy cove.

I paddled toward it as hard and fast as my body would allow. When the bow touched the sand, I popped out of the canoe like I was shot from a cannon. My refuge wasn't much, but I wasn't complaining. With a small fire glowing from the sparse driftwood, I settled against the cliff's base and watched the squall roll by.

The reality of my position became somewhat unsettling. What little firewood there was lay directly against the sheer rock wall. This was also where the beach terminated. Looking across the open water, I could see the cliffs on the other side of Norton Bay, some forty miles away. The cauldron from here to there boiled. To get to that side I would have to follow the coast for over 100 miles. That wasn't the most pressing problem—firewood was at a premium, maybe two days' worth, and drinking water didn't exist.

That day passed slowly, as did the next. There was only one change in the weather; it got colder. I left a pan filled with saltwater overnight to get an estimate of the temperature. *Cold as hell,* I learned. By morning, it was frozen solid. Combined with the wind chill, the billowing air felt like it had plunged below zero degrees. Dryness crept in. Even a light snow would have helped, would have helped provide fresh water. Never escaping this cove would end my journey with a cruelly ironic twist. I envisioned the title of my obituary, "Canoeist Dies of Thirst." All I could do was wait.

With impatience I stalked up and down the tiny beach, willing the wind to slacken. On the third day it did, though it was far from calm. Nevertheless, I used this brief respite to get to another beach an hour down shore. Fortunately, firewood was abundant, and huge, brown, swampcicles hung from the surrounding cliffs. These were harvested and converted into drinking water.

Soon the wind returned to gale-force and sea ice coated the towering rocks from spray that had escaped the pounding waves. Once, the demon got under the overturned canoe and sent it tumbling down the beach toward huge rocks and certain destruction. Halting its progress, I lashed it stoutly to an enormous boulder protruding from the sand. I needed to get out of the wind. That wasn't possible, but I found a small niche underneath a slight overhang that provided some comfort, as well as protection from rocks and ice that could fall from the 100-foot cliffs. Snared among the driftwood, I found a 55-gallon barrel, and was able to start a roaring fire. Now I was able to sit against the cliff, feet to the stove, book in hand, and wait, all in *relative* comfort.

For three days snow constantly swirled across the narrow beach in the unrelenting wind. Since I couldn't read my only book for the umpteenth time, my mind turned to winterizing. Out came a ragged coat I found near Old Shaktoolik. I sewed the many holes and a long rip beneath the arm to secure the remaining down. Removing the zipper from my useless raincoat, I stitched it to my rejuvenated coat, directly over the mangled one.

Next came a faded Army hood complete with cheap, thin, coyote-fur fringe, that I had picked off the floor at Alstrom Trading Company in the abandoned Fish Village. Soaked then and wet now, it was sewn to the coat collar. The musty smell of mold had permanently saturated it. Unable to do much with my worn pants, I stitched the holes in my mismatched gloves.

In my mind, I was preparing for the worst. Things were going to get tough if I had to stay here much longer. Firewood was getting limited and so was the food. I began to give thought to somehow caching the canoe and ending this trip on foot; it would require a rough climb out of there. I didn't relish the idea, but a decision had to be made soon. I crawled as deep as possible into the niche and waited.

Day four passed, then day five. I broke down and dug into the library for the book. Firewood had to be wrestled from the sand, the easy pickings were gone. Ice coated the rocks as far as the spray could reach. Sleep was starting to come more and more easily as fatigue set in, with rice and tea providing little nourishment.

Wind and waves still battered Cape Denbigh as day six faded; day seven passed unchanged. I didn't know what time I had drifted to sleep, but when I awoke to start my eighth day in isolation, something was wrong. It had to be close to daylight though darkness still covered the cove. I lay next to the cold barrel in silence. That was what was wrong, the silence.

There was not a sound. Its unnaturalness was an omen. For 170 hours the waves had beat their drum. Now there was nothing. Only the occasional spark fleeing the depths of the cold barrel broke the tranquility. I re-kindled the fire and with anticipation, knew that within hours, I could paddle out.

Soon firelight belching from the barrel dimly lit the cliffs while white smoke weaved through snowflakes. Occasionally a flicker would reflect off the overturned canoe, giving some depth to the darkness. The long, brown icicles that had been picked from the surrounding cliffs were now an ice-block in the frying pan. This was balanced on logs across the top of the barrel, heating for a morning cup of tea. Then, with hands and back to the barrel, I stood looking into the darkness, waiting for any indication of morning's light.

Not a swell sounded against the rocks in my vigilance. At even a hint of light, I was going to get into that canoe and paddle until exhausted. Finally, it came, a splash of gray on the horizon. It was a curtain of despair. For miles and miles, as far as I could see, there was ice. The ocean had frozen.

Norton Bay had frozen; it was over.

I had to try. Thickening ice cracked, parting around the canoe. Progress developed from bad, to worse, to impossible. Inches of ice, frozen from spray, caked the exposed hull. After four grueling hours, I veered inland. Behind me lay a broken path, forced through winter's inauguration. My journey by canoe was over. I struggled the ice-laden canoe onto the snow-covered beach, knowing now that the only way out was on foot.

A long, thin grove of poplar trees lined the back of the beach. With great effort, I dragged the ice-covered canoe into them and erected two crossbars to hold the now-useless craft off the ground. Inside the overturned canoe I cached the guitar, tripod, 800mm camera lens, and anything else deemed not worth carrying 250 miles. What remained in my pack was the tent tarp, rifle with five shells, sleeping bag and pad, camera, cooking gear, ax, two handfuls of rice, and three tea bags.

The tent would be left behind to conserve weight. Now,

procrastination meant little. A light snow fell as I stretched the tarp over a slanted pole to form a shelter. By evening I crawled under the crude shelter knowing the calm weather would help thicken the river ice and make crossings safer. It was a small consolation.

The weight awoke me. Six inches of new snow had collapsed the sanctuary. It was just as well since there was enough light to leave. Kicking through the snow revealed my frying pan and cup. Breakfast was restricted to tea, whose bag was returned to the food box to be used again.

Visibility was limited by a storm that raged above the cliffs, sending swirling snow down in sheets to settle on the white beach below. While hoisting the fifty-pound pack of remnants, a glance toward the overturned canoe revealed it had swiftly developed a camouflaged, winter coat. *One hell of a canoe trip,* I repeated to myself as I turned and started the walk to Nome. All that lay behind me now were memories and tracks through the deepening snow.

There was little choice but walk, as Nome lay only 250 miles away.

Within a quarter mile, I confronted sheer cliffs that jutted into the frozen ocean. Steep fractured rocks beckoned as long, white, snowy fingers blew from their tops. On the ascent I slid, sweated, and swore. At times I was forced to drop the pack, worm past an obstacle, and then hoist the pack up behind me by rope. My pants and gloves became drenched from sweat and crawling on my hands and knees in the cold snow. After two hours I climbed over a snow-packed cornice and stood on the plateau above.

The flat summit was no place to linger. My clothes froze immediately in the blinding wind. While the snow was over the tops of my Sorrels, I trudged across the cliff tops with a cocked arm across my eyes. Finding a steep decline in the tundra, I weaved through high hummocks for three hours before regaining the beach. Another hour brought me to a small amount of driftwood. It was nearing dark and I was going no farther.

All night the wind threatened to sail my protective tarp into the frozen sea. By morning it had slackened, and a small patch of blue graced the otherwise gray sky. As the day lightened, I struggled the frozen Sorrels over dry socks. It took a mile's walk along shore before the liner's stiffness thawed into yesterday's wet sweat. I left without breakfast, for no more driftwood showed through the snow where darkness forced last night's camp. What little there was had been consumed in last night's fire.

Progress was slow as many small rivers laced the area, each containing a varying thickness of ice. At each crossing, I would set the pack down and crawl across the ice, pounding the ax in front of me. When the ax head disappeared, which it often did, a hasty retreat would be made.

After two days at this lagging pace, I angled inland in search of the high-water line, hoping to find wood for the night's fire. The long day ended hours later at an overturned, rotten, wooden boat that was tangled among a long, gray band of barkless driftwood.

While having my bowl of rice surrounded by my adversaries, the hummocks, I thought about the last few days and felt lucky to have been able to cross two major rivers that flowed through these pimpled plains, the Ungalik and Inglutalik Rivers. I knew there would be more. I eyed a six-foot, tripod trail-marker near the boat. A quick night's shelter was constructed by blanketing the winter trail marker with the tarp. Peering from the tepee, I watched huge clouds from the northwest obliterate the evening stars. But, beneath those darkening clouds reflected signs of life, for far away, twinkled the village lights of Koyuk.

When I awoke, an eerie haze covered the land. A whiteout of mixed fog and ice crystals obscured every landmark. The feeble lights of Koyuk had shown directly over the rotted boat from my shelter so I followed that bearing across uncompromising, snow-covered hummocks. After four hours, I stood in relief, on the bank of the Koyuk River. A snowmachine trail split the frozen river in two. It led directly into the village.

An energetic dog announced my arrival, and three men poured from the nearest house. "Hello, hello, where you come from?" one asked.

"New Orleans," I replied as I shook each hand in turn.

"We thought you were frozen," the one named Dave Otten said. "The radio and newspaper said you were many days out of Shaktoolik and feared lost." Each of them was smiling openly and seemed genuinely happy to see me. It took a few seconds to understand, but these people thought I was dead. "Come in and have coffee," Dave said. Gladly, I followed the trio into Dave's house.

After twenty minutes, one of the guys had heard enough and dashed away to radio the state troopers with the news that I wasn't dead yet. As Mrs. Otten fixed a supper of fried grayling and rice, Dave worked on me to go hear their church choir after dinner. Finally, I relented, ran Dave's electric razor across my face, and marched with them to the tiny church. It had been a long time since I had heard a church choir.

My attendance was embarrassing. Dave conducted the prayer meeting and after the opening hymn said, "We have with us today a young man who came all the way from Louisiana, who was lost and found his way to Koyuk, by the name of Jerry Pushcar."

As if that wasn't bad enough, he asked me to stand up. I knew I smelled like a burning outhouse. A moldy, matted-dog smelling army hood dangled from what was left of my tattered coat, and in many places my union suit peered through my ragged pants. And yet, he wanted me to stand up. When he asked a second time, I stood.

My face flushed as all those brown eyes stared at me. I stayed uncomfortably warm even after sitting down. The homage wore on. Kids wandered in and out at will. Behind me a body slumped against the corner of a pew, head down, snoring heavily. I wasn't far from joining him when Dave said, "Now for the closing, we will sing hymn number 327 for Jerry Pushcar." Curious, I flipped to that page of the hymnal. It was titled "Seeking the Lost." We returned to Dave's home for evening tea.

What a busy place! Even kids came in, stood by the door with shy heads held low, snuck a cautious look at me, and then silently slipped back out. "You sure get a lot of people in and out," I said to Dave.

"Yah," he replied, "when someone new comes to town everybody wants to see them." The unaccustomed warmth of the indoors was having ill effects on me. My eyes began to droop. I was grateful when the last visitor left, and darkness filled the cabin.

In my sleeping bag on the pine floor, I awoke to the invigorating smell of coffee brewing. Mrs. Otten was bustling around the kitchen preparing eggs, sourdough pancakes, and bacon. Dave came into the kitchen, stepping over me to get there, and poured the coffee. I could take the hint. At 5:00 A.M., it was time to get up. Breakfast didn't take long. After we emptied the coffee pot, I packed. Working on the dishes, Mrs. Otten offered to pay my airfare to Nome. *Nice gesture from a good woman,* I thought appreciatively, but I had to decline.

Grayness crept into the quiet morning when I hoisted my pack to leave. Appropriate thanks and goodbyes were exchanged. As I set out for the edge of town in the dim light, Dave shouted, "Come back anytime. You are always welcome here." *Someday,* I hoped.

A stiff morning trudge took me west-southwest out of Koyuk under a low, gray sky, through bands of spruce, and across desolate, snowy tundra. Stretching away to the horizon on my left was Norton Bay, the surface still and crowded with ice. Gentle hills rose to my right as the Seward Peninsula passed beneath my feet. The slight stiffness wore off quickly as I was refreshed and enjoying the feel of dry boots and socks. It was a pleasure that lasted less than an hour. Before the lights of Koyuk disappeared behind me, I sank to my knees in a small creek. It was aggravating, as everything had been thoroughly dried that night.

About mid-afternoon, I reached a conical structure near the mouth of a small river. It appeared to be a driftwood tepee and a good place to get out of the weather. That is until I peered inside. On the sandy floor lay two ribs and the jawbone of a human skull, apparently an old Eskimo burial site. Leaving it untouched, I walked until dark, camping six miles from Bald Mountain and a cabin that

Dave had suggested.

"Good place to spend the night," was his description of it. The old cabin door creaked as I pushed it inward the following afternoon, having made it to the shadow of Bald Mountain. The low, gray, log structure stood vacant. Inside, the rusted stove still proved capable of warming the one room while the sagging walls turned back most of the winter winds. Fuel for the night was obtained with a dull, rusted bow saw and patience.

As darkness imposed on the shortening day, I stacked wood beside the glowing stove. A kerosene lamp with no mantle stood in the center of a rickety table. Matches were wasted until I noticed the wick dangling an inch above the fuel. Checking the shelves and darkened corners produced no additional kerosene, so I filled the glass bulb with leftover tea, floating the kerosene to the wick. There was some sputtering, but soon a glow spread across the table with ample light to page through a ten-year-old, centerfold-less Playboy Magazine.

After a comfortable night's sleep, I wired the door back shut, cut behind Bald Mountain, followed the beach all day, and then crossed a frozen lagoon to a long sand spit called Moses Point. Dave explained to me that this was a lively place in the summer months due to the salmon fishing season. In winter it lay deserted, evidenced by the many, small, one-roomed plywood shacks lining the beach. Some were locked, some were open and littered with garbage, and some were drifted in with snow. I peered in each as I made my way along the beach until coming to a rotting tent collapsed by the snow. With room for a body on one side, it was here I spent the night.

The last of morning's darkness found me walking down the Moses Point runway. Winds had whisked the snow from the graveled lane making my stroll seem effortless. Days were short and nights long, the sun now only allowing eight hours of lightness. In its rays, I covered 14 miles, which put me within five miles of the village of Elim.

"Stay in the camp just around the bend there at Iron Creek," a cigarette-inhaling local volunteered, "nobody will mind." He had stopped on his snowmachine to inquire what I was doing, as others had earlier, talking long enough to finish a smoke. With a flick, the butt arched through the air, and he was off before it hissed in the snow. Shouldering the pack, I headed around the bend for the cabin on Iron Creek.

The Iron Creek Cabin was an un-insulated ten-foot by twelve-foot plywood shack. I had no complaints, as a fire was immediately started in the wood cook stove. Smoke soon seeped from every orifice of the stove, as I frantically searched for the damper lever. Thick, gray smoke rolled under the header of the flung-open plywood door. Through watering eyes, I groped until I felt the metal latch tucked beneath the cast iron top.

Waiting outside until the smoke cleared, I reentered and closed the door to enjoy the heat. It was a stove-hugger sort of night, as most of the heat went up and out the plywood ceiling. It was also heaven compared to lying on the frozen tundra trying to hug an open fire.

Two hours after closing the Iron Creek cabin door, I was in Elim. The first stop was the store. Two candy bars were purchased with some of my few remaining dollars. With no place to go, I sat on an icy, 55-gallon oil drum near the store's front, savoring each bite. An ancient thermometer dangling from a bent nail read ten degrees below zero. Squirming to redistribute the cold being sucked from the chilling barrel, I heard, "Care for some coffee?"

Pushing the half-frozen wad of an Oh Henry! bar into my cheek, I of course said sure. The voice was clad in faded Carhartts, bunny boots and a beaver hat. Following him, Bob Loftgren, to his home, I met his wife Sally. Fresh coffee was already on the wood stove, spreading its aroma throughout the house.

Many stories were swapped over the coffee pot until food replaced the cups. Though it smelled delicious, it was new to me. Three large bowls were set on the table. One contained boiled *oogruk*, or seal meat, in another floated boiled oogruk intestines, and in the third, mounded a majestic concoction prepared with salmon berries.

All eyes watched discreetly as I cut a length of intestine in two and put a piece in my mouth. Chewing noncommittally, I put the other half in and speared another section from the bowl. "God damn!" Bob roared with laughter, "you *are* a sourdough!" I didn't bother explaining that when the food pack was nearly empty, food took on a different meaning. Besides, it wasn't any worse than moose nose.

Thanking the Loftgrens, I took my leave hoping to find some sales at the store. Disappointed, I stood in line with a few dry goods behind a man who introduced himself as Paul. Still broad-shouldered at ninety, flecks of gray hair showed around the bottom of his stocking cap. He was the eldest person in the village. "You can sleep in the clinic tonight if you want to," he said while pulling his hat tighter over his head, "and if you do, come to my house for supper at six o'clock. It's the blue house on the other side of town." While we faced each other over a moose roast, Paul's wife and daughter took the remaining seats. Conversation was quiet but not strained.

After the meal Paul and his wife retired to the living room, leaving their daughter to do the dishes. My offer to help was met with refusal. "You know my father thought you were dead," she said. "He was very impressed when he heard you had walked into Koyuk." This, from a man who had lived his life here, and without a doubt had been through things that I couldn't begin to imagine. I felt humbled.

I left early. Everyone wished me well and predicted we would meet again in Nome. The walking was rough. By nightfall, only ten miles separated me from Elim. But I was at the Walla Walla shelter cabin, or at least what was left of it.

At one time it stood tall. It was a log cabin erected for the postal mushers who lost their livelihood with the introduction of airplanes in the 1930's. Although the remains of a stove lay in the middle of the floor, any stovepipe lay collapsed in a pile of rust. A six-inch hole emitted light through the stove jack directly above the derelict aparatus.

It works in a tepee, maybe it'll work here, I hoped while kindling a fire. The thick smoke went up but not out. Those were some tough folks, I had to admit, as I stood outside waiting for the snow-doused fire to die and the smoke to dissipate. Defeated, I curled up in the bag in a corner and watched the stars appear through the smoke hole.

Breakfast was a cup of coffee. The sky was clear and stars still bright in the blackness when I shouldered the pack and left the comforts of the cabin to face the Walla Walla portage. Theoretically, the portage, or winter trail in my case, is a twelve-mile *shortcut* over hilly tundra that cut across the base of Cape Darby, which jutted 15 miles into the ocean. I followed the trail to the tree line. Then, it vanished. There was nothing to indicate the path that wove through the 1,500-foot hills. All that could be seen was a faint light on the horizon and snow.

As soon as I crested the first hill, a blast of wind, seemingly out of nowhere, met me; soft, knee-deep snow developed immediately. Scant hummocks, blown free of snow, dotted the distant landscape but offered little relief from the dragging drifts. Constant glare blinded me, reflecting off the solid, white ground. The sun stared superficially from a clear blue sky. In wind-filled valleys, it was cold. On the ridges, it was staggering.

At midday, I ate what little I had while on the move, wanting only to get across these hills and back onto the ocean, where firewood laid waiting. My clothes were wet with sweat. Winter clothes at the Nome post office teased me, as the relentless wind sliced its way through my shabby wardrobe. A rock point, miles away, broke the uniform horizon. This was my guide through troubled waters. Keeping it in front of me assured a relatively straight course.

All afternoon I waded up and down the snow-filled valleys, and still there was no sign of the ocean. The guidance rock faded and faded until it was lost in darkness. With nightfall the temperature dropped drastically. Crackling sounds now accompanied each step. My clothes were freezing as I walked.

Swirling above the windy, moonless night were the Northern Lights. Many times, I stumbled and fell, as I advanced toward a beckoning star in the west. Lying in the snow, I gave serious thought to crawling into the sleeping bag. Only visions of a blazing fire at the ocean kept me from it. I'd get up, brush the snow off, and convince myself that it couldn't be much farther. I'd been walking all day and it was only twelve miles.

There came a time in the night when, though I could see little, I knew I had been going downhill for a long time. My once perspiration-soaked, now-frozen gloves were numbing my hands, so I stuffed them in the pack and continued with my hands down the front of my pants.

Finally, the terrain leveled, and the snow depth lessened. Plodding on, I was weary, near-totally exhausted, and very, very cold. I'd been stumbling in the dark for hours, and it suddenly occurred to me that I could walk right onto the frozen ocean and not recognize the difference between snow-covered tundra and snow-covered ice. Alone in the dark, it was a frightening thought. My limits were being approached, and I gave thought to the deadly cold creeping through me. My feet were numb, and I cursed each time they clumsily slid between half-exposed hummocks.

I became gradually aware of a faint noise. Standing still in the starlit night, I listened. It worried me that I couldn't identify it. I readied my rifle, straining my ears into the darkness. There it was, a *whoosh, whoosh, whoosh.* It continued without break. I realized it was the surf, the wind had blown the ice out to sea. It was a glorious relief.

It was another hour before I reached the shore, but I gained clarity, knowing that I was near rejuvenation. Finally, black water contrasted with the white snow, and there were piles of driftwood. Dumping the pack, I sat on the frozen sand, leaning back against a log. My hands and feet were as cold as they had ever been. After the 14-and-a-half-hour trek, my biggest ambition was to just sit. But I knew I couldn't *just* sit.

Pushing twigs and dry grass together, I struck matches with trembling, blue hands. Blessed flames danced and spread. Chills formed deep inside me, and I couldn't control the shaking. While the fire grew, I staggered to the ocean's edge as dry heaves racked me again and again. My stomach in agony, I dropped to my knees. With an icy finger jammed down my throat, soon all that had been in me lay strewn across the snow.

The fire warmed my hands, but for the next hour I wished it hadn't. The pain in my fingertips was excruciating. As the piercing sensation in my hands finally faded, I was able to work on my feet. Packed with snow, my boots were frozen solid. The socks were frozen to the liners, and the liners were frozen to the boots. It took thirty minutes to rip the liners from the boots while a million pins and needles jabbed and twisted in my feet. The rest of my thawing clothing was removed, and nearly naked, I crawled into the cold sleeping bag.

Exhausted as I was, sleep evaded me. I loathed the thought of getting up to stoke the fire. Warmth slowly returned to my body as I watched steam rise from the drying clothes and disappear into the night. Even though I was out of the dying wind, the air remained cold. I would learn the following day that the wind chill factor was sixty degrees below zero.

Three times during the night, muscles cramped in a simultaneous state of failure and fight. I sat straight up and felt a knot the size of my fist bulging at the back of my thigh. Through clenched teeth I would straighten the leg and feel the muscle slowly relax. The knots never really vanished. Instead, they lay dormant, waiting to swell and seize at the slightest movement.

When the sleepless night ended, I limped around the fire and tugged the stiff, smoke-impregnated clothes over my head. The sun was yet a long way from topping the Walla Walla hills. I did not feel well. Breakfast was rice and tea, not because I didn't want to tax my stomach, but because that was all there was. All I could say about the trek over Walla Walla was that it hadn't been much of a way to spend Halloween.

Dressed, more or less dry, more or less ready, I shrugged the pack onto my back and continued along the coast. Golovin was six miles away. Light-headed and weak, I came to impassable, ice-covered cliffs blocking the beach. They forced a detour up low cliffs that provided a continuous field of snow-filled hummocks. Alternating between the hummocks and the shore for hours drained what little reserves I had left. Finally, sitting on a stump, I stared down a long sandy beach, and Golovin was at the end of it. I willed myself up.

It was 2:30 P.M. when I stiffly entered the Golovin store. The thermometer tacked to the window jamb read twelve below zero, probably the warmest part of the day. Lingering in my quest for groceries, I relished the warmth before spending my last eight dollars. I had little incentive to leave, walk until dark, and crawl into a cold sleeping bag somewhere along a frozen beach, but with little choice, I shouldered the pack and walked on.

A snowmachine trail led northwest out of Golovin, skirting Golovin Bay. Plodding on for five miles into the coming darkness brought me to the Kachuik River. Here stood three small fishing cabins. Two were guarded with padlocks, but the third stood empty, its doorway a yawning hole.

Peering inside the eight-by-eight hovel revealed a wooden sleeping platform and a homemade, five-gallon wood stove. Both were heaped with snow. The four-pane window above the tiny stove lacked one of its components. Plywood, two-by-four studs, and a tin roof were a thin barrier against winter. I didn't care. It was a place to rest and shake off the lingering effects of Walla Walla. Hopefully its owner would not care either.

First came snow removal. With cupped hands and the side of my boot, I took what I could out the door. I collected driftwood in a growing wind. There wasn't much, but I muscled what I could from the grips of winter. As snow began to fall, I pulled a leaning sheet of plywood and shook it from its resting place. It was big enough to cover the door opening. Pried against the doorjamb from the inside by a piece of driftwood, it would definitely help the situation. After stuffing my shirt into the broken windowpane, I lit the little stove.

It wouldn't even melt the frost off the tin roof. As it huffed and puffed, a southerly wind was working into a feverish pitch. I was thankful that it was the little building that was totally exposed, and not I. Snow soon swooped down in earnest and before dark, a raging blizzard blew horizontally across the earth. As the hut swayed, I hung the tent tarp on the south wall to divert some of the wind. It floated to the ceiling like a magic carpet. Driftwood was stacked on its bottom to hold it in place. Pushing the bed close to the stove as the wind howled outside, I slept.

It was daylight when I opened my eyes in the depths of the sleeping bag. I was amazed that the place was still standing. That didn't mean that the inside of my shelter wasn't covered in snow. Forcing myself out of my only comfort, I dressed and lit the little heater. What snow I could gather went out the doorway. The two cabins just fifty feet away were occasional shadows. While the storm still raged, I was going nowhere.

There was little to do. I occupied the time by spreading my attention between the book and the bag. Read a chapter, sew a few burn holes, read a chapter, sew a few burn holes. Although this got me through the day, as night neared, I longed for a light, as 16 hours couldn't be slept away. Fortunately, I had found a block of canning wax behind the stove while removing snow.

For a while I felt lucky that it didn't melt because it was close to the stove. I hoped it would melt in an empty baby food jar on top of the stove. One knife-cut sliver was added at a time, none wasted. When finished, the liquefied wax nearly filled the jar. A piece of twine tied to a twig spanning the mouth dangled to the bottom of the wax. It was set aside to solidify. That didn't take long, quickly melting a round hole through the snow to the floorboards. Seeing how it wasn't the high-dollar, dripless paraffin, I smashed the glass from around my newly-minted candle, and I was ready to face the night.

If not for the feeble light in the window, four, masked snowmachine riders probably wouldn't have stopped. As I un-propped the plywood, they filed in. "Hi, Jerry!" one of them said. Removing their snow-encrusted face masks and goggles, they said they had just stopped to get warm. *Boy, did they come to the wrong place!*

"We heard on the radio how you swam in the ice water for your canoe," one of the two men said.

"Yah, in your underwear!" giggled his wife.

Is nothing sacred anymore? I flushed.

It turned out that one of the men's parents owned the fish camp and said I could stay here until next spring for all they cared.

"Boy, that's real bad weather out there," someone complained.

"Well, you can spend the night here if you want," I offered. There were no takers, claiming that they had to get to Golovin for a bingo game. Again, barricading the plywood door, I heard their machines roar into the dying storm. Much colder air had invaded what little heat I had accumulated in my bunker. The candle flickered twice and went out.

Over a tasteless bowl of oatmeal, I thought about trampling through a foot of new snow, finding no great enthusiasm. The wind had decreased considerably, allowing huge snowflakes to float down. The layover had done wonders for my health, though that wasn't saying much, relative to the night on Walla Walla. I knew I still wouldn't be going 100 percent—but I was alive. Propping the plywood over the doorway from the outside, I started along the edge of Golovin Bay. It glistened with a foot of overflow.

Visibility was limited by the snow, and I stayed well away from the steaming water. Nearing the end of the bay, I headed straight west toward land, hoping I was beyond the water's reach. Walking on early ice is always tense, but it looked good and I had no problems. Then, near dark, the bay ended. I was at the base of the rocky point that marked the western end of Walla Walla portage. No encore seemed necessary.

Walking west of the point for a mile uphill produced the only shelter around. It was probably a trickle of a creek in the summer as a very thin line of willows faded toward the hilltop. Finding any shoots taller than waist-high was a challenge. It was a pencil line on a field of white.

Dead willows were broken off and added to the group that I cradled in my arms, as I followed the tiny ravine upward. When I had my arms full, I camped. The sticks produced little more than a hot supper. Then, like an old dog, circling before lying down, I kicked snow from the tundra, made my bed, and waited for the return of the short daylight hours of winter.

Coldness crept upward through the valley as I lay in the darkness waiting for any sign of light. At the slightest hint, I shook the snow from the sleeping bag, packed, and headed west-southwest toward the ocean. It was a breeze compared to Walla Walla, half as long and windless. Still, it was five hours among the snow and hummocks before reaching the sandy shore. Shortly, the beach was blocked by sheer cliffs. I could have reached their tops before twilight but didn't know what awaited me. Here, I knew quite well—tons and tons of life-giving driftwood.

Like the Valley of 10,000 Smokes, gray wisps seeped through the sand-covered campfire the next morning. It lay behind me as I crested the high, jagged cliffs. The wind was finally on my side, for it had exposed long, level, rock surfaces, then died. Not a hummock was in sight, and it was a joy walking, even in Sorrels. High above the dark water I walked, seeing that the wind had pushed the ice to a thin, white line across the horizon. As the sun peered from a clear blue sky, nothing in my world stirred until I climbed out of a narrow ravine.

Roaring fifty feet above me and gaining altitude, a Cessna with blue and white wings banked to the left. Finishing its circle, it took aim and descended, coming right at me. Seemingly six-feet off the ground, it passed with the sound of a racecar, disappearing over the cliff toward the ocean. Although their intention must have been to make me duck, that plan didn't make any sense, as I'm only five-foot-ten.

What more could you want for the final fifty miles of a 9,000-mile journey, than a cliff-top view of the Bering Sea?

Traveling the tops of the cliffs as if time didn't matter, I took-in the ice-covered ocean and the snow-tipped mountains to the north.

By midday, I stood scanning across a valley. Weathered, lonely buildings were clustered a quarter-mile from the ocean. *When easy gold ran out, the people must have, too.* A tilted gin pole spoke of earlier times. It was a ghost town, a place called Bluff. I left the leisure of the cliff tops.

Though tolerable, the depth of the snow increased as I reached the lower elevation of the buildings. Junk lay everywhere, half-buried in the snow. Even though progress and the beach still beckoned, I couldn't pass exploring the wreckage.

Whether it was exploring or snooping, I exhibited no prejudice, roaming from one building to another, checking them all. Not much daylight remained as I entered what appeared to be the mess hall. Plates and silverware still littered a long wooden table. Pots and pans lay scattered. Even the wood stove in the corner was in disarray, its pipes littering the floor. With bailing wire, I made it operational enough to cook with. When daylight had fully waned, I climbed onto the table, entered the sleeping bag, and slept with my crumbs.

Darkness was overabundant. I couldn't sleep through the entirety of its hours. In the blackness I tossed and turned, staring into nothingness. Waiting for daylight, I was glad that it was a wide table, as little creatures scurried around me. A flashlight would have been nice, even a chunk of wax from behind the stove. But it was forced patience that dominated, until finally, fixtures began to appear as black globs on the wall and ceiling. Within minutes of adequate light, I was out the door and down the beach.

For eight miles the terrain was fragmented. *Climb to the cliff tops, then descend to the beach, climb to the cliff tops, then descend to the beach.* It would have been easier with breakfast, but finally, flat lands spread before me. After a quick lunch I continued. Significantly less snow had fallen here, and the ocean was relatively free of ice. The tide was out, exposing a highway of frozen sand, made just for walking. After two hours I saw what looked like the roof of a cabin, far down the beach. If I hurried, I could make it before dark.

It was a log cabin in good shape—except that the south wall was gone, as well as half of the west wall, and it was also filled with four feet of sand. 55-gallon barrels abounded so I stood one on end beneath the unsupported roof corner. *Don't need to be squished, after all.* It was seemingly made to fit. With the wobbly roof corner stabilized, I checked the back of the cabin.

There was an attached shed, buried to the roof with driftwood.

Whoever built this cabin gravely underestimated the fury of this ocean. Another salvaged drum was sacrificed by the ax. Only one piece of rusted stovepipe could be located, so the stove was put to use half in and half out of the cabin. Since most of the smoke escaped to the outside, and unfrozen, soft, white sand shifted beneath the sleeping bag, I was cozy.

With the luxury of a shed buried in firewood, it amounted to one comfortable night. I took the time to eat breakfast as the day lightened, then left the cabin, knowing that the partial structure didn't have many years before the ocean finished its reclamation.

The beach was easily walked, though a stiff offshore wind blew stinging swirls of snow. Coming to a river, I could see a group of buildings toward the north. I hated to leave the frozen beach, but the river crossing was not safe. *Inland it must be.* I headed north across miles of hummocks. After three hours, I was standing on a dirt road that ran between a few old cabins higher on the plateau and a large, two-story building that appeared to have seen many winters. This place had to be Solomon.

A weathered-gray sled lay on the roof of the porch of the two-story structure. It looked like it could have been an old store, or a roadhouse. The porch door lay open, and I crossed the threshold beneath a set of reindeer antlers before knocking on the inner door. It swung slightly inward at my knock. "Anybody here!" I shouted into a huge, empty room. "Anyone home?" I shouted again.

To the left was a wall of empty shelves. Halfway down the other wall stood a barrel stove guarded by a rocking chair, its shredded, wicker seat dangling toward the floor. Other than that, the room was empty. I closed the door, crossed the porch, and walked the road to see what else Solomon had to offer.

Rounding a slight curve, I noticed white wood smoke rising from what appeared to be a new, red-painted house. "What?" came the response to my knock on the door. "What!" came the grumbled shout again.

Oh boy. I grew apprehensive.

"What ya want? Use the other damn door," a gruff voice commanded. I went around the house and used the back door. "Oh, hi," the short, stocky man said, eyeing my disheveled state. "I thought you was my sister."

I asked him if he thought anyone would mind if I spent the night in the old, two-story building at the other end of town. Since it had been empty for a long time, he doubted anyone would care.

When introductions were exchanged, he started talking about the new house he was building. "Yup, Solomon's gonna grow, maybe next year, so I built me a new house," the grizzled old-timer commented. When I asked why there was a tank with pipes coming out of it, he said, "Don't know much about all that plumbing stuff, lived in a cabin all my life, and I got a real good outhouse right out there." I could see the small out-building through the window where he pointed as he continued.

"Wiring it was sure a mess. Don't know if it'll ever work, but I guess it don't matter anyway 'cause there's no electricity." Before I returned to the vacant roadhouse, he passed along a bit of information I didn't need to hear. "Ain't no jobs in Nome during the winter," he said, "and a one-bedroom place with a kitchen will cost you at least $400 a month, if you can find one." It was not good news for someone with 19 cents in their pocket.

With peeling fingers compliments of Walla Walla, I started a small fire in the barrel stove to take the chill from the room, and then explored my surroundings. There was one empty room and another. A kitchen in the back had cupboards with peeling paint and a rusted sink. A staircase led to the second floor. Beneath the landing was a box that contained a few newspapers from months ago. As I thumbed through them, one of the headlines took me by surprise, Elvis was dead.

I ascended the creaking wooden steps. There was a multitude of rooms, some empty, some containing mattress-less bedframes attached to rusted, wrought-iron headboards. Only one thing broke the monotony of the many rooms, a Playboy centerfold taped to the wall, pierced by two well-placed darts.

Supper was quick and easy. Afterward I sat next to the window reading one of the old newspapers in what was left of the day's light. I watched as a car's headlights crossed a distant bridge and came down the road. When it stopped just outside the window, the passenger door flew open. I didn't know if it was a visit or an eviction.

A man dashed across the snow and stood behind a barrel under the window. If there had been no glass in the windowpane, from where I sat, I could have poked the guy in the ear. He checked his surroundings—poorly, I might add—then undid his fly, relief flooding his face. Temptation to rap on the glass was great, but the opportunity passed and he dashed back to the truck before disappearing in a cloud of snow and dust.

The day was well lit when I left the old roadhouse the next morning. Walking the road required little effort. Whenever the Sorrels seemed heavy, I just thought of Walla Walla. I also thought of Nome, now only 34 miles away. As I took in the ocean lapping the sands below me to my left, family also came to mind. I hadn't talked to them in months, though that would be resolved in a few days. Today was November 10th.

Rotting driftwood was piled on both sides of the road, a solemn warning of the ocean's reach. After four hours I came to the end of a long, straight stretch of highway. A bridge was being built across the outlet of Safety Sound, and a temporary bridge allowed construction vehicle passage. It was the only way across. I'd walk a bit and then step aside as a truck crept by. After the fifth or sixth game of chicken, I reached the other side and was on my way again.

"Want a ride!" someone called from the cab of a dump truck.

"No, I'm just walking into town. Thanks anyway!" I answered. He nodded at me skeptically, shifted gears, and headed toward Nome.

Four men to my left worked on a guardrail. "If you can make it down to my house, I've got an extra bedroom," a guy shouted through a brown facemask, "it's about eight more miles down the road, a big white house at the foot of the mountain."

I acknowledged his offer and added I would stop if I made it that far. Another eight miles would round the day's mileage to twenty; my old bones still had that much in them. The road leveled after walking down the long incline to the bridge and I could see the hump of a mountain before me. It looked a long eight miles away. To my left stood a two-story rusting, galvanized, tin building. An orange windsock flopped limply above its roof, waiting for a gust of wind. Electrical wires ran to a smaller building and a permanently stalled truck adorned the front yard. A sign braced above the front porch stated Safety Roadhouse Beer Gas Snacks. It was a welcome sight, if it weren't for the door and windows being cloaked in plywood, closed for the winter.

As the bridge crew headed back to town, I cleared off the road. More slowed with ride offers; none were accepted. Camps appeared along the road, becoming more abundant the closer I got to the mountain. They were of all shapes and sizes and many seemed dangerously close to the ocean. Most incorporated silver-and-rust colored corrugated tin in some way.

Soon, they dimmed into darkness. I walked and walked knowing the end of eight miles couldn't be much farther. Just staying on the road in the darkness became a chore as no light seeped through the cloud-covered night. Finally, I came to a building where light from a window spread across the white snow. With a slight limp, I found the door and knocked.

Pounding on the door three times produced a figure in the doorway. "Is this the big white house at the foot of the mountain?" I asked feeling foolish, able to see in the fading light that it was red.

"Huh?" the older man said blankly.

"I'm looking for a big white house below—"

"Come in! Come in!" he exclaimed, ending my plea. "Had supper yet?"

We sat at the kitchen table where the 62-year old retired man introduced himself and speculated, "You must be that guy who's walking. It's hard to believe you're only 16 miles from your destination. Jeez, you came a helluva long way." It wasn't long before his wife placed a huge plate of moose and potatoes in front of me, followed by a pot of steaming coffee.

I sipped the coffee slowly, not anxious to return to the darkness. Alas hospitality was not to be abused, so I thanked my hosts, hoisted the pack, and started for the door. "If anyone asks what took you so long, tell them you stopped to *B.S.* with the Warrens!" the generous man called out as he aimed a flashlight, lighting my path to the road. Then, I limped into the darkness, looking for a big house at the foot of the mountain. It took an hour, but even in the darkness I couldn't miss the big white house.

"Come on in," the guy responded after answering my knock. "Hi, I'm Kavik Hahn," he stated. We went to the living room. The fireplace roared, illuminating years of beachcombing that ornamented every wall and shelf. Kavik excused himself and soon returned with a platter of fried ptarmigan legs and breasts. Over these we talked until midnight, mostly about the history of Nome. Though it was late, Kavik entertained me as long as possible, until he acknowledged that he had to be up early to get back to the bridge. Following him up a narrow staircase, I was assigned a bedroom to the left of the landing. I gladly slid the switch of a borrowed flashlight off. With my head on a real pillow, sleep was effortless.

When the sun had risen, Kavik was already gone. I lounged in front of the now cold fireplace, knowing today would be the last day. Nome lay 14 miles away. I couldn't help but ponder my fate as I jingled the dime, nickel, and four pennies left in my pocket. Three event-filled years had brought me here, and now I knew and understood my capabilities. Nonetheless, it was sad and strange for my journey to be ending.

A sucker stick lolled around my mouth as I stared into the gray ashes. The hard, sugary top had long been devoured. It hadn't been much for breakfast, but it was enough. A small *puff* of dust rose from the fire's ashes as the white paper stick landed. I then hoisted my pack for the last time and started to finish what began so long ago.

I reached my destination Nov. 12, 1977 at 5:36 P.M.

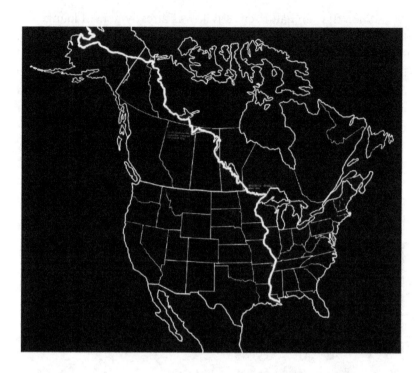

366

December 14, 1977

Mr. Jerry Pushcar
c/o The City of Biwabik
Office of Mayor R.G. Woods
Biwabik, Minnesota 55708

Dear Mr. Pushcar:

    I would like to join the many Minnesotans who are proud to congratulate you on your recent dangerous and thrilling adventure across this country. I am sure that the experiences that you had and the new territory that you visited will remain as most reassured memories.

    Please accept my best wishes and congratulations on your safe return. I wish you much future success.

    With warm regards.

Sincerely,

Walter F. Mondale

Walter F. Mondale